Operations and the Management of Change

Vic Gilgeous

University of Nottingham

Pearson Education Limited
Edinburgh Gate
Harlow
Essex CM20 2JE

and Associated Companies around the world

Visit us on the World Wide Web at:
www.pearsoned-ema.com

First published in Great Britain in 1997

© Pearson Professional Limited 1997

The right of Vic Gilgeous to be identified as author of this work
has been asserted by him in accordance with the Copyright,
Designs and Patents Act 1988.

ISBN 0 273 62507 1

British Library Cataloguing in Publication Data
A CIP catalogue record for this book can be obtained from the British Library

10 9 8 7 6 5 4 3 2

Typeset by Pantek Arts, Maidstone, Kent
Printed and bound in Britain by Clays Ltd, St Ives plc.

The Publishers' policy is to use paper manufactured from sustainable forests.

CONTENTS

Bury College
Learning Resources
Woodbury Centre

Part 1 INTRODUCTION

1 Managing change   3

What is change? · The change process · Main change factors · Key dimensions for managing operations and change · Approach to change · Perceptions of change · Change perspectives · Conditions for success · Barriers to successful change · People and change · A model for managing change · Overcoming pitfalls in the change process · The need for an operations and change strategy · Summary · Review and discussion questions · Assignments · References

Part 2 CLARIFYING WHAT NEEDS TO BE CHANGED

2 Operations and change strategy   35

The need for an operations and change strategy · Vision and business strategy · Process and content of an operations and change strategy · Clarifying what needs to be changed · The people in the change process · Operations and change initiatives · Making it happen · Executive assessment of focus and action plan · Strategy development considerations · Prominent approaches to operations strategy development · Strategy implementation · Case study: The Clearview Company – Development of an operations and change strategy · Summary · Review and discussion questions · Assignments · References

3 Performance objectives   71

The performance objectives · What is quality? · The gurus of quality · Achieving quality · Requirements for quality · Management of quality · Measurement of quality · Quality cost breakdown · Difficulties with quality · The benefits of quality · Speed · The   benefits of speed · Ways to achieve a fast operation · Assessing performance and making improvements · Dependability · Achieving dependability · Speeding up development · Flexibility · System flexibility · Types of resource flexibilities · Measuring flexibility · The benefits of flexibility · Improving flexibility · Cost · The process of pursuing the performance objectives · Action planning for performance objectives · Case study: The Clearview Company – Establishing Clearview's objectives · Summary · Review and discussion questions · Assignments · References

v

PREFACE

ABOUT THIS BOOK AND HOW TO USE IT

Introduction

Change management is about recognising the need for change and determining how to provide an effective response to it. Operations management is concerned with creating the products and services upon which we all depend. Although operations management is becoming less technical, less technique- and technology-orientated, if we cannot address the attendant problems of managing the change and the people involved, we are wasting our time. In my consultancies and teaching as a university lecturer I place emphasis on the importance of managing change in the operations area. This book does the same.

Currently Britain and other advanced economies are experiencing change on a dramatic scale. Competing organisations and the people within them are having continuously to face these changes. No one is immune unless they want to get left behind. There are many reasons for these changes, with the main ones being economic (bigger, freer, global market place), social (changing workplace and skills), environmental and technological. The difficulty is that each year the pace of change accelerates and becomes more unpredictable.

Change is difficult and complex to manage

In most organisations, change is difficult and complex to manage. Some organisations are very successful at handling change, whereas most do a poor job. Why is this so? Unfortunately many organisations are unwilling or lack the vision, the drive, the supporting culture and management competence and workforce abilities to cope when things need to be changed. It is these organisations that will continue to be outperformed and which are ultimately doomed to perish.

Best practice companies excel at managing change

For an organisation to continue to grow and achieve long-term success, it must develop the key ability to recognise the need for change and be capable of managing change in their operations.

According to the BIM/DTI/CBI latest management surveys, a key competitive strength of organisations which are deemed best practice or 'world class' is that they excel at managing change in their operations. They know that the ability to manage change is at the heart of effective operations management. Therefore, for an organisation to be successful it is important that you and the people within it can understand and conceptualise what the management of change within an operations management context is, how it is decided, what needs to be done and how it can be achieved.

What managing operations and change involves

All the changes from the strategic level must be identified, linked down and integrated with the operating level. At the strategic level this will involve being aware of the need to change through influences from the customer, competition and the environment. It is then necessary to clarify what needs to be changed in operations to meet the new challenges. The senior management or sponsors of the change will need to have the vision to direct and support those who will manage the change, the change agents. In turn they will need to understand how to plan and control operations and know how to harness both operations management and change initiatives, making use of their expertise and the best available management practice. This will necessitate changes in the organisation's process, structure, people and culture, and analysis and redesign of these main facets of the organisation must become a way of thinking. Thus the needs, fears and resistance of those involved in the change process need to be understood and managed. At all levels the power that the contribution of effective management of operations and change can make to an organisation needs to be recognised and acted upon in a way that becomes part of the organisation culture.

Managing change and operations is a key competence that must be built into the very fabric of the company. Such competences can be fostered through extreme efforts to educate, train, communicate, listen and reward. In essence the organisation must become a 'master of managing change in operations'. The extent to which the people in the organisation have or can acquire such competences will define the organisation's potential for success. Therefore it is imperative that there be a process which affects every individual, whereby people with such capabilities can be acquired or developed.

THE AIM OF THIS BOOK

The aim of this book is to provide management students and practising managers with an understanding of, and a guide to, managing the complexities of managing change in operations. Throughout, the material is presented in a clear, well-structured and interesting way with the purpose of:

- improving understanding and developing knowledge of managing change and operations management
- developing management skills and competence in the area of managing operations and change
- showing how an organisation can effectively manage operations and change.

Why this book combines managing change and managing operations

A year ago I attended a one-day seminar entitled 'Managing Change'. It was well attended with people from advertising, retail, manufacturing etc. At the start, the presenter asked everyone what they hoped they would get from the seminar. Being an operations person I was particularly interested in the reply from a chap who was the operations director of an international swimwear manufacturer. He said:

> The trouble is, when it comes to initiating and implementing changes in our operations to become more competitive things fail. I feel that we are poor at managing the change process and getting our people involved.

At the end of the seminar before everyone drifted off, people's comments on it were quickly invited and overall everyone said that it had been excellent and they thought that they had learned a lot about what change involved and how it could be managed.

Before leaving I managed to catch the operations director chap on his own and I asked him what he thought. He said:

Well, it was good, but the trouble is that all the examples and exercises used dealt with changes that aren't really related to the way things are in operations. I feel that now I understand more about the process of change, but how do I apply it to managing operations?

He asked me what I thought. I replied:

Unfortunately the literature and courses on operations management do not deal with the issues of managing the change involved, and it is important that they should. Essentially I think that operations managers know what needs to be changed but they don't know how to go about doing it. The same is true for change management; in this area the change issues of operations management are not understood and they are therefore neglected. It would be a great help if there was a book on managing change from an operations management perspective.

'I would certainly buy it,' he said.

Only half the story

My quickly-found reply was based on my considered belief and experience that courses, books and presentation on the process and management of change are presented by people who, although experts on the change process, know and have little appreciation of the practice of operations management. Naturally such people tend to be from widely different backgrounds and use different terminologies and rationales as the basis for their material and teaching.

In particular, the operations management area deals more with the technical, hard issues, in contrast with the management of change area which emphasises more the softer, processal, organisational and people issues involved with change. As a consequence of being informed or taught in this way, students as well as managers, when dealing with operations management, are only presented with half the story.

Taking an integrated view

Many books on change are either too general or too theoretical and they do not deal with the application of change management principles to actual operations and how they should be managed. Many books on operations management are too technical and lengthy, and neglect the management of the change process involved and the important aspects of managing people using the latest key management ideas and approaches. Consequently, because of the integrated way in which today's businesses operate, students and managers, presented with such partial knowledge and skills, will, together with their organisations, suffer. Both the subject areas or disciplines of operations management and managing change need to be taught in an integrated manner.

For operations managers

Students of operations management and operations managers using this book should feel comfortable because it is written from the perspective of determining what needs to be done in operations management and then effectively managing the change that is necessary. Thus a feature of the book is that it adds to the traditional knowledge set of operations management to deal with the knowledge and skills needed to manage the change process involved.

For managers of change

Those many managers and students who read texts and go on courses on how to manage change have here a book which puts change in a real context; that is, how successful companies adopt change management principles to manage their operations. Here there is the opportunity for the student or manager to acquire knowledge and skills outside the usual abstract framework that is presented in many texts on change.

DISTINCTIVE FEATURES

Practical real-world insight and examples

The book uses many illustrations of actual practice from industry and commerce and makes reference to the literature on managing operations and managing change that abound in journals, newspapers, magazines and other books. Also, the author makes use of his industrial and managerial experience by using material gained through consultancy, presenting management courses and supervising student projects in this area. And last, but not least, are those experiences gained from everyday life in and out of the office.

Latest management ideas and approaches

In a concise, straightforward way the book comprehensively provides an in-depth examination of the topic from the point of view of the latest knowledge, approaches and models presented by researchers and writers on the topic. In doing so it covers all the relevant literature, the latest management ideas, and provides checklists of methods to manage operations and the associated changes effectively. It looks at strategy development and considers the harder, technical initiatives of operations management such as TQM, MRP, JIT and OPT, as well as the softer, people-orientated management initiatives such as teams, empowerment, the learning organisation and business process re-engineering.

A learning and reference resource for managers and students

To provide the reader with an understanding of each particular element of managing change in operations, each chapter clearly states its objectives. It explains what the topic is, why it is important, and how it integrates with the other chapters so as to provide an overall, effective approach to managing change from an operations management perspective. The text is interspersed with information, tips, advice, illustrations, current real-life case studies, case histories and approaches the successful practitioners use when they manage in this particular field. At the end of each chapter is a summary, as well as questions which encourage the reader to consider the information and main issues presented. The assignments are intended to provide the reader with problems and tasks on managing change in operations that he/she would be faced with in an actual operating environment in an organisation. The intention is to enable students and managers to understand the subject and develop their knowledge in it so they can relate what they are reading to their own organisations and situations. In this way, the reader should become a more competent person and better equipped to manage change in operations.

WHO THIS BOOK IS FOR

This book is suitable for students, managers and trainers.

Students

- **Undergraduates** on Business Studies and Management degrees will find clear explanations, conceptual underpinnings and a structured approach which reflects the work of leading practitioners in the subject.
- **Students on Certificate and Diploma courses**, which include business studies and management functions, should find the practical discussions and exercises enhance their understanding of business and management and the change issues they will face in their working lives.
- **Postgraduates** on specialist Masters' degrees, Master of Business Administration (MBA) courses and the Diploma in Management Studies (DMS) will find the input, the latest management knowledge and approaches, the critical approach to issues and development exercises in the text can be used to develop their knowledge and skills in the area.

Managers

Senior or middle managers and supervisors concerned either directly or indirectly with manufacturing and operations and their associated change programmes can use the book as a development programme to enhance their understanding of the area and develop their management skills.

Trainers

Trainers can use the book as the basis of in-house development programmes that can be adapted to the specific needs of a company. As such, it can be used to develop the managerial expertise of managers and supervisors who are involved with manufacturing and operations and their associated change programme. It can also be used as a training tool aimed at improving an organisation's effectiveness in respect of managing operations and change.

OUTLINE OF THE BOOK

As a complete course of study

The book can be used as a complete course of study on managing the change process from an operations management perspective whereby the reader studies each chapter in the order presented. In this way the design of the book enables the reader to work in a structured and progressive way, as follows:

Part 1: Introduction, where Chapter 1: Managing Change deals with the process of change and managing change.

Part 2: Clarifying what needs to be changed contains Chapters 2–5 on operations management, dealing with formulating strategy, performance objectives, operations activities and planning and controlling operations.

Part 3: The initiatives that make operations work, where Chapter 6 provides an up-to-date examination of prominent initiatives in operations management; namely, total quality management (TQM), material and requirements planning and manufacturing resource planning (MRP), just-in-time (JIT) and optimised production technology (OPT).

Part 4: The people in the change process, where Chapter 7 deals with the sponsors of change, the change champions and people in operations who have to make the changes work (the 'change partners'). Essentially it deals with how people should manage the change process and deal with those who conduct or are affected by the changes.

Part 5: The initiatives of change, in which Chapters 8–11 deal with the initiatives that are prominent in facilitating change in today's successful organisations; namely, teams, empowerment, the learning organisation and business process re-engineering.

Part 6: Making it happen, in which Chapters 12–14 concentrate on key management ideas and approaches, personal and management development and continuous improvement.

Alternative pathways

Readers may wish to dip into specific sections of the book to increase their knowledge and understanding in a particular area. The following shows the different pathways that can be chosen, depending on the knowledge, experience and preference of the reader:

Change management

Here is a pathway for someone with a knowledge and/or experience of operations management who is interested in change management and effective management of change in operations. The reader could skip Chapters 2–6 which focus on operations management. It is recommended that the reader studies and completes Chapter 1 to get an overview of the main elements involved in managing change, and how to go about identifying the main causes of problems in this area and the actions necessary to overcome them. Chapter 1 can be followed by Chapter 7 which deals with the people in the change process and how they should be managed, and Chapters 8–11 which focus on the initiatives of change: teams, empowerment, the learning organisation and business process re-engineering. Finally, read Chapters 12–14 which deal with key management ideas and approaches, personal and management development and continuous improvement, which act in an integrated way to provide a platform for effective management of change in operations.

Management of operations

This pathway is most suitable for someone with knowledge and/or experience of management of change who is interested in operations management and effective management of operations while in a state of change. Again it is recommended that the reader studies and completes Chapter 1 to get an overview of the main elements involved in managing change. Chapters 2–5, which focus on clarifying what needs to be changed in operations, should be studied, followed by Chapter 6 which is concerned with important operations management initiatives. Chapters 8–11 could be skipped. Chapters 12–14, which deal with key management ideas and approaches, personal and management development and continuous improvement, and which integrate the earlier chapters to provide a platform for effective management of change in operations, should then be covered.

Operations and change initiatives

The reader may wish to focus on more specific pathways relating purely to the latest initiatives in operations management or change management, in which case the reader should to go to:

Part 3: The initiatives that make operations work, Chapter 6, which deals with the latest philosophies, systems and approaches prevalent in operations management

or

Part 5: The initiatives of change, in which Chapters 8–11 concentrate on the initiatives of change: teams, empowerment, the learning organisation and business process re-engineering.

ABOUT THE AUTHOR

Vic Gilgeous is a lecturer in the Department of Manufacturing Engineering and Operations Management at the University of Nottingham.

He initially served his time as an engineering apprentice in the aerospace industry. In his 16 years in industry he worked as an aeronautical design engineer, a systems design engineer and a production manager, latterly being Airbus Controller at British Aerospace.

He holds an Higher National Diploma in Aeronautical Engineering, a Master's degree from Cranfield in Industrial Engineering and Administration and a Doctor's degree in Management in collaboration with the University of Oxford. He is also a chartered engineer.

He has published numerous research papers on operations management and is the author of *Structured Workshops for Improving Manufacturing Effectiveness*, published by Gower Publishing in 1995.

Vic was the Course Director of the Nottingham University School of Finance and Management Master of Business Administration programme and has acted as Nottingham University's external liaison adviser for the University of Derby's engineering degree. He is an external examiner for its management development programme. He has also sat on various validation panels for management programmes at the University of Humberside, where he is currently an external examiner for its International Modular Management Masters Programme.

Vic has considerable experience in running his own short courses on management and has acted as an adviser to many companies, as well as undertaking consultancy work for BAe, W.H.Smith, European Gas Turbines, John Players, The Society of Logistics Engineers, NATO Maintenance and Supply Agency (NAMSA) and Humberside County Council.

Vic's research is in the area of operations management, managing change, operations strategy and the core competences necessary for business effectiveness.

ACKNOWLEDGEMENTS

A very special thank you to the most special person in the world, my wife Vicky. She has always put me first and is a tremendous source of help and love. Without her I would not have been able to write this book or any other.

To the memory of my mother who died last year. She often asked how the book was coming on and would have been proud to see it published. She had to make sacrifices to bring up three sons in the difficult years of the 1930s and '40s. Through her strength of character and determined and positive approach to life she showed all around her how to tackle the many changes that life brings.

Many thanks to the very professional publishing team, my editor, Annette McFadyen, and in particular Penelope Woolf, senior publisher, who spent time reading my work, made detailed comments and offered advice.

To Caroline Brierley-Banga, secretary at Nottingham University, who went beyond her normal secretarial duties to type up many of the case illustrations for this book.

To Joe Marshall, lecturer in Organisation Development at The University of Derby, who pointed me in the right direction concerning the most appropriate literature on the management of change.

To the students of the MSc module that I teach entitled 'Managing Operations and Change', who have acted as a sounding board for my ideas on the subject.

To my employers, Nottingham University, who enable me to pay my bills and put bread (as well as some jam) on my table.

Much time has been spent attempting to ensure that this book is free of errors, omissions, and misinterpretations. However, having written this book, if they do occur I take the responsibility for them, and comments from readers would be appreciated.

Vic Gilgeous
May 1997

PLAN OF THE BOOK

PART 1: INTRODUCTION
Chapter 1 **Managing change**

PART 2: CLARIFYING WHAT NEEDS TO BE CHANGED			
Chapter 2 **Operations and change strategy**	**Chapter 3** **Performance objectives**	**Chapter 4** **Operations activities**	**Chapter 5** **Planning and controlling**

PART 3: THE INITIATIVES THAT MAKE OPERATIONS WORK
Chapter 6 **The operations initiatives of TQM, MRP, JIT and OPT**

PART 4: THE PEOPLE IN THE CHANGE PROCESS
Chapter 7 **The people in the change process**

PART 5: THE INITIATIVES OF CHANGE			
Chapter 8 **Teams**	**Chapter 9** **Empowerment**	**Chapter 10** **The learning organisation**	**Chapter 11** **Business process re-engineering**

PART 6: MAKING IT HAPPEN		
Chapter 12 **Key management ideas**	**Chapter 13** **Personal and management development**	**Chapter 14** **Continuous improvement**

PART 1

Introduction

CHAPTER 1

Managing change

OBJECTIVES

The objectives of this chapter are to:

- explain what change is and why it is important to organisations
- describe the change process and the change activities involved
- provide an awareness of the main factors that will need to be considered when developing a change programme
- examine the business dimensions that support the change process
- appreciate the importance of the perceptions of change and the variety of ways of monitoring change and the issues and problems involved
- identify the conditions which are likely to achieve successful change and how they can be created
- examine the barriers to successful change, the politics of the situation, and the ways in which individuals, groups and organisations view particular change situations
- appreciate the use of the Intervention Strategy Model (ISM) and the eight stages involved
- explain why it is necessary to develop an 'operations and change strategy' and outline the main components of such a strategy.

WHAT IS CHANGE?

Change is generally a response to some significant threat or opportunity arising outside of the organisation. According to Pettigrew:

> *Changes within an organisation take place both in response to business and economic events and to processes of managerial perception, choice and actions. Managers in this sense see events taking place that, to them, signal the need for change.*

In this sense it is important that an organisation continually monitors what is happening around it; that is it develops a sense of awareness which stems from realising the need to set in motion changes that will keep it in, or ahead of, the game.

The opening line of a recent DTI report, *How the Best UK Companies are Winning*, reads:

> *Winning UK companies are led by visionary, enthusiastic champions of change.*

This idea of change is evident in the ideas of many writers on management. Michael Jordan cites one of the management defects which leads to the failure of a company as being:

> *...failure to respond to changing circumstances...*

and he then goes on to divide this further into:

> *old attitudes towards employees; out-of-date products; obsolete plant and equipment; out-of-date marketing; an ageing board of directors; no computers.*

It is evident that for the organisation to survive, let alone thrive, change needs to be considered by management at all levels. It is necessary to consider what the causes of change are and what actually needs changing.

The main causes of change that give rise to change programmes being initiated can be classified as follows:

- **External causes of change** can be as a result of changes in the level of technology used, market place changes, customer expectations, competitor activities, quality and standards, government legislation or political values, as well as changes in the economy. Depending on their current situation and aspirations, different companies will react to these external stimuli in different ways.
- **Internal context of change** relates to management philosophy, structure, culture, and the system of power and control.

Good and bad organisations

Although some organisations are very successful at implementing change, most companies do a poor job. The difference can lead to organisations either being successful or being destroyed.

Ignorant, reactive organisations

Organisations that do not change due to ignorance will be the first to fail. Next to go will be those organisations which just react to change. That is, they witness change and see it as a disturbance requiring major or minor adjustment. The response of these organisations is to ask:

- What are the disturbances?
- What do we need to adjust?

These organisations are generally in the majority and change is usually a response to some significant threat from outside.

Visionary, proactive organisations

For organisations to survive and excel they must constantly scan what is happening in their area of business and try to anticipate problems in the market place. Organisations that continually seek to determine what is going on and why, and seek to accommodate and benefit from the changes, are acting in a proactive manner. The typical approach of these organisations would be to ask:

- What is happening, *vis-à-vis* what changes are perceived as being important?
- What is our current situation?
- Given what we are about, what do we need to do to move in the right direction?

This proactive approach to change suggests a 'vision-building' approach requiring strong leadership and a clear view of the direction in which the company is moving. The persons directing the change must believe that change is necessary, perhaps even mandatory.

Change is difficult and complex

The management of change is different to many of the tasks in organisations which can be completed using known procedures and routines. We seem to be able to solve complicated technical problems but fail miserably at implementing even the simplest changes. For example, with respect to the 'people aspects' of change, how do you implement change without creating resistance and without threatening employee security? Managing change involves considering many such imponderables that are continuously changing. It relies on managers scanning their environment to discover what is happening, making sense of it, and finally reacting and taking decisions. Most importantly, it relies on managers understanding what organisation change entails and what has to be present for it to be successful. Consequently, for most organisations change is difficult and complex to manage.

THE CHANGE PROCESS

Lewin proposed a change model which describes the necessary stages for successful change to occur.

The three-step model of change

1 **Unfreezing** the present level requires confrontation meeting or a process of re-education which might be achieved through team building.
2 **Moving** to the new level requires developing new behaviours, values, and attitudes.
3 **Refreezing** the new level seeks to stabilise the organisation at a new state of equilibrium to ensure that the new ways are safe from regression.

A feature of this model is that it recognises, and takes into account, the important fact that, with many change programmes, things may revert back to what they were, unless permanence of the new level is included in the objective.

Managing the change process

Managers wanting to introduce change should recognise that change occurs slowly and moves through a series of stages. In the first instance, the need for change must be recognised. Then it is necessary to define where the company stands relative to the problem, where it wants to be, and how it is going to get there. With respect to the way the change process needs to be managed, Lewin's three-step model can be expanded to show that the following sequential set of activities needs to take place:

1 recognising the need for change
2 defining problems
3 identifying where the company is relative to the problem
4 searching for alternatives
5 defining goals (identifying where the company wants to be after the change)

 6 preparing for change
 7 unfreezing (loosening the organisation so that it can change)
 8 moving (consciously managing the process of change)
 9 arriving (realising when the goals have been met)
10 refreezing (stabilising and reinforcing the change).

This process is summarised in Fig 1.1, where the major elements in the process are:

● recognising the need for change
● preparing for change
● unfreezing the organisation
● managing the change
● refreezing (stabilising) the organisation afterwards.

Phases of planned change

Based on a review of over 30 models of planned change, Bullock and Batten show that change activities, of the type listed above, fall into four phases, shown in Fig 1.2. They are:

1 **Exploration phase**: becoming aware of the need for change; deciding whether to make specific changes and commit resources to planning the changes; searching for a consultant or facilitator to assist with planning and implementing the changes; establishing a contract with a consultant which defines each party's responsibilities.

2 **Planning phase**: understanding the organisation's problem or concern; collecting information in order to diagnose the problem; establishing change goals and designing appropriate actions to achieve these goals; getting key decision makers to approve and support the proposed changes.

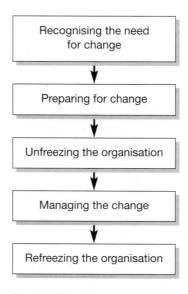

Fig 1.1 The change process

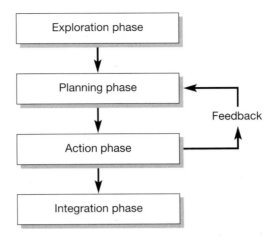

Fig 1.2 The four phases of change

3 **Action phase**: implementing the changes derived from the planning, including arrangements to manage the change process, evaluating the implementation activities and feeding back the results to make any necessary adjustments.

4 **Integration phase**: consolidating and stabilising the changes so that they become part of normal everyday operations; reinforcing new behaviours through feedback and reward systems and gradually decreasing reliance on the consultant.

MAIN CHANGE FACTORS

Before embarking on a change programme, one needs to obtain an overview of the situation. Wilson suggests that this can be done by considering the following broad parameters:

Scale. What is the scope and size of the programme? Is it a pilot study in a section or department? Perhaps you have selected a particular unit, or maybe your plans entail changing the whole organisation.

Investment. Change can rarely take place without considerable investment. How it is defined in monetary terms will depend on your organisation. Is the sum to be spent the annual change budget figure or does it include additional money?

Timescale. How long do you envisage that the total change process will take? Are you including the time spent on research and planning the change programme? How will the end of the programme be determined – when the operation is working to target or when a change of philosophy and culture has taken place?

Changes. The nature of the changes that are taking place needs to be appreciated. These may range from a change in current operating methods through to a complete change of organisation philosophy. The approach required and the investment needed will be different for each level of change.

Impetus for change. The reasons for embarking on the change programme need to be known, since these will determine, to some extent, its direction and style. Is the change to do with organisation survival or development, since the implications of the strategy adopted can be quite different?

Strategy. What is the nature of the strategy driving the change process? Is it, for example, revolutionary in nature, happening to a very short timescale with many casualties? Or does it have a much longer timescale and grow organically with the full support and co-operation of the organisation's employees? Perhaps it is neither of these and change is introduced piecemeal or on a project-by-project basis.

The areas above can be adapted to form a questionnaire that can be used to assess the impact and magnitude of a change. By considering the above parameters of change, the sponsor of change and the change agent will get a feel for the nature of the change and any dangers that might impede the optimal route forward.

KEY DIMENSIONS FOR MANAGING OPERATIONS AND CHANGE

The change process should be based on an operations and change strategy which stems from the organisation's business strategy. The business strategy provides the overriding business dimension which is prepotent in directing the degree of emphasis in the change process that should be placed on three important dimensions which support it: the technology dimension, the innovation dimension and the organisation dimension.

The business dimension

The business dimension refers to the overall strategic direction and competitive position of the company. It is necessary first to audit the company's current business situation and its existing strategy; that is, to obtain a clear assessment of the organisation's operations, what opportunities there are, and where problem areas exist. Once the way forward has been agreed, the next step would be to determine the strategies in the main business areas of the company, i.e. finance, marketing, personnel, operations etc. With respect to operations, for example, this would involve determining the objectives of quality, delivery, flexibility and cost that would need to be pursued to fulfil the competitive criteria. Thus the basis is formed for determining the best technology, innovation and organisation dimensions.

The technology dimension

Technology influences productivity improvement pervasively. It is the combination of processes and technology in terms of equipment and hardware through which a product or service is produced or delivered. The systems of combined processes and technology have a great deal to do with productivity improvement and are key ingredients in continuous improvement. Certainly the new technologies are the catalysts that help foster effective operations and organisational change.

The innovation dimension

Successful change or improvement, by definition, often requires innovation; that is the introduction of something new: a new method or device, a better idea, an improved piece of hardware. For example, advances in microcomputers and robotics have enabled new equipment to perform faster and smarter. The time to market may be reduced through new processes like rapid prototyping; restructuring to improve organisational effectiveness may be achieved expeditiously through business process re-engineering. Whatever the nature of the innovation, it is important to know that in many organisations success can be achieved through having a culture of innovation and rapid response to change. Exhibit 1.1 illustrates this point for Iceland Frozen Foods Ltd.

Exhibit 1.1

The innovation dimension at Iceland Frozen Foods Ltd

According to chairman and founding partner Malcolm Walker, Iceland's culture is young, innovative and fast moving – 'like a person running very fast'. It is 'high risk' tolerant and able to accommodate failure and learn from it. 'We are a "have a go" company. We make quick decisions. If our ideas work, fine. If they don't, we take a quick step back and move on again.'

Quick response to change is essential in food retailing – 'It's a fashion business,' says Walker. Iceland launches at least 200 new products every year. Every Monday morning, the Board meets to look at the previous week's sales and make decisions for the week ahead.

What sort of employees can handle such rapid change?

The company employs young entrepreneurial people, who are expected to take a high degree of responsibility. 'We like people who are bold and innovative, who make decisions and then stand by them. Even junior managers are expected to take a high degree of responsibility.' Everyone is expected to come up with ideas for improvement. 'We are good at communicating upwards,' says Walker. 'A good idea from an area manager's meeting can be implemented countrywide in a very short time.'

Iceland has an unbroken growth record and an unbroken profit record and is a perfect illustration of the success of a culture of innovation and rapid response to change. Malcolm Walker believes in winning. 'Being second best is never enough. We have to be the best.'

Source: Walker, M. (1994).

The organisation dimension

Technology and innovation alone are not sufficient to ensure successful change. Although technology and innovation can make an organisation highly competitive, the organisation dimension recognises that it still needs people to make it work.

It is people in the organisation that advocate change and it is people that both ensure and enable it to take place. That is, there will be people, both managers and workers, who implement change, and others in the organisation who will be influenced by it. Their total involvement in any change process is the vital ingredient for success. Clearly then, any programme of change involves a high degree of skill in managing the people aspect of the organisation dimension, since people are at the very centre of the change.

The organisation dimension can be divided into two major areas: organisation design and job design. Organisation design involves restructuring and cultural change to utilise the new technology, innovations and people in the best way to deliver what the customers want. Job design, beside being concerned with the design of the job, involves skills, work groups and payment systems.

Changing features of job and organisation design

According to Tranfield and Smith, if we look more closely at these areas, some features of a more effective way of managing change are emerging. These features are shown in Table 1.1.

Changing feature of managing inter-organisational relationships

Also, according to Tranfield and Smith, the difference between the past and emerging patterns in the relationships between an organisation and its customers and suppliers can be seen, which is a shift away from confrontation and a move to a more co-operative, long-term relationship.

Table 1.1 Changing features of managing the organisation

Features of job design	
Past	*Emerging*
Single skilled	Multi-skilled
High division of labour	Integrated tasks
Long skill life cycle	Short skill life cycle
Skill life greater than employee life	Skill life less than employee life
Individual work/accountability	Teamwork/accountability
Payment by results	Alternative payment systems
Supervisor controlled	Supervisor supported
Low work discretion	Increased flexibility/autonomy
Features of organisation design	
Past	*Emerging*
Sharp line/staff boundary	Blurred boundaries
Pyramid authority	Simultaneous tight/loose
Vertical communication	Network communication
Multi-level hierarchy	Flat structure
Bureaucratic/mechanistic	Temporary/organic
Formal control	Holographic adjustment
Functional structures	Product/project/customer-based
Status differentiated	Single status
Rigid/non-participative	Flexible/participative

APPROACH TO CHANGE

There are various ways in which change can be introduced and it is necessary that managers should appreciate what these are so that they can carefully attempt to choose the most useful one. Kotter *et al.* provide a description of the available alternatives that arise from the choice of four types of variable:

1 the amount of time required
2 the degree of planning
3 the type of involvement
4 the use of power.

These represent four strategic options for the management of change, as shown in Table 1.2.

The four variables, depicted in Table 1.2, illustrate the range of extremes in managing operations and change. In making the choice between the extremes, the effect of the tactics chosen needs to be appreciated. For example, a manager adopting the approach indicated on the right-hand side of Table 1.2 would introduce change slowly in a very controlled and thoroughly planned manner. This is an *evolutionary* approach and explicit is the need to be comfortable with each new situation before moving on to the next stage. Typically, with an evolutionary approach, many people will be involved in planning and implementing the change programme, taking great care to be patient, get people involved and minimise resistance. Consequently, much investment and effort would be put into education, problem-solving training, organisational development, supervisory retraining and teambuilding to achieve this.

The left-hand-side of the table depicts changes which are more *revolutionary*. Such changes are often planned by a few people and implemented in a rapid manner by those who agree with the changes or those who are coerced to do so. At first the rapid changes may excite the doubters and induce them to help make change work. However, there is a great chance here that the situation may become unsavoury, involving conflict and casualties, since those who resist will suffer.

Table 1.2 Strategic options for the management of change

Revolutionary change	Evolutionary change
Pace	
Rapid changes	Slow changes
Structure	
Clearly planned	Not clearly planned initially
Involvement	
Little involvement of others	Lots of involvement of others
Approach to resistance	
Overcome resistance	Minimise resistance

Source: Adapted from Kotter, J. P., Schlesinger, L. A. and Sathe, V., *Organisation*, p. 360, Richard D. Irwin, Inc., Homewood, Illinois, 1986.

Key situational variables

Between the endpoints of each of the change continuums there is a range of approaches, any of which a manager may adopt. According to Kotter *et al.* the key situational variables that can help a manager decide which approach to take are:

- the amount and type of resistance that is anticipated
- the position of the initiators *vis-à-vis* the resisters, in terms of trust, power, etc.
- the locus of the relevant data for designing the change and the energy needed for implementing it
- the stakes involved.

Therefore, in attempting to manage effectively all of the stages in the change process, different managers will adopt different change styles, and managers wishing to embark on a change programme need to understand the change process and adopt a style that will increase the chance of being successful.

PERCEPTIONS OF CHANGE

Managing perception is very important, since the management process is perceiving, assessing and then making a decision. As perception is the first stage of the process, if it is faulty then everything else that follows is also faulty.

Depending upon their level in the organisation, managers will have differing perceptions of the problems and opportunities associated with change. It is a fact that the higher people are in the organisation, the more they see and understand of the board-room problems, but they can lose a feeling for life at the operational level. Balancing these sometimes opposing perceptions is a crucial task for the change makers.

CHANGE PERSPECTIVES

Wilson states that:

> *The perspective is the conscience of the change process. It is a mechanism that the change makers set up to enable them to receive valid feedback on the effects of their change. In their passion for pushing through the programme, they can sometimes overlook or under-estimate conditions being created in certain groups of people or parts of the organisation which could seriously jeopardise their plans.*

Therefore, before the change programme commences, it is necessary to incorporate into the programme ways of keeping in touch so that the change problems that arise can be appreciated and any areas that are experiencing difficulty can be identified. There are many different mechanisms that can be used for achieving this, and some, defined by Wilson, are presented below:

Newsletter. Regular update on the change programme circulated to all employees.

Attitude surveys. Structured interviews and questionnaires to a representative sample of employees.

Management by wandering around. Management policy to walk around the organisation regularly and seek employees' views on the change programme.

Consultants. Organisation employs outside consultants to provide an objective outside view.

Briefing sheets. Regular summaries produced by the change makers for managers to brief their teams.

Joint project groups. Management/union/employee groups to implement parts of the change programme.

Steering committee. Selected management/union/employee committee to oversee the change programme.

Video. Make and show a video film on the progress towards change to all employees every six months.

Roadshows. Structured presentation by senior managers to all employees every six months.

Change centre. Construct a centre to house the change project team. Display progress charts and allow free access to all employees.

Publications. Publish discussion booklets on the main elements of the change process.

Consultative committee. Managers consult with employee representatives on change plans and progress.

Progress charts. Project progress charts circulated to employees.

Poster campaign. Posters displayed on notice boards informing staff of progress.

CONDITIONS FOR SUCCESS

Making the right changes that will benefit the company, while bringing along the people within it, doesn't just happen by chance. Particular foundations and structures need to be created and developed. The following are conditions under which success is likely:

Direct, active involvement of senior management

Peters and Waterman provide evidence of how effective change in organisations is fostered by visible top management support. If others lower in the hierarchy see the senior people giving their time and emphasising and enthusing about certain changes, then the message will soon get around that they are not just paying lip service to those changes. They will see that the senior managers are committed to change and are willing to lead by example in order to bring others along to facilitate it.

Starting afresh: The green field approach

Sometimes, as the old saying goes, 'you have to be cruel to be kind'. That is, it is a waste of time perpetuating the existing ways; be they certain systems, technology, processes, products or, yes, even certain people. The necessary changes may be impossible to achieve unless the 'old' system is altered.

In the BBC 'Trouble Shooter II' series, Sir John Harvey Jones provided a striking example of this when he visited an Indian textile weaving company. During a factory tour Sir John exclaimed, *'This is worse than the dark satanic mills that Dickens wrote about.'* Certainly the noise and working conditions were such that in this country, through legislation and company ethics, the mill would not have been allowed to operate. Sir John pointed out that, because of high land prices in that locality and the low contribution the company was experiencing, it would be better for all concerned if the place was shut down. The money could be used to adopt a green field approach and open up a new factory. Eventually, the managers took the advice and considered that by starting afresh they could, using the right technology and people, build up larger markets and employ more people than before.

Many companies, like the one mentioned above, are slowly dying on their feet. They have not yet been faced, like so many have, with the stark choice between survival or death. They may feel that closing down or green field options are unrealistic. However, they may be forced to take such measures unless they can retrieve the situation by drastically changing or stopping their current practices.

Praise as well as pay for results

People want to be adequately remunerated for their effort, and profit-sharing schemes, gain sharing and share options are examples of remuneration systems that can achieve this. Studies of operations managers in Clementson show they are not dissatisfied with their monetary rewards but are unhappy about the amount of recognition they are given. For example, a comprehensive school at the bottom of the league table had embarked upon a change initiative to improve its situation. Changes were made, such as every pupil being in uniform, an increase in attendance, greater interest and higher scores in mathematics. Successes were achieved but it was evident that the spirit for change and improvement was lacking. When, however, the headmaster took the action of having a party, or going on a trip, or generally finding some way to mark the occasion and celebrate the change, then things really started to take off and improvements became easier to achieve and more frequent.

Use of individual skills capabilities and innovativeness

Selecting, developing and making the best use of individuals are vital activities, because an organisation is only as good as the competency of the people within it. First, people need the technical knowledge and skills so that they can participate in making useful decisions, solving problems and creating new ideas. It is most important that such knowledge and skills are directed in the right areas to achieve the organisation's desired business outcomes. To achieve this, the competences of individuals, both personal and interpersonal, need to be continuously upgraded in the areas of business and management and performance improvement.

Creating the conditions for change

It is important that we consider the elements which create the conditions that allow change to take place successfully. To move towards an organisation's vision, to implement its strategies, requires change – often quite radical change. This usually means that people in the organisation are required to do new things in new ways within new structures. For some, this will bring benefits. For other people, though, the reverse may be the case. Organisations, therefore, need to create a readiness for change among their employees, and be aware of the possibility and causes of resistance, and deal with these at an early stage. The summaries following are what Burnes considers are necessary in organisations to create a readiness for change:

Make people aware of the pressures for change. Employees should be informed of the plans for the future, the competitive-market pressures being faced, and the performance of the key competitors.

Give regular feedback on the performance of individual functions and areas of activities within the organisation. The organisation should draw attention to any discrepancy between actual performance and desired present and future performance. It allows those concerned to begin to think about how this situation can be improved and prepares them for the need for change.

Publicise successful change. To create a positive attitude towards change, the organisation should publicise the change programmes which are seen as models of how to undertake change and the positive effects it can have for employees. This does not mean that mistakes should be hidden or poor outcomes ignored.

There are other steps which need to be taken to deal with causes of resistance at an early stage:

Understand people's fears and concerns. Change does create uncertainty and people may resist or be unco-operative. These fears need to be recognised and attention given to solving these types of problems.

Encourage communication. One way of avoiding the uncertainty that change can promote is to establish a regular and effective communications process – one which gives both the context for and the details and consequences of proposed changes.

Involve those affected. Involvement promotes understanding and overcomes potential resistance; lack of involvement creates suspicion and leads to resistance.

Exhibit 1.2 illustrates how multinationals like Hewlett-Packard, Motorola, 3M, Rank Xerox, Ricoh, Philips Electronics and Ericsson manage their change programmes better through the managers becoming more personally involved in the process and appreciating that the use of systems like budgeting and cost allocation, remuneration, promotion, management information and personnel assessment can be used to modify behaviour.

The need for the right culture

Much of the above, and indeed what follows, requires organisations to have cultures which encourage and support these activities. Handy pointed out that just as there are many different organisational structures, practices and procedures, so too are there different cultures. However, rather than being separate, Handy argued that each type of organisational structure has its own matching culture. These act to reinforce and legitimise each other. However, if the two are not matching, or if one changes and the other does not, then the likelihood is that conflict will arise. In any case, the types of behaviour and procedures involved in bringing about successful change require cultures which encourage flexibility, autonomy, group

Exhibit 1.2

How multinational CEOs make change programmes stick

Transforming major organisations with thousands of employees is a complex and arduous task, especially when the aim of change is to alter the behavioural patterns of all the employees. In exploring top management teams from Hewlett-Packard, Motorola, 3M, Rank Xerox, Ricoh, Philips Electronics and Ericsson the following lessons were learnt.

Change cannot be captured in a cook book approach. It is a transformation process with an heuristic nature and a balancing act of acceptable push and pull between corporate headquarters and the business units. But top management can actively direct and influence the change by first altering their own behaviour and becoming more personally involved in the process and engaging in at least four major areas of activities:

1 **Legitimacy**. Managers need to devote ample time and attention to ensure that the change is seen by all members of the organisation as legitimate and often the only way to advance the organisation.
2 **Formulating objectives**. Top management teams need to formulate objectives which are significant for all business units, irrespective of their current performance levels and circumstances.
3 **Managing reviews**. Business managers need to understand better the process and learn why things fail or succeed through observation, fact-based analysis, experimentation and improvement.
4 **Changing systems**. Systems like budgeting and cost allocation, remuneration, promotion, management information and personnel assessment are responsible for directly influencing 80 per cent of the behaviour of employees and therefore changing these systems has a major effect on a company.

Source: Adapted from Bertsch, B. and Williams, R., 'How multinational CEOs make change programmes stick', *Long Range Planning*, Vol. 21, No. 5, pp. 12–24, Copyright 1994, with kind permission from Elsevier Science Ltd., The Boulevard, Langford Lane, Kidlington OX5 1GB, UK.

working, etc. If the organisation's culture does not support these activities, then change will be much more difficult and may not be successful. Therefore, if organisations do not have a culture which matches how they wish to operate in future, they must create one.

Change through the right focus on processes, people and culture

Duncan Pummel, Manufacturing Systems Manager with Caradon Mira, questions what organisations need to change in order to meet competitive pressures. He asks if their changes are covered adequately by

- processes
- people
- culture.

He suggests that many projects fail because the environment and people issues are not addressed and that the technical project is only one part of the equation. His comments on what organisations need to change in order to meet competitive pressures are summarised in Exhibit 1.3.

Exhibit 1.3

What organisations need to change in order to meet competitive pressures

A Operational processes

When considering operations processes such as manufacturing we often tend to take the following traditional approach to change with the emphasis on spending money: the more the better, introducing staff functions and questioning effectiveness. A new view of process improvement should be:

- Understand the process.
- Understand why it fails.
- Understand the cause of the failure.
- Improve the process by tackling the cause.

This follows closely the Kaizen approach of continual improvement.

B People

An old view could be that management and supervision knew best and so told people what to do. Generally we have had a lack of respect for people. So if we are to become more competitive we have to change the way we treat people. People are now looking to be treated in a different way. The general culture has changed and industry can reflect these changes by:

- Respecting all people in the business. They have skills which you should use to the utmost.
- Working in teams rather than individually. The power of a team is again a case where 2+2 =5.
- Enabling and empowering people to make process changes.
- The role of supervision and management changes. Instead of directing people what to do and how to do it, the new role of management/supervision can be one quoted by Tom Peters – 'cops turned coach'.

C Culture

The culture of an organisation is very important as it supplies the context within which process and people changes takes place. It may help change the culture of an organisation if senior management:

- develop a vision of how they see the organisation in the future
- develop improvement strategies which move the company from where they are to where they see themselves in their vision
- communicate the vision and strategies to everyone in the organisation.

Source: Adapted from Pummell, D., 'Changing the manufacturing and people culture, or can 2 + 2 = 5?', *Control*, August/September, pp. 29–33, 1994, The Institute of Operations Management.

Successful change programmes begin with results

Schaffer and Thomson argue that most corporate change programmes mistake means for ends, process for outcome, and in doing so do not achieve any real bottom-line performance improvements. It is argued that change programmes can succeed if they begin by being results-orientated. Exhibit 1.4 provides an example of a results-driven improvement process that focuses on achieving specific, measurable operational improvements and achieves them within a few months.

BARRIERS TO SUCCESSFUL CHANGE

Barriers that impede the change process

Those managing the change must be aware of the nature of the resistance they will face by other managers as well as workers. The cause can often be traced back to difficulties in the organisation – its structure, its power centres, its culture. These difficulties must be addressed before unfreezing can take place. People may become stubborn and defend the status quo. They may aggressively challenge the credibility of any change proposals. Alternatively, they may feign co-operation while covertly seeking to jeopardise the change programme. Table 1.3 describes many of the barriers that impede companies in their change efforts.

In a similar vein, Woodcock and Francis talk about unblocking the organisation. They identify 14 categories of blocks:

1 unclear aims	8 unfair rewards
2 unclear values	9 poor training
3 inappropriate management philosophy	10 personal stagnation
4 lack of management development	11 inadequate communication
5 confused organisational structure	12 poor teamwork
6 inadequate control	13 low motivation
7 inadequate recruitment and selection	14 low creativity.

Table 1.3 Perceived barriers to change

- Performance measures will kill us if we do these things.
- The union will never hear of this.
- The consultant doesn't have hands-on manufacturing experience.
- Does management understand all that this implies?
- What does this do to our existing capital spending plans?
- The supplier is unreliable.
- Marketing can't forecast well enough.
- Engineering and schedule changes won't permit zero inventories.
- Our equipment won't meet a zero defects requirement.
- How can we deal with 'their' mindset?
- Management has no real manufacturing understanding or appreciation.
- They'll never accept all this disruption.

Source: Bell, R. R. and Burnham, J. M., *Managing Productivity and Change*.

Exhibit 1.4

Successful change programmes begin with results

In 1988, one of the largest US financial institutions committed itself to a 'total quality' program. At the end of two years of costly effort, it did not report any bottom-line performance improvements – because there were none. In a 1991 survey of more than 300 electronics companies, sponsored by the American Electronics Association, 73 per cent of the companies reported having a total quality program under way, but of these, 63 per cent had failed to improve quality defects by even as much as 10 per cent. We believe this survey understates the magnitude of the failure of activity-centered programs, not only in the quality-conscious electronics industry, but across all businesses.

There are six reasons why the cards are stacked against activity-centered improvement programs:

1 Not keyed to specific results.
2 Too large scale and diffused. One company identified so many activities in so many places, it required a complex chart just to describe them.
3 Results is a four-letter word. It is a brave manager who insists on seeing a demonstrable link between the proposed investment and tangible payoffs in the short term.
4 Delusional measurements. Companies proclaim their quality programs with the same pride with which they would proclaim real performance improvements. The Malcolm Baldrige National Quality Award encourages such practices by awarding high marks to companies that demonstrate outstanding quality processes without always demanding that the current products and services be equally outstanding.
5 Staff- and consultant-driven. In many cases, managers seek this outside help because they have exhausted their own ideas about improvement. So, when staff experts and improvement gurus show up with their evangelistic enthusiasm and bright promises of total quality and continuous improvement, asking only for faith and funds, managers greet them with open arms.
6 Bias to orthodoxy, not empiricism. Because of the absence of clear-cut beginnings and ends and an inability to link cause and effect, there is virtually no opportunity to learn useful lessons and apply them to future programs. Instead, as in any approach based in faith rather than evidence, the advocates – convinced they already know the answers – merely give more dedication to the 'right' steps.

A Harvard Business School team headed by Michael Beer analyzed a number of large-scale corporate change programs. As the authors colourfully put it, 'Wave after wave of programs rolled across the landscape with little positive impact.'

The alternative is a results-driven improvement process that focuses on achieving specific, measurable operational improvements within a few months. The results-driven path stakes specific targets and matches resources, tools, and action plans to the requirements of reaching those targets.

Consider the case of the Morgan Bank which yielded significant service improvements and several million dollars of cost savings within the first year of the initiative. The case illustrates four key benefits of a results-driven approach that activity-centered programs generally miss:

1 Companies introduce managerial and process innovations only as they are needed. Results-driven projects require managers to prioritize carefully the innovations they want to employ to achieve targeted goals.
2 Empirical testing reveals what works. Because management introduces each managerial and process innovation sequentially and links them to short-term goals, it can discover fairly quickly the extent to which each approach yields results.
3 Frequent reinforcement energizes the improvement process. There is no motivator more powerful than frequent successes ... managers and employees can enjoy the psychological fruits of success ... builds management's confidence and skills for continued incremental improvements.
4 Management creates a continuous learning process by building on the lessons of previous phases in designing the next phase of the program.

Source: Shaffer, R.H. and Thomson, H.A., 'Successful change programs begin with results', *Harvard Business Review*.

Other barriers to change

Although the barriers described above can have an effect on the change process, it is necessary to understand the factors that lie behind resistance to change. Beckhardt lists these as being:

1 The existence of a credibility gap between top management's statement of philosophy, values, and practices and its actual behaviour.

2 The use of canned solutions or pieces of a change programme that are not based on specific change goals. Comments like 'We need a CAD/CAM system because everyone else has one' are not likely to occasion productive change. In other words, is it imitation or innovation?

3 A short time perspective or an unrealistic expectation of short-term results.

4 An overdependence on or improper use of external or internal consultants. This is buying expertise, being unwilling or unable to develop it, and can be a major barrier.

5 A lack of communications and integration of change efforts among various levels of the organisation.

6 The search for quick solutions or cook book prescriptions for organisational effectiveness.

Three important additions to the above list need referring to. First, the culture of the organisation may pose a barrier to change. For example, a 'no mistakes allowed' culture may prevail. This may be symptomatic of a risk-avoidance strategy on the part of managers. The effect is that it will adversely limit the plans and actions of many in the organisation. Experimentation and innovation should be accepted as a natural part of the change process. Peters and Waterman noted that risk-taking and occasional failure often accompany successful change:

> A special attribute of the success-oriented, positive, and innovative environment is a substantial tolerance for failure.

Second, the hierarchies in which people manage can separate them from a common sense of purpose. Communications from top to bottom and from bottom to top may be infrequent, inconsistent, and give rise to misunderstandings. Finally, the barrier to change can lie within every person. The individualism of the West may spurn innovativeness which is an essential asset in many market places, but the spirit of the East which accepts teamwork and group goals certainly underpins bringing such assets to the market.

Analysis of both change and resistance forces to identify an appropriate change path

According to Strebel, programmes based primarily on the change drivers, ignoring the forces of resistance, are as prone to failure as those dealing primarily with the forces of resistance, ignoring the change drivers. What is needed is the choice of a change path based on a diagnosis of both the forces of change and resistance.

Strebel identifies three basic forms of change forces:

● established trends in the socio-political, economic, technological, competitive, and organisational environments

- turning points that reflect the limits to the established trends (limits to the existing resources, capacity investment, growth) and the stimuli promoting new trends (innovation, life cycle shifts, new players)
- internal change drivers in the form of organisational shifts, new managers, and change agents.

The forces of resistance, which are the response of the company's internal and external stakeholders to the change requirements, he identifies as four basic forms:

- rigid structures and systems reflecting organisations, business technology, and stakeholder resources that are not consistent with the forces of change
- closed mindsets reflecting business beliefs and strategies that are oblivious to the forces of change
- entrenched cultures reflecting values, behaviours and skills that are not adapted to the forces of change
- counterproductive change momentum driven by historical or other change drivers that are not relevant to the most urgent forces of change.

Strebel presents a 'change path diagnostic', shown in Fig 1.3, which makes it possible to identify an appropriate change path for a given situation.

Studies using the change path diagnostic were conducted on Nabisco, Scandinavian Airlines System (SAS), BP, Harley-Davidson, Nestlé and Seiko. In each case it was possible to make a choice between the eight different change paths. Strebel's main conclusions were:

- When the change forces are strong, the key issue is whether, and when, the resistance will be overcome. Resistance that is capable of dominating the change forces gives the company the choice of adapting with limited renewal, or resisting. By contrast, change forces that cannot be neutralised, must be fully adapted to – either with slow, deep revitalisation when there is enough time and resources available, or with sharp, rapid restructuring when time is short.
- When the change forces are weak and have yet to affect performance, the key question for initiating proactive change is whether the forces can be readily identified. If so, the most appropriate change path is determined by how open or closed the organisation is to change.
- If the change forces themselves are difficult to identify, the challenge is to create a mobilising sense of discomfort with things as they are.
- To adapt to more than one change force, a change campaign is required in the form of a sequence of change paths, to deal with the stronger change forces first, thereby clearing the way for exploiting the weaker ones.
- The change campaign must be ongoing; as soon as companies stop dealing with change forces, they run into trouble, as illustrated by the studies with both SAS and Harley-Davidson.

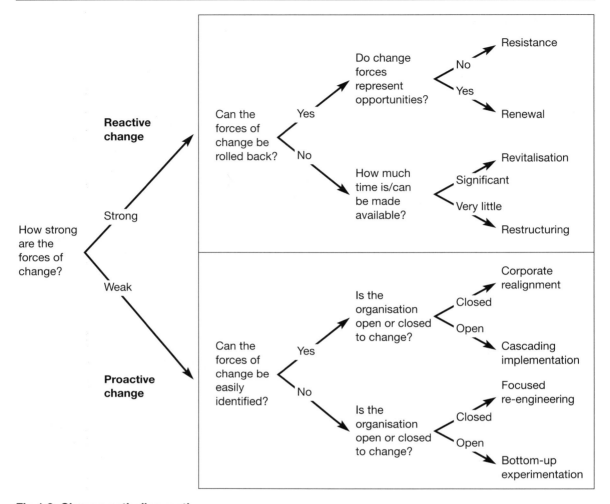

Fig 1.3 Change path diagnostic

Source: Strebel, P., 'Choosing the right change path', *California Management Review.* Copyright © 1994, by The Regents of the University of California. Reprinted from the *California Management Review*, Vol. 36, No. 2. By permission of The Regents.

PEOPLE AND CHANGE

The approach to change and people

Change programmes should be instigated which are designed to question the basic order and bring about the right type of changes. The approach to change should contain a management process which is orderly, systematic and enables plans to be developed which lead to the choice of effective actions from the many different avenues open to the organisation. Management of the change process is not an easy task. Change often causes both internal conflicts in people and external conflicts between people, departments, and companies. To effect the change, the manager must have influence in the company and the ability to create in others the need to do what will succeed.

Politics, people and power

Although the need for change can be recognised and acknowledged, some very important questions need addressing which are central to the change process being successful. How widespread is the perceived need for change? How much support is there for change? Who sees the need for improvement or change in the dimensions of process, technology, systems or people? What changes in these dimensions are necessary? How are people best involved in the change process? Who should be involved and in what ways? How will the technology–people–process–systems interface work? Finally, those involved in managing the change must explore the politics of the situation. Where are the power and influence centres? What votes are needed to win?

Accommodating the losers in the process

Since change can be viewed as a threat instead of a benefit, people may not have the commitment to the vision that the change makers would like. Consequently, understanding the different perceptions those people have and how to manage them successfully is an important aspect of managing the change process. However, irrespective of the messages conveyed about the potential benefits of any significant change programme, there will inevitably be winners and losers. Some of the pain and difficulty can be avoided if those managing the change build checks into the process which consider how the change is being perceived. For example, who might perceive themselves to be the winners or the losers in the change process, and why? By taking more notice of the possible reactions of the potential losers and dealing with them early enough, major disruptions may be avoided.

People may consider they will lose out because their level of responsibility appears to be being reduced. Through the changes they see a reduction in their perceived relative status – a common worry nowadays in the management ranks of an organisation, as operating teams become more self-managing and there is less need for supervisors and middle managers. Similarly, both professional and craft people, respectively, may feel threatened as some of their skills, and hence bargaining power, are transferred elsewhere through the introduction of new technology, computer systems and people becoming more multi-skilled.

Factors that influence the way change is viewed

According to McCalman and Paton there are a number of influential factors which combine to mould the way in which individuals, groups and organisations view particular change situations:

- organisational culture
- source of change: internal/external
- social background: inhibits collaboration
- education history: topical management ideas
- employment history: the 'them and us' mentality
- style of management: could possibly be at odds with it
- problem ownership: involvement and commitment of the problem owner is essential
- experience: judged in terms of their past ability to cope with change; will influence the expectations of all concerned.

To manage these sort of problems the change makers must have the ability to overcome any personal prejudices regarding the change. They must plan carefully for the change, skillfully introduce it, and handle resistance, bearing in mind the political ramifications within the organisation. It needs to be appreciated that directives from the top are very likely to produce mediocre results unless they are designed to point the way (the Japanese say, 'Give the idea to the people') and provide support for implementation efforts. This can be achieved by ensuring that the views, as well as prejudices, exhibited by all other affected parties are taken on board. To do this, those managing the change must be able to develop the necessary relationships with both those who support and those who will be affected by it. It is through these means that the chances of managing the change through to a successful conclusion are greatest. The change must then be stabilised.

A MODEL FOR MANAGING CHANGE

The Intervention Strategy Model

Management processes and structures may be described in systems terms, and many believe that change situations may be effectively managed through the application of systems thinking. The Intervention Strategy Model (ISM) takes a systems approach and, in a structured manner, handles the analysis and implementation of a change situation. It is a most useful change model for adopting when the impending or existing change situation exhibits tendencies towards the 'hard' end of the change spectrum, that is, the change is quantifiable, structured, mechanistic, systems or technically-orientated; in short, where the change problems are scientific or engineering related, although it could find use in 'softer' situations, typical of the kind of problems found in personal relationships and where emotional responses are predominant. The term 'intervention strategy' is used because the methodology adopted by the model is that of successfully intervening in the working processes of the original system, with the purpose of bringing about an effective change in that system.

Incorporated within the ISM is the Systems Intervention Strategy (SIS) developed by the Open Business School and the Total Project Management Model (TPMM), a product of the University of Glasgow Business School. All three models have been extensively tried and tested on countless practising managers and their associated organisations.

The following is a summary of McCalman and Paton's description on the phases of intervention and the stages of the ISM.

The three phases of intervention

The three basic phases of the ISM for the problem owner and possibly a supporting management team are shown in Fig 1.4. The definition phase involves the in-depth specification and study of the change situation, both from an historical and futuristic view; the evaluation phase generates and evaluates the potential solution options; and the implementation phase develops the action plans which should successfully introduce the outputs of the design phase.

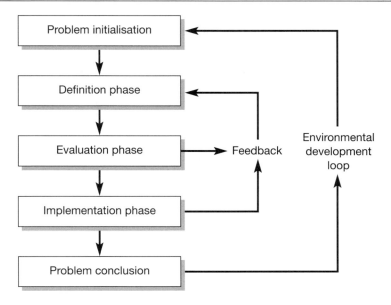

Fig 1.4 The basic phases of the Intervention Strategy Model

Source: Reprinted with permission from McCalman, J. and Paton, R. A., *Change Management: A guide to effective implementation*. Copyright 1992 Paul Chapman Publishing Ltd., London.

Before embarking on a formal and detailed journey through these stages, it is advisable to conduct a 'quick and dirty' analysis of the change problem. In this way the key factors associated with the change can be addressed.

During each of the phases, the systems affected should be constantly monitored, both internally and externally, to check and revamp, if necessary, the assumptions, objectives, information and analysis. Consequently, iterations are a feature of this approach to a change problem. And the purpose of identifying the environmental development feedback loop, which links the final outcome with the initial situation, is to illustrate that the change cycle is never complete.

The individual stages associated with each phase of the model are shown in Fig 1.5.

The stages of ISM

Phase 1: Definition and identification of the appropriate problem owners

- **Stage 1: Problem/system specification and description**. Develop an understanding of the situation. Use diagrammatic techniques, meetings and historical data.

- **Stage 2: Formulation of objectives and constraints**. The objectives need to be prioritised and considered further to include the options for achieving them. As a result the various options for their pursuit can then form the basis of an implementation strategy. Constraints become apparent because of the requirement for resources which are scarce.

- **Stage 3: Identification of performance measures**. Having decided on the objectives of the change programme, it is important to formulate appropriate quantifiable performance indicators or measures, such as costs, savings, volume, labour and time,

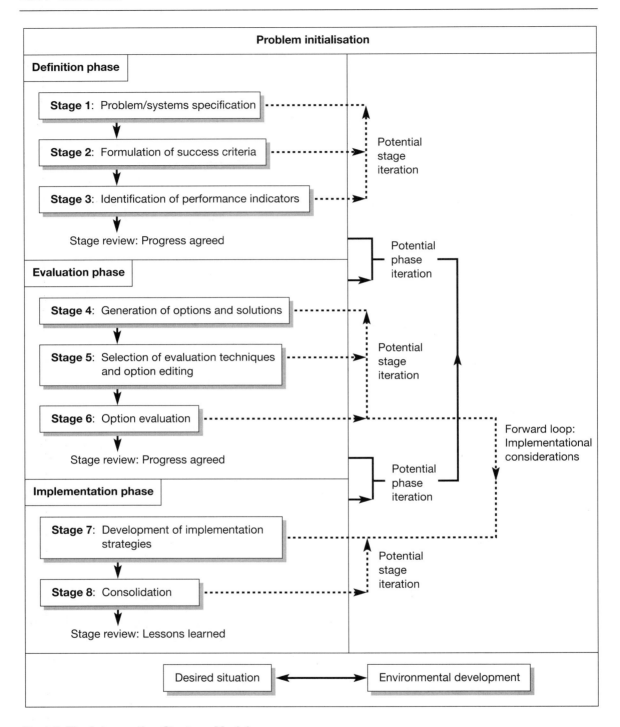

Fig 1.5 The Intervention Strategy Model

Source: Reprinted with permission from McCalman J. and Paton, R. A., *Change Management: A guide to effective implementation.* Copyright 1992 Paul Chapman Publishing Ltd., London.

for each one. If this is not done then it becomes difficult for the problem owner to evaluate the options that are generated. Such measures can also be entered on the objectives tree.

Phase 2: Evaluation

- **Stage 4: Generation of options or solutions**. This is best done as a group exercise using one of the wide range of techniques available, such as brainstorming, focus groups, meetings and workshops. If members of the group involved have limited knowledge of each other then some form of team-building exercise may be necessary.

- **Stage 5: Selection of appropriate evaluation techniques and option editing**. Here the options are considered in greater depth to establish their true viability. Techniques such as systems diagrams, simulation, investment analysis and cost–benefit analysis will assist in weeding out the weak options and will form the basis of the final evaluation.

- **Stage 6: Option evaluation**. Options are evaluated against the previously-determined priority for each objective. It is not worth rushing this phase. Time spent getting it right first time is seldom wasted.

The first two phases are not considered complete until all those involved agree with the decisions and conclusions reached. This develops ownership of the problem of those involved.

Phase 3: Implementation

- **Stage 7: Development of implementation strategies**. There are essentially three basic implementation strategies:

  1 pilot studies leading eventually to change
  2 parallel running
  3 Big Bang.

  Pilot studies provide the opportunity to review the change in the safest way and learn how possibly to approach it better. However, pilot studies delay full implementation and it must be appreciated that the environment does not stand still and more time is given to those who may wish to resist the change. When the proposed changes can greatly affect other areas it may be best to adopt a parallel-running implementation strategy and slowly phase out the old system as the new becomes more reliable and understood. Big Bang implementation maximises the speed of change but it can also generate the maximum resistance, at least in the short term.

- **Stage 8: Consolidation**. It is necessary to maintain the establishment of the new system and carefully ward off any encroachment of old systems and practices, unless it can be proved they have merit in the new order.

OVERCOMING PITFALLS IN THE CHANGE PROCESS

Bridges explains that each step in the change process has its own pitfalls. His tips on how to overcome them are shown in Table 1.4.

Rules for successful change

Pugh discusses several rules for change:

1 Work hard at establishing the need for change. Make sure there is an agreement on the need for change in all relevant departments.

2 Don't only think out the change, think through it. Consider the coming changes in job content, tasks, methods of working, group relationships, autonomy or authority and status.

3 Initiate change through informal discussion to get feedback and participation. Make an effort to appreciate all views about the coming changes.

4 Positively encourage those concerned to give their objections. People who object to changes could form a new source of resistance. Therefore it is important to know who objects and why.

5 Be prepared to change yourself. Change is not just for other people; it also concerns the manager. Appreciate opinions and ideas from others in the organisation.

Table 1.4 Overcoming pitfalls in the change process

Step in change process	How to ensure success
Letting go	Identify who is losing what
	Accept losses
	Inform people
Managing neutral zone	Encourage creativity
	Set path
Launching new beginning	Timing
	Clarity: purpose, picture, plan, part people play
	Watch for slower people
Non-stop change	Do exercises; what if …?
	Mission
	Sell problems, not solutions (by coaching)
Taking care of yourself	People are not machine X operators, but can be assigned anywhere to add value

6 Monitor the change and reinforce it. Ensure when the changes are made that progress continues. Communicate positive sounds to people who deserve them.

THE NEED FOR AN OPERATIONS AND CHANGE STRATEGY

To enable all of the above to be co-ordinated in order to manage the changes involved in operations management, it is necessary to develop an 'operations and change strategy'. To be complete such a strategy would require the following stages:

1 The need to clarify what operations need to be changed to meet the changing needs of the business. Such a strategy process would define the performance objectives that are to be pursued, the operations activities needed to achieve them, together with necessary detail on the plans and control systems.

2 The consideration of the most appropriate operations initiatives for the pursuit of the operations activities.

3 The need to consider fully the people who are involved in the changes, be they leaders, followers or objectors.

4 The most appropriate initiatives of change to adopt. Clearly, the use of restructuring and teamwork will assist, but what about the merits of empowerment or becoming a learning organisation?

5 Most importantly, how to make it all happen. What needs to be known here is which management approaches really work, how the organisation and the people within it can be developed and how the system can be continually improved.

These five stages are explained in detail in the following chapter, 'Operations and change strategy'.

SUMMARY

- Change is generally a response to some significant threat or opportunity arising outside of the organisation. Organisations that do not change due to ignorance will be the first to fail. For organisations to survive and thrive they must constantly scan what is happening and develop an awareness of what actually needs changing in order to move in the right direction.

- The change process was described by Lewin as three stages: unfreezing, moving, and refreezing. The major elements in managing the change process are: recognising the need for change, preparing for change, unfreezing the organisation, managing the actual change, and refreezing (stabilising) the organisation afterwards. These change activities fall into four phases: the exploration phase, the planning phase, the action phase and the integration phase.

- The following factors need to be considered when developing a change programme: the scope and size of the programme, the amount of investment required, the timescale, the nature of the changes that need to take place, the impetus for change (is it for survival or development?), the nature of the strategy on the revolutionary–evolutionary continuum.

- The business dimension is prepotent in directing the degree of emphasis in the change process, and three important dimensions which support it are: the technology dimension, the innovation dimension and the organisation dimension.

- Perceptions of change are very important because management bases its decisions on what it perceives is happening and needs to change. The higher people are in the organisation's hierarchy the more they see and understand of the strategic issues, but they can lose a feeling for life at the operational level. Therefore, it is necessary to incorporate into the programme ways of keeping in touch so that the change problems can be appreciated and any difficulties identified.

- The conditions which are likely to lead to successful change are: the direct, active involvement of senior management; starting afresh, for example a green field approach; praising as well as paying for results; the use of individual skills capabilities and innovativeness. The right conditions for change need to be created and this involves: making people aware of the pressures for change, giving regular feedback on the performance of individual functions and areas of activities within the organisation, publicising successful change, understanding people's fears and concerns, encouraging communication, involving those affected and having the right culture.

- Barriers to successful change need to be identified. Their cause can often be traced back to difficulties in the organisation, in its structure and its culture.

- The approach to change should reflect the politics of the situation, power bases, and how people can best be involved in the change process. The way in which individuals, groups and organisations view particular change situations should be considered, and in particular notice should be taken of the potential losers if major disruptions are to be avoided.

- The Intervention Strategy Model (ISM) handles, in a structured manner, the analysis and implementation of a change situation. The stages of the ISM are: Stage 1 – problem/system specification and description; Stage 2 – formulation of objectives and constraints; Stage 3 – identification of performance measures; Stage 4 – generation of options or solutions; Stage 5 – selection of appropriate evaluation techniques and option editing; Stage 6 – option evaluation; Stage 7 – development of implementation strategies, and Stage 8 – consolidation.

- To manage the change in operations effectively it is necessary to develop an 'operations and change strategy'. Such a strategy would require the following: First, the need to clarify what needs to be changed in the operations; second, deciding on the most appropriate operations initiatives for the pursuit of the operations activities; third, the need to consider fully the people who are involved in the changes; fourth, the determination of the most appropriate initiatives of change to adopt, and fifth, how to make it all happen.

REVIEW AND DISCUSSION QUESTIONS

1 Explain what change is and why it is important to organisations.

2 Discuss the importance of the perceptions of change, the variety of ways of monitoring change and the issues and problems involved.

3 Outline the conditions in an organisation that are likely to achieve successful change and explain how they can be created.

4 Outline possible barriers to successful change and explain how they might be overcome.

ASSIGNMENTS

1 The managing director has asked you, a senior operations manager, to provide him/her with an outline of a presentation you are to make to other managers on how change might best be managed in the organisation. The main focus of your presentation concerns the main factors you consider need to be taken into account in order to assess the nature and magnitude of the changes. Also, what particular aspects of the business would best support the change process?

2 In the role of a change consultant, you have been asked to give a talk on how to identify the barriers to successful change in a typical organisation, what the success factors for change are and what approach an organisation might use to make its change process run effectively. What would be the main points of your talk?

REFERENCES

Beckhardt, R., *Organisational Development Strategies and Models*, p. 131, Addison-Wesley, Boston, 1969.

Bell, R.R. and Burnham, J.M., *Managing Productivity and Change*, South-Western Publishing Co, Cincinnati, Ohio, 1991.

Bertsch, B. and Williams, R., 'How multinational CEOs make change programmes stick', *Long Range Planning*, Vol. 21, No. 5, pp. 12–24, 1994.

Bridges, William, *Managing Transitions: Making the most out of change*, Nicholas Brealey Publishing, London, 1995. Previously published in 1991 by Addison-Wesley, USA as *Managing Organisational Transitions*.

Bullock, R.J. and Batten, D., 'It's just a phase we're going through: A review and synthesis of OD phase analysis' in *Group and Organisation Studies*, Vol. 10, pp. 383–412, December 1985.

Burnes, B., *Managing Change: A strategic approach to organisational development and renewal*, Pitman Publishing, London, 1992.

Clementson, S., *The Skills and Capabilities of Manufacturing Managers: Esteem, motivation and job satisfaction*, BSc dissertation, Department of Manufacturing Engineering and Operations Management, University of Nottingham, Nottingham, 1995.

DTI, *How the Best UK Companies are Winning*, report published jointly by the DTI and the CBI, designed and produced by CGI London Limited, 1994.

Handy, C., *Understanding Organisations*, Penguin, Harmondsworth, 1986.

Jordan, M.G., *Production Management Systems*, SME, Dearborn, Mich.

Kotter, J.P., Schlesinger, L.A. and Sathe, V., *Organisation*, p. 360, Irwin, Homewood, Ill., 1986.

Lewin, K., 'Group decision and social change' in Maccoby, E.E., Newcomb, T.M. and Hartley, E.L. (eds), *Readings in Social Psychology*, Holt, Rinehart & Winston, New York, 1958.

McCalman, J. and Paton, R.A., *Change Management: A guide to effective implementation*, Paul Chapman, London, 1992.

Paton, R.A. and Southern, G., *Total Project Management*, University of Glasgow Business School Working Paper Series, 1990.

Peters, T.J. and Waterman, R.H., *In Search of Excellence: Lessons from America's best-run companies*, Harper & Row, New York, 1982.

Pettigrew, A., *The Awakening Giant: Continuity and change in Imperial Chemical Industries*, Blackwell, Oxford, 1985.

Pugh, D. S. in Mabey, C. and Mayon-White, B., *Managing Change*, pp. 108–12, Paul Chapman, London, 1993.

Pummell, D., 'Changing the manufacturing and people culture, or can 2 + 2 = 5?', *Control*, pp. 29–33, Aug/Sep 1994, The Institute of Operations Management, Coventry.

Schaffer, R.H. and Thomson, H.A., 'Successful change programs begin with results', *Harvard Business Review*, pp. 80–9, Jan/Feb 1992.

Strebel, P., 'Choosing the right change path', *California Management Review*, Vol. 36, No. 2, pp. 29–51, 1994.

Tranfield D. and Smith, S., *Managing Change*, IFS Publications, Kempston, Bedford, 1990.

Walker, M., Comments of Malcolm Walker, Iceland Frozen Foods Ltd, Wales. Reproduced in *Competitiveness – How the Best UK Companies at Winning*, report published jointly by the DTI and the CBI, designed and produced by CGI London Limited, 1994.

Wilson, T.W., *A Manual for Change*, Gower, Aldershot, 1994.

Woodcock, M. and Francis, D., *Unblocking Your Organisation*, Gower, Aldershot, 1990.

PART 2

Clarifying what needs to be changed

CHAPTER 2

Operations and change strategy

OBJECTIVES

The objectives of this chapter are to:

- define an operations and change strategy
- provide a framework for operations and change strategy development, the main components of which are:
  - clarifying what needs to be changed
  - the people in the change process
  - the initiatives of change
  - making it happen
  - formulating a coherent operations and change strategy
- provide tips for sound strategy development, including:
  - being proactive and being involved in the strategy formulation
  - linking and aligning operations capabilities with market requirements
  - agreeing and communicating task priorities
  - considering the trade-offs, focus and flexibility
  - seeking strategic flexibility
- preview the features of operations strategy development by considering three prominent approaches, namely those of Hill, Platts and Gregory, and Slack
- provide an action plan for operations and change strategy development
- illustrate some of the practical issues and problems associated with operations and change strategy development by reference to the Clearview Company case.

THE NEED FOR AN OPERATIONS AND CHANGE STRATEGY

Organisations that compete more effectively than others are those which have a strategic direction and are better managed. Organisations deemed excellent or 'world class', in most cases, attribute their success to managing their operations effectively. A key feature of such achievement is having the strategic direction for managing operations which is provided by the operations strategy. However, an operations strategy has to be enacted and it is here that the organisation can face problems with managing the associated change. To provide a strategic direction for the change process, it is necessary to have a change strategy. The two areas are interdependent and a mechanism is needed to provide a strategic direction for managing the changes involved with the operations. This can be achieved by developing a strategy for operations and change *together* so that they are properly integrated and can relate to each other. This is an *operations and change strategy*.

An **operations strategy** can be defined as:

> *a process which establishes the objectives and activities in each part of the operation in order continually to support and enhance the organisation's competitive position or effectiveness.*

A **change strategy** can be defined as:

> *a process which considers what is needed in the future to achieve the organisation's desired aims and establishes an approach to managing the change, considering the key players, the barriers and the enablers of change.*

An **operations and change strategy** can be defined as:

> *a process which establishes the objectives and activities and how the associated changes, in terms of the key players, the barriers and the enablers of change, are best managed in each part of the operation in order continually to support and enhance the organisation's competitive position.*

VISION AND BUSINESS STRATEGY

Vision

The senior managers in the organisation need to brainstorm to develop a vision of what they think the organisation should be in the future. This may be based on the products and markets and style of company they would like to pursue and which they foresee could be successful in the long term. Having agreed on the vision, it is necessary to formulate a strategy that will fulfil it. It then becomes necessary to assess the company's current position so that it can establish the extent of the task. At this point the vision may be reconsidered and refined.

Three lessons on vision

Exhibit 2.1 outlines one company's experiences of attempting to develop a strategy that challenged existing structures, functions and jobs.

Business strategy

An organisation's business strategy sets the objectives for the various functions or parts of the business, such as operations, marketing, personnel, finance, product development, and so on. The business strategy covers the longer term of three to five years ahead and it should specify what are the strategic objectives and how the organisation is to compete. This will depend upon the situation regarding the customers, the market, the competitors and the finances available, as well as technological and environmental issues. The business strategy should outline what needs to be done over the next year or so, and usually it is reviewed annually or if the situation alters in some significant way.

Exhibit 2.1

Three lessons on vision that benefited Process Control Inc.

Process Control Inc. (PCI) employs a staff of 395, is the European manufacturing arm of an American conglomerate, and is located in the Midlands area of the UK. PCI specialises in the production of electronic printed circuit boards (PCBs) and process control equipment.

In working to implement major changes in the way its work was organised, the company learnt three fundamental lessons. The first was that the senior management team needed to share and support a common vision of where the organisation was going and how to get there. The second lesson was that a common vision – a common purpose – could only emerge and be realised when managers worked as a cohesive and stable team committed to being open and honest with each other. The final lesson was that time was needed for the Chief Executive Officer (CEO) to build the team, to take people slowly through the ideas and arguments. To summarise, a fundamental lesson for all organisations is that radical changes involving human factors require a stable and committed management with the time to develop a common vision to which everyone can be committed. The process cannot be rushed, otherwise dissent and uncertainty will emerge rather than vision and commitment.

Source: Adapted from Burnes, B. and James, H., 'Human factors in manufacturing: The need for a consistent strategy', *International Journal of Human Factors in Manufacturing*. Reprinted by permission of John Wiley & Sons, Inc.

PROCESS AND CONTENT OF AN OPERATIONS AND CHANGE STRATEGY

The preparation of a coherent operations and change strategy will be facilitated by bringing together information about:

- the company's markets and products
- the performance objectives sought and the supporting key activities
- the masterminding of the change, the change champions and people affected by the change
- the hard and soft initiatives of change – total quality management, just-in-time, teams, empowerment etc.
- the enablers of change, i.e. the key management ideas and approaches, personal and management development, and continuous improvement.

The above can be presented as five stages (*see* Table 2.1) that a company needs to complete in order to have an integrated operations and change strategy. The stages are as follows:

- **Stage 1**: Clarifying what needs to be changed
- **Stage 2**: The people in the change process
- **Stage 3**: Operations and the change initiatives
- **Stage 4**: Making it happen
- **Stage 5**: Executive assessment of focus and action plan

Table 2.1 Framework for the operations and change strategy process

Stages	*What is involved?*
Stage 1 **Clarifying what needs to be changed**	• Evaluate market requirements • Judge company performance against performance of the competition • Decide on performance objectives • Decisions in the key activity areas
Stage 2 **The people in the change process**	• The approach to change • The people involved • The conditions for change • The losers and barriers to change • Communication, feedback and rewards
Stage 3 **Operations and change initiatives**	• Total quality management (TQM) • Material requirements planning (MRP) • Just-in-time (JIT) • Teams • Empowerment • Business process re-engineering • The learning organisation
Stage 4 **Making it happen**	• Key management ideas approaches • Personal and management development • Continuous improvement
Stage 5 **Executive assessment of focus and action plan**	• Assessment report collating all the information from stages 1 to 4 • Meetings between directors, managers and relevant personnel • Action plans prepared

CLARIFYING WHAT NEEDS TO BE CHANGED

Evaluation of the market requirements

To ensure its long-term prosperity, every single business enterprise that faces free competition needs to achieve some form of maintainable advantage over its competitors. In practice this means understanding and anticipating the needs of the customers and then outperforming the competition in respect of certain 'critical' needs.

The performance objectives

The customer needs relating to a product or service can be interpreted as being what a company can provide in terms of the following performance objectives:

- quality
- speed
- dependability
- flexibility
- cost.

These critical areas of performance are the factors which determine how products or services win orders in the market place. Several authors – Hill, Slack and New – have defined what they perceive to be the performance objectives that an organisation should seek to attain. The wording used by the authors may vary, but the objectives involved are essentially constant. These objectives are defined in Fig 2.1.

Fig 2.1 Performance objectives of a product/service to give competitive advantage

Establishing the priority of performance objectives

As mentioned, the relative importance of performance objectives depends on:

- the customer needs
- what the company's competitors are doing, how well they are doing it, and how strong they might be at attracting existing as well as new customers in the area in which the organisation competes.

Another important factor here is:

- at what stage of the product life cycle the product or service stands.

Order-winning and order-qualifying objectives

For each product or family of similar products, these objectives can be divided into what Terry Hill describes as 'order-winning' and 'order-qualifying' objectives. Order-qualifying objectives are the objectives upon which the company has to perform at least as well as the competition in order even to be considered. Order-winning objectives are the objectives upon which products actually win orders in the market place. Some order-qualifiers may have the potential to become order-winners, but it is more likely that they become order-losers if they fall below the market qualifying level.

It is the needs of the customers which define those objectives that are important for a particular product or service, and it is the performance of the main competition which determines the levels of performance required for each of the important objectives.

Changing performance objectives in the product/service life cycle

The relative importance of performance objectives can vary according to the stage of the product life cycle that the product or service has reached. The life cycle of the sales of a product or service is generally described as comprising four stages: introduction, growth, maturity and decline. According to Kotler, products and services require different marketing, financial, operations, purchasing and personnel strategies in each stage of their life cycle. This has implications for the way in which operations should be managed, since different objectives will be sought by the customer as the product or service moves from being new through to its maturity and decline.

Through this process it is possible to establish how good the organisation should be at achieving quality or speed or dependability or flexibility or cost. That is, what is the priority of its performance objectives? Most importantly, the organisation needs to understand what is required to achieve each objective.

The importance of speed, flexibility and timeliness

Exhibit 2.2 illustrates how three companies achieved competitive superiority by focusing, not only on the cost and quality of products, but also on speed, flexibility and timeliness.

Structural and infrastructural decisions

Once the various performance objectives for each product or product family have been prioritised, decisions have to be made as to how the key operations areas can support and continually enhance the desired competitive positions.

Exhibit 2.2

7–Eleven Japan, Federal Express and Benetton focus on speed, flexibility and timeliness

I (Shin-ichi Itoh, NEC Corporation, Tokyo, Japan) want to begin my discussion of competitive superiority in the 1990s by looking at what types of strategies have been adopted at present by those companies that have attained rapid growth.

The first example I wish to examine is 7–Eleven Japan. Their competitive superiority lies in their ability to assess their customers' needs accurately, and in real time, thanks to their point-of-sales (POS) information system. In short, they know which products sell quickly and which ones do not move at all. 7–Eleven is overwhelming their competitors in terms of both sales and profits.

My second example is Federal Express of the US. This company modified conventional direct delivery between cities by implementing centralised sorting of all parcels at individual locations to improve the reliability of delivery service (sorting is a task where the possibility of errors is extremely high). The company then linked all these sorting centres together in a network to create its delivery system. Federal Express is able to deliver a package within 24 hours anywhere in the US. Furthermore, it has reduced the rate of wrong deliveries to less than 0.1 per cent, and has earned immense trust from its customers.

My third example is Benetton, a manufacturer of apparel. As you know, a great reduction in lead-time improves the accuracy of demand forecasting. Benetton reversed the conventional organisation of its manufacturing process, revolutionising the process so that the clothes were dyed after being stitched together. As a result of adopting this strategy, the degree of error in forecasting was reduced. Now, a mere 25 years after its founding, Benetton is growing rapidly and is now a world-class manufacturer.

What do these examples of success demonstrate? The answer is that we have entered an age when customer satisfaction depends, not only on the cost and quality of products, but also, to a great extent, on speed and timing. At present, what the world wants above all else is time, or, to express it more precisely, what everyone wants is speed, flexibility and timeliness.

Source: Adapted from Itoh, S., 'Customer-oriented Manufacturing', *International Journal of Human Factors in Manufacturing*. Reprinted by permission of John Wiley & Sons, Inc.

Hayes, Wheelwright and Clark refer to this in terms of a number of structural and infrastructural decisions which need to be co-ordinated in the process of formulating a manufacturing (or operations) strategy.

Structural (process) decisions

Decisions need to be taken on:

- amount of total capacity to be provided
- how the capacity should be broken up into specific production facilities
- the kind of production equipment and systems with which to provide the facilities
- which materials, systems and services to produce internally and which to source from outside the organisation (and the kinds of relationships to be established with suppliers).

Infrastructural (policies and systems) decisions

Decisions need to be taken on:

- human resource policies and practices, including management selection and training policies
- quality assurance and control systems
- production planning and inventory control systems
- new product development processes
- performance measurement and reward systems, including capital allocation systems
- organisational structure and design.

The structural decisions are referred to as the 'bricks and mortar', with the infrastructure referring to the management policies and systems that determine how the bricks and mortar are managed. Hill argues that most companies have access to much the same processes and technologies, and that most elements of infrastructure are equally universal. What, he suggests, differentiates organisations is the degree to which the operations processes and infrastructure are matched to the performance objectives. It is this match of structure and infrastructure, and how they are to be combined to achieve operational objectives, which constitutes the manufacturing (or operations) strategy.

It is the complexities and intricacies of this match which makes a competitive advantage which originates within the company's operations so difficult to imitate. Hence, the use of an operations strategy can help companies create a more sustainable advantage over their competitors.

Key activities and the attainment of performance objectives

In an organisation the key activity areas in which the structural and infrastructural decisions take place are typically:

- design and product
- process
- customers and suppliers
- human resources
- controls and systems.

These key activity areas are discussed in detail in Chapter 4. Within each of these areas there are key activities which can support the attainment of the objectives sought. It is necessary to determine which key activities in a key activity area are necessary to support each performance objective and hence fulfil the business requirements. For example, Gilgeous shows how information from a manufacturing audit of a manufacturing concern in the West Midlands, with a turnover of £15 million, showed that of the five key activity areas mentioned above, the decisions being made in area of 'human resources' did not appropriately support the strategy. Analysis showed that the problems in this area boiled down to:

1 The level of motivation and positive attitudes.
2 The level of knowledge, experience and skills.
3 The thoroughness and effectiveness of selection, development and training.
4 The need for a participative management style.

Of these it was realised that the problem mainly lay with 'the level of knowledge, experience and skills'. In far too many organisations this level of analysis is not carried out and therefore the crucial decisions concerning the alignment of the key activity areas towards a common strategic goal simply does not happen, with the result that businesses fail.

THE PEOPLE IN THE CHANGE PROCESS

Knowing now what is needed in the future in the organisation's key activity areas it becomes possible to consider the people aspect of the operations and change strategy process. In particular:

- the approach to change
- the people involved
- the conditions for change
- the losers and barriers to change
- communication, feedback and rewards.

The approach to change

The pace of change will influence the degree of planning and involvement and the approach taken to resistance. In making a choice between the extremes of adopting a slow evolutionary pace and a rapid revolutionary one, the effect on the tactics chosen needs to be appreciated.

The people involved

When managing the change process, some critical questions need to be answered. Who owns the change? Who is supposed to implement the change and on whom will the change have an impact? This involves considering three sets of people: the sponsors of change, the change champions and the partners in change.

The conditions for change

To manage change effectively particular foundations and structures need to be created and developed. The conditions under which success is likely are when an organisation has the right culture; direct, active involvement of senior management; the right people; and has made attempts to create the right conditions for change.

The losers and barriers to change

The potential losers in the change programme can be workers or managers, and both need to be listened to. They may feel they could become losers because they may foresee bad aspects of the change that could affect many. Their suggestions might prove invaluable in averting some major problems. With knowledge of their concerns it may be possible to accommodate their wishes and get them to contribute positively, rather than negatively, to the change programme. Allowing them to express their fears and concerns often provides an outlet for more overt hostility which could derail the change programme.

Communication, feedback and rewards

People will accept change more readily if they are made aware of the pressures for change. It also helps to publicise successful change and give regular feedback on the performance of individual functions and areas of activities within the organisation. Also, the change makers need to have a mechanism that enables them to receive valid feedback on the effects of the change. In their passion for pushing through the programme, they can sometimes overlook or underestimate conditions being created in certain groups of people or parts of the organisation which could seriously jeopardise their plans. Therefore, before the change programme commences, it is necessary to incorporate into the programme ways of keeping in touch so that the change problems that arise can be appreciated and any areas that are experiencing difficulty can be identified. There are many different mechanisms that can be used for achieving this: for example, newsletters, attitude surveys, management by wandering around, consultative committees etc. Further, people want to be recognised and adequately remunerated for their effort, knowledge and skills. ICL strives to achieve all this through its management of change which attempts to bring together the right people, organise them effectively, and provide the right systems tools.

Exhibit 2.3 illustrates the importance ICL attaches to the management of change when pursuing the strategies needed to achieve a competitive edge.

Exhibit 2.3

ICL: Strategies for competitive edge and the management of change

ICL is the wholly-owned subsidiary of STC plc and the largest British supplier of information technology systems, with an annual turnover in excess of £1.3 billion. The company has been through a period of transition over the past four years. This transition followed a clear process of realignment, but the most significant common theme was the importance of people, attitude, and organisation.

In summary, the company's route to gaining a manufacturing competitive edge is to:

- determine what provides competitive edge within the market environment concerned
- determine the strategies needed to achieve the edge
- change the attitudes of the people and set in place the system necessary to focus on the strategy
- decide on and quantify the key measures, and communicate progress and relevance regularly and widely.

To achieve this will probably mean implementing different organisation structures to bring together this design, manufacture and configuration with the markets. Whatever the requirements are, the way to achieve them is through the management of change – bringing together the right people, organised effectively, and with the right systems tools.

Source: Adapted from Powell, R., 'Manufacturing as a source of competitive edge', *Industrial Management & Data Systems*.

OPERATIONS AND CHANGE INITIATIVES

Hard initiatives

The use of different initiatives to support the operations and change strategy can be classified as either *soft* or *hard*. The hard initiatives are involved with the technical and system aspects of the company's product and processes and the systems, technology and equipment needed to design, plan, execute and control them. Some hard initiatives that are popular and which organisations employ to support the performance of the activity areas in a company are:

- **Total quality management (TQM)**: the focus on quality throughout the organisation; quality being a strategic issue involving everyone and every process in the organisation.
- **Material requirements planning (MRP)**: a system for scheduling dependent demand items.
- **Just-in-time (JIT)**: a philosophy of manufacturing, initially developed by the Japanese, used to ensure that the right quantities are purchased and made at the right time with little or no waste.
- **Optimised production technology (OPT)**: seeks to improve productivity through the use of an analytical technique which aims to synchronise production.
- **Computer integrated manufacture (CIM)**: the planning and control of manufacture using computers and technology.

Soft initiatives

The soft initiatives are those which harness the capabilities of people through initiatives such as:

- **Teams**: a small number of people with skills directed to a common purpose who are set on achieving objectives for which they are mutually responsible.
- **Empowerment**: devolving responsibility all the way down the organisational hierarchy to those individuals who have the relevant understanding to make the best decisions.
- **The learning organisation**: an organisation that facilitates learning to develop and compete successfully.
- **Business process re-engineering**: a strategy-driven, top-down reappraisal and redesign of the total business. Although encompassing many soft initiatives, the comprehensive nature of this approach means that it will inevitably encompass hard initiatives.

These hard and soft initiatives are shown in Fig 2.2. The nature and potential of these initiatives needs to be understood and questions concerning their use in a particular situation need to be asked. In particular, how applicable to the situation is each initiative, what features of the initiative need to be focused on and improved, and how effective is each initiative at contributing to good business performance?

MAKING IT HAPPEN

It is the enablers of change who instigate key management ideas and approaches, personal and management development, and continuous improvement.

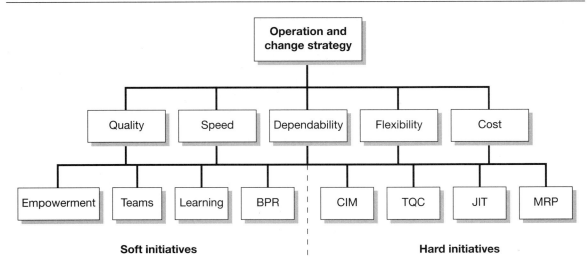

Fig 2.2 Soft and hard initiatives

Key management ideas

Making things happen means changing the way things are done in an organisation. To assist in this process it helps to focus on:

● understanding prominent management ideas and approaches
● the nature and importance of organisation culture
● the need for the right type of structure and organisation
● the pursuit of organisation development
● consideration of stress at work and its effects on people.

Personal and management development

If changes are to happen effectively, then it becomes important to address work lifestyle and how it can assist with job satisfaction, career development and people giving their best to their organisation. Managers need to appreciate the nature of the skills they need and how they can assess and develop themselves as a manager. They need to pursue their personal and career development in a professional way, making use of career development programmes, mentors and objective feedback.

Continuous improvement

Continuous improvement is a process of ongoing improvements which aggregate over time to provide visible proof that things are getting better. The Japanese call this *kaizen*. Important in this is the development of the management procedures involved in improvement programmes, which focus on waste, use of procedures and standards, employees' involvement, improvement teams and suggestion schemes.

EXECUTIVE ASSESSMENT OF FOCUS AND ACTION PLAN

The focus on what needs to be changed in operations and how it should be managed should be decided through considering the management's views at executive level meetings. The basis for discussion should be an assessment report collating all the information from Stages 1 to 4. This should provide a sound foundation for the process of managerial learning and discussion concerning the formulation of a coherent operations and change strategy.

Action plans can then be prepared which define the operations and change strategy objectives together with detail on how, and with what resources, the different functions, key activity areas, and project groups are going to contribute to their attainment.

STRATEGY DEVELOPMENT CONSIDERATIONS

The state of evolution of many companies regarding their strategic approach to managing operations can be recognised as falling into one of four stages, varying from poor to excellent, as shown in Fig 2.3. Essentially, Hayes and Wheelwright consider that the four-stage model depicts the progressive shift in aspirations of a company from negative and operational to positive and strategic.

Unfortunately, many companies operate at Stages 1 or 2 with little or no emphasis on the development of a strategic approach. The following quote sums up the dismal situation Buffa saw regarding the lack of a coherent strategy in many US companies:

> We are losing our competitive edge, not because we don't know how to market the product or finance it. It is because we sometimes produce the wrong product for the market. Our prices and quality are not competitive, or our product is not available in the market place. In short, we have not learned how to develop a manufacturing strategy to support the strategic plans of the enterprise.

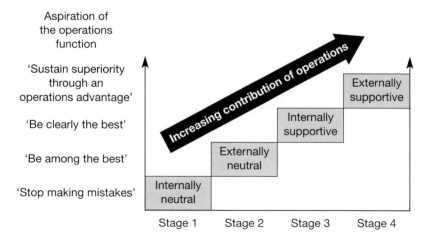

Fig 2.3 Four-stage model

Source: Hayes, R.H. and Wheelwright, S. C., *Restoring Our Competitive Edge: Competing through manufacturing*, Copyright © 1988. Reprinted by permission of John Wiley & Sons, Inc.

47

Since then many organisations have made great strides in their understanding and practice of strategic management. With respect to operations, some of the considerations that go towards developing an effective and realistically possible operations and change strategy are now recognised, and these are:

- operations being proactive and being involved in the strategy formulation
- linking and aligning operations capabilities with market requirements
- agreeing and communicating task priorities
- considering the trade-offs, focus and flexibility
- seeking strategic flexibility.

Operations being proactive and being involved in the strategy formulation

It is important that operations become involved early in the corporate debate with other main functions like marketing and finance so that they can provide an informed awareness to other executives of what operations can currently offer the business. On the other hand, people in operations need to know what they should be doing to meet the needs of the business. At all costs, operations staff should not allow themselves to be told what to do by senior managers and executives who may have mainly focused on marketing and finance issues. Operations should strive to be involved early in the making of joint decisions as to the most realistic way operations can support the businesses competitive requirements. If this is not done and corporate decisions are made without understanding what operations can offer, the business is wasting that potential and it could soon become vulnerable in the market place.

Linking and aligning operations capabilities with market requirements

For an operations strategy to be of use it must be closely aligned with other functional strategies, and they must all be in line with the overall business strategy, the purpose of which is to meet the customers' needs and provide the business with a sustainable advantage over the competition in the markets in which it chooses to compete. To achieve this it is necessary for operations to be aware of the business needs in the market place and the corresponding action that needs to be taken at the operations level to support these needs. Exhibit 2.4 illustrates the benefits the National Bicycle Industrial Company realises from establishing strong links between manufacturing and marketing.

Exhibit 2.4

A new relationship between manufacturing and marketing

In today's markets where mass customisation is superseding mass production, the significance of the link between manufacturing and marketing becomes ever more crucial. For example, the National Bicycle Industrial Company in Kokubu, Japan, is already producing made-to-order bicycles. The customer has a choice of 11 231 862 variations, and the made-to-measure bicycles are delivered within two weeks of the order being placed. Prices are only 10 per cent higher than ready-made models. For this level of customisation to be achieved, in what would traditionally have been a mass production process, there are extremely close links between the marketing and manufacturing functions.

The need to align operations with business needs

It is a fact that the right actions taken at the operational level can give the company the competitive advantage that it needs. The aim is to determine how the operations capabilities can best be utilised and developed so as to provide a competitive advantage. It may be that the operations need realigning to achieve this. That is, the skills, systems, process, technology and management style etc. must be suited to the current needs of the business. However, it must be appreciated that it can take many months, perhaps years, to reorientate operations capability. Therefore, information on any misalignment between what operations can offer in relation to the competition and what the market wants now and in the future needs to be known quickly and in some detail. This sets the basis for effective operations strategy development. Research carried out by Hayes and Wheelwright for manufacturing highlights the problem of misalignment:

> *Again and again we have found the root cause of a 'manufacturing crisis' has been that a business's manufacturing policies and people... have become incompatible with its competitive needs.*

The danger of misalignment between manufacturing capabilities and market requirements is strikingly illustrated by the US company Babcock and Wilcox (B&W) in an extract from 'The Great Nuclear Fizzle' case presented in Exhibit 2.5.

Exhibit 2.5

Babcock and Wilcox (B&W) in the US

In the late 1960s B&W entered the nuclear pressure vessel business. This new market place was markedly different from that of steam pressure vessels in which the company currently operated. B&W had invested $25m in a new green field site at Mount Vernon on the Ohio River to make the nuclear pressure vessels. To its eventual dismay, B&W realised that the key activity areas in manufacturing at the Mount Vernon plant were not suited to the production of nuclear pressure vessels. The plant and equipment, labour, supervision, engineering support and organisational style required for the fossil fuel boilers were entirely different to those required for the nuclear pressure vessels. This resulted in it incurring major delivery delays against critical delivery dates. Through a court case, B&W was ordered to release its work to others. This resulted in 50 per cent of B&W's work-in-progress going to its major competitors. In creating work for them it cost the company at least $50m, which was more than twice B&W's total capital investment.

Death in a dry bathtub
B&W's inaction to reorientate its manufacturing strategy led to this classic case of the wrong manufacturing mix for the job. This nearly resulted in bankruptcy of once one of the biggest and most successful companies in this field. The personal consequences to certain of the individuals involved can also be dire and this is illustrated through the following gruesome tale about the fate of John Paul Craven, the man directly responsible for the Mount Vernon plant: 'Less than a month after taking over as chief executive from Nielsen, Zipf scheduled a meeting at the Mount Vernon plant with Craven and Austin Fragomen, vice president for manufacturing. The meeting was set for a Monday morning. During the preceding weekend Craven told friends that for the first time in his life he thought his job was getting beyond him. Sometime on the Sunday afternoon or evening before his scheduled meeting with Zipf, Craven took off his clothes and climbed into a dry bathtub in his $250-a-month apartment at Akron's luxurious Carlton House. Then he slashed his ankles, cut his throat, and stabbed himself in the heart with the serrated eight-inch blade of a butcher's knife.'

Source: Meyers, H.B., 'The Great Nuclear Fizzle at Old B&W', *Fortune*, © 1969 Time Inc. All rights reserved.

Agreeing and communicating the priorities of performance objectives

At each stage of the strategy development process it must be made clear, communicated and agreed what the business objectives are, what the performance objectives are that operations should pursue and what needs to be done in the key activity areas to fulfil these objectives.

An example

The study information in Table 2.2 shows a company's current and required priorities. Here, the vice presidents (VP) considered the current and required priorities of the performance objectives for various product groups. From this they made decisions concerning where more, or less, emphasis should be placed with respect to each one. When the manufacturing managers (MM) were asked to assess the priorities of the performance objectives for the various product groups, a different set of priorities emerged. The questions that need to be asked are: Is there a procedure for determining the priorities of performance objectives? How adequate is the procedure? Are the priorities of the performance objectives, once determined, properly agreed and communicated? Are there any differences in perception among senior managers in the organisation as to what the priorities of the performance objectives are? If there are any differences, why do they exist?

Considering the trade-offs, focus and flexibility

Trade-offs

Academic debate continues as to the nature and effects of trade-offs. In this debate some say that if you want more of one thing you must accept less of something else – the common trade-off dilemma. They insist that, however good you get at minimising the effects of trade-offs, they will not go away because there is no such thing as a free lunch. Two examples of trade-offs follow:

1 Industries which experience higher volume demand usually have more costly dedicated facilities but they benefit through economies of scale, whereby the higher volumes they experience bring them decreasing costs per unit (*see* Hayes and Wheelwright). However, as their facilities become more dedicated they become less flexible and are therefore more vulnerable to changes in the market. The classic trade-off here is one of low cost versus flexibility.

2 When faced with a widely-fluctuating demand (the situation of high inventories versus fluctuating production), should a company adopt a chase–demand strategy, a level production strategy, or a mix of the two? Whichever policy is chosen will result in either high inventories or fluctuating production. One answer would be to reduce the effects on manufacturing by smoothing demand through clever marketing and price discounts etc. Another way would be to choose the appropriate levels of production (the strategy decision) that will meet the fluctuating demand as well as satisfying the other performance objectives being sought. In summary, the real trade-off problem becomes one of deciding whether to reduce the need for an appropriate strategy countermeasure, to choose the best strategy to deal with the situation, or a mixture of the two. Other examples of typical trade-offs are:

Table 2.2 Differences between current and required priorities

	Cost		Quality		Dependability		Flexibility	
	VP	MM	VP	MM	VP	MM	VP	MM
Product 1:								
As is	42	44	17	15	25	26	16	15
Should be	28	46	24	16	31	26	17	12
Needs more (less)	(14)	2	7	1	6	0	1	(3)
Product 2:								
As is	26	20	37	43	24	22	13	15
Should be	26	30	36	38	26	20	12	12
Needs more (less)	0	10	(1)	(5)	2	(2)	(1)	(3)
Product 3:								
As is	34	36	27	28	23	19	16	17
Should be	34	38	29	24	24	20	13	18
Needs more (less)	0	2	2	(4)	1	1	(3)	1
Product 4:								
As is	24	34	30	22	19	17	27	27
Should be	39	44	20	25	23	15	18	16
Needs more (less)	15	10	(10)	3	4	(2)	(9)	(11)
Product 5:								
As is	45	37	21	14	18	31	16	18
Should be	22	31	24	13	35	35	19	21
Needs more (less)	(23)	(6)	3	(1)	17	4	3	3

Criteria totals for VP and MM for each priority = 100.
Source: Wheelwright, S. C., 'Reflecting corporate strategy in manufacturing decisions', *Business Horizons*. Reprinted from *Business Horizons,* February 1978, Table, p. 65. Copyright 1978 by the Foundation for the School of Business at Indiana University. Used with permission.

- more versus less volume in a particular product range
- delivery time versus capacity utilisation
- more versus less product mix
- more versus less of the same products
- quality versus absolute cost
- labour productivity versus capital productivity.

Challenging the trade-offs
Many organisations are concerned as to how they can best manage what they see as an apparent trade-off situation. Others see this argument as a 'red herring' which detracts from the main aim of trying to get better at everything simultaneously. They provide evidence to the contrary, showing that improvements in one so-called trade-off dimension do not have to be accompanied by a downgrade in performance in its

traditional trade-off counterpart. For example, through their approach to managing quality and the systems and technology they employ, many operations have avoided the trade-off between quality and cost.

Focus

Many companies experience difficulty in being efficient when they produce a variety of goods in changing and diverse markets. However, the problem can be approached and benefits achieved through the use of focused facilities, focused plants and the use of plants within a plant. Skinner (1969) cites many examples of the benefits of doing this. The principle being followed here is that 'simplicity and repetition breed competence'. This is true, but the need to focus and the benefits to be gained from it depend upon the complexity of the business, the changing nature of the market and the current capabilities of the company and its competitors.

Examples of a process focus

According to Skinner (1992), companies which successfully develop innovative production processes typically enjoy powerful, sustainable competitive advantage. This arises in industries such as chemicals, plastics, steel and paper. Here, process superiority enables firms to produce a better or lower-priced product or improved service, thereby creating a superb strategic position for gaining an unassailable market position.

Mini steel mills, for example, have succeeded during the last 15 years due almost entirely to their development of radically different steel mills from the large, integrated conventional mills. The origin and rapid growth of McDonald's was based on the innovative development of a total process for cooking and presenting fast foods. The rise and present predominance of the Japanese in the semiconductor industry is due in large part to their ability to produce semiconductors with outstanding performance, because of the production processes they developed. Wholesale process innovation in the Japanese automobile industry has accounted for much of its success.

Lessening the need for focus

The need for focus can be lessened through the fact that modern, sophisticated management and operations can provide the needed flexibility while remaining competitive; for example, the use of manufacturing cells, and self-managing teams using computer-aided design (CAD) and rapid prototyping devices. Also, firms now automate using flexible manufacturing systems (FMS) which can cope speedily with high volumes and yet switch quickly to different products.

Seeking strategic flexibility

The real problem that a business needs to address is how to achieve the right mix of capabilities for the present in the operations area and yet balance this with the need to move as swiftly as possible to satisfy future business needs, maybe with a different mix of capabilities. In a nutshell, if a company can get this balance right, and change it quickly, it has strategic flexibility and it will soon be rated as an excellent company.

PROMINENT APPROACHES TO OPERATIONS STRATEGY DEVELOPMENT

An organisation can develop its own approach to operations strategy development or it can adapt one of the many proprietary approaches or the approaches presented in the literature by both practitioners and academics. Three operations strategy approaches prominent in the quality literature on operations management are the Hill, the Platts and Gregory and the Slack procedures.

The Hill procedure

Hill's five-step operations strategy development procedure (shown for manufacturing operations) is depicted in Table 2.3. A feature of the approach is that it shows the links in the strategy process between the corporate and operations level. Step 1 is concerned with the long-term corporate objectives of the organisation to which the operations strategy contributes. Step 2 is concerned with the development of the marketing strategy to achieve the corporate objectives. Here, the marketing mix is defined in terms of product range, mix, volume etc. This step, in effect, identifies the products or service characteristics and the nature of the market. In Step 3 the marketing strategy is translated into what is important to the operation in terms of winning business or satisfying customers. Hill divides the factors which win business into order-winners and qualifiers. Step 4 is concerned with co-ordinating the structural (process) characteristics of the operation; and Step 5 is concerned with the infrastructural (policies and systems) aspects of the operation.

Table 2.3 The Hill operations (manufacturing) strategy procedure

Step 1	Step 2	Step 3	Step 4	Step 5
Corporate objectives	*Marketing strategy*	*How products win orders in the market place*	*Operations strategy*	
			Process choice	*Infrastructure*
• growth • profit • return on investment • other financial measures	• product markets and segments • range • mix • volumes • standardisation versus customisation • level of innovation • leader versus follower alternatives	• price • quality • delivery speed and reliability • colour range • product range • design leadership	• choice of alternative processes • trade-offs embodied in the process choice • role of inventory in the process configuration	• function support • manufacturing systems • controls and procedures • work structuring • organisational structure

Source: Hill, T.J., *Manufacturing Strategy: The strategic management of the manufacturing function.* Reprinted by permission of Macmillan Press Ltd, Basingstoke.

The Platts and Gregory procedure

The Platts and Gregory procedure has three stages and it makes explicit the comparison between what the market wants and how the operation performs. This approach is different to that of Hill in which the operations strategy is developed from the customers' view of competitive factors. The Platts and Gregory procedure uses a 'profile analysis', shown in Fig 2.4, to identify any gaps between the needs of the market and operations performance.

In Stage 1 the market position is assessed in terms of the opportunities and threats posed to the organisation. In Stage 2 the capabilities of the operation are assessed in order to establish how much it contributes towards achieving the desired performance identified in Stage 1.

In Stage 3 the various strategic options open to the organisation are considered. The aim is to select a strategy which best satisfies the scenarios presented in Stages 1 and 2.

The Slack procedure

Slack's procedure enables the organisation to establish priorities of the operations performance objectives based on what is important to the customer and how well the organisation achieves these objectives relative to the competition. Essentially it combines the features of both the Hill and Platts and Gregory approaches, and provides a graphical view of the priorities of the performance objectives.

The procedure involves three steps:

Step 1 is concerned with establishing the operations objectives. This involves determining how important each of the performance objectives is to the way in which each product or product group competes. The best way of achieving this is in a workshop setting, involving personnel from manufacturing, marketing and product development. A clear, ranked set of competitive performance objectives for each product and each product group is needed. The objectives should be determined by the customers' needs. Slack proposes a nine-point importance scale which can be used to rank the various performance objectives as being order-winning, order-qualifying or less important. For each of the performance objectives (quality of product, delivery reliability, price etc.), a value representing its relative importance to the way the product competes is assigned.

Step 2 is concerned with judging company performance against that of the competition. Competitors provide a standard against which any manufacturing company should measure itself. This step involves assessing the company's performance, with respect to each of the performance objectives, against that of the competition. Although competitors' performance is sometimes difficult to judge, Slack suggests another nine-point scale to determine the comparative performance of each of the performance objectives.

Step 3 involves prioritising the objectives by analysis of the 'gap' between the importance and performance of each one. It is this 'importance/performance gap' which gives an indication of the priorities which should be set. The importance/performance matrix, shown in Fig 2.5, provides a useful tool for graphically representing the two scales and showing any gaps.

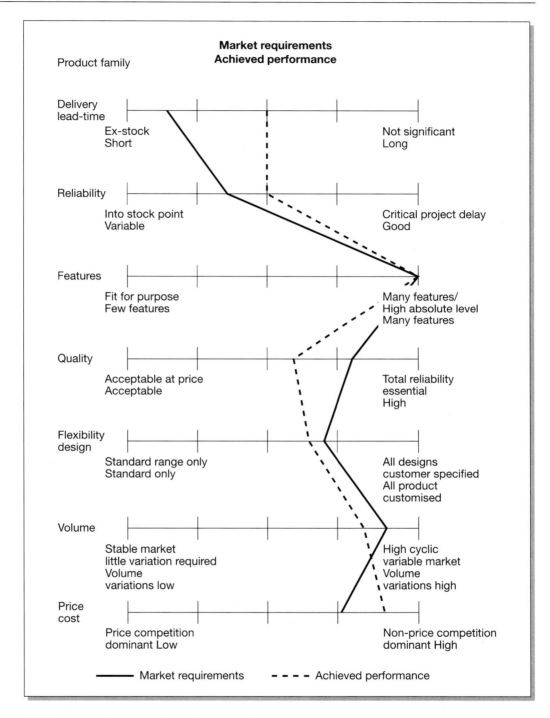

Fig 2.4 Use of profiling in the Platts and Gregory procedure

The importance/performance matrix explained

Referring to Fig 2.5:

- The 'Importance' axis relates to the customers and the 'Performance' axis relates to the competition.
- The 'Appropriate' zone: The lower edge of this boundary is the level of performance below which the company, in the medium term, would not wish the operation to fall.
- The 'Improve' zone: Any performance objective which lies below the lower bound of the appropriate zone will be a candidate for improvement.
- The 'Urgent Action' zone: Items in this zone are those for which importance is high but performance is far below what it ought to be. Business is probably being lost as a result and action is obviously required. Short-term aims must be to raise the performance of any objectives lying in this zone up to at least the improve zone.
- The 'Excess' zone: This zone contains items for which the performance is high but the importance is low. In these areas performance is far better than would seem to be warranted, and perhaps too much effort is being expended for too little gain. Resources might be better employed improving items in the urgent action zone. Ideally, all performance objectives would lie well inside the appropriate zone.

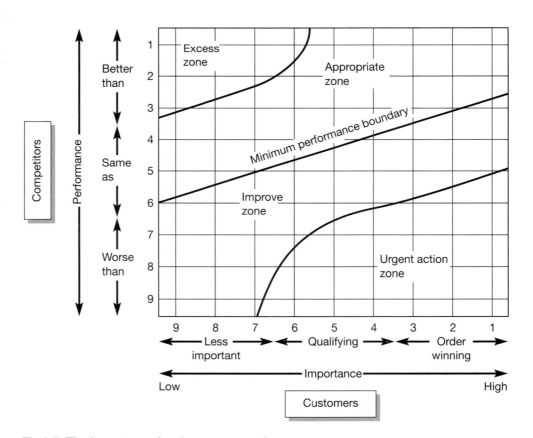

Fig 2.5 The importance/performance matrix

STRATEGY IMPLEMENTATION

Many good strategies and their associated plans, after much planning and many meetings, fizzle out and fail to materialise. In short, many of our strategies simply are not happening. The problem is that managers are not good at successfully implementing a strategy: they have not got the skills to install or put into operation changes called for in a strategic plan. Successful installation of these changes often depends on obtaining the involvement, co-operation, endorsement or consent of those power centres that will operate the plan, be served by it, or be influenced by its operation. In realising this problem, Hambrick and Cannella Jr concluded that the major difference between competitive success and failure for numerous firms they studied lay more in matters of strategy implementation than formulation.

Patterns of behaviour for effective implementation of strategy

The patterns of behaviour for the effective implementation of strategy at the plants studied by Hambrick and Cannella Jr can be summarised as follows:

1 Obtain broad-based inputs and participation at the formulation stage.
2 Carefully and deliberately assess the obstacles at the formulation stage.
3 Make early, first-cut moves across the full array of implementation levers – resource commitments, submit policies and programmes, structure, people and rewards.
4 Sell, sell, sell the strategy to everyone who matters – upwards, downwards, across and outwards.
5 Steadily fine tune, adjust and respond as events and trends arise.

According to Hambrick and Cannella Jr, three things need to be focused on in order to implement a strategy successfully:

1 Preliminary groundwork

Broad-based inputs on formulation
One of the most effective aids to implementation is to involve people early on in the development and debate of strategic options.

Deliberate assessment of obstacles
The strategist must comprehend that the implementation setting is not benign. A variety of obstacles – generally known but just as generally overlooked – can and will intervene to prevent the new strategy from unfolding. The effective strategist must have a careful understanding of these obstacles:

- *Internal obstacles*: The success of a strategy primarily depends on marshalling resources within the business itself. Human and material limitations make this difficult.

- *External obstacles*: The strategist must also navigate around obstacles outside the business unit. The most obvious counterforce is competition, but the general economic and technological environment can also intervene to impede a new strategy.

2 The early use of implementation levers

Once the strategist has secured various inputs, settled on the new strategy, and carefully assessed the major obstacles, he or she is ready to start taking substantive implementation actions. The five major areas the strategist must consider are:

Resource commitments
- What level of resources should be directed at each product or market?
- What level of resources should be placed behind each competitive weapon?

Submit policies and programmes
- What actions will each submit need to take?
- According to what timetables and with what outlays?

Structure
- How should roles and relationships be organised?
- How should information flow and decisions get made?

Rewards
- What behaviours and outcomes should be rewarded?
- What should be the types and amounts of rewards?

People
- What personal and professional qualities will be needed in the business?
- How will these qualities be attained?

3 Selling strategic change

A new strategy, because it involves change, will provoke resistance from those who either have a vested interest in the old strategy or cannot foresee the positive aspects of the new one. To build support, a major selling job is needed, and the efforts of persuasion, according to Hambrick and Cannella Jr, must proceed in four directions: upwards to superiors, downwards to subordinates, across to other organisational units, and outwards to external stakeholders.

Selling upwards
Executives at the corporate level need to be sold on the merits and viability of a strategy. As the stewards of corporate resources, they expect to see careful analysis and supporting data for the strategy, not only at the time it is being proposed but also while it is being implemented.

Selling downwards
Communicating with employees in the business is the type of implementation selling about which we hear most. Employees are the people who will make the strategy work, and their full understanding is required.

Selling across
A business unit is often dependent on other units of the company for services or assistance in strategy implementation. For example, sister units that provide raw materials,

technology, sales, or services often need to be 'sold' on the new strategy and their role in it.

Selling outwards

The strategist relies on external constituencies for success in implementation. These external parties are no different from insiders in their potential for scepticism and anxiety about the new strategy. The effective implementer will be alert to these problems and develop means for overcoming them.

Selecting tactics to implement strategic plans

According to Nutt (1989), a major cause of implementation failure is that many managers are shortcutting the implementation process by minimising their involvement with it. To avoid an implementation failure, strategic managers should consider increasing their involvement, or the involvement of key stakeholders, during implementation-related activities.

In over 90 per cent of the strategic planning cases that were studied by Nutt (1987) four types of tactics – intervention, persuasion, participation, and edict – were used by managers to implement strategic plans.

The intervention tactic

Implementation activities for the intervention tactic begin when a manager is delegated the authority to make changes required by a strategy. The manager creates a need for change in minds of key people by reforming the system(s) to be changed. Current performance is compared to a standard to make this performance seem unacceptable.

The participation tactic

In participation implementation a manager initiates planning by stipulating strategic needs and an arena of action, using a priority-strategic option. The development of the option is then delegated to a group. The group members are carefully selected so that key points of view and information are represented.

The persuasion tactic

In persuasion implementation a manager delegates the development of ideas consistent with priority-strategic directions to technical staff or consultants. This delegation occurs in one of two ways. Either the manager assigns project development to an expert; or experts approach the manager with an idea that may help to realise a priority-strategic aim and obtain the authority to develop the idea.

The edict tactic

Managers use an edict when directives are issued that call for plan adoption – the use of power, instead of a process, being the dominant theme. The manager announces the plan and prescribes the expected behaviour using a memorandum, formal presentation, or on-the-job instruction.

Links with Lippitt and Mackenzie's strategic implementation tactics

Nutt provides a framework, Table 2.4, which links the above strategic implementation tactics to those proposed by Lippitt and Mackenzie.

Case studies of strategic planning conducted to test the framework found that a high proportion of failures applied implementation tactics that differed from those recommended by the framework. A 94 per cent success rate was observed when recommended tactics were used, compared to a 19 per cent success rate when non-recommended tactics were used. The framework seems particularly useful in identifying conditions under which participation and persuasion tactics and edicts could be profitably used. The analysis also revealed a tendency for strategic managers to invest too little of their time in implementation. Low-involvement approaches were preferred. In 93 per cent of the failures, tactics that appeared to be minimising the strategic managers' involvement were applied. This tendency to be expedient had strategic managers delegating to an expert (e.g. a member of staff) or issuing an edict, when participation or intervention would have been a better tactic.

Implementing strategy at Lucas and Bosch

Much of what has been said above is reflected in the experiences of Lucas Industries plc and Robert Bosch GmbH, depicted in Exhibit 2.6. Here it was found that a strategy will have a better chance of being implemented successfully if the changing strategies are progressive, i.e. if they enable each change to be built on the best of what has been achieved in the past, and also, if there is a two-way communication between the people who have to make it happen and the strategist who plans the changes.

Table 2.4 Linkage of the Lippitt and Mackenzie (L&M) tactics and strategic implementation tactics

L&M tactics	Strategic implementation tactics
• Consultation	• Persuasion
• Form an implementation committee to shape plan	• Intervention or participation
• Form a planning group to develop plan	• Intervention or participation
• Ask a standing committee to monitor plan	• Participation
• Power	• Edict
• Solve	• Intervention

Source: Nutt, P. C., 'Selecting tactics to implement strategic plans', *Strategic Management Journal*, Vol. 10, pp. 145–61, 1989. Reprinted by permission of John Wiley & Sons, Ltd.

Exhibit 2.6

Important strategic considerations for Lucas Industries plc and Robert Bosch GmbH

The study reveals two important considerations:

1 Stability in company strategy formulation

At Lucas the emphasis has been on making a 'step change' to achieve competitiveness. In other words, the company has undertaken a transformation of its performance in order to arrive at its destination of 'competitiveness' in the automotive components industry. Bosch, on the other hand, is competitive. Its sales are strong, its employment growing and its R&D an integral part of the overall operations of the company. There is in the company a feeling of the progression of strategy: it is not static, it is changing. But each change is built on past experience and past knowledge. Here, the emphasis is on strategic continuity throughout the period, with incremental adaptation to change.

2 The relationships between the strategists and the grass-root operations

In light of an examination of the way strategy is transmitted to the plant level and diffused into actual working practices, it is argued that the relationship between strategists in the company headquarters and the grass-root operations at plant level is central to understanding company performance. The conclusion here is that the company must balance the degree of decentralisation against the central control of strategy, if it is to implement its technology efficiently at a plant level but still develop its core technologies.

Source: Adapted from Harding, R., 'Technology, human resources and turbulent change in Lucas and Bosch: A plant-level study', *British Journal of Management*, Vol. 5, pp. 261–73, 1994. Reprinted by permission of John Wiley & Sons, Ltd.

Five approaches to strategic implementation

Bourgeois and Brodwin consider that implementation is best treated as an issue of gaining prior group commitment through coalitional decision making, or as a question of total organisational involvement through a strong corporate culture. They review the evolution of these approaches, developing four models to characterise them, and suggest a fifth one, with strategy emerging in an almost-implemented form from within the firm.

1 **The commander model** closely follows the traditional approach to business policy and/or strategic planning. It addresses strategic 'position' only, and essentially guides the CEO in charting his/her firm's destiny. Here, the CEO uses economic and competitive analyses to plan resource allocations in the achievement of explicit objectives. The model contains a strong bias towards centralised direction.

2 **The change model**, so called because it usually concerns the adoption and implementation of a new strategy, emphasises how organisational structure, incentive compensation, control systems, and so forth, can be used to facilitate the execution of a strategy.

3 **The collaborative model** involves the consideration of multiple inputs to group decision making at senior levels, and involves top management in the formulation process to secure commitment. The strategy should emerge as a negotiated outcome.

4 **The cultural model** seeks to implement strategy through the infusion of a corporate culture throughout the organisation. Here, lower levels participate in the design of means to perpetuate strategic direction, and are inculcated with a set of values which influence work-related behaviour.

5 **The crescive model** involves 'growing' strategy from within the firm and examines strategy issues in terms of 'strategy developers' and 'strategy implementers'. This approach draws on managers' natural inclinations to want to develop new opportunities as they see them in the course of their day-to-day management.

To highlight the differences in abbreviated form, Table 2.5 summarises the five models in terms of the strategic management question each addresses and the CEO's role in each.

The five models represent an increasing intention to bring implementation forward in the strategic management process. The first three models assume 'after-the-fact' implementation. Experience shows that, remarkably, the cultural model, which requires a large amount of time invested in consensual decision making, pays off with almost instant implementation. A similar claim can be made for the crescive model: by the time the strategy alternative has come forth with a champion attached to it, most of the energy in formulation has been expended and the strategy is practically in its implementation.

Table 2.5 Five strategic implementation models in brief

Model	CEO's strategic question	CEO's role
1 Commander	'How do I formulate the optimum strategy?'	Rational actor
2 Change	'I have a strategy in mind; now how do I implement it?'	Architect
3 Collaborative	'How do I involve top management to get commitment to strategies from the start?'	Co-ordinator
4 Cultural	'How do I involve the whole organisation in implementation?'	Coach
5 Crescive	'How do I encourage managers to come forward as champions of sound strategies?'	Premise-setter and judge

Source: Bourgeois, L. J. III and Brodwin, D., 'Strategic implementation: Five approaches to an elusive phenomenon', *Strategic Management Journal*, Vol. 5, pp. 241–64, 1984. Reprinted by permission of John Wiley & Sons, Ltd.

CASE STUDY: THE CLEARVIEW COMPANY

Development of an operations and change strategy

Clearview manufactures a variety of shower units for domestic and overseas use. Although small in terms of the 65 staff, the turnover is currently £4.5 million and rising. The company offers a wide range of both gravity-fed and powered shower units and considers that its superiority over the main competition, besides its range, is that its shower units are easy to install and simple to operate: facts which please both the installers and the users.

The executive structure is as follows:

Managing Director:	Mike Bennett
Operations Director:	George Dickinson
Marketing Director:	Don Whittaker
IT and Communications Director:	Andrew Brown
Finance Director:	Jean Dilworth
Personnel Director:	Bernard Gill
Personnel Manager:	Fiona
IT and Communications Manager:	Nick
Finance manager:	Eric

It was still only January and the executive committee, under the leadership of the Managing Director, Mike Bennett, had met three times already, the purpose being to thrash out a new operations strategy for the company. The last meeting centred around a product review that Don Whittaker, the Marketing Director, had conducted in the Autumn. This looked at the current and future customer base and considered what was important to the customers and what main problems, if any, the company was experiencing with its products. The meeting had also been concerned with reviewing how well the company's products and services performed relative to the competition.

This was the fourth meeting and it was hoped that a new operations strategy could be finalised.

At the start of the meeting, Mike called upon Don to summarise the pertinent aspects of the product review that had been discussed at the previous meeting.

Don began, 'As you know I instigated a product review to look into some of the main problems we are experiencing with our customers. In summary, we have been able to identify eight manufacturing performance objectives with which the customers identify.

First, quality of design. The installer and the user both put the ease of installation and simplicity of operation at the top of their list. This reflects the quality of the design of the shower units.

Second, price. The customers are willing to pay a little more for a better quality shower unit, but quality standards are rising across the industry, and prices for shower units of a similar rating and performance are tending to even out.

Third, delivery reliability. Delivery reliability is important because the Consumer Protection Act now requires that we endeavour to honour installation date promises made to the customers. We can be proud of our delivery reliability, but in order to achieve this, high stocks of finished units are carried, which pushes up costs.

Fourth, skills availability. Although the customers are happy with how well our showers perform when they have been installed, they have expressed dissatisfaction with the quality of any retiling that has had to be done on the wall surround of baths and showers. The survey we conducted shows that our plumbers make a poor job of this and, as a result, many customers have complained and asked that the shoddy tiling be made good or that they be recompensed. This adversely affects our image. However, we see this as a skills problem and are seeking to solve it through retraining or hiring more proficient plumbers.

Fifth and sixth, parts quality and supplier lead time. Strong customer dissatisfaction has arisen because certain shower unit models have started to leak water within months of being installed. The trouble has been traced back to difficulties with achieving dimensional tolerance during our manufacture, and sloppy inspection is also a problem. When this happens, our policy is to repair the leaky showers by fitting new sets of replacement seals and washers, and our plumbers are instructed to do this. The seals and washers are purchased from outside and, to compound the problem, their 'off-the-shelf availability' is poor. This has resulted in customers having to wait longer than they should for their showers to be repaired. Again, this puts us in a bad light. It has also resulted in us having to pay excessive warranty claims, and we are currently losing money on service repairs. These most serious problems of parts reliability and supplier lead time must be addressed immediately.

Seventh, new product flexibility. Shower units with more novel features are not considered to be important to the customer at the present time but could become more so in the future.

Eighth, manufacturing lead time. Currently, delivery lead time is not a problem and therefore considered unimportant. The rise in demand for these products could eventually cause problems and alter this situation.'

Mike thanked Don for his report and then spoke to George Dickinson, the Operations Director, 'George, Don has been feeding you with this product review stuff over the last few weeks. I hope that you have done your homework and have got some idea of how we fare relative to the competition in these areas?'

George replied, 'Well, from the benchmarking studies we have conducted we are better than our competitors in terms of the quality of our designs. Also, our delivery reliability and our manufacturing lead time are about the same as those of most of our competitors. Unfortunately, our costs and new product flexibility do not compare well with the rest. However, our main problems lie with our skills availability, parts quality, and supplier lead time, where we are consistently worse than most of our competitors.'

George continued, 'So, if we consider this information on how we perform relative to the main competition in conjunction with what Don says is important in winning orders, then, as I see it, our most serious problems are concerned with skills, parts reliability and supplier lead times. The activities that are next in importance, and to which we need to attend to ensure that improvements are made, are cost, delivery reliability and new product flexibility. The activities that could be kept ticking over until our more important issues have been dealt with are our quality of design and manufacturing lead time.'

George then handed out documentation which defined the operations performance objectives based on his analysis. He continued, 'The next step is to find out what needs to be done in the company's key activity areas to fulfil these performance objectives. By incorporating this information into our operations strategy we should be in a position to provide sufficient guidance to draft out plans and implement the changes required in our operations.'

Mike asked George if such plans would incorporate the people in the change process. George replied saying that the people aspects would be addressed in the operations strategy in terms of recruiting and retraining to improve the skills needed to address Clearview's quality and new product flexibility problems. Mike responded by saying that George's comments on the people aspects lacked detail and seemed very parochial.

George said, 'I wouldn't disagree but you did ask me to detail the operations strategy and that's what I have done.'

'Yes, thank you George', responded Mike, 'You have done what I requested and provided an operations strategy which clarifies what needs to be changed in our operations. I suppose it is my fault for providing such a narrow brief. What I also need to know is the organisational and people implications of managing the changes in our operations. This should be made explicit in our operations strategy from the start. Since we know what needs to be done in the operations, it should not be too difficult to integrate in with the operations the people and organisational issues in the change process. What we need, I suppose, is a strategy which establishes the operations objectives and the changes needed, in terms of how our people can be involved to help us be more competitive.'

Mike asked Bernard Gill, the Personnel Director if he had any thoughts on this. Bernard Gill baulked at this, saying that he agreed with the sentiment but was not prepared to give some kind of off-the-cuff answer and that the details needed to be thought out. Andrew Brown, the IT and Communications Director, supported Bernard Gill on this.

'I'm extremely annoyed', Mike exclaimed. 'I wish certain people would use their initiatives more and get together before these formal meetings to sort things out. We are just wasting time. Look Bernard! And you, Andrew! Get together to thrash out the details on this. Meet with the others to check things out and modify them, if necessary, but be ready to present an operations and change strategy, of the type we have discussed, at this executive in two weeks' time. If you feel you need an outside view, contact John; here is his business card. He is a consultant who has proved to be useful to Clearview in the past. Bill his charges against your accounts equally.'

At the next executive meeting, Bernard Gill presented to Mike and the executives a strategy which he hoped would be an integrated operations and change strategy.

Bernard announced, 'We have met and defined our operations and change strategy as *"a process which establishes the objectives and activities and how the associated changes, in terms of the key players, the barriers and enablers of change, are best managed in each part of the operation in order continually to support and enhance the organisation's competitive position"*.

First, we need to clarify what needs to be changed in our operations. I won't go over this in detail, since it involves what George said previously in terms of defining our performance objectives and then determining what needs to be done in our key activity areas to achieve them. Since our last meeting, we have decided that it is important to make explicit, and integrate into our operations and change strategy, directives on managing the people in the change process and the change initiatives that are to be employed. Being passed around now is our final report. This details the requirements on the sponsors of the change process – namely, us. Also there is information on who will champion the change process, the "change champions" or "operations change teams" that need to be created, and how we on the executive are to act as facilitators to them. I suggest that we need about seven people in the operations team. I suggest Fiona, Nick and Eric. Can the executive agree to this and suggest other managers whom they think would be up to this job? Next we present the considerations that need to be made concerning the people involved or affected by the changes. We call these the "partners" in change. What we are proposing is that Clearview pursues its objectives, working under the banner of particular initiatives of change. Such initiatives that we have considered to be essential so far are: continuing with our hard initiatives like computer-integrated manufacturing, total quality control, just-in-time and material requirements planning, but putting emphasis also on softer initiatives like "teams", "empowerment" and "the learning organisation". I'll hand you over to Andrew to go through the rest of the report.'

Andrew continued, 'As you know, at our meetings and with the guidance of John the consultant we have explored ways of making the strategy happen so that we can write this into the operations and change strategy. Also, we have done some initial field work to establish some basic competences that we wish to develop at Clearview in order to make things happen more efficiently: things like introducing new management ideas that have been found to be effective, a personal and management development programme, and a continuous improvement programme. But first we need to ascertain how each initiative, through the capabilities we have, can best support the objectives we have set for our operations. This will require the identification of the particular capabilities necessary to support each of our company initiatives. For example, as you can see from the report, in pursuing learning we will need to concentrate on capabilities such as a learning approach to strategy, a learning climate, inter-company learning, self-development opportunities etc.

It will then be necessary to identify the difference between the current level of performance or activity of each of these capabilities and the level of performance necessary for each of them to achieve the performance objectives.'

Mike interrupted, 'Sounds a bit technical and long-winded. Are you sure that we can do it?'

Andrew replied, 'Well, as the report details, this will require collating information from the senior managers in each key activity area to show how these initiatives and their necessary capabilities support the achievement of Clearview's performance objectives from the perspective of their area. We have the know-how and software to speed up the data collection process.'

Andrew then went on to explain that at the meetings they had held over the last two weeks they had also considered the details of new management ideas and approaches and a management development programme that they thought was necessary at Clearview to assist in implementing the changes. They had also defined a framework for making continuous improvements once the agreed changes were starting to be implemented.

Mike said, 'I am happy with the feel of this. Things are starting to come together now. Thank you all for all your hard work. Great, lets go for it. We shall meet in two weeks' time to go through the plans in detail. I want to know our major milestones and timescales. I am happy with Bernard's suggestions as to the initial composition of an "operations change team". Can the rest of you feed suggestions to Bernard for additional team members and leave it to him to set the team up? Oh, by the way Jean,' he said to Jean Dilworth, the Finance Director, 'can you give me an idea of the cost of all this and draft up a timescaled budget?'

SUMMARY

- An operations and change strategy can be defined as 'a process which establishes the objectives and activities and how the associated changes, in terms of the key players, the barriers and the enablers of change, are best managed in each part of the operation in order continually to support and enhance the organisation's competitive position or effectiveness'.

- A vision of the business is what the senior managers in the organisation think the organisation should be in the future. This may be based on the type of products and markets and style of company they would like to pursue and which they foresee could be successful in the long term.

- A business strategy seeks to fulfil the vision through satisfying the needs of the customers, the different interests of the shareholders and the people in the business, bearing in mind the constraints imposed by the competition and the environment.

- There are five stages that a company needs to complete in order to have an integrated operations and change strategy:

  - **Stage 1: Clarifying what needs to be changed**. This requires evaluating the market requirements, judging company performance against that of the competition; deciding upon the performance objectives and identifying the key activities that can help fulfil them.

  - **Stage 2: The people in the change process**. This concerns the approach to change, the people involved, the conditions for change, the losers and barriers to change, communication, feedback and rewards.

  - **Stage 3: Operations and change initiatives**. For example, teams, empowerment, the learning organisation and business process re-engineering.

  - **Stage 4: Making it happen**. The identification and capability of the unique range of competences necessary to support the change initiative. Also the enablers of change – the key management ideas and approaches, personal and management development, and continuous improvement.

  - **Stage 5: Executive assessment of focus and action plan**. The bringing together of information from the above stages; deciding, through executive discussion and assessment, where effort is to be focused, and then developing an action plan.

- Regarding strategy, operations should not act in a reactive role but be involved early in the corporate debate.

- Operations capabilities need to be linked and aligned with market requirements. In this way task priorities can be agreed and communicated.

- Different decisions in operations lead to different results. To achieve operational effectiveness the trade-offs involved need to be understood.

- The trade-off situation can be challenged and situations can be created where improvements in one so-called trade-off dimension do not have to be accompanied by a downgrade in performance in its traditional trade-off counterpart. It is possible to improve different performance objectives simultaneously.

- The problems associated with complexity and diversity in operations can be addressed and to some extent overcome by adopting the principles of focus.

- Strategic flexibility means having the ability to identify the business's core enablers to competitiveness and then ensuring that they have a high degree of competence and can respond quickly to support the business.

- Companies can develop their own operations strategy or adapt one that has been published by practitioners or academics. Three prominent approaches are those of Hill, Platts and Gregory, and Slack.

REVIEW AND DISCUSSION QUESTIONS

1 In what ways do you think the five-stage operations and change strategy development process described in this chapter addresses, or fails to address, the problems of providing strategic direction for managing the change in an organisation's operations? If it fails to address the problems, what modifications would you suggest might be necessary to enable it to do so?

2 Consider that your company is in the situation described by Assignment 2 below. What might be the trade-offs that need to be made in the different performance areas, how might they be challenged and what use could be made of the concept of focus?

3 Reference was made in this chapter to a four-stage model depicting the progressive shift in aspirations of a company from negative and operational to positive and strategic. Discuss how a company may decide at what stage it is currently operating, and explain what might be the benefits and difficulties associated with progressing from Stage 3 to Stage 4.

4 Contrast the Hill, Platts and Gregory, and Slack approaches to operations strategy development in terms of their strengths, and discuss what might be the practical difficulties associated with using each approach.

ASSIGNMENTS

1 Compare and contrast the Slack operations strategy development procedure and the five-stage procedure for operations and change strategy development presented in the chapter, and explain what you think are the strengths and drawbacks of each.

2 Consider yourself in the role of an operations director for a company which operates, as it has done for many, many years, in the leisurewear market, providing good quality, up-market, expensive, traditional leisurewear for yachtsmen and sailors. It is the board's intention to broaden the company's scope and move into a wider leisure and sportswear market and continually offer new novel designs which are good quality and moderately priced. As operations director you have been asked by the managing director to present a new operations strategy to the board. Explain the main features of this strategy and the means by which it will change the existing operations in order to realign them with the new, intended market.

REFERENCES

Bourgeois III, L.J. and Brodwin, D., 'Strategic implementation: Five approaches to an elusive phenomenon', *Strategic Management Journal*, Vol. 5, pp. 241–64, 1984.

Buffa, E. S., *Meeting the Competitive Challenge*, Irwin, Homewood, Ill., 1984.

Burnes, B. and James, H., 'Human factors in manufacturing: The need for a consistent strategy', *International Journal of Human Factors in Manufacturing*, Vol. 2, No. 1, pp. 67–9, 1992.

Gileous, V.G., 'Strategic concerns and capability impeders', *International Journal of Operations and Production Management*, Vol. 15, No. 10, pp. 4–29, 1995.

Hambrick, D.C. and Cannella Jr, A.A., 'Strategy implementation as substance and selling', *The Academy of Management Executive*, Vol. 3, No. 4, pp. 278–85, 1989.

Harding, R., 'Technology, human resources and turbulent change in Lucas and Bosch: A plant-level study', *British Journal of Management*, Vol. 5, pp. 261–73, 1994.

Hayes, R.H., Wheelwright, S.C. and Clark, K.B., *Dynamic Manufacturing*, Free Press, New York, 1988.

Hill, T.J., *Manufacturing Strategy: The strategic management of the manufacturing function*, 2nd edn., Macmillan, Basingstoke, 1993.

Itoh, S., 'Customer-oriented Manufacturing', *International Journal of Human Factors in Manufacturing*, Vol. 1, No. 4, pp. 365–70, October 1991.

Kotler, P., *Marketing Management*, Prentice Hall International, 1991.

Lippitt, M. E. and Mackenzie, K. D., 'Authority-task problems', *Administrative Science Quarterly*, Vol. 21, No. 4, pp. 643–60, 1976.

Meyers, H. B., 'The great nuclear fizzle at old B&W', *Fortune*, Time Inc., November 1969.

New, C.C., 'World class manufacturing versus strategic trade-offs', *International Journal of Operations and Production Management*, Vol. 12, No. 6, pp. 19–31, 1992.

Nutt, P.C., 'Identifying and appraising how managers install strategy', *Strategic Management Journal*, Vol. 8, pp. 1–14, 1987.

Nutt, P.C., 'Selecting tactics to implement strategic plans', *Strategic Management Journal*, Vol. 10, pp. 145–61, 1989.

Platts, K.W. and Gregory, M.J. 'Manufacturing audit in the process of strategy formulation', *International Journal of Operations and Production Management*, Vol. 10, No. 9, p. 5, 1990.

Powell, R., 'Manufacturing as a source of competitive edge', *Industrial Management & Data Systems*, Vol. 91, No. 1, pp. 19–23, 1991.

Skinner, W., 'Manufacturing – missing link in corporate strategy', *Harvard Business Review*, p. 136, May/June 1969.

Skinner, W., 'Precious jewels: companies that achieve competitive advantage from process innovation', *International Journal of Technology Management*, Special Issue on Strengthening Corporate and National Competitiveness through Technology, Vol. 7, Nos. 1/2/3, pp. 41–8, 1992.

Slack, N., *The Manufacturing Advantage: Achieving competitive manufacturing operations*, Mercury, London, 1991.

Wheelwright, S.C., 'Reflecting corporate strategy in manufacturing decisions', *Business Horizons*, p. 65, February 1978.

CHAPTER 3

Performance objectives

OBJECTIVES

The objectives of this chapter are to:

- explain the five basic performance objectives that contribute directly to an organisation's competitive advantage
- provide an understanding of what each of the performance objectives means and what their achievement can mean to an organisation
- present a process of achieving the performance objectives, by
  - developing definitions of the 'first-level' performance objectives, establishing priorities, agreeing on the timescale and the sequence in which the objectives are to be attained
  - defining and quantifying the 'second-level' performance objectives that are directly subordinate to the first-level objectives
  - creating a performance policy to provide guidance on how the objectives are to be pursued, what resources are needed to achieve them, and how these can be marshalled in an integrated way
  - measuring how well the objectives are achieved and how well the supporting process performs.

THE PERFORMANCE OBJECTIVES

A strategy for operations and change should reflect the goals of the organisation and the needs of the market place and translate those needs into performance objectives. There are five basic performance objectives, and the organisation gains competitive advantage by outperforming competitors in one or more of these. They are:

- quality
- speed
- dependability
- flexibility
- cost.

Each of the performance objectives is pursued differently and the achievement of each brings a different benefit to an organisation.

Quality is about doing things right – wanting to satisfy customers by providing goods and services which are 'fit for their purpose'.

Speed is about doing things quickly – delivering goods or services to the customer as soon as they would like them.

Dependability is about doing things on time – keeping the delivery promises which you have given to your customers.

Flexibility is about being able to change what you do to satisfy changed requirements or to cater for unexpected occurrences.

Cost is about wanting to do things cheaply – to give good value at a low cost and still achieve a satisfactory return.

WHAT IS QUALITY?

The quality of a product or service is a measure of the extent to which it satisfies the customer. Owing to increased consumer awareness and widespread availability of quality offerings, customers are becoming more discriminating. This means that those organisations that strive to provide high-quality offerings stand a greater chance of maintaining and attracting customers than their competitors. Conversely, if the customer perceives the quality to be poor, they will take their business elsewhere. Therefore, best quality means better business, and those organisations that put quality before all else, including short-term profit, will be the ones that prosper the most.

Product quality and process quality

Chase and Aquilano divide quality into two categories: *product quality* and *process quality*.

Product quality
The level of quality in a product's design will vary according to the market segment it is aimed at. For example, the technical capabilities, quality of workmanship, materials, testing and availability of service employees for telescopes to be sold to professional astronomers will be different to those for telescopes offered for sale to amateur star gazers. Similarly, the offerings of a quality restaurant in terms of the quality and variety of the food, the furnishings and décor, the courteousness and helpfulness of waiters etc. should be vastly different to other places where food can be purchased, for example, cafeterias, fast food outlets and pubs. People will pay a premium for the provision of superior quality features. However, all people want a level of quality commensurate with their expectations and outlay. To establish the appropriate level of product quality, it is necessary to define the requirements of the customer. Over-designed products which display excessive quality may be viewed as being unnecessarily expensive. Conversely, customers may be turned off by under-designed products, since they may be willing to pay a little more for a product or service that they perceive as offering greater benefits.

Process quality
Whether we are talking about telescopes for professional astronomers or for amateur star gazers, or the offerings of a quality restaurant versus a cafeteria, process quality is

critical. Essentially, customers want products or services without defects, that consistently conform to the specifications they contracted for, have come to expect, or saw advertised. Process quality aims to achieve this by meeting design specifications and producing error-free products. To achieve consistent process quality, managers need to design and monitor operations to ensure the process capability is adequate.

THE GURUS OF QUALITY

As quality is so important to the success of an organisation, much has been said and written on the topic. Exhibit 3.1 lists the 'quality gurus', each of whom has contributed important and different perspectives on the attainment of quality.

Exhibit 3.1

The gurus of quality

Juran	● fitness for purpose and breakthrough
Deming	● statistical process control
	● plan–do–check–act
Feigenbaum	● Quality system
Crosby	● conformance to requirements
	● cost of quality
Taguchi	● total loss to society
	● continuous reduction of variation

ACHIEVING QUALITY

The following are three main ingredients for achieving quality:

- requirements for quality
- management of quality
- measurement of quality.

These are looked at in more detail in the following sections.

REQUIREMENTS FOR QUALITY

Know who your customers are and what they want

BS 5750 defines quality as '*the totality of features and characteristics of a product or a service that bear on its ability to satisfy a given need*'. Another simpler definition by Juran is '*fitness for purpose*'. Whatever definition is offered in the move towards providing quality, we need to define what the customer wants. An important prerequisite to this is that you know who your customer is. Your customer is the decision maker who agrees the purchase, as well as the user of your product or service. This can refer to people inside the company's operations, the 'internal customers', as well as those outside, the 'external customers'. Satisfying them can be just as important as satisfying the external customers. So, let's say we have identified the customer. This is where the first problem emerges: the problem of a difference between what the customer perceives as being their quality requirements and what the provider sees. Some of these requirements of the customer and supplier are shown in Fig 3.1.

Note, in Fig 3.1, that the first two requirements are agreed. This is because whether you are delivering on the fifth day of the year of the monkey, according to a Chinese calendar, or paying the price in Japanese yen or Israeli shekels, both the provider and the customer know the exact time and price. The question mark against the other requirements like finish, noise, colour etc. is there to illustrate that there can be a potential source of misinterpretation between the supplier and the customer.

Acquire knowledge of competitors' quality performance levels

Even though an organisation can make significant quality improvements, it needs to understand what the competition is doing. The fact is that potential customers can buy elsewhere and they will if they can get better value.

Get your design right

The quality of design depends in the first instance on having a clear definition of the customer requirements. These requirements have then to be embodied in the design. How well this is achieved is a function of the design concept and how well the finished offering fulfils the requisite performance features like reliability, durability, serviceability etc. A value feature of the design will be the achievement of good performance of these features while keeping down the costs of providing the product or service. This can be achieved by adopting the use of value engineering principles.

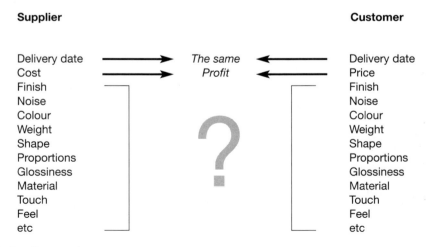

Fig 3.1 Quality requirements

Another feature of good design of a product or service is the ease and speed with which it can be provided. Speed of early design can be improved through the use of rapid prototyping, and concurrent engineering approaches can facilitate the speed and quality of the whole design and make process.

Another important feature of good design is the quality of the specifications. It must be agreed that they are appropriate, sufficiently detailed and that they are achievable. They need to be communicated to the right people who need to understand what they mean. Misunderstanding and misinterpretation of specifications is a major reason for loss of quality.

Availability of personnel trained in quality matters

All employees need to have the ability to do what is expected of them right first time. To do this, clear definitions of what is expected are needed. It is then necessary to acquire people with the requisite skills or train them so they can monitor their progress to see that the quality is being achieved.

Capable process and systems

Good process design, the appropriate level of technology, adequate transportation, handling, storage and distribution facilities are necessary features of good quality. To plan and control the processes requires the establishment and documentation of quality systems. However, a word of caution: it is not possible to control people through the application of systems. People can always thwart systems and find ways of getting around them. They can also make others think that the system is working. It is necessary to persuade people to help to achieve the objectives set and make it possible for them to do so. Although systems help and are necessary, the most useful asset is the people.

Assessing customer satisfaction

Obtaining a few opinions on the level of customer satisfaction is not rigorous enough. An organisation must know who its customers are and then stay close to them. This should be achieved by continually measuring and monitoring service and product performance across a range of carefully considered and well-defined objectives based on customer needs and expectations. When required, the organisation must respond quickly to customer requirements, being obsessive about quality and service. This requires commitment, communication and inspired leadership.

Everyone has a responsibility for quality

All employees, starting with the Chairperson, Chief Executive and Directors, need to be held accountable, not only for what they do, but for what they achieve with respect to quality. Being effective with regards to quality means everyone, starting at the corporate level, being accountable for quality.

The adoption of a philosophy of continuous quality improvement

An organisation must never stop striving to improve the product or service and the way jobs are done. They must believe that defects are neither acceptable nor inevitable.

MANAGEMENT OF QUALITY

For an organisation to say that it practices Total Quality Management (TQM) is not enough for it to pursue good quality products and espouse quality slogans. Quality has to be pervasive throughout the organisation, and to achieve this some fundamental issues need to be addressed, such as:

- management commitment
- quality policy and objectives
- planning
- quality improvement programme
- employee participation
- quality management system.

Management commitment

Commitment to quality from the most senior managers must exist if the people in the organisation and its systems, processes, products and services are to be of a high standard of quality. Implicit in this is the senior management possessing a clear understanding of quality, its importance, and how it can be achieved. The commitment to quality should be expressed in terms of the senior management's active support and provision of adequate resources to achieve the objectives set.

Quality policy and objectives

The maintenance of a defined quality policy statement which is well publicised will assist the company to demonstrate to its employees, customers and suppliers its commitment to total quality. The quality policy should be a clear statement of intention that is achievable in practice. Where possible, it should quantify performance standards and it should be easy to understand by everyone in the organisation. The use of this document makes it possible to audit and assess the performance of the organisation's quality systems.

Planning

Many managers attempt to manage in 'personal control mode'. They may do this because they fear giving away authority, or they may not know how to plan and delegate their work. As management of quality is too complex for one person to be able to control everything, the manager in personal control mode can often fail to cover many important situations, and things can drift out of control. This often leads to the manager 'fire fighting' in an attempt to retrieve the situation. Many managers think that this style of managing is attractive and macho. Experience has shown that quality is improved at lower costs, and more quickly, if more time is spent planning for things to happen. Planning for quality means planning to do the job right first time. Such planning reduces the occurrences of 'fire fighting' and is a more cost-effective method of management which the organisation would be wise to adopt at all levels and in all parts of the company. Exhibit 3.2 provides an illustration of how Cadillac's disciplined approach to planning has assisted with improvements in quality, earning Cadillac the 1990 Malcolm Baldrige National Quality Award.

Exhibit 3.2

The Cadillac quality story

Since 1985, a turnaround has occurred: Cadillac has demonstrated continuous improvement in both quality and customer satisfaction. The story of Cadillac's transformation – the people, systems, processes, and products responsible for the improvement – earned Cadillac the 1990 Malcolm Baldrige National Quality Award, the first American automobile company so honoured. One of the main strategies behind the transformation was Cadillac's disciplined approach to planning, the main objective of which is to institutionalise continuous improvement of products and services. This strategy has assisted the continuous improvement in quality, productivity and customer satisfaction measures. Since 1986 (through 1990), warranty-related costs have dropped nearly 30 per cent. Productivity at the Detroit-Hamtramck Assembly Centre has increased by 58 per cent, and lead time for a completely new model has been cut by 40 weeks.

Source: Adapted from Cadillac Motor Car Division, *Cadillac, The Quality Story.*

Toyota, Xerox, Rolls Royce and BAe are all organisations that subscribe to this approach of planning and problem solving, which can be expressed as five steps:

1 **Evaluate**: Define the situation and the problem; state the objectives.
2 **Plan**: To achieve the objectives.
3 **Do**: Implement the plan.
4 **Check**: Is the plan achieving the objectives?
5 **Amend**: Corrective action to improve performance and encourage never-ending improvement.

Quality improvement programme

An open-mindedness on the part of managers to proposals concerning quality will assist in the development of improvement programmes. This may require them seeking outside advice and expertise on quality issues. Core expertise inside the organisation can be maintained through careful selection to ensure that the right people are hired, and also through a commitment to training for quality and tapping people's expertise when they are working in teams on quality improvement programmes.

Employee participation

Emphasis should be placed on creating people's awareness of quality through the organisation's communication system. People's attitudes towards their own responsibility for quality should be reinforced by educating them on the importance of quality. Training in problem solving and the actual skills to perform a quality task will facilitate their participation. Most importantly, the achievement of quality, like any objective, requires the recognition that people are the most important resource.

A quality management system

The quality system should have all processes mapped. Supervision and control of quality, where possible, should be in the hands of those performing the tasks. Line and processes should possess adequate process capability, i.e. they should be statistically capable. Focus should be on the prevention, rather than the detection, of errors and faults in all areas and all departments. To maintain quality of supplies, attention should be on supplier management. Here, concentration should be on supplier selection, approval, co-operation, service and rating. The quality management system should be customer driven, cost-effective, aiming at a zero-defect product or service to the customer. The management should ensure that people's success in making the systems work is recognised and that they are rewarded.

MEASUREMENT OF QUALITY

Cost of quality

The measurement of quality is a quantitative indicator of change. It serves as the 'scorecard' to determine effectiveness of quality programmes. One of the main and effective ways to measure quality is by measuring quality costs. The categories of quality costs are shown in Fig 3.2.

Costs of conformance

The costs of conformance are the costs of investing to ensure that all activities are right first time, on time, every time. In this category is the *cost of prevention*. This is the cost of any action taken to prevent or reduce failure. Such costs are:

- quality engineering
- education/training
- instrument calibration
- supplier certification
- prevention maintenance
- quality system administration
- improvement projects.

The *cost of appraisal* is the cost of assessing the quality achieved. Such costs are:

- acceptance testing
- inspection and testing

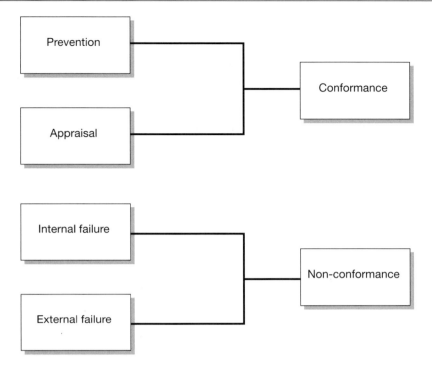

Fig 3.2 Categories of quality costs

- quality reporting
- quality audits
- stock checking
- administrative checking
- evaluations at customers' sites
- in-process inspection.

Costs of non-conformance

The costs of non-conformance are the costs incurred by *failing* to ensure all activities are right first time, on time, every time. In this category is the *cost of internal failure*. This is the cost arising from the failure to achieve the quality specified, *before* the transfer of ownership to the customer. Such costs are:

- scrap
- rework
- troubleshooting
- analysis of defects and failures
- reinspection and retest
- lost production due to poor material
- engineering changes due to poor design
- downgraded product.

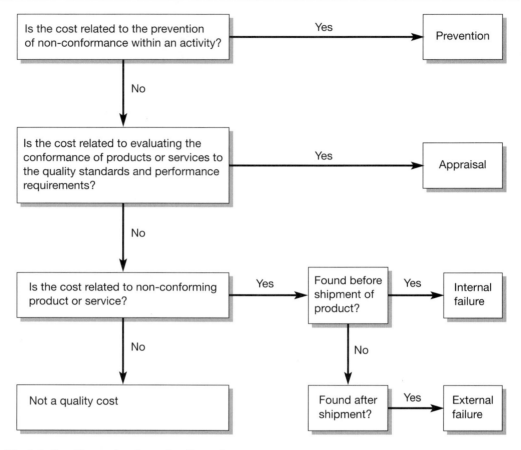

Fig 3.3 Quality cost categories flow chart

The *cost of external failure* is the cost arising from the failure to achieve the quality specified, *after* the transfer of ownership to the customer. Such costs are:

- complaints administration
- product or customer service
- product liability
- product returns
- product recalls
- product replacement
- marketing errors.

Figure 3.3 shows a flow chart which can be used to determine a quality cost category.

QUALITY COST BREAKDOWN

Figure 3.4 shows the cost of quality breakdown for a typical organisation.

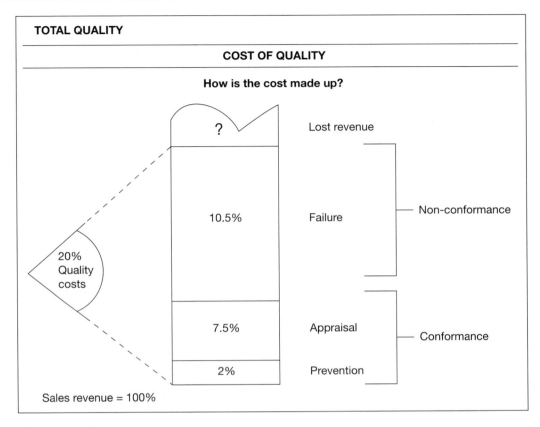

TOTAL QUALITY

COST OF QUALITY

How is the cost made up?

?

Lost revenue

10.5%   Failure

Non-conformance

20% Quality costs

7.5%   Appraisal

Conformance

2%   Prevention

Sales revenue = 100%

Fig 3.4 Quality cost breakdown

Source: Reproduced with kind permission of Andrew Owen, Partner, Coopers & Lybrand, Nottingham.

Typically, quality costs are 20 per cent of the sales revenue. As shown, failure can be expensive and prevention costs are less than failure costs. Failure costs are caused through mismanagement, and they can be reduced, along with the costs of appraisal, by emphasising prevention of poor quality occurring in the first place.

Exhibit 3.3 illustrates how D2D, ICL's contract electronics manufacturing subsidiary, reduced its costs of non-conformance by an average of £2 to £3 million per annum and beat the best to win the European Quality Award.

Quality maturity profile

In striving to improve the above dimensions of quality, an organisation needs to recognise where it is in respect of any transition it needs to make. That is, it needs to know its current position and what it needs to do. To assist in this process, Table 3.1 shows certain quality characteristics that organisations exhibit at each stage of progression, from being a complete 'innocent' regarding quality to being excellent.

Exhibit 3.3

D2D reduces costs of non-conformance to win the European Quality Award

'At D2D, quality is not a religion. It is seen as a competitive differentiator for the business but also as something that must provide value for money,' added Alastair Kelly, managing director of D2D. 'Since 1980, staff productivity has improved by over 300 per cent and the company has reduced quality losses, or costs of non-conformance, by an average of £2 to £3 million per annum.'

Although implementation of the European Foundation for Quality Management (EFQM) total quality model has been instrumental in business performance improvement, Kelly emphasised that the awards signify neither perfection nor a signal to let up. 'This year's self-assessment,' he says, 'will drive further improvement over the entire business, with the aim of improving today's quality score of around 700, out of a possible score of 1000, to 850 by 1996.'

Source: Adapted from 'D2D – Beating the best', *Quality Today*. Published by Nexus Media Ltd.

Table 3.1 Quality maturity profile

Stage / Characteristic	Innocence	Awareness	Understanding	Competence	Excellence
Quality approach	Reactive	Quality improvement	Prevention	Designed-in	Innovation
Corporate leadership	Not involved	Assumes responsibility	Supports process focus	Measures total performance	Stimulates creative responses
Data collection and analysis	Haphazard	Collecting and analysing data	Using information	Continuous improvement of process	Advanced methods and techniques
Quality assurance	Quality department	Management	Knowledge transfer to staff	Quality at source	Shared company-wide
Type of quality assurance	Inspect and correct	Try new procedures	Process control	Real-time market feedback	Innovative improvement
Customer relations	React to worst complaints	Internal customer recognised	Plan to requirements of customers	Improvement plans linked to customer	Customers aid innovation
Supplier relations	React to worse defects	Education	Joint quality analysis	Long-term strategic partnerships	Mutual work to prepare for market evolution
Quality cost (% of income)	Over 20%	15–20%	8–15%	3–8%	Cost to society
Education and training	Little	Techniques	Planned	Company-wide	Continuous

Source: Reproduced with kind permission of Andrew Owen, Partner, Coopers & Lybrand, Nottingham.

DIFFICULTIES WITH QUALITY

The foregoing has dealt with the main features and means of achieving quality. There can be many reasons why a company may experience difficulty when it attempts to provide its customers with a high-quality product or service. These could be inadequate information, little or no training, poor management, lack of management support, poor attitude towards quality, poor planning, lack of resources etc. In each case it is down to the management to investigate the main reason, or reasons, why the company may be experiencing difficulty with quality. Managers should indicate the *extent of difficulty* they think their company is experiencing in attempting to achieve quality. Many of these difficulties can be overcome when the management appreciates that it needs to change its basic assumptions about quality. Table 3.2 shows the type of assumptions that need to be changed.

Table 3.2 Changing quality assumptions

From	To
Reactive	Proactive
Inspection	Prevention
Acceptable quality level	Zero defects
Production-orientated	Organisation-orientated
Blame placing	Problem solving
Quality versus operations	Quality and operations
Quality costs more	Quality costs less
Operations only	Product design, process design and operations
Quality department problems	Purchasing, R&D, marketing have quality problems
General managers not evaluated on quality	Quality performance part of general managers' review
Quality is technical	Quality is managerial

THE BENEFITS OF QUALITY

A precondition to all improvements is an improvement in the quality performance of operations. With this comes the following benefits:

Improved customer service, internal as well as external

Better quality directly improves customer service and helps build up business. Good quality also makes life easier inside the operation; that is, it provides internal customer satisfaction, which can be as important as satisfying external customers.

Reduction of costs

Improved quality assists in the reduction of costs. This is because fewer mistakes are being made in each operation and therefore less time is spent correcting these mistakes and the fuss they cause.

Increase in dependability and productivity

The consequences of poor quality mean that problems have to be sorted out, which takes up the management's time. The result is that more mistakes could be made and the process becomes more unreliable. On the other hand, if more things are done right first time, less time has to be spent on rectifying mistakes. This leads to operations being more stable, more productive, efficient and dependable.

Satisfaction and security

People want to work in an environment that strives for quality; one that respects and rewards their talents. Given such conditions, people's self-esteem and personal development will thrive and so should improvements in quality. In turn, the chances are that customers will receive higher quality products and services and the business will reap the benefits, thereby maintaining the security of the people in the organisation.

SPEED

Speed outside the operation

Speed of delivery (external to the operation) is important to the customer since it determines how long they have to wait to receive their products or services. Speed is also about the availability of goods, and if the customer wants immediate service then off-the-shelf availability is essential. In this situation, if the goods are not available, there is a good chance that the customer might take their business elsewhere.

The speedy delivery of goods and services to the operation's (external) customers enhances the operation's offering to the customer. Quite simply, for most goods and services, the faster a customer can have the product or service, the more likely he or she is to buy it. To some operations, for example parcel delivery, speed is particularly important.

In most situations, customers want their goods and services quickly, and therefore speed influences their decision on whether or not to buy and also what they are prepared to pay. Here, the ability of a firm to provide a reliable, fast delivery allows it to charge a premium price for its products.

Speed inside the operation

Speed is equally important inside the operation, since it can save money, reduce costs and benefit the customer. Here, we are concerned with the shortest possible elapsed time between receiving a customer's order and fulfilling it. An acceptable delivery time could be a year or more for a highly-sought, customised product, say a Morgan car; several weeks for elective eye surgery; and minutes for a fire engine. Companies can shorten delivery times by speeding up their decision-making processes, by the speedy movement of materials and information inside the operation, and by storing inventory (manufacturing) or having excess capacity (manufacturing or service).

Relationship between external customers' demand waiting time and the total throughput time in manufacturing

Speed involves the whole throughput cycle, and Fig 3.5 shows the relationship between the external customers' demand waiting time, D, and the total throughput time – to manage the flow of materials and information – P. P and D depend on the type of manufacture.

In a 'make to stock' situation, e.g. a steel stockist, D is the time for transmitting the order, processing the order, picking and packing the order and transporting it to the customer. The make cycle involves the purchase cycle, scheduling work in the manufacturing process, withdrawing materials and parts from stock, and processing them. Here, the demand time is very short compared with the total throughput cycle.

In a 'make to order' situation, e.g. Aerospace companies, D is the same as P.

Most companies lie between these two extremes and operate with more than one P and more than one D for their range of products. Generally, the demand time, D, is very short compared with the total throughput cycle, P, for most companies. The greater P is than D, the higher is the proportion of speculative activity, i.e. work carried out on the expectation of receiving a firm order – speculative because P is greater than D and because of demand forecast uncertainty. Reducing the P–D ratio takes some of the risks out of manufacturing planning.

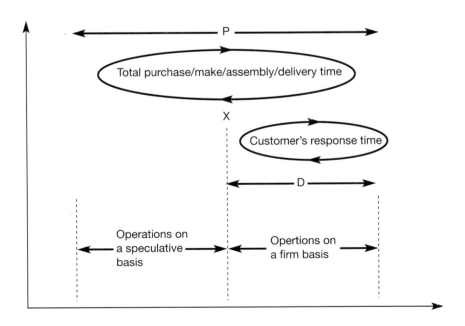

Fig 3.5 Relationship between P and D

Source: Slack, N., *The Manufacturing Advantage*.

THE BENEFITS OF SPEED

Reducing the time to the right of point X in Fig 3.5 reduces delivery lead time and customers get their goods faster. Therefore, for the same amount of speculative production, competitiveness is increased and the company gets its revenue sooner.

Time is the yardstick

Owen, in his article 'Time is the yardstick', emphasises how – reducing lead and cycle times, cutting lot sizes, speeding a product from concept to production, moving parts through the plant on the fast track, accelerating orders, delivering in days instead of weeks – time is the source of competitive advantage. Squeezing time out of the process does uncover the sources of inefficiency and quality problems. Eliminating them does cut costs and improve quality. In the same article, similar comments are made:

> 'Managing businesses by cycle time,' says Nigel Southway of Cycle Time Management Inc. (Toronto, Canada), 'will soon be essential.'

> 'Lead time reduction is not a tactic,' says Rajan Suri, Director, Center for Quick Response Manufacturing, University of Wisconsin-Madison, 'It is an organisational strategy led by top management.'

Exhibit 3.4 highlights the benefits of speed experienced at Beloit Corporation, Dayton Reliable Tool & Mfg Co., and M/A–Com.

The internal benefits of responsiveness

The internal benefits of responsiveness can be listed as follows:

- Speed reduces speculative activity.
- Speed allows better forecasts to be made.
- Speed reduces overheads.
- Speed lowers work-in-progress.
- Speed exposes problems.
- Speed can provide protection against slippage.
- Speed enables freeze time to be planned.

Speed reduces risks

Although no one can predict the future, forecasting tomorrow's events is far less of a risky business than forecasting next year's. This means that most companies will have greater confidence in their forecasts for shorter sales periods than in their forecasts for longer periods.

WAYS TO ACHIEVE A FAST OPERATION

Possible points for consideration in speeding up operations are as follows:

1 Confusion and ignorance causes delays; for example, hold-ups while priority and urgent jobs jump the queue. This can be avoided by thorough planning and agreement over timings and resources.

Exhibit 3.4

The benefits of speed at Beloit Corporation, Dayton Reliable Tool & Mfg Co., and M/A–Com

Making time the metric at Beloit

Lead time for delivery of Beloit Corporation's (Beloit, WI) huge paper-making machines was 16 months; parts took 14 to 16 weeks. Beloit adopted a total employee involvement programme. Three months after the programme began, rolls were flowing through the shop in as little as eight days.

Spotting the rocks at Dayton

Dayton Reliable Tool & Mfg Co. (Dayton) provides precision progressive tooling systems for the aluminum can industry. Dennis T. Casey, the company president, decided the best attack on delivery dates was a cellular approach. Casey says work-in-progress is down 75 per cent and manufacturing cycle time dropped 90 per cent. Lead time is down only a week, although parts are made much faster, because of the backlog of orders. The accelerated manufacturing cycle will soon clear that away, says Casey. All delivery dates are now firm, with 100 per cent on-time performance in the cell.

Continuous flow at M/A–Com

New commercial customers' pressure produced major changes at M/A–Com, which makes silicon and gallium diodes for radio-frequency and microwave devices. Like many defense contractors, the company found time a major obstacle. Product life cycles measured in years had to become months. Bob Lynch, engineering manager, installed a pull system in a cellular operation run by a team at the company's Burlington Semiconductor Operations (Burlington, MA). Wafer fabrication lead times, 8.5 weeks in July 1991, had dropped to three weeks by March 1992. Work-in-progress was halved while weekly shipments increased; cycle time was cut 75 per cent.

Source: Adapted from Owen, J. V., 'Time is the yardstick', *Manufacturing Engineering*.

2 Everyone should think in terms of speed and performance, which should be measured in terms of throughput times. Typical problems here can be inherently slow data transmission media; decision-making delays over credit control, part orders, and scheduling of work; delays to ensure full loads in transportation, or delays for the Master Production Control (MPC) system to be run.

3 It is important that 'throughput efficiency' be known, i.e. the ratio of actual value-adding time to elapsed time for materials to go through the operation.

4 Where possible, the operation should be protected from unexpected variation in demand. Otherwise there will be an erratic work flow and this can lead to backlogs of work in the factory.

5 Emphasis should be placed on internal dependability, quality and flexibility. For example, quality failures can delay throughput twice over due to the reordering of products which fail quality standards or the rework of components or products which fail quality standards.

6 Separation reduces the imperative for speed; functions should be put close together.

7 Attention should be paid to bottlenecks in the flow of production, say to identify overloading in one part of the order cycle.

8 Decision making should be simplified and streamlined and decisions should be made by the lowest competent authority.

9 Batching of work for processing is one of the major causes of delay in operations. For example, large batch sizes incur long process set-up times, and there can be transportation delays in moving batches of work around the plant.

10 Focus should be on eliminating the 90-odd per cent of the throughput time when no value is being added to the product.

ASSESSING PERFORMANCE AND MAKING IMPROVEMENTS

It is important to get everyone thinking in terms of speed. This can be done by measuring performance in terms of throughput times, prioritising the importance to the company of speeding up particular operations, and asking what are the ways in which these operations can be speeded up? Important questions that need to be asked are:

Total throughput time, P
- For each of your main products (product groups), what is the total throughput time, P, i.e. the time taken to manage the flow of materials and information?
- In what ways could the throughput cycle be speeded up/improved?

Customers' waiting time, D
- For each of your main products (product groups), what is the external customers' demand waiting time, D, i.e. the time for transmitting the order, processing the order, picking and packing the order and transporting it to the customer?
- In what ways could the delivery cycle be speeded up/improved?

Total manufacturing time, M
- For each of your main products (product groups), what is the total manufacturing time, M, i.e. the time taken to withdraw materials and parts from input inventories and process them?
- In what ways could the make cycle be speeded up/improved?

Total purchase time, C
- For each of your main products (product groups), what is the total purchase time, C, i.e. the time for replenishment of the input stocks – involving transmitting the order to suppliers and awaiting their delivery?
- In what ways could the purchase cycle be speeded up/improved?

By focusing on these areas in this way the potential savings can be huge.

Competitive superiority through a time-orientated competitive strategy

Exhibit 3.5 illustrates how NEC Corporation, Tokyo, Japan, achieves competitive superiority through a time-orientated competitive strategy.

Exhibit 3.5

NEC Corporation achieves competitive superiority through a time-orientated competitive strategy

Time is becoming the most important differentiating element for achieving competitive superiority in today's age; those who can manage time efficiently will attain great success. A time-orientated competitive strategy can be described as a company-wide management strategy that aims to reduce the total lead time required to adapt to changes in the market.

I (Shin-ichi Itoh, NEC Corporation, Tokyo, Japan) would like to close by emphasising four points.

First, NEC Corporation's time-orientated competitive strategy is definitely our inventory minimisation programme. Characteristics such as the drastic nature of our targets and the pursuit of revolutionary ideas and methods through joint activities by line workers and the staff are all part of the innovation represented by our activities.

Second, the strategy is necessary, not only for lead-time reduction in a physical sense, but also for reduction of lead time needed for management, decision making, and interfacing. In short, since time saving, as a concept, encompasses effects such as reduced costs and improved quality, integration-orientated ideas are extremely important.

Third, there is the need for sophisticated utilisation of information. In the 1990s, there will be a flood of information. In this type of situation, intelligence will be essential, in terms of being able to extract essential information in a timely manner, being able to use it strategically, and being able to use it in order to save time.

Finally, all attempts to improve combined strength and management capabilities ultimately rest on people. The ability to cultivate people suited for strategic IE, that is, the ability to cultivate people who have pride and capability in manufacturing and who are receptive to value and awareness reform, will be the deciding factor in determining who triumphs in this age of time-based competition.

Source: Adapted from Itoh, S., 'Customer-oriented manufacturing', *International Journal of Human Factors in Manufacturing*.

DEPENDABILITY

Dependability outside the operation

Dependability means doing things in time for customers to receive their goods or services when they were promised. This means 'on-time delivery', and it can be measured as the frequency with which delivery-time promises are met. Manufacturers measure on-time delivery as the percentage of customer orders shipped when promised. In a service situation, say a fast-food outlet, on-time delivery can be measured as the percentage of customers who wait longer than a minute to be served.

Dependability inside the operation

Inside the operation dependability is also just as important since internal operations act as customers to each other. Consequently, operations where internal dependability is high, for example delivering material or information on time, will be more effective than those where it is not.

What dependability achieves

Dependability saves money because it reduces the ineffective use of time which translates into extra cost in the operation. The disruption caused to operations by a lack of dependability affects more than time and cost. One can imagine the benefits of operations which are dependable. Trust is built up and this enables particular operations to focus on improving their own effectiveness without the worry of being let down by others. This provides a level of stability and confidence on which to progress.

ACHIEVING DEPENDABILITY

Possible requisites for delivery dependability are:

1 Investigating the benefit of investing in the dependability of process technology because of the resulting benefits in process dependability.

2 Each and every department taking responsibility for and emphasising internal supplier development.

3 When delivery reliability is excellent, advertising this fact to the customer.

4 Improving the dependability of operations through improved manufacturing flexibility.

5 Monitoring progress closely so as to improve dependability.

6 Attempting to maintain delivery integrity by providing an early warning of a late order.

7 Seeking stability of operations through improving the dependability of internal operations.

8 Considering the ways in which the dependability of the delivery cycle can be improved, and planning ahead to avoid problems which can affect delivery dependability.

9 Considering the ways in which the dependability of the purchase cycle may be improved.

10 Giving careful thought to the proper measurement of delivery dependability, and making it a key measure of operations performance.

11 Not overstretching capacity – in fact any spare capacity should be used to improve dependability.

SPEEDING UP DEVELOPMENT

In today's competitive environment where many organisations are using approaches such as rapid prototyping, concurrent engineering and use of computer-aided design and manufacture, the need for rapid 'development speed' is essential. This is a measure of how quickly a new product or service becomes available, and covers the elapsed time from concept through to design and then production. Being the first to get a new product or service on to the market gives a company a lead from which, in today's turbulent business environment, the competition might not recover. For example, development speed of software is especially important in the computer games industry where the saving of days on the launch of a new game can mean the difference between success or failure.

Ways of speeding up development

New product development and time to market can be speeded up in many ways, for example by:

- speeding up product development
- including the whole development cycle
- concentrating on developing non-value-adding
- simplifying decision making
- putting stages close together
- protecting the process from disturbances
- stressing internal dependability
- stressing quality operations
- measuring performance in terms of speed.

In relation to the above, a company should consider how well it performs. This may result in it reconsidering the importance it should attach to speeding up 'new product time to market'.

Many companies seek to maintain or increase their customer base by focusing on the competitive priorities of development speed and fast delivery time. This is referred to as *time-based competition* (*see* Krajewski and Ritzman, 1996) and is where managers carefully define the steps and time needed to deliver a product or service, and then critically analyse each step to determine whether time can be saved without compromising quality.

FLEXIBILITY

Today's companies are having to cope with changing customer needs, rapid development of technology and new, keen competition. They need to be flexible if they are to survive and operate effectively; that is, they need to have the ability to change what they do and how they do it quickly.

Flexibility is the ability to change, to do something different. According to Slack:

> *Flexibility means being able to change the operation in some way. This may mean changing what the operation does, how it is doing it, or when it is doing it, but change is the key idea.*

According to Chase and Aquilano:

Flexibility, from a strategic perspective, refers to the ability of a company to offer a wide variety of products to its customers. Flexibility is also a measure of how fast a company can convert its process(es) from making an old line of products to producing a new product line. Product variety is often perceived by the customer to be a dimension of speed of delivery.

REASONS FOR FLEXIBILITY

Flexibility is needed for the following reasons:

1 **To cope with the variety of activities:** For example to cope with a wide range of parts and products and to adapt products to customers' needs, i.e. to customise; to adjust output levels to suit varying demand, and to deal expeditiously with changing priorities on orders.

2 **To maintain performance under short-term uncertainty:** For example, to cope with plant breakdowns, unexpected changes in demand; to provide adjustments in capacity, and to cope with supplier unreliability.

3 **Because of long-term uncertainty:** For example, because there is no clear idea about the nature of manufacture in the future or the capacity needs in the future, the operations need to be flexible to cope with new products and changing markets.

4 **To cope with ignorance of other functions' plans or company strategy:** Flexibility is useful here because it can help overcome the problems caused by ignorance or lack of any accurate plan or forecast for the future – basically, bad management. The problem is that if flexibility is used to compensate for lack of dependability, it is wasted. The lack of dependability should be tackled directly.

SYSTEM FLEXIBILITY

To satisfy changing customers' requirements, organisations will require their operations to change. This can be accommodated through the following types of system flexibility:

* product/service flexibility
* mix flexibility
* volume flexibility
* delivery flexibility.

Product/service flexibility

Product/service flexibility is the operation's ability to introduce new products and services.

Krajewski and Ritzman refer to this type of flexibility as 'customisation'; that is, the ability to accommodate the unique needs of each customer with ever-changing product or service designs. Often, products or services which are tailored to individual preferences do not have long lives. A trainer may design a fitness programme that is unique to the individual. The life of that service can vary from month to month depending on the progress of the individual. Alternatively, a customised car may last for years. Therefore, to achieve customisation the operation system must be flexible to handle specific customer needs and changes in designs.

Mix flexibility

Mix flexibility means being able to provide a wide range or mix of products and services. The majority of operations do not dedicate all their resources exclusively to a single product or service. Consequently, such operations will need to change between activities and they will be more effective at doing this if they are flexible.

Volume flexibility

Volume flexibility is the ability to accelerate or decelerate the rate of output or activity quickly to handle fluctuations in demand. The time between peaks may be years, as with the cycles in the construction industry or public sector educational resource requirements; or it may be months, as with a health farm or the manufacture of heating appliances. It may even be hours, as with the demand for a hospital's rescue and emergency helicopter. Operations in most cases are faced with widely fluctuating demand, and if they are 'inflexible' they may face serious consequences on customer service, operating costs, or both.

Delivery flexibility

Delivery flexibility is the ability of operations to react to changes in the timing of delivery requirements. This may be due to services and goods being required earlier or at a different time from that initially thought. It may also be due to operations reshuffling delivery priorities in order to create a more efficient schedule.

TYPES OF RESOURCE FLEXIBILITIES

The system flexibilities that are required should dictate the type of 'resource flexibilities' needed, these being:

- the process technology
- the human resources
- the supply networks.

Resource requirements

Table 3.3 shows the implications on resources for different types of system flexibility. This information can be used to consider the implications of using each of the three resources to improve the flexibility of a company's operations.

MEASURING FLEXIBILITY

The flexibility of systems can be measured in terms of:

- **Range flexibility**: how far the operation can be changed. This represents the system's ability to be bent. This would be over a longer term.
- **Response flexibility**: how fast the operation can be changed. This represents the ease with which the system can be moved. Usually this would be in the shorter term.

Table 3.3 Resource implications of system flexibility types

Resources	Product flexibility	Mix flexibility	Volume flexibility	Delivery flexibility
Process technology	• Range of process capability • Capability of design technology	• Range of process capability • Process change times • Scale and integration of process	• Total process capability • Speed with which processes can be focused on required product range	• Total process capacity • Speed with which processes can be focused on required product range
Human resources	• Range of design skills • Range of process skills • Transferability of labour	• Range of process skills • Direct/indirect task transferability	• Overtime capability • Transferability of labour	• Overtime capability • Transferability of labour
Supply networks	• Supply of design and process labour • Ability to modify process technology • Project management skills	• Purchased items lead times • Rescheduling capability	• Ability to recruit new and/or temporary labour • Ability to organise subcontract supply • Order processing and forecasting sensitivity	• Purchased items lead times • Ability to recruit new temporary labour • Ability to reschudule activities

Source: Slack, N., *The Manufacturing Advantage*.

Types of range and response flexibility that can be measured for different system types are presented in Table 3.4.

Table 3.4 The range and response dimensions of the four system flexibility types

Product flexibility type	Range flexibility	Response flexibility
Product flexibility	The range of products which the company has the design, purchasing and manufacturing capability to produce	The time necessary to develop or modify the product and processes to the point where regular production can start
Mix flexibility	The range of products which the company can produce within a given time period	The time necessary to adjust the mix of products being manufactured
Volume flexibility	The absolute level of aggregated output which the company can achieve for a given product mix	The time taken to change the aggregated level of output
Delivery flexibility	The extent to which delivery dates can be brought forward	The time taken to reorganise the manufacturing system so as to replan for the new delivery date

Source: Slack, N., *The Manufacturing Advantage*.

THE BENEFITS OF FLEXIBILITY

The benefits of flexibility relate mainly to speedier operations. For example, if operations are flexible they are more capable of providing a fast service. In this case, *flexibility speeds up response*.

Developing a flexible operation means that the other operations, or internal customers, will benefit. This is *flexibility inside the operation*. If, say, an emergency unit in a hospital is flexible in 'changing over' from one task to the next, then this *flexibility saves time*.

Internal flexibility can also help when unexpected occurrences play havoc with an operation's schedules. Often, internal flexibility helps keep the operation on schedule, that is *flexibility maintains dependability*.

IMPROVING FLEXIBILITY

Reducing the need to be flexible

Before you rush to improve flexibility, it is wise to ascertain how much flexibility is necessary. It may be that the need for flexibility can be reduced by an 'avoidance strategy'.

For example, can the operation compete on a non-flexible basis by matching market segmentation with product segmentation, i.e. by having strict limits on product range? The need to be flexible can also be reduced by making things less complicated, say by variety reduction programmes or modular design. Also, the need for flexibility can be confined to particular operations. This may be achieved by separating the more standard product lines from those processes which deal with more variety and hence need to be more flexible.

Defining the operations objectives

For the company's operations to be effective it is necessary first to define the objectives of speed, dependability and cost that flexibility can assist. It is then possible to consider ways in which flexibility can support these objectives.

Clarifying the need for flexibility

It is important to clarify why you need flexibility, and to do this it is necessary to refer back to the reasons for flexibility, namely:

- variety – response flexibility
- short-term uncertainty – response flexibility
- long-term uncertainty – new product and volume flexibility
- ignorance.

Whichever of these reasons are prominent will indicate the type of flexibility to develop.

Knowing the ranges and response dimensions of flexibility

In most situations the more things that are changed, the longer it takes. These are the dimensions of flexibility, i.e. range and response, which will be different for different situations. Therefore, to improve flexibility it is necessary to have this information, which can be obtained by drawing range–response curves. These curves show the range or extent of change possible for varying response times, and this gives an idea of system capability. Figure 3.6 shows the range–response curves for the volume flexibility of two plants, A and B.

Developing flexible resources

Different system flexibility requirements imply different operational resources. Therefore, it is necessary to differentiate between the contribution to flexibility to be gained from the three types of resource areas mentioned earlier: process technology, human resources, and supply networks.

COST

In many markets the attraction to the buyer is being able to buy the product or service at the lowest cost. Usually, what is being purchased is a standard commodity and the

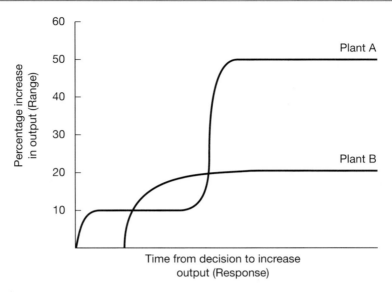

Fig 3.6 Range-response curves for the volume flexibility of two plants

Source: Slack, N., *The Manufacturing Advantage*.

customers use the cost to determine whether or not to purchase. This segment of the market often deals with large volumes and companies see the potential for making huge profits. Therefore, competition is keen and companies strive to win by lowering prices in order to attract customers. If they cannot keep the costs of producing their product or service to a minimum, they will fail.

There are, however, companies whose strategy is not to compete on price. These companies will still be interested in keeping their costs low, since every pound saved is another pound extra to their profits. Consequently, companies world-wide are interested in keeping costs low. To do this they need to address their expenditure on:

- staff costs (the money spent on employing people)
- facilities, technology and equipment costs (the money spent on buying, looking after, operating and replacing the operation's 'hardware')
- material costs (the money spent on the materials consumed or transformed in the operation)
- wastage and scrap
- overheads.

First, they need to appreciate the different ways in which they can attack costs. Costs may be approached at three levels:

1 Tackle head on, directly.

2 Understand the strategic drivers of cost.

3 Understand what the operational costs are and the effect that the other performance objectives of quality, speed, dependability and flexibility have on cost.

Tackle costs head on

This means cutting out surplus resources directly and appropriately balancing them to match the level of output required.

Strategic costs

The following strategic determinants of cost have a major impact on an operation's cost structure:

- the volume of outputs for each product group
- the variety of products or activities for which the manufacturing function is responsible
- the variation in output expected from the operation.

Volume costs

In the shorter term, volume effects are largely a matter of higher throughput spreading the fixed costs of production over a great number of products produced. For most companies, the volume cost curve is not smooth since costs will increase with, say, extra shifts or additional plant. The cost curve is also not certain since there is considerable management discretion as to when to commit the plant to 'fixed cost breaks'. This is agreeing to extra fixed costs and thereby having a fixed cost break due to, say, extra shifts commencing or new plant being acquired.

In the longer term, the volume of output may allow changes in the way the company uses its technology, or even the acquisition of more economic technology.

Usually, as volume increases, the tendency is for variety per unit volume to decrease, so each part of the system has fewer different tasks to perform in each time period. This will reduce the changeovers, which will free up capacity and avoid many of the quality problems associated with changeover.

Long-term volume cost effects include economies of scale; that is, the plant's cost will not double when capacity doubles. However, there are also diseconomies of scale: organisation complexity is one, increasing formality another. The potential for communications being distorted can also increase.

Managers should be able to answer questions about their own economies of scale. Where do fixed cost breaks occur? Which parts of the plant are likely to become bottlenecks? At what levels of output do alternative technologies become viable?

Variety costs

High product variety is often accompanied by high parts variety, process variety, and routing variety, which contribute to complexity, the root cause of variety-related costs. High variety requires a more complex technology, which requires increased complexity of control systems and materials handling. All this usually leads to higher capital and operation costs.

Less quantifiable are the effects of variety on overhead costs. These include the cost of supporting the increased complexity of the operation. Increased variety of input materials and bought-in parts means more purchasing effort, records, standards, inventories and co-ordination. It means more drawings, more product specifications, more process routes and logistics, all of which need organising. It

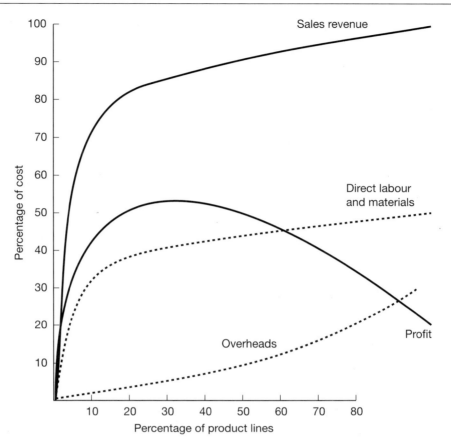

Fig 3.7 The Pareto view of variety-related costs and revenue

Source: Slack, N., *The Manufacturing Advantage*.

means more finished goods inventories, space, and co-ordination. No wonder high variety makes it harder for the operation to move down the learning curve. Certainly, accounting systems cannot reflect all the disruptive effects of variety.

The effects of variety can be seen by a Pareto view of the volume–variety relationship, shown in Fig 3.7.

The curves of Fig 3.7 show that:

- 80 per cent of sales revenue is represented by 20 per cent of the product lines.
- Direct labour and material costs follow a similar pattern to the sales revenue curve.
- The complexity effects of variety are evident as higher overhead costs at the tail of the variety distribution.
- The cumulative profits peak at a point typically below 50 per cent of the product range produced, i.e. the higher volume lines subsidise the lower volume ones.

Although variety can be an important part of competitiveness, management should attempt to accommodate it in a cost-effective manner. This can be achieved by:

1 differentiating between perceived and actual variety by looking at standardisation and simplification of design.

2 increasing product mix flexibility by making the plant more flexible and able to change more quickly and cheaply from one product to another.

3 limiting the effects of variety on the plant by keeping different types of manufacture apart, i.e. focused manufacture.

Variation costs

Companies that chase demand

Companies that alter their production levels in order to meet anticipated demand follow a 'chase demand' strategy. Manufacturers of goods such as garments and heating appliances, whose requirements peak at certain times of the year, adopt this strategy. Adjustments either way can be achieved through the use of overtime, undertime, hiring or laying-off people, subcontracting, shorter working week etc. Whichever approach is adopted, these company's will have to pay a premium on adjusting their output levels.

Companies that have level production

Alternatively, some organisations have a fairly constant rate of production and use their inventories to buffer them against fluctuations in demand. This is a 'level production' strategy. The motor car manufacturers and many mass production and process-type industries produce in this manner. The additional costs here will be inventory related, such as interest on capital, space, insurance, deterioration, obsolescence, and so forth.

Most companies, because of their products, processes and the costs involved, find it best to operate using a mixture of the two extreme strategies.

Strategic cost trade-offs

The impact of strategic costs is significant and managers have to have a reasonable idea of how costs will respond to changes in volume, variety, and variation.

It is understood that high volume, together with low variety and a steady, predictable demand, keep manufacturing costs low; whereas low volume, high variety and fluctuating demand exact a cost penalty. Therefore, managers have to seek ways of minimising the cost penalties which low volume, high variety and high variation produce. They also have to make sure that other managers who can influence manufacturing cost, even though they may work in other areas of the company, should play their part in keeping these costs under control.

Operational costs

Operational costs can be classified as direct labour, materials and overheads. Many companies, when embarking on cost-cutting exercises, tend to concentrate on direct labour. Since most operations spend less than 20 per cent of their costs on direct labour, this approach is questionable. Many plants spend twice as much on purchase material as on direct labour, and they do not attempt to measure purchasing performance realistically.

These costs for a typical company are illustrated in Exhibit 3.6.

Exhibit 3.6

Typical factory costs

A factory's total costs vary depending upon the type of industry. For example, the cost of direct labour can vary from less than 1 per cent to over 40 per cent. On average this cost is around 15 per cent. The cost of bought-in materials and parts can vary from over 80 per cent to less than 20 per cent, but an average is about 55 per cent. Overhead costs on average are around 30 per cent.

The example below provides typical factory costs, overheads and profit per sales of 100.

Materials	54
Direct labour	14
Overheads	26
Tax	2
Profit	4
TOTAL SALES	100

Consideration 1: Stricter supervision and revised work methods

Through stricter supervision and revised work methods the company has reduced its direct labour costs.

Question
What would be the percentage improvement in profit resulting from a 1% reduction in direct labour?

Calculation

Direct labour	$= 14 - 1\% = 13.86$
Profit before tax	$= 6 + 0.14 = 6.14$
Profit after tax	$= 4 + 0.093 = 4.093$ (pro rata)
Therefore the profit increase	$= \dfrac{0.09 \times 100}{4}$
	$= 2.33\%$

Answer
A 1% reduction in direct labour would provide a 2.33% improvement in profit.

Consideration 2: Efficient use of indirect labour

Through making more efficient use of indirect labour, e.g. less activities of checking, packing, chasing, the company has reduced its overheads.

Question
What would be the percentage improvement in profit resulting from a 1% reduction in overheads?

Calculation

Overheads	$= 30 - 1\% = 29.7$
Profit before tax	$= 6 + 0.3 = 6.3$
Profit after tax	$= 4 + 0.2 = 4.2$ (pro rata)
Therefore the profit increase	$= \dfrac{0.2 \times 100}{4}$
	$= 5\%$

Answer
A 1% reduction in overheads would provide a 5% improvement in profit.

Consideration 3: Reduction in scrap and standardisation of parts

Through a reduction in scrap and standardisation of parts in the finished products the company has made more efficient use of its bought-out materials and parts.

(continued)

Exhibit 3.6 continued

Question
What would be the percentage improvement in profit resulting from a 1% saving in material?

Calculation (Similar process to above.)

Answer
A 1% saving in material would provide a 9% improvement in profit.

Consideration 4: Reduction in the prices of its main product range
Through a reduction in the prices of its main product range, made possible by a programme of standardisation and variety reduction, the company sells more of its products.

Question
What would be the percentage improvement in profit resulting from a 1% increase in sales?

Calculation (Similar process to above.)

Answer
A 1% increase in sales would provide a 16.67% improvement in profit.

The typical factory costs in Exhibit 3.6 illustrate that a one per cent saving in bought-out materials and parts can mean more than three times the cost savings of a one per cent improvement in direct labour costs. The case also illustrates that a one per cent reduction in overheads can mean over twice the cost savings of a one per cent improvement in direct labour costs.

Performance objectives and cost

But what about overheads: how is it possible to reduce the level of overheads referred to earlier? A reduction in overhead costs can be achieved largely through improvement in cost performance of the performance objectives: quality, speed, dependability and flexibility.

- **Speed**: Faster throughput means materials and parts will spend less time in inventory.
- **Dependability**: Improvements in internal dependability mean less time is spent chasing up late operations.
- **Quality**: Higher quality means a reduction in scrap and reworking.
- **Flexibility**: Improving changeover flexibility means throughput time can be reduced.

Therefore, we can see that one important way to improve cost performance is to improve the internal operations by achieving improvements in internal quality, speed, dependability and flexibility. The implication of this is very important because it tells us about the relationship between the external and internal aspects of operations performance. All organisations can reduce the cost of their operations and in so doing delight customers and improve their profit.

Cost and the other performance objectives

Research conducted on a number of European manufacturers, by Ferdows and De Meyer, shows that manufacturing improvement is based on first achieving a mini-

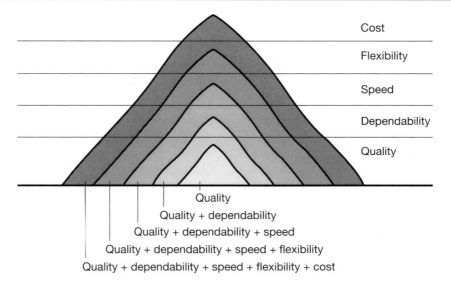

Quality
Quality + dependability
Quality + dependability + speed
Quality + dependability + speed + flexibility
Quality + dependability + speed + flexibility + cost

Fig 3.8 The sandcone model of manufacturing improvement

Source: Slack, N., *The Manufacturing Advantage.*

mum acceptable level of quality. Then issues of internal dependability and then over-all dependability need to be tackled, while still pursuing quality improvement. The next stage is to focus on speed, leading to making improvements in flexibility while continuing to improve the other objectives of quality and dependability. The research suggests that only at this stage should costs be tackled head-on. The researchers depict this cumulative improvement process in terms of the sandcone model, shown in Fig 3.8. The figure shows how cost reduction relies on a cumulative foundation of improvement in the other performance objectives.

THE PROCESS OF PURSUING THE PERFORMANCE OBJECTIVES

It is important that everyone knows what objectives are being pursued. It is also important to know how they are to be pursued, what resources are needed and how these can be marshalled in an integrated way. If this is not done, there is a strong possibility that there will be an overlap of effort across functional areas, responsibilities and departments. A performance policy should provide guidance in this respect. Necessary detail in the policy would be:

- definition and priority of first-level objectives
- definition and magnitude of second-level objectives
- timescale and sequence of pursuing the objectives
- means of achieving the objectives
- measuring how well the performance objectives are achieved.

Definition and priority of first-level objectives

The operations and change strategy process referred to in the preceding chapter, if followed, will result in the determination of a definition and priority of the 'first-level', or 'top-level' objectives. For example, a first-level quality performance objective could be:

Nature: Improve overall quality of finished goods.
Priority: Higher than the other performance objectives of delivery, flexibility and cost.

Definition and magnitude of second-level objectives

Definition

It is now possible and necessary to define the objectives that are directly subordinate to the first-level objectives, i.e. the second-level objectives. For example, the first-level objective of 'Improve overall quality of finished goods' might be achieved in a company through the pursuit of the following second-level subordinate objectives, which can be defined as:

- improve incoming material
- improve process inspection
- improve process capability
- improve operator training.

Magnitude

The magnitude of these second-level objectives can be quantified as the change in performance from the present state to the desired state. For example, the magnitude of the second-level objective 'improve incoming material' could be quantified as '*up to 3% improvement in AOQL*'; that is, the Average Outgoing Quality Level (AOQL) of incoming material needs to be improved by up to three per cent.

Timescale and sequence of pursuing the objectives

The timescale and the sequence in which the objectives are to be attained need to be agreed upon. The timescale will depend on the nature of the task the objective implies and the emphasis on and resources put into its attainment. With regard to the sequence of pursuing objectives, this will depend on how much has already been achieved and what more needs to be done, as well as the priority assigned to them. The senior management of the company may wish to take the advice of Ferdows and De Meyer and pursue the fulfilment of the objectives in a cumulative way. If a company were starting from scratch, this would mean pursuing essential quality objectives, and then building on them in a cumulative way through the pursuit of delivery objectives, then flexibility, then cost.

Means of achieving the objectives

The responsibility for achieving each of the first-level objectives should be assigned to the most senior managers in the organisation. Their task should be to become familiar with their assigned objective(s) at both levels, assessing its validity in terms of its definition, relative priority and magnitude. They should be held personally responsible for being actively involved with and supporting the attainment of the objective(s). Objectives should be pursued through teams led by the senior manager.

Table 3.5 Action plan

Action plan	Comments
Understand what each of the first-level performance objectives means and what they can achieve.	
From the operations and change strategy process develop definitions of and establish priorities among the first-level objectives.	
Agree on the timescale and the sequence in which the objectives are to be attained.	
Define the second-level performance objectives that are directly subordinate to the first-level objectives. Quantify the magnitude of the second-level objectives as the change in performance from the present state to the desired state.	
Create a performance policy to provide guidance on how the objectives are to be pursued, what resources are needed to achieve them and how these can be marshalled in an integrated way.	
Articulate and communicate clearly what the performance objectives are.	
Assign the responsibility for achieving each of the first-level objectives to the most senior managers in the organisation. Ensure that commitment and leadership comes from the Chief Executive.	
Pursue the achievement of the performance objectives through teams led by the senior managers and staffed by people who have, or can marshal, power in the organisation.	
Develop plans for the attainment of the performance objectives.	
Measure how well each performance objective is achieved relative to its performance target set by the strategy. Where possible this should be measured quantitatively.	
Provide recognition and reward for those involved in achieving the objectives. Honour not just the success but the attempt.	
Tell everyone what has been achieved.	

Measuring how well the performance objectives are achieved

An important aspect of the management process involved in achieving the performance objectives is their measurement. It is important because, in the strategy development process, it is imperative to know how well the company is performing relative to its main competitors. One way of determining this is to measure how well the company is achieving a particular performance objective relative to its performance target set by the strategy. Where possible, this should be measured quantitatively; for example, a quality goal can be expressed as a percentage achievement. Where this is difficult, or impossible to do, a qualitative measure can be used. One way of doing this is to measure on an ordinal Likert scale from, say, 1 to 5 to ascertain how well the performance objective has been achieved, where 1 = not at all, to 5 = completely.

ACTION PLANNING FOR PERFORMANCE OBJECTIVES

It is important that the managers agree on what actions need to be taken to define and achieve the performance objectives necessary to maintain competitive advantage. (It is also important that students understand these.) The points referred to in Table 3.5 will assist this process, and both managers and students should be encouraged to make use of it and make their own notes in the spaces provided as a means of developing it further to suit their particular circumstances.

CASE STUDY: THE CLEARVIEW COMPANY

Establishing Clearview's objectives

Earlier meetings with the executives had been held to resolve strategy issues relating to market requirements and how best Clearview could compete. This meeting with the executives was the second one Mike, the Managing Director, had called to resolve what Clearview's performance objectives should be and how things should be managed to achieve them.

Mike listened intently as Don, the Marketing Director, presented the list of performance objective priorities that had been decided at the previous meeting (shown as Table 1 below).

Don explained, 'Our most serious problems are concerned with skills, parts reliability and supplier lead times. I have presented these objectives as category A in Table 1 in front of you. Their achievement is crucial in terms of the company's success, since it is these areas in which we are consistently worse than our competitors, and they are most important to our customers. Therefore, the highest priority should be assigned to their achievement.'

Don continued, 'Those objectives in category B are next in importance, whereas those in category C could be kept ticking over until the more important issues have been dealt with. At our earlier meeting it was decided that eight areas of project activity would be particularly important to the achievement of these objectives.'

Don then presented the list of the project activities and how they support the company's main performance objectives (Table 2).

Table 1 Priority of Clearview's performance objectives

Performance objectives	Concern category (A = most important)
Quality of design	C
Cost	B
Delivery reliability	B
Skills availability	A
Parts quality	A
Supplier lead time	A
New product flexibility	B
Manufacturing lead time	C

Table 2 Project activities and their support of performance objectives

Project activities	To support performance objectives
1 Continued emphasis on Total Quality Management (TQM)	To improve quality of parts
2 Reducing manufacturing lead time	To reduce manufacturing lead time
3 Improving design quality	To improve the quality (ease of installation and use) of design
4 Skills assessment and retraining	To improve skills availability
5 Alternative sourcing of supplies	To reduce supplier lead time and improve parts availability
6 Improving delivery reliability	To improve delivery reliability
7 More novel designs	To improve new product flexibility
8 Continued emphasis on Just-in-Time (JIT)	To reduce costs and therefore enable competitive pricing as well as reducing manufacturing lead time

Don then handed over to Jean Dilworth, the Finance Director, with whom he had worked to collect cost and sales data regarding the achievement of the project activities. Jean handed round Table 3 which showed the estimated overall cost of pursuing the project activities and the overall percentage improvement in sales, per £100,000 spent on pursuing the different project activities over the next two years that Don estimated should occur if they were achieved.

Using this information, Jean explained what package of improvements would be most cost-effective to the company; that is, what level of improvement, either Stage 1 or Stage 2, should be made for each performance objective sought, bearing in mind the extent of improvement needed, the costs involved and the resultant improvement in sales.

Table 3 Improvement in sales for each project activity achieved

Project activities	Sales improvement % per £100 000 spent	
	Stage 1[1]	Stage 2[2]
Improving design quality	8.2	9.3
Introduction of Just-in-Time	3.2	3.4
Improving delivery reliability	7.8	7.5
Skills assessment and retraining	25.4	15.7
Introduction of Total Quality Management	12.1	10.7
Alternative sourcing of supplies	33.8	28.9
More novel designs	12.3	9.2
Reducing manufacturing lead time	2.6	4.1

[1] Stage 1 improvement = bringing those activities where the company performs worse than the competition up to the same level as most competitors.

[2] Stage 2 improvement = bringing those activities for which the performance is about the same as most competitors up to a considerably higher level than the nearest competitors.

Mike thanked Jean and Don for their work and said 'All this information needs to be coalesced to provide a clear picture of what needs to be done. I want you all to meet again to provide a definitive definition and priority of these first-level objectives. For example, if a first-level objective is 'improve skills' and another is 'improve supplier lead time', what are their relative priorities and over what timescale can we expect them to be achieved?

He then went on to overview what he saw as the process for achieving the performance objectives. 'As I said, before we can do anything we need a clear definition and priority of our first-level objectives. This you are meeting to decide upon. It will then be possible and necessary to provide a definition and magnitude of the objectives that are directly subordinate to the first-level objectives, that is the second-level objectives.'

Mike then asked George, the Operations Director, if, for example, one of Clearview's first-level objectives was 'improve overall quality of finished goods', what the second-level subordinate objectives might be.

George, taken aback by this instant request, spluttered, 'Well, off the cuff, although I think everything is okay regarding the quality of our finished goods, I suppose if it was not then we would need to improve our incoming material, improve our in-process inspection and then improve our process capability. Oh, and of course improve our operator training.'

'Thank you, George,' said Mike. 'So as you can see, each of the first-level objectives leads to second-level objectives which need to be achieved. It will then be necessary to determine their magnitude. This will need to be quantified as the change in performance from the present state to the desired state. For example, if, as George said, a second-level objective was "improve incoming material", we would need to quantify this in terms of a percentage improvement needed in the quality of the incoming material. So, as you can see, this is a substantial task, but it is one that is important and necessary, since the timescale and the sequence in which these objectives are to be attained need to be agreed.'

Mike then said he had considered the means of achieving the objectives and he went on to outline them. 'I shall assign each one of you with the responsibility for achieving one or more of the first-level objectives. Your task will be to become familiar with the objective at both levels, assessing its validity in terms of its definition, relative priority and magnitude. I shall hold each of you personally responsible for being actively involved with and supporting the attainment of that objective.'

Mike then started on the task of assigning responsibilities, but Fiona, the Personnel Manager, who was standing in for Bernard Gill, spoke up. 'I am not happy about all this', she said. ' You ask us to go away and see to it that the objectives are achieved without providing any substantive policy or guidance on how we are to do this. For example, with the executives each pursuing particular objectives, how can we ensure that the resources needed to achieve them are marshalled in an integrated way? What are we to do if overlap occurs across functional areas, responsibilities and departments? – and they will. Also, we still seem to be considering the traditional ways of improving our operations, like continuing with total quality management and just-in-time. No thought seems to have been given as to whether or not we are developing the competences we need at Clearview to pursue all our objectives.'

Mike responded, 'It's easy to criticise, but what do you suggest we do?'

Fiona replied, 'I'm not criticising, I'm trying to help. It's just that in today's working environment we should be thinking more in terms of how we can better utilise team working, empowering people and becoming a learning organisation. In this way we can continually develop a range of competences that will enable us to pursue our current objectives as well as those objectives that become important in the future. That is, we should be pursuing an enabling structure that will give us strategic flexibility and thereby give our customers the best possible deal.'

Andrew Brown, the IT and Communications Director, interrupted. 'Nice speech, but I think this empowering and learning organisation stuff is just psycho babble!'

Mike said, 'Okay everybody, listen! I don't know all the answers and, I suppose, neither does Fiona. So let's not condemn Fiona's ideas, or mine, before we have had a proper chance to consider them in detail. Otherwise, we could go around in circles if we are not careful. Could I ask you all to go away and have a few quiet corridor and coffee room type meetings to mull things over. Then I will convene a meeting at which you can raise your points in a more informed way and make a decision as to whether or not my ideas, or Fiona's, are feasible. However, let me give you a word of warning. Don't reject the ideas unless you have better ones that you can table to me. '

SUMMARY

- There are five basic performance objectives that contribute directly to an organisation's competitive advantage, namely: quality, speed, dependability, flexibility and cost.

- Each of the performance objectives is pursued in a different way and their achievement brings different benefits to an organisation.

- Quality is about doing things right – wanting to satisfy customers by providing goods and services which are 'fit for their purpose'.

- Speed is about doing things quickly – delivering goods or services to the customer as soon as they would like them.

- Dependability is about doing things on time – keeping the delivery promises which you have given to your customers.

- Flexibility is about being able to change what you do to satisfy changed requirements or to cater for unexpected occurrences.

- Cost is about wanting to do things cheaply – to give good value at a low cost and still achieve a satisfactory return.

- Individual performance objectives support and reinforce certain other performance objectives, but all performance objectives support cost.

- A structured process can be followed which will enable the performance objectives to be achieved.

- First-level performance objectives need to be defined and their priorities established, along with the timescale and the sequence in which they are to be attained.

- Second-level performance objectives that are directly subordinate to the first-level objectives need defining and quantifying.

- How well the performance objectives are achieved can be measured directly.

REVIEW AND DISCUSSION QUESTIONS

1 Outline what aspects of quality you think a supermarket (your company) should pursue, giving the reasons why.

2 In what ways can the speed and dependability of a company's operations be improved?

3 Compile a shortlist of the types of flexibility a company might wish to possess. Use the shortlist to discuss:

- the benefits of having these types of flexibility
- the resources needed to provide these flexibilities
- how these flexibilities could be measured.

4 There are different ways in which an organisation could attack its costs. How would you suggest a private water utility (your company) goes about doing so?

ASSIGNMENTS

1 Assume that you are the assistant to the managing director of your company (a super-market). Provide him/her with details concerning each of the main items on the agenda of a meeting he/she is to chair at which the company executives are expected to discuss the detail and validity behind the establishment of the company's performance objectives.

2 You have been asked to prepare a policy document on how your company's (a private water utility) performance objectives are to be pursued. What do you think should be the main features of the policy document and what problems might be encountered in pursuing the objectives?

REFERENCES

Cadillac Motor Car Division, *Cadillac, The Quality Story,* Cadillac, Detroit, Mich., 1991.

Chase, R.B. and Aquilano, N.J., *Production and Operations Management: Manufacturing and services*, 7th edn, Richard D. Irwin Inc., London, 1995.

Crosby, P.B., *Quality is Free*, McGraw-Hill, New York, 1979.

'D2D – Beating the best', *Quality Today*, pp. 8–9, January 1995, Nexus Media, Swanley, Kent.

Deming, W. E., *Quality, Productivity, and Competitive Position*, MIT Centre for Advanced Engineering Study, Cambridge, Mass., 1982.

Feigenbaum, A.V., *Total Quality Control*, 3rd edn, McGraw-Hill, New York, 1983.

Ferdows, K. and De Meyer, A., 'Lasting improvement in manufacturing performance: In search of a new theory', *Journal of Operations Management*, Vol. 9, No. 2, pp. 168–84, 1990.

Itoh, S., 'Customer-oriented manufacturing', *International Journal of Human Factors in Manufacturing*, Vol. 1, No. 4, pp. 365–70, 1991.

Juran, J.M., *Quality Control Handbook*, 3rd edn, McGraw-Hill, New York, 1979.

Krajewski, L.J. and Ritzman, L.P., *Operations Management: Strategy and analysis*, 4th edn, Addison-Wesley, Wokingham, 1996.

Owen, J.V., 'Time is the yardstick', *Manufacturing Engineering*, pp. 65–70, November 1993.

Slack, N., *The Manufacturing Advantage*, Mercury Books, London, 1991.

Taguchi, G., *On-line Quality Control during Production*, Japanese Standards Association, Tokyo, 1987.

CHAPTER 4

Operations activities

OBJECTIVES

The objectives of this chapter are to:

- provide an understanding of an organisation's operations activity areas
- demonstrate the need to provide a process for tracing the links down from the strategic to the operations level
- illustrate that, in companies that are deemed to be excellent, each has a unique range of company-specific initiatives
- explain the importance of audits and the establishment of appropriate performance measures in operations
- explain that the competency level of an operational activity can positively affect business performance and provide a method of assessing it.

TYPICAL OPERATIONS ACTIVITY AREAS

The pursuit of different performance objectives is made possible through making decisions and conducting the activities in the businesses operations activity areas, which typically are the:

- design and the product
- process
- customers and suppliers
- human resources
- controls and systems.

In respect of these activity areas, three main issues need to be addressed:

1 the relative importance of each activity area in its support of the strategic performance objectives: to ascertain this it is necessary to determine what are the links down from the strategy to the operations level
2 what needs to be done in the activity areas to support the performance objectives: this is dependent on the relative importance of each activity area, referred to above, and on
3 how well the activity areas perform.

In the first place it is necessary to understand what the activity areas are and how they operate.

UNDERSTANDING THE ACTIVITY AREAS

To make the right decisions in the activity areas in order to support the performance objectives, it is necessary to understand what each area comprises and what it can do. All this needs to be documented as a process specification, or a standard operating procedure (SOP), for each activity area, in terms of the following detail:

- policies and plans
- structure
- staffing and budgets
- operating standards and procedures.

The SOPs should be reviewed annually or when important changes are made. An SOP should be used for the purposes of training and induction and as a basis for 'continuous improvement', based on the procedures and standards contained within it.

The operations activity areas of a business all interlink and they are depicted pictorially in Fig 4.1.

Design and the product

Essentially, a good design is one in which the requirements of the customer are adequately met. This means that the customer requirements have been understood or anticipated by the producer and that they have been fully and accurately specified at the design stage. Different designers or design teams will interpret customer requirements differently, and accordingly their designs will differ.

The choice of design has a significant effect on the type of product offered to the customer in terms of its functional performance, appearance, cost, and so on. This is because the design specification tends to fix many of the downstream process planning and manufacturing variables, such as the type of labour, material and equipment to be used.

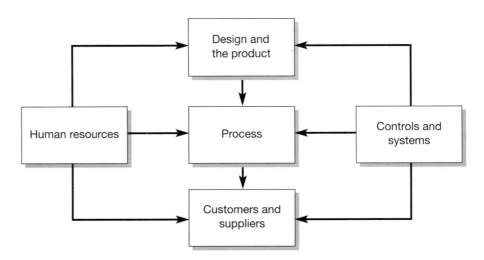

Fig 4.1 Operations activity areas

This in turn will influence the type of product offered to the customer in terms of its cost, availability, functionability, durability, resale or scrap value etc. These product features tend to be utilitarian but many features can be related to feelings the owner may have concerning the possession of a particular product. The product may be rare, expensive, customised, beautiful. It may confer a feeling of security or status on the owner.

Close links between the factory floor and design

The Bonas Machine Company (see *Management Today*, November 1995) employs 430 people and is a force in the textile machinery business, with around half the world market for electronic Jacquard machines. Its outstanding features are a wide range of improvement techniques implemented with unusual thoroughness. Close links have been established between the factory floor and the design engineers. (A large sign in the design office reminds the 21 software, firmware and mechanical engineering staff that 85 per cent of manufacturing costs are incurred at the design stage.) These days, as a design engineer explains, screws have been eliminated in favour of push-type fittings.

Wider product offerings are important

Today the term 'product' connotes a wider meaning than the physical item or product offering itself, and more offerings based around the provision of the product are available. For example, the customer could be offered guidance as to what might be the best choice from a range of products, together with advice as to the most appropriate means of financing the purchase.

From the point of view of the supplier, the success of the product will depend on how well it sells, what it sells for and how costly and difficult it is to resource, produce and get to the customer.

New product design and development

The factors that affect the success of product mainly relate back to basic design considerations such as the use of standard components, modularisation, and generally taking into account how the design affects the method of manufacture. Taking care at the design stage helps to ensure that the customer gets a good quality product that has been produced as efficiently, quickly and economically as possible.

Exhibit 4.1 illustrates how W.A. Baxter & Sons Ltd can provide a quick response to changing customer needs because of the expertise of its new product development unit.

Process

Of major concern is how to establish and maintain the right type of manufacturing process and so manage it in the most effective way for the company as a whole. Processes will vary and can range from conventional machines and equipment to fully-automatic, dedicated, computerised plant and equipment. Manufacturing processes are notoriously difficult to change quickly and their effective utilisation depends on how well the process characteristics of the plant match the requirements of the market.

Exhibit 4.2 illustrates how W.H. Smith & Sons (Tools) improved the throughput rate of its high temperature processes by using robots to replace operators.

Exhibit 4.1

Rapid new product development at W.A. Baxter & Sons Ltd

One company that seems to have proved itself very capable of coping successfully with today's market place, through the anticipation of market trends and providing quick response to changing customer needs, is W.A. Baxter & Sons Ltd. Known internationally for its 'family of fine foods', the company also has its own way of organisational learning: that of remaining a family-owned and managed business.

Over the past four generations, the Baxter family has driven the company forward. From the humble beginnings in 1868 of a small grocer's village store has grown a new multi-million pound factory located on the banks of the River Spey in Scotland. Today's £40 million food-manufacturing organisation, which sells products worldwide, employs over 600 people.

The company's major strength is its new product development unit, which is backed by a commitment to total quality. 'It is continuously creating new products to fulfil a consumer demand that helps keep the Baxter company ahead of its competition,' stated group managing director Audrey Baxter … She added, 'Clearly, it is a great advantage if business leaders can get on the road and find out for themselves what the customer requires … and by having worked in partnership with customers to create new products for an ever-expanding market.'

It is the company's experience, maintained Baxter, that manufacturers and retailers should work closely together to develop the new products that will appeal to today's more discerning consumer. It is such an approach that leads to exciting product development and mutual benefit.

Source: Adapted from Lee-Mortimer, A., 'Competing through new product delivery', *World Class Design to Manufacture*.

The correct level of process capacity needs to be established, bearing in mind that more and more capacity is unleashed every time more of the various types of waste in the process, e.g. overproduction, waiting time, transport time, product defects etc., are eliminated. Many problems associated with waste can be solved at very little cost through improved housekeeping and workplace organisation. It is also important to make machine improvements, have adequate maintenance, and have sensible automation and machine selection. The result should be a more effective process with better compliance to schedule, fewer machine breakdowns, lower defect rates, and prompt exposure of problem areas.

The whole manufacturing process can be streamlined further by small lot production, made possible through quicker set-ups and changing to a product-orientated layout.

Cell manufacturing and flexible manufacturing systems are attempts to improve the flexibility of processes and so facilitate quicker response to the market. In many cases they represent substantial capital investment.

Exhibit 4.3 illustrates how Premier Exhaust Systems' outstanding cell manufacturing capability enabled it to become winner of the Midland Region Best Factory of the Year in 1993.

Human resources

People form the main criterion for success in any organisation, and an aim of human resource management is to treat people with the utmost care and respect, since the

Exhibit 4.2

W.H. Smith & Sons (Tools) uses robots to improve high temperature process throughput rate

W.H. Smith & Sons has no connection with a better-known company of the same name, purveyors of newspapers and ballpoint pens on the high street. Smith's employs 320 people and its main activity is just-in-time manufacture and supply of low-cost, quality thermoplastic mouldings to some of Britain's most demanding industrial customers – a list that includes Black & Decker, Honda, Nissan, Rover and Toyota. Outstanding features of the company, that won it the Household & General Best Factory Award in the Best Factory Awards 1995, were continuous improvement, tool-making and engineering capability, process control and corporate culture.

The company is generally ready to take lessons from others; however, Black & Decker has in the past been a particular spur to excellence, encouraging Smith's to advance towards its vision of being a world-class supplier. A benchmarking visit to Kodak at Annesley near Nottingham, after that plant was named Factory of the Year in 1992, provided more inspiration. So did a visit to Lego, in Denmark, which has 'an incredible 1200 moulding machines on one site'.

One idea thrown up by the Lego trip was to use robots to handle mouldings and surplus sprue from injection machines which were at greater temperatures than an operator could tolerate. Designed and built by Smith's own engineers, the robots have halved the cycle time from 20 seconds to 10 seconds – 'doubling throughput at a stroke'. Nissan, too, has proved extremely helpful. A supplier-development engineer from the Japanese-owned factory helped to establish continuous improvement groups and set the company on the way to achieving the BS 5750 standard.

Source: Adapted from 'W.H. Smith & Sons (Tools), Household & General Best Factory, Engineering Industry Best Factory Awards 1995', *Management Today*, Haymarket Publications.

organisation's competitiveness depends upon their actions. This means that the selection of the right individuals should be considered as an important organisational task, as should be the task of training and educating people within the organisation. People should be listened to and their actions carefully considered and acknowledged. Everyone's potential should be considered and current abilities should be tapped to the full. Leading companies place great emphasis on the qualifications, training and skill of their employees, and companies which employ skilled, committed and enthusiastic people tend to be the most successful.

Exhibit 4.4 illustrates how SIV UK, through extensive use of training and the unquestionably high calibre of its management and workforce, became the Most Commended Company in the 1993 Engineering Industry Best Factory Awards.

People must be considered as an integral part of a manufacturing system and not as an 'afterthought'. Even with the most advanced manufacturing technology, people play a key role in determining the organisation's ability to convert that technology into competitive advantage.

However, the ability of managers to achieve the setting and culture in which people will commit to change and improvement is not commonplace. Acquiring the right culture and people with the appropriate level of skills will provide an advantage, but for continued success people must be adequately motivated. The use of incentives and

Exhibit 4.3

Premier Exhaust Systems' outstanding cell manufacturing capability

Premier Exhaust Systems stood head and shoulders above every other entrant to win the 1993 Engineering Industry Best Factory Award for Midland Region Best Factory of the Year. The Coventry factory, which is part of the Unipart Group, employs 200 people and uses just-in-time to manufacture exhaust systems for a variety of vehicles. In all, some 130 different systems are produced from 500-odd components, which are either bought-out or fabricated in-house.

Manufacturing tasks are overwhelmingly cell-based. Dedicated (or semi-dedicated) cells occupy most of the factory. Changeovers are, in consequence, minimal, which helps to ensure reliability of delivery. The managing director, Burns, claims, 'In three years of delivering to Rover, we've never failed to deliver on time.' The trouble with dedicated plant in a batch production factory is that machine utilisation is inescapably low; around 30 per cent of the equipment is idle at any one time. Nevertheless, productivity and yield both benefit from the fact that set-ups are almost permanently in place. One of the team leaders, Debbi Clapham, suggests that machine changes are now far less of a problem than material changes: she is worrying about how to reconfigure her cell in order to cope.

A lot of machinery has been crammed into the available space. Within each cell the machines are tightly knitted together, which has helped to drive down throughput times. Inventory is now turned over 30 times a year, compared to six times in the first 12 months of operation. The judges of the award were impressed by the pace of work at Premier, among the highest of any factory visited. The combination of dedicated machines and dedicated personnel has produced, Burns believes, 'the highest sales-per-square-foot in the industry'.

Source: Adapted from 'Premier Exhaust Systems, Midland Region Best Factory of the Year, Engineering Industry Best Factory Awards 1993', *Management Today,* Haymarket Publications.

Exhibit 4.4

SIV UK's extensive use of training and high calibre of its management and workforce

SIV, an Italian company (although now 50 per cent owned by Pilkington), makes 'Sicursiv' vehicle windscreens. Its UK subsidiary is Coventry-based.

The company takes raw windscreens from its Italian parent, attaches fittings, lugs etc. on two robotised assembly and curing lines, and delivers the products to Rover 'just-in-time'.

Three-quarters of the workforce have spent time working alongside their opposite numbers on the tracks at Rover and Unipart. Many have also visited Honda and other suppliers. There is extensive use of training, and the calibre of management and workforce is unquestionably high. Definitely a model of how to do it.

Source: Adapted from 'SIV UK, Most Commended Company, Engineering Industry Best Factory Awards 1993', *Management Today,* Haymarket Publications.

reward schemes are important here, as are the day-to-day relationships between line managers and operatives. Also, participative management techniques, involving the sharing of information and problems, and managers showing trust in the operatives, have been shown to result in high levels of motivation and commitment.

Exhibit 4.5 summarises how Land Rover's accessability of its managers and the development and empowerment of its employees won the company the 1993 Most Improved Factory Award.

Other examples of companies that make the best of their people to become best practice companies are:

Glaxo

Glaxo produces pharmaceutical products for distribution around the world. One of the company's outstanding features is its employee commitment. Where there had been demarcation, there is now flexibility. Operatives perform tasks that were formerly carried out by craftspeople and operatives undergo company-sponsored training in their own time, with the aim of becoming multi-skilled. Delivery performance has improved from a mere 15 per cent dispatched on time to over 90 per cent in the past couple of years.

Kimberly-Clark

Kimberly-Clark's Flint Mill produces industrial wipers. It emphasises that its process technology provides only a portion of its competitive edge. A high-quality workforce is important too. General manager Ken Haselden happily admitted to 'paying over the odds' to attract and retain the best. There is a formal training plan for every employee, with clear progress paths identified. Learning by rote is an anathema here: even the mundane tasks have a properly thought-through syllabus – well written and clearly

Exhibit 4.5

Land Rover's accessability of its managers and the development and empowerment of its employees

Land Rover, Solihull, won the 1993 Most Improved Factory Award. The director, Terry Morgan, comments that every employee takes part in quality circle discussion. Every employee is individually appraised and has his or her own personal development file.

Empowerment is no mere buzzword, Morgan insists. On the track, where the specifications of successive vehicles can differ considerably because of the wide range of options, Errol Bell and his team demonstrate what this means in terms of flexible working. Bell points out a block of empty offices – 'That's where the managers used to be.'; also an open-plan arrangement of desks between the tracks – 'That's where they are today.' Managers are not only more accessible, they are fewer in number, and the scope for continuous improvement has increased. 'As long as the new process is better, there's no reason why anything can't be changed,' says Bell.

Source: Adapted from 'Land Rover, Most Improved Factory, Engineering Industry Best Factory Awards 1993', *Management Today*, Haymarket Publications.

illustrated – that takes the initiate through the learning process. Once they are trained, employees are empowered to take on more responsibility and broaden their roles.

Merck, Sharp & Dohme

Merck, Sharp & Dohme's Cramlington factory is one of its four plants in the UK. It is also one of the US pharmaceutical giant's lowest-cost manufacturing units, reports Brian Lumsden, senior director of UK operations. Here 200 staff produce almost 2.8 billion tablets and capsules annually, with a sales value of $2 billion.

Again, this factory considers one of its outstanding features is people management. Continuous improvement teams have cut cleandown times from as much as 300 man-hours to 40, achieving substantial savings in energy, fuels and maintenance costs. Cramlington is not only a lean organisation, it is also a learning one. All employees will receive ten days' training this year and everyone will also be individually appraised. 'Reverse appraisals' take place biannually.

Controls and systems

The last few years have seen the development of several systems and approaches for managing production and planning, scheduling and expediting orders. These are material requirements planning (MRP), manufacturing resource planning (MRP II), *kanban*, just-in-time (JIT), total quality management (TQM) and optimised production technology (OPT).

In very different ways these approaches strive to make the manufacturing processes more effective, and they can yield dramatic reductions in cost as well as improvements in service, usually without the need for heavy capital investment in new plant.

Linking the strategy to the operational level

An organisation's ability to implement successfully and gain advantage from any of these approaches depends, in the first place, on how well the business strategy has been translated to specify what kind of control systems are necessary. Gilgeous demonstrates an approach for linking the strategic needs of a business to the operational level. Through the use of the approach it becomes possible to identify operational areas of concern which, if not improved, could definitely impede the company's progress towards being more competitive.

For many companies the pressure is on to provide different options, new models and new products. If these requirements are to be met, the production facilities and systems of such companies will need to be more responsible and flexible. This is where the use of computers and networked systems, both in the office and factory, come into play. Such systems can be complex, requiring a high level of employee skills and knowledge. If systems are too complex then progress may be thwarted. Simpler, straightforward systems encourage participation and understanding by everyone.

Exhibit 4.6 explains how Honeywell moved away from MRP II to electronic data interchange (EDI) and faxed *kanban* cards as a preferred system to eliminate invoices and provide tighter control. Its suppliers now provide direct-to-line replenishment of components and raw materials.

Exhibit 4.6

Honeywell uses EDI *kanban* cards to control replenishment

Honeywell's Motherwell factory employs 850 people and produces thermostats, controllers and switches. Among customers for these products are the likes of Boeing, Bosch, Electrolux and Rolls Royce. Its outstanding features that won it the Outstanding Achievement in a Specific Area Award in the 1995 Best Factory Awards are automation, component replenishment, cell design and operation.

Although Motherwell has been an MRP II Class A site for over ten years, current thinking at the plant is moving away from this technique, McDougall explains. Electronic data interchange and faxed *kanban* cards (known as 'faxbans') are currently the preferred means of transmitting requirements to suppliers. A van calls on every supplier within a 40-mile radius daily, picking up that day's components and raw materials which it delivers direct to the appropriate production cell.

Under this system, invoices have been eliminated. 'Once a week we tell our suppliers what we think we've received, and every fourth week we send them the money,' says John McDougall, the unit's director of manufacturing. Inspectors, goods inwards personnel, procurement and planning people – all these have been redeployed. They are now engaged in the manufacture of products rather than the shuffling of paper.

Source: Adapted from 'Honeywell, Outstanding Achievement in a Specific Area, Best Factory Awards 1995', *Management Today*, Haymarket Publications.

If a system is to achieve its objectives it must be adequately controlled as well as properly designed. An effective system of control is one that measures what is important to the business and has a bias towards revenue generation rather than cost containment. Also, the standards used in control systems should be scrutinised as to their accuracy and relevance.

Process Industry Best Factory 1995 achieved through process control

David Fletcher is the operations manager at Shell UK's Lubricants Centre at Stanlow on the Wirral, the Process Industry Best Factory 1995 (*see Management Today*, November 1995). He comments that the factory's strength lies in its ability to blend, to a very tight specification, a wide range of oils for almost every conceivable application.

Virtually every stage is computer-controlled. From the initial receipt of base oils, through blending and the mixing of additives and on to the 10 240 pallet-space automated warehouse, human beings have little more than a monitoring role. 'We have 10 000 control loops out there, the same as a medium-sized refinery,' says Fletcher. Automatic guided vehicles shuttle back and forth bearing batches of oil to the load cells, which hold the secret of the plant's tight blending accuracy: so accurate that, in spite of increasingly rigorous specifications, it has been possible to cut the number of laboratory analyses by as much as one-third, to 8000 per month.

Action plans for control

Wherever possible, information about the business should be made visible and shared since this encourages people's involvement in solving problems and taking corrective action. Action plans devised to control and improve situations should be generated with the participation and consensus of the people involved in the situation. Similarly, such plans should be implemented by those people who will be responsible for their operation.

Customers

Customers need to be consulted and their requirements established. Such requirements may be as follows:

- information availability – range, prices, delivery timescale
- advice – business, technical
- completeness of package – e.g. finance options when purchasing a car.

These requirements need to be clearly understood and defined. Other customer needs are more difficult to define, but nevertheless they can mean very much to the customer. For example:

- courtesy and politeness
- quick response to inquiries
- desire to please
- honesty.

Inattention to these aspects can often lose business.

Obtaining this information requires getting to the customer or potential customer in the first place and then being able to attract their custom. It is the responsibility of everyone, especially the marketing function and those in closest contact with the customer, to make efforts to have sufficient numbers of suitably-trained staff. In particular, marketing needs to ensure that the sales force is adequate and strategically located and that expert care and time is given to deciding the extent and nature of the advertising and promotions.

Staff should also possess good product knowledge and should constantly seek improvement by feeding back information relating to the products and business performance of the company, together with any suggestions for improvement.

Good public relations and customer satisfaction

The Bonas Machine Company places importance on good public relations and customer satisfaction. One aspect of its work is where the purchasing staff take the visitor through the family-based supplier rationalisation programme.

Suppliers

A company's purchasing policy should be aimed at seeking the best service from its suppliers while maintaining awareness of new alternative sources. Information on a company's suppliers should be accurate, and up-to-date records should be kept relating to volume of business, quality, price, delivery, degree of satisfaction with the service offered and advantages of doing business with the supplier. Analysis should provide vendor ratings which can be used to form the basis of improving service from existing suppliers. Information on alternative sources of supply for important items will also need to be sought, and the policies relating to single or multiple sourcing will need to be examined.

It helps if buyers meet regularly with the design and manufacturing areas and have a clear understanding of quality requirements and the adverse effects that poor supplier service can have on a company. Also, the fostering of good relations and improved communications with the main suppliers would be spurred if senior personnel in the company made visits themselves or provided the resources to ensure closer contact.

Single versus dual sourcing

GPT, which is jointly owned by GEC and Siemens, employs 2100 people and manufactures telecommunications switching equipment (*see Management Today*, November 1993). According to the company, single sourcing is highly fashionable these days. Management at its factory in Edge Lane acknowledges the reasons for cultivating customer/supplier partnerships, but insists on multiple sourcing nevertheless. Manufacturing costs in electronics are generally noted for their high bought-out content, which indeed has become something of an Achilles' heel. 'It's always nice to have a little competitive edge,' says procurement manager Janet Butler. She is equally blunt about GPT's objective of maximising the cash balance by way of its payment terms – 90 days from the end of the month of delivery. Suppliers are assessed, incidentally, not only on their quality and delivery, but also on their EDI capability.

The secrets of a best factory

The best factories in the UK surveyed in 1992 had ten vital characteristics in all (see *Management Today*, November 1992). It should be noted that the key activity areas discussed above contain many of these characteristics, which are:

1 an integrated management team
2 commitment to quality
3 the exploitation of key process technologies
4 a highly-trained workforce
5 operator empowerment
6 simple systems
7 visible operational performance signs
8 attention to detail
9 customer service focus
10 response flexibility.

Improving the key activity areas

According to Christopher Jones, the total quality manager at Unisys, key business process (key activity areas) improvement should be driven both 'top-down' and 'bottom-up'. At Unisys, in common with other companies such as ICL and the Rover Group, every work group is empowered and expected to use its measures of process performance to identify, prioritise and implement 'local' improvements. These improvements focus on ensuring that the groups' outputs conform to the agreed customer requirements and/or on improving the efficiency of the processes involved. Proposed process changes should be reviewed by the process owner prior to implementation to determine their contribution to the overall performance of the business process involved.

Jones considers that key business process management, in conjunction with the other elements of strategy, can contribute towards the significant enhancement of business performance sought by senior managers today.

LINKING OPERATIONS ACTIVITIES TO THE STRATEGY

Review of foundation work

There is a need to trace the links down from the strategic to the operational level to make explicit which operational activities need to be focused on in order to provide the business with a sustainable advantage over the competition. With respect to strategy development, only a few authors have proposed any practical means by which a manufacturing or operations strategy may be developed: Hill (1985), Slack, Platts and Gregory, Gunn, New and Hayes, Wheelwright and Clark. Fewer approaches stress the need for a close link between customer requirements and shopfloor activities and provide guidance on the availability of an approach that is practical enough to be realistically used by operational managers. Work on this by Gilgeous (1995a) presents a process of manufacturing strategy development which links the strategic needs of the business through to the operational level in order to determine and prioritise the operational areas of strategic concern in a company; that is, to identify the extent to which particular problems in a given operations activity area would, if not addressed, stop a company from being able to pursue effectively a chosen strategy.

A PRACTICAL PROCESS TO DETERMINE THE LINKS

Deciding upon the needed operations activities and their relative importance

To determine how to plan the operations activities to pursue the main business objectives, it is necessary to define, prioritise and put a timescale to what the previous chapter described as 'first-level' and 'second-level' objectives. Given the objectives to be pursued, decisions then have to be made as to what management activities and what operations areas and their associated activities are necessary to support them. It then becomes necessary to determine the relative management effort that should be placed on

- each activity area relative to another;
- each activity in each activity area.

This can be achieved by the following:

Identifying the activity areas and associated activities. Within each activity area there are activities which can support the attainment of the performance objectives sought. These activities need to be recorded, and this information, for all objectives across all activity areas, then needs collating.

Establishing the relative importance of each activity area and its respective activities to the achievement of each performance objective. To collect the data and perform this analysis speedily and sift out respondent bias, an Analytical Hierarchical

Programming (AHP) methodology can be employed (*see* Saaty, 1980), the purpose of the analysis being to ascertain the nature and amount of work to be done in each activity area to support the objectives. These tasks should be co-ordinated by the teams responsible for each of the objectives.

Initiatives that support the key activity areas

It should be apparent now that there is a need to determine how important each activity area is to the achievement of each performance objective. It is also necessary to determine what are the initiatives that underpin the performance of each activity area. Fieldwork in companies that are deemed to be excellent, conducted by Gilgeous (1995b), shows that each has a unique range of competences or 'enablers' that fall into different domains of company-specific initiatives or programmes. Some of the main initiatives that an organisation can pursue are teams, empowerment, the learning organisation and business process re-engineering. These are discussed in Part 5 'The initiatives of change' in Chapters 8 to 11. The fieldwork also shows that how well the operations activities are performed depends on the quality and effectiveness of the initiatives or programmes the company pursues and the capability of the enablers. An example of a particular company's initiatives and the enablers of empowerment, researched by Gilgeous and Gilgeous (1996) are shown in Fig 4.2.

Identifying initiatives and their emphasis in a particular organisation

Obviously, the initiatives companies currently pursue may remain or change over time. For example, total quality management (TQM) is still considered an important initiative in the 1990s, whereas management by objectives (MBO), popular in the '50s and '60s, is considered less important. Work study is important in certain areas, but because of its technical nature, it needs to be run in parallel with other initiatives. Research continues with the so-called 'best practice companies' to identify which initiative(s) need to be focused on in today's operating environment to help the company achieve excellence in manufacturing.

PERFORMANCE OF OPERATIONS ACTIVITIES

Manufacturing performance measures

In his book on performance measures for world-class manufacturing, Maskell justifies the need for manufacturing measures as opposed to narrow financial measures. He outlines measurement methods for manufacturing, with particular emphasis on quality management, continuous improvement and strategy. He argues that companies must use the results in a positive way to encourage problem solving and innovation towards continuous improvement. Other work in this area has been carried out by Hall and Turney. In their book *Measuring Up* they emphasise the importance of measures to achieve manufacturing excellence. They focus on three broad areas of people, process and quality, with particular focus on goals for continuous improvement. The book concludes with how to measure up, and discusses the accuracy and inaccuracy of the measurement process and performance indicators.

Performance measurement and benchmarking, specifically in manufacturing planning and control systems, has been extensively researched at UMIST (*see* Kennerley,

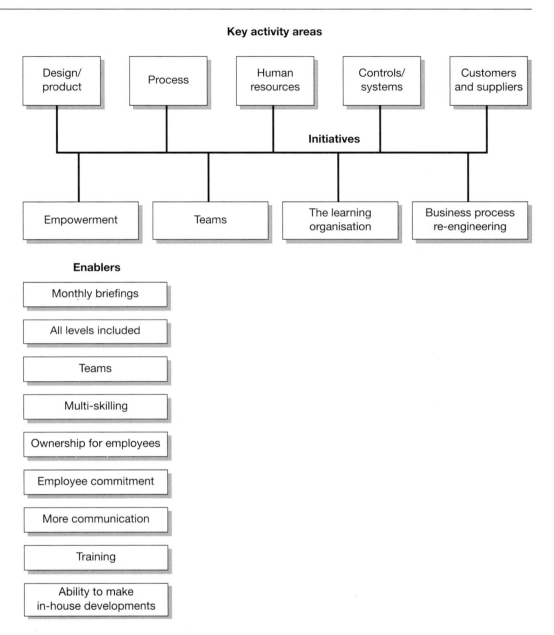

Fig 4.2 Supporting initiatives and enablers

Davies and Kochhar, 1996). The researchers there have looked at ways of linking manufacturing planning (including materials, machines, processes, people and suppliers) with overall strategic measures. They found that (at the manufacturing planning level) performance measurement 'tends not to be' directly or explicitly related to practices, and is often not linked to the strategic objectives of the organisation. Findings from these projects provide some pointers for product development, but manufacturing and strategic considerations are the main focus.

Performance measurement systems

The Manufacturing Engineering Group at Cambridge University (Neely, Gregory & Platts, 1995) has worked extensively on performance measurement design systems; what makes a good performance measure (Neely, Richards, Mills & Platts, 1995) and strategy issues (Neely *et al.*, 1994). They have carried out a thorough review of literature in the field, covering everything from financial, quality and manufacturing methods used today to flexibility measures and others that are emerging. The Cambridge researchers highlight the need for predictive performance measures (in the same vein as statistical process control (SPC) for quality control). A performance measurement record sheet, for use in both industry and academia, has introduced a means of analysis and a checksheet that can be used to make theoretically appealing performance measures practical. This forms part of the group's wider aim of developing a comprehensive performance measurement system.

A collaborative project involving Liverpool, Strathclyde and Loughborough Universities is investigating integrated performance measurement systems for manufacturing organisations. The objective of the research is to provide industry with a comprehensive set of tools, techniques and procedures to allow self-audit of existing performance measurement systems against a reference model, as a means of continuously improving the system. Strathclyde University is investigating specifically the use of tools and techniques (such as customer focus, process modelling, cause and effect analysis and quality function deployment (QFD)) for designing integrated performance measurement systems. This research is similar to the work at Cambridge in that they are attempting to devise a comprehensive measurement system, with emphasis on strategy rather than specific processes or stages of development.

During work towards her PhD on performance measurement systems, Crawford analysed six manufacturing companies whose specific focus was on just-in-time (JIT). Her results included the following findings:

1 Few criteria are required to detect improving or worsening performance.
2 Performance criteria must be measured in ways that are easily understood by those whose performance is being evaluated.
3 Performance data should be collected, where possible, by those whose performance is being evaluated.
4 Specific numeric standards are not required [for inventory and quality criteria]: improving trends are needed.
5 Performance to schedule criteria must evaluate group, not individual, work.
6 Graphs should be the primary method of reporting performance data.
7 Performance data should be available for constant review.
8 The reporting system must not replace frequently-held performance review meetings.

Hronec introduces the 'quantum leap model of performance' in companies. He discusses the need for vertical (strategic, top-down) measures and horizontal (process-based) measures. Within this framework, Hronec advocates a six-step implementation procedure for introducing a performance measurement system into the company.

Sink and Tuttle, in their book on planning and measurement in organisations of the future, describe a performance improvement planning process. This includes organisational systems analysis (for strategic vision and analysis); creation of planning assumptions upon which the plan will be based (to raise awareness of expectations of the result); development of tactical objectives (translating strategy into achievable action items); formation of action teams and development of the plan of action; continued development and management of the evaluation system. They then propose a general measurement methodology to implement this. This includes many of the general principles of management, such as continuous improvement, project management etc., but is captured in a practical, appealing way that makes it popular.

Other work in this area includes that by Zairi who explored the connection between performance measurement systems and TQM; and Globerson who compiled a useful 'do's and don'ts' list in the design and development of an effective performance measurement system. Globerson states that the main objective is a decision support system that provides information. He considers a closed management loop to be a major ingredient with 'realisation of potential improvement, either by an individual or by an organisation, depending on the existence of a feedback system that provides performance information'. He recommends that, for measures to be successful, they must be derived from strategy and relate to specific and realistic goals. Furthermore, they should be based on quantities that can be influenced by the user or the user in conjunction with others. The preferred form of data collection is using data that are automatically collected as part of a process, with ratios rather than absolute numbers being the best guides.

Exhibit 4.7 illustrates the importance of measurement at the Granite Rock Company.

The use and value of audits

Self-assessment audits, usually led by the quality function, are designed to encourage a formalised approach to process improvement in all areas of the business. Supporters consider such audits to be a very effective way of analysing strengths and weaknesses, which should highlight where to deploy resources for maximum effect. Critics argue that audits are cumbersome, too bureaucratic, and that they slow down improvement initiatives and sap enthusiasm.

Requirements of ISO 9000 and quality awards

Previous attempts at a systems approach to assessment have been made, most famously by the establishment of Britain's own quality system standard BS 5750 and the equivalent worldwide quality standard ISO 9000. Within the last ten years, the latter has become a universal standard and even a prerequisite for business. It is undoubtedly a step forward, but does have limitations in that people quickly began to concentrate on 'conforming' and following the system to the letter, rather than looking for improvements. This is necessary to a certain extent as it ensures ongoing accreditation, but it also inhibits innovation and continuous improvement.

The Malcolm Baldridge Quality Award, developed in the USA, provides a quality management framework to help companies towards implementing best practices. It is divided into seven categories:

- leadership
- information and analysis
- strategic quality planning
- human resource development and management

Exhibit 4.7

The importance of measurement at the Granite Rock Company

'Measurement is what it's all about,' says Val Verutti, quality-support manager for Granite Rock Co., in Watsonville, California. 'If you set goals and lofty ideas, without means of measuring, you're just kidding yourself. You've got to have ways of finding out if improvements really are improvements.'

Granite Rock is a 386-employee, family-owned company that manufactures construction materials of many kinds: aggregates, ready-mix concrete, gravel, asphaltic concrete and so on. The volume and accuracy of its measurements, among other things, won it a Malcolm Baldridge National Quality Award in 1992, in the small-business category.

The criteria for the Baldridge Award were in fact a wake-up call to Granite Rock's managers, Verutti says; as they began applying those criteria to the company, they became aware of the need for better measurements. 'When they start asking for three years of trend data,' Verutti says, 'and you don't have one measure in place, that gives you a clue right away.'

None of this measuring is done for its own sake. Jack Leemaster, general manager of Granite Rock's southern concrete and building materials division, told a Baldridge Award conference last year that the company attaches great importance to selecting the right information to be tracked because that data 'organises the quality process for the entire company'.

Bruce W. Woolpert, president and CEO, started by setting about a dozen 'baseline goals' as measures of the company's performance; the number grew to 57 in 1992 and 66 in 1993. The baseline goals, Woolpert says, 'are the specific action areas that we're going to focus on' every year in support of Granite Rock's nine corporate objectives. 'This is what makes the corporate objectives come alive.'

Through customer surveys, Granite Rock identifies the factors most important to its customers – not just throughout the company but in each of its markets as well.

Granite Rock has been successful at measuring customer preferences accurately – it stayed profitable and almost doubled its market share during the severe California recession – but doing so is not a simple matter.

Source: Adapted from Barrier, M., 'Learning the meaning of measurement', *Nation's Business*.

- management of process quality
- quality and operational results
- customer focus and satisfaction.

These categories are attributed with varying weights according to their importance. The main aim is to enable companies to benchmark key processes, and this requires them to understand themselves before benchmarking against others. This approach has been adopted across the world, with variations including the European Quality Award and the Australian Quality Awards. Although the Baldridge Award deals with the overall performance of the organisation rather than concentrating on specific processes or products, it is useful as a guide to companies who do not know how to approach measuring their activities.

Auditing the activity areas

Exhibit 4.8 presents possible statements that could be used to ascertain the relative performance of each activity in each activity area.

THE COMPETENCE OF ACTIVITY AREAS

Competence in operations

A firm that positions itself in Stage 4, according to Wheelwright and Hayes should perform better than a similar firm which is in a lower stage. However, performance means different things at different levels of the organisation. It can mean, for example, financial performance, marketing performance or manufacturing performance. Since we are concerned with strategic operations effectiveness, the direct impact will be at the operations level. The work done on performance measures in this respect mainly relates to manufacturing performance measures. However, Kim and Arnold noted that the field of manufacturing strategy does not have a well-defined set of performance measures to test frameworks or theories or to measure overall manufacturing capability. This predicament was acknowledged by Nemetz, who stated that:

> The manufacturing environment has changed in such a way that old performance measures are no longer meaningful. Neither the academic nor the industrial community has yet established new standards for assessing general performance ... Without publicly reported, standardised measures of performance, there is no straightforward method for conducting manufacturing research.

Financial and market performance measures cannot accurately demonstrate manufacturing performance because they are affected by other functional areas. Instead, the concept of 'manufacturing competence'* is more relevant. Researchers like Cleveland *et al.*, Vickery *et al.*, and Kim and Arnold have shown that manufacturing competence is a measure of manufacturing performance and it positively affects business performance.

Cleveland *et al.* proposed the concept of manufacturing competence as the link between business strategy and manufacturing operations. The subsequent works of Kim and Arnold and Vickery *et al.* improved the conceptual foundations of manufacturing competence. These three studies are reviewed and compared below.

Framework of Cleveland et al.

Cleveland *et al.* defined manufacturing competence as:

> the preparedness, skill, or capability that enables manufacturers to prosecute a product-market specific business strategy.

They suggested that competence is a variable rather than a fixed attribute and accordingly should be rated on a continuous scale. Their framework is defined as the relationship of four principal constructs, namely: business strategy, production

---

*Cleveland *et al.* and Vickery *et al.* called this concept 'production competence'. However, I will take the view of Kim and Arnold, who argued that by using competitive priorities as the operationalising vehicle, the concept of production competence is broadened and therefore it should be called manufacturing competence.

Exhibit 4.8

Audit statements for activity areas

Design and product

Designs and product range are constantly updated.

Products are developed using multi-functional teams (design, engineering, marketing, manufacture, finance).

Suppliers, distributors and customers are involved in new product development.

The product and the manufacturing process are developed together.

The design of the product makes production/assembly a foolproof task.

The tolerance and accuracy of the product design does not place too much stress on manufacturing.

The product design facilitates ease of testing, installation, commission, use and maintenance.

A reduction in the number of parts and/or having common parts in our products is sought.

The product is of good quality.

The product is reasonably priced.

Product availability and choice is adequate.

The product is reliable in use.

The product performance is superior to that of its competitors.

The product offers features which are not available from the competitors' offerings.

The market requirements for our type of product are continually sought.

Process

Items are produced across a sales range at a rate that is in proportion to the customer sales mix.

Continuous efforts are made to ensure that the process is capable of consistently producing products to the requisite specified quality standards.

Efforts are made to reduce the level of defective items produced.

Improvements in the layout of the process lines take place.

Where possible machines are being grouped to produce specific product lines or families of products or parts.

Moves towards improving the flow of work are continually being made.

Efforts are made to eliminate bottlenecks and reduce queues in the process.

A set-up time reduction programme is being pursued.

Efforts are made to reduce the manufacturing lead time.

Ways of possible automation are proposed and acted upon.

More efficient and versatile machinery and equipment is being made available.

An effective maintenance programme aimed at improving machinery and equipment and reducing machine downtime is in operation.

More and more operatives are being given the responsibility for things like quality, maintenance, workplace tidiness, output, and organisation of work.

A reduction in the levels of raw material, in-process inventories and finished goods stocks is continuously being pursued.

Improvements and reduction in material handling are taking place.

Human resources

The company encourages its management and workforce to develop themselves and has programmes in place to facilitate this.

The company provides in-house training.

When prospective employees are considered for recruitment a careful selection procedure is adopted.

Employees are encouraged to participate in company improvement programmes.

Employees are given paid time off in order to obtain professional training and qualifications related to their job or vocation.

Group or individual performance is recognised and rewarded financially.

Individual or group achievements are recognised and rewarded in some way by the company.

Management communicates with the workforce and listens to what they have to say.

The development of a multi-skilled flexible workforce is sought.

The company operates a selection of attractive schemes on pensions, savings, insurance and health care.

Social occasions and informal get-togethers are encouraged and promoted by the company.

Employees are appraised and given constructive feedback on their performance.

The company has a benevolent approach with its employees and acknowledges loyalty and efforts.

In the past the company has sought a policy of secure and continuing employment for its employees.

Overall the level of remuneration and benefits offered by the company is quite satisfactory.

Controls and systems

There is an openness and sharing of company information.

Information generated is generally accurate and up to date.

The use of modern systems and approaches like material requirements planning (MRP), just-in-time (JIT), total quality management (TQM) etc. are sought.

Overall the systems are straightforward and easy to use.

Training in the use of systems is given.

The systems of planning and scheduling are effective.

The systems for controlling inventory are effective.

Planning and controlling for good quality is of paramount importance.

The office and factory communication systems are linked together and accessible.

Every area has performance measures that are realistic and meaningful.

People are encouraged to improve and develop systems.

Changes in systems are made through consultation and involvement of the people who use them.

People have more and more authority and control over the systems they use.

Employees are involved in measuring how their systems perform.

The performance of different areas of the factory are made visible.

Customers and suppliers

We listen to our customers and follow up complaints.

We regularly visit our customers and assess opportunities for closer links.

We emphasise our service and product offerings in the customers' terms.

Quality is always defined in terms of the customers' perceptions.

We emphasise the intangible attributes of our products and services.

Customer satisfaction is measured.

Compensation and performance evaluation is tied directly to customer satisfaction.

Our sales and service people are highly valued.

Our supplier relationships are based on close co-operation; suppliers are seen as partners.

Thorough procedures for the selection and evaluation of new suppliers are in place.

Main suppliers are liaised with to get the best possible product and service from them.

The number of different suppliers the company deals with is effectively being reduced.

Vendor appraisal is used to accredit our suppliers.

Our suppliers provide good value and take appropriate action for non-conforming goods or late delivery.

Our main suppliers have effective systems for ensuring that their products and services are of a high standard.

process, manufacturing competence, and business performance. The business performance was measured using seven attributes, four of which represent manufacturing performance: cost, quality, dependability, and flexibility. Market share and growth rate represent marketing performance, and financial performance is measured by pre-tax return on assets. In manufacturing they identified the following nine performance areas: adaptive manufacturing, cost-effectiveness of labour, delivery performance, logistics, production economies of scale, process technology, quality performance, throughput and lead time, and vertical integration. The researchers used regression analysis and found that manufacturing competence is positively correlated with business performance.

Kim and Arnold's framework

An alternative framework, shown in Fig 4.3, was proposed by Kim and Arnold.

Kim and Arnold used the notion of competitive priorities as the vehicle for operationalising the concept of manufacturing competence. They argued that:

> The framework of competitive priorities has been one of the major building blocks in manufacturing strategy research. In his seminal paper, Skinner called it the missing link in corporate strategy... the literature in manufacturing strategy has conceptualised this linkage between the business strategy and the manufacturing function with the framework of competitive priorities.

Kim and Arnold identified 15 competitive capabilities which they classified into five categories, namely: price, flexibility, quality, delivery and service, as shown in Table 4.1.

Table 4.1 List of competitive capabilities

Price	Manufacture with lower cost than competitors.
Flexibility	Make rapid design changes. Introduce new products quickly. Make rapid volume changes. Make rapid product mix changes. Offer broad line of products.
Quality	Manufacture with consistently low defect rates. Provide high performance products. Offer reliable products.
Delivery	Provide fast delivery of products. Deliver products on time as promised.
Service	Provide effective after-sales service. Provide product support effectively. Make products easily available (broad distribution). Customise products to customer needs.

Source: Kim, J.S. and Arnold, P, 1993.

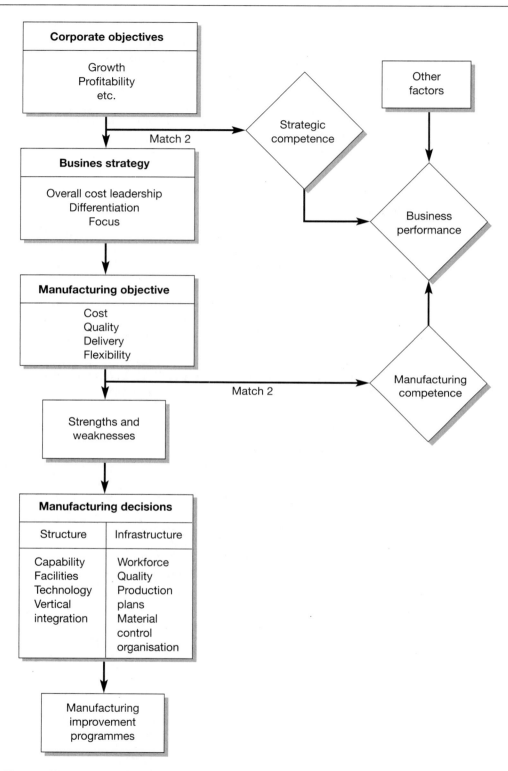

Fig 4.3 Kim and Arnold's framework of manufacturing competence
Source: Kim, J. S. and Arnold, P., 1993.

Kim and Arnold then used seven-point scales to rate responses of firms with respect to the importance that they perceive and the strength they possess in each of the 15 capabilities. They used this information to determine a competence index of the competitive capabilities of each firm. By exploring the correlation between competence indexes and the business performance, Kim and Arnold observed that:

- in some industries, the concept of competence was not able to explain the business performance
- two firms can be equally competent even though their strengths and weaknesses are considerably different.

Framework of Vickery et al.

Vickery, Droge and Markland's framework of manufacturing competence, in comparison with the other two frameworks, contained a larger set of 31 competitive capabilities. This research showed that the best performance resulted from a sound manufacturing competence coupled with a strategy that is based on differentiation. The worst performance resulted from a weak manufacturing competence combined with a strategy that emphasises differentiation as its primary objective and cost as the second objective.

Assessing the frameworks of manufacturing competence

Preparedness

The frameworks of manufacturing competence devised by Cleveland et al., Kim and Arnold, and Vickery et al. did not give any indication of how 'prepared' manufacturing is. To prosecute a product-market specific business strategy requires capabilities that are sustainable. So, in order to depict a better representation of manufacturing competence, it is more revealing to include, not only how much has been achieved at a certain point in time, but also how prepared a firm is to achieve the target performance, and how competitors are catching up. This is analogous to a race where a participant has to worry, not only about how well he or she is doing at a particular moment, but also how difficult it is to finish the remaining distance, and how the other competitors are performing.

The importance of sustainability

Manufacturing competence is a relative measure of manufacturing performance. It gives the assessment of competence of one manufacturer relative to others. Since the importance of capabilities change over time, a manufacturer has continuously to upgrade its competences to stay competitive. In this context, Hill (1989) suggested the notions of order-winning criteria (OWC) and order-qualifying criteria (OQC). To qualify for an order, a firm must meet the OQC, and to be in contention of winning orders, it has to meet the OWC for its industry. Hill also noted that, over time, OWC can change to OQC. The reason is that companies are always replicating the capabilities of one another, and so whatever advantage a firm has is not sustainable for very long periods of time. Consequently, sustainability of capabilities can be an important aspect of competence.

The potential for improvement

For firms that have not yet reached their targeted level of performance, there is still scope for improvement. The potential for achieving this unfulfilled performance is dependent on the ease or difficulty of achieving capabilities. If, for example, a firm finds it difficult to develop certain capabilities, then its preparedness for achieving higher performance will be low.

These points are endorsed by Coyne who states that one of the conditions that makes a competitive advantage meaningful in strategy is that:

> the difference in important attributes and the capability gap [superior performance relative to other firms] can be expected to endure over time.

This statement also implies that if a firm is at a disadvantage with respect to the capability gap, it must have the potential to fill it in order to neutralise its competitors' advantage. If this view is taken into account, then it can be argued that there are at least four dimensions that constitute manufacturing competence. These dimensions are:

1 the importance of capabilities
2 the strength or performance in these capabilities
3 the sustainability of achieved performance
4 the potential for achieving unfulfilled performance.

Cumulative development of capabilities

The concept of manufacturing competence can be extended still further by incorporating the model of cumulative competitive capabilities. Nakane was one of the first researchers to notice that, not only are some successful manufacturers competing on all priorities, but they follow a specific sequence in their quest to build capabilities. The sequence that he observed starts with quality, followed by dependability, cost, and flexibility, respectively.

Ferdows and De Meyer had similar observations for their sandcone model. However, their sequence differed in that cost came last. They described their model as follows:

> To build cumulative and lasting manufacturing capability, management attention and resources should go first towards enhancing quality, then, while the efforts to enhance quality are further expanded, attention should be paid to improve also the dependability of the production system, then, and again while efforts on the previous two are further enhanced, production flexibility should also be improved, and finally, while all these efforts are further enlarged, direct attention can be paid to cost efficiency.

The arguments presented for extending the concept of manufacturing competence indicate that there is quite a scope for improving this important concept, and hence the frameworks reviewed might not be able to capture the 'true' manufacturing competence. Cleveland et al. realised this point by stating that there are other ways to operationalise this concept. Extending this concept or finding other ways to operationalise provides scope for further research on this topic.

Establishing a competency index for operations activities

The competency level can be measured as the average level of competency of the key activities in their support of each objective. For a particular activity area this depends on the *performance* of operations activities, how *difficult* they are to achieve, and how quickly, or the *speed* with which, the key activities can be accomplished. This is referred to as the *competency index*, which can be defined as:

$$C = P \times E \times S$$

where:

C = competency index

P = performance – in terms of how good the operations activities are at supporting the operations performance objectives. This could be assessed using the audit information presented earlier.

E = ease of change. This means the ease with which the enablers can achieve the fulfilment of the key activities needed to achieve the objective. This can be measured as the weight of the blocks to the enablers. Blocks will vary depending on the company and the particular situation. Examples are:

- attitudes
- trade union resistance
- shopfloor objection
- pay differentials
- craft demarcation
- staff turnover.

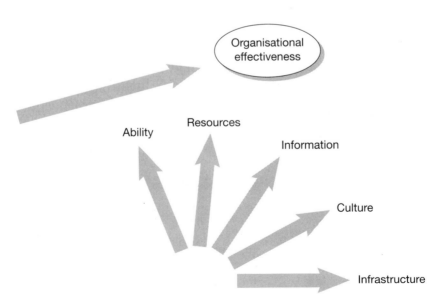

Fig 4.4 Key areas of capability in an organisation

Identifying the blocks

To identify and examine the blocks to progress or improvement in the operations activities, an impedance methodology has been developed. The methodology demonstrates the importance to organisational effectiveness of the five key areas of

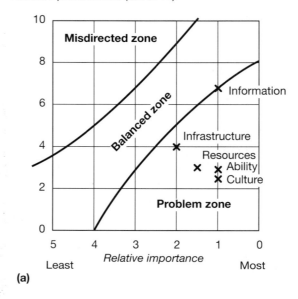

(a)

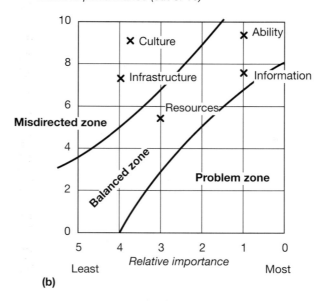

(b)

Fig 4.5 Impedance methodology results at Company X
(a) Impedence matrix for the outbound logistics department
(b) impedence matrix for the marketing and sales department

capability within companies; namely, *abilities, resources, information, culture* and *infrastructure* (*see* Fig 4.4), and how the lack of such capabilities can impede the improvement of the operations activities which are essential to the pursuit of the company's strategy. The methodology can be used to identify which capability weaknesses are having a deleterious effect on particular areas of strategic concern.

An example of the use of the methodology was tested in Company X, a subsidiary of an international American corporation with a turnover of $50 million (1992–3), which designs and manufactures a popular brand of jeans and leisurewear. The results (Fig 4.5a) show an impedance matrix for the company's *outbound logistics department,* indicating that the company has serious problems with all five capabilities. The impedance matrix presented in Fig 4.5b for the *marketing and sales department* shows the capabilities of 'information', 'resources' and 'abilities' to be balanced. That is, where they need to be strong they are, and where strength is not important the capabilities are accordingly less strong. The capabilities of 'culture' and 'infrastructure', however, are misdirected. That is, their performance is not important to the success of the marketing and sales department.

S = speed of change. This means how quickly the key activity can be completed, given the magnitude of the task, the strength of any blocks that may exist, and the ease with which the enablers can overcome it.

A worked example of competency index

To illustrate how a competency index can be determined in practice, a worked example for the determination of a similar measure called a 'potential', developed by Easingwood and Arnott, is presented in Exhibit 4.9.

ESTABLISHING HOW WELL THE PROCESS PERFORMS

To check the above process, which seeks to establish the extent to which the operations activities support the achievement of the performance objectives, it is necessary to measure how well particular performance objectives are being achieved in order to see if 'the medicine is working'. That is, for each objective sought, there should be a high correlation between the level of its performance and the level of competency of the operations activities that support it.

Measuring the performance level of objectives

The level of the performance of an objective can be measured in terms of how well the objective itself has been achieved. Where possible, this should be measured quantitatively as, say, a rate or a volume. Sometimes, however, this is impossible or difficult, and qualitative measures have to be used. Here, a manager can be asked to record his/her responses on an ordinal scale, in order to establish how well the performance objective has been achieved.

Using these measures it is possible to obtain an overall measure that represents each performance objective's 'competency'. The higher the competency of operations activities and their associated performance objectives, the further along the road towards excellence the company is likely to be.

Exhibit 4.9

Priorities in services marketing

How can managers prioritise the value of the different areas of marketing activity that their company engages in? One approach is to calculate a single measure called a 'potential':

Potential = (scope for improvement) $\times$ (sensitivity to change) $\times$ (ease of change) x 0.8 [1]

where 1 = low and 5 = high.

High values indicate areas that score reasonably well on all three components (i.e. impact company performance, offer scope for improvement, can be improved). Such areas ought to be prime candidates for management attention and action. The table shows the three areas of marketing activity with the highest score. [2]

Areas of marketing activity	Score	Rank
Managing of customer contact staff generally	32.19	1
Determining 'best' price	31.95	2
Training of customer contact staff	30.02	3

It is these three areas which deserve to be given high priority by marketing managers, according to the sample. Improvements are especially likely to lead to better company performance.

[1] By multiplying by 0.8 potential has a maximum score of 100.
[2] 141 service companies were surveyed and the results from interviewing 36 marketing managers generated 26 areas of marketing affecting corporate performance.

Source: Adapted from Easingwood, C.J. and Arnott, D.C., 'Priorities in services marketing', *International Journal of Service Industry Management.*

It is now possible to measure the extent of correlation between the competency level of the activities and the performance level of the objectives they support. If the correlation is positive and high, this shows the correct level of management emphasis is being placed on the appropriate operations activities.

ACTION PLANNING FOR OPERATIONS ACTIVITIES

The action-planning table given in the last chapter can now be expanded, as shown in Table 4.2, to help managers to define and achieve performance objectives.

Table 4.2 Action plan

Action plan	Comments
Define what are the key activity areas that support the attainment of the performance objectives	
Record which key activities in each key activity area are necessary to support each objective. Collate this information, for all objectives, across all key activity areas.	
Collect information on how important each key activity is to the achievement of each objective.	
Determine what company's initiatives and enablers underpin the performance of each key activity.	
Determine how important the underpinning enablers and initiatives are to the performance of each key activity.	
Develop a plan for the attainment of the performance objectives. The plan to show the key activities that need to be completed and what initiatives and enablers are involved.	
Measure how well each performance objective is achieved relative to its performance target set by the strategy. Where possible this should be measured quantitatively.	
Measure the competency index for each objective. That is how good the enablers are at achieving the key activities. This will depend upon the performance of the organisation's enablers, the strength of any blocks to their achievement and the speed with which the key activities can be accomplished.	
Establish the level of correlation between the performance level of each objective and the average level of competency with which the key activities support each objective.	
Provide recognition and reward for those involved in achieving the objectives. Honour not just for success but for the attempt.	
Tell everyone what has been achieved.	

SUMMARY

- The pursuit of different performance objectives is made possible by making decisions and conducting the activities in the business's operations activity areas. Such operations activity areas typically concern design and the product, process, customers and suppliers, human resources, and controls and systems.

- To enable a business to achieve a sustainable advantage over the competition it is necessary to determine the relative importance of each activity area in its support of the strategic performance objectives. This can be achieved by tracing the links down from the strategy to the operations level to make explicit which operations activities need to be focused on.

- A practical process for determining the links is to:
  - define and prioritise the first- and second-level objectives, the timescale and sequence of pursuing them, together with the means of achieving them
  - determine the relative importance of each activity area and its associated operations with respect to the pursuit of these objectives.

- Fieldwork in companies that are deemed to be excellent shows that each has a unique range of competences or 'enablers' that fall into different domains of company-specific initiatives or programmes. Some of the main initiatives that an organisation can pursue are teams, empowerment, the learning organisation and business process re-engineering.

- Research shows that it is important to establish measures in order to predict and pursue operations (manufacturing) excellence. At the operations planning level, performance measurement tends not to be directly or explicitly related to the strategic objectives of the organisation.

- A widely-sought aim of companies and researchers is to develop a comprehensive performance measurement system, tools, techniques and procedures to allow self-audit of existing performance against a reference model as a means of continuously improving the system.

- For measures to be successful, they should be derived from strategy and relate to specific and realistic goals. They should be based on quantities that can be influenced by the user or the user in conjunction with others.

- Audits are designed to encourage a formalised approach to process improvement in all areas of the business. ISO 9000 and quality awards have become a universal standard and even a prerequisite for a business.

- Many of the performance measures used in operations are not meaningful in terms of accurately demonstrating the ability of operations to support the business strategy. Researchers such as Cleveland *et al.*, Vickery *et al.*, and Kim and Arnold have shown that a measure of competence of operations (manufacturing) performance can be established, and that it positively affects business performance.

- The competency level of an operation activity can be established in terms of how well it supports the operations objectives. For a particular activity area this depends on the performance of operations activities, how difficult they are to achieve (depending on the strength of any blocks to their achievement), and how quickly, or the speed with which, the key activities can be accomplished. This can be measured and calculated as a 'competency index'.

● For each objective sought there should be a high correlation between the level of its performance and the level of competency of the operations activities that support it.

REVIEW AND DISCUSSION QUESTIONS

1 Describe the types of activities that are conducted and decisions that have to be made in two operations activity areas of a business.

2 In what ways can an operations activity area support the performance objectives of a business?

3 Discuss the significance of establishing the links from the strategy level down to the operations level.

4 Describe a process for determining which operations activities need to be focused on.

ASSIGNMENTS

1 Consider yourself in the role of an operations manager. You have been requested by the director to outline your views on audits and performance measures in operations. Couch your reply in terms of their potential value as well as any disadvantages.

2 Consider a measure of competence of operations performance that could possibly be established in your (a typical) organisation. Explain how its pursuit would positively support the operations objectives and how it could be measured.

REFERENCES

Barrier, M., 'Learning the meaning of measurement', *Nation's Business*, pp. 72–4, June 1994.

Bonas Machine Company, Factory of the Year and Electronics Industry Best Factory, *Management Today*, pp. 98–100, November 1995.

Cleveland, G., Schroeder, R. and Anderson, J., 'A theory of production competence', *Decision Sciences*, Vol. 20, No. 4, pp. 655–68, 1989.

Coyne, K.P., 'Sustainable competitive advantage – what it is, what it isn't', *Business Horizons*, pp. 54–61, Jan/Feb 1986.

Crawford, K.M., *An Analysis of Performance Measurement Systems in Selected Just-In-Time Operations*, University of Georgia, PhD thesis, order number 8812059, 1988.

Driva, H., 'Literature review on performance measures', Chapter 2, Draft PhD thesis, 1996.

Drucker, P.S., *The Practice of Management*, Harper & Row, New York, 1954.

Easingwood, C.J. and Arnott, D.C., 'Priorities in services marketing', *International Journal of Service Industry Management*, Vol. 2, No. 2, pp. 20–37, 1991.

Ferdows, K. and De Meyer, A., 'Lasting improvement in manufacturing performance: In search of a new theory', *Journal of Operations Management*, Vol. 9. No. 2, pp. 168–84, 1990.

Gilgeous, V.G., (a) 'Strategic concerns and capability impeders', *International Journal of Production and Operations Management*, Vol. 15, No. 10, pp. 4–29, 1995.

Gilgeous, V.G. (b) 'Impedance Methodology: Two cases of its use', *Advances in Manufacturing Technology IX*, Proceedings of the XIth National Conference on Manufacturing Research, Taylor & Francis, pp. 671–5, 1995.

Gilgeous, V. G. and Gilgeous, M., *Towards Manufacturing Excellence Using Initiatives*, 12th National Conference on Manufacturing Research, University of Bath, September 1996.

Glaxo Manufacturing Services, Household Products Best Factory, *Management Today*, pp. 116 & 117, November 1994.

Globerson, S., 'Developing a performance criteria system', *International Journal of Production Research*, Vol. 23, No. 4, pp. 639–46, 1985.

GPT, Electronics Industry Best Factory 1993, *Management Today*, pp. 105 & 106, November 1993.

Gunn, T.G., *Manufacturing for Competitive Advantage: Becoming a world class manufacturer*, Ballinger, Cambridge, Mass., 1987.

Hall, R. W. and Turney P. B., *Measuring Up: Charting pathways to manufacturing excellence*, Business One, Irwin, Homewood, Ill., 1991.

Hayes, R. H., Wheelwright, S.C. and Clark, K.B., *Dynamic Manufacturing: Creating the learning organisation*, The Free Press, New York, 1988.

Hill, T.J., *Manufacturing Strategy*, Macmillan, London, 1985.

Hill, T., *Manufacturing Strategy: Text and cases*, Irwin, Homewood, Ill., 1989.

Honeywell, Outstanding Achievement in a Specific Area, Best Factory Awards 1995, *Management Today*, pp. 125 & 126, November 1995.

Hronec, S., *Vital Signs: Using quality, time and cost performance measurement to chart your company's future*, Amacom, New York, 1993.

Jones, C. R., 'Improving your key business processes', *The TQM Magazine*, Vol. 6, No. 2, pp. 25–9, 1994.

Kennerley, M., Davies, A. and Kochhar, A. K., 'Manufacturing strategy, performance and best practices – the contribution of manufacturing planning and control systems', *Proceedings of the 3rd EurOMA Conference*, London Business School, pp. 363–8, June 1996.

Kim, J.S. and Arnold, P. 'Manufacturing competence and business performance: A framework and empirical analysis', *International Journal of Operations and Production Management*, Vol. 13, No. 10, pp. 4–25, 1993.

Kimberly-Clark, Best Process Factory, *Management Today*, pp. 60 & 61, November 1992.

Land Rover, Most Improved Factory, Engineering Industry Best Factory Awards 1993, *Management Today*, pp. 96–7, November 1993.

Lee-Mortimer, A., 'Competing through new product delivery', *World Class Design to Manufacture*, Vol. 2, No. 2, pp. 37–40, 1995.

Maskell, B., *Performance for World Class Manufacturing*, Productivity Press, Cambridge, Mass., 1991.

Merck, Sharp & Dohme, Household & General Highly Commended, *Management Today*, p. 113, November 1995.

Nakane, J., Ferdows, K., Miller, J.G. and Vollman, T.E., 'Evolving global manufacturing strategies: Projections into the 1990s', *International Journal of Operations & Production Management*, Vol. 6, No. 4, pp. 6–16, 1986.

Neely, A., Mills, J., Platts, K., Gregory, M. and Richards, H., 'Realising strategy through measurement system design', *International Journal of Operations and Production Management*, Vol. 4, No. 3, pp. 140–52, 1994.

Neely, A., Gregory, M. and Platts, K., 'Performance measurement system design', *International Journal of Operations and Production Management*, Vol. 15, No. 4, pp. 80–116, 1995.

Neely, A., Richards, H., Mills, J. and Platts, K., 'What makes a good performance measure?', Proceedings of the 2nd EurOMA conference, Twente, Holland, pp. 362–71, June 1995.

Nemetz, P.L., 'Bridging the strategic outcome measurement gap in manufacturing organisations' in Ettlie, J., Burstein, M. and Fiegenbaum, A. (eds), 'Manufacturing strategy: the search agenda for the next decade', Proceedings of the Joint Industry University Conference on Manufacturing Strategy, Ann Arbor, Mich., 1990.

New, C.C., Competitive Edge Manufacturing Workshop Participant Documentation, School of Management, Cranfield/Department of Trade and Industry, London, 1987.

Platts, K.W. and Gregory, M. J., 'Manufacturing audit in the process of strategy formulation', *International Journal of Operations and Production Management*, Vol. 10, No. 9, p. 5, 1990.

Premier Exhaust Systems, Midland Region Best Factory of the Year, Engineering Industry Best Factory Awards 1993, *Management Today*, pp. 90–95, November 1993.

Saaty, T.L., *The Analytical Hierarchy Process*, McGraw-Hill, New York, 1980.

SIV UK, Most Commended Company, Engineering Industry Best Factory Awards 1993, *Management Today*, p. 96, November 1993.

Shell Lubricants Centre, Process Industry Best Factory 1995, *Management Today*, p. 116, November 1995.

Sink, D.S. and Tuttle, T.C., *Planning and Measurement in your Organisation of the Future*, Industrial Engineering and Management Press, Norcross, Georgia, 1989.

Skinner, W., 'Manufacturing: Missing link in corporate strategy', *Harvard Business Review*, pp. 136–45, May/June 1969.

Slack, N.J., *The Manufacturing Advantage*, Mercury Books, London, 1991.

Total Quality Management, Fact Sheet 29, Institute of Personnel Management, May 1990.

Vickery, S.K., Droge, C. and Markland, R.E., 'Production competence business strategy: Do they affect business performance?', *Decision Sciences*, Vol. 24, No. 2, pp. 435–55, 1993.

Wheatley, M., 'The secrets of a best factory', *Management Today*, p. 70, November 1992.

Wheelwright, S.C. and Hayes R.H., 'Competing through manufacturing', *Harvard Business Review*, pp. 99–109, Jan/Feb 1985.

W.H. Smith & Sons (Tools), Household & General Best Factory, Best Factory Awards 1995, *Management Today*, pp. 110–11, November 1995 Haymarket Publications, London.

Zairi, M., *Measuring Performance for Business Results*, Chapman & Hall, London, 1994.

CHAPTER 5

Planning and controlling

OBJECTIVES

The objectives of this chapter are to:

- **explain the basic management function of planning, the process and main considerations involved**
- **explain what is involved in planning and controlling operations**
- **describe the process of scheduling, loading and sequencing operations.**

PLANNING AS A BASIC MANAGEMENT FUNCTION

Planning is the first and one of the most important of four basic management functions:

1 **Planning** – setting objectives and deciding how to accomplish them
2 **Organising** – allocating resources to accomplish tasks
3 **Leading** – guiding human resource efforts to accomplish tasks
4 **Controlling** – monitoring accomplishment of tasks and taking necessary corrective actions.

Planning and controlling are interrelated. *Planning* establishes what is intended to happen in the future. It tells people the way to go and what to do. In this way, plans establish the standards of control. *Organising* brings people and other resources together to fulfil the intended plan. *Leading* is the process of managing how best people should work to utilise these resources. *Controlling* is dealing with changes that might throw things off course and ensuring that the plans progress as they should. Through this process, planning leads to controlling which might lead to further planning. The relationship between planning and controlling is shown in Fig 5.1.

THE NEED FOR PLANNING

Research shows that both large and small firms that have formal planning systems achieve better financial performance than those that do not. Planning attempts to co-ordinate the efforts made in the organisation so that the managers and staff are heading in the right direction. In considering the future, the organisation can control events and take action for unexpected occurrences in an attempt to maintain the intended future course.

The main benefits of planning are shown to be:

- focusing managers' attention on objectives that can generate results
- helping managers to set priorities

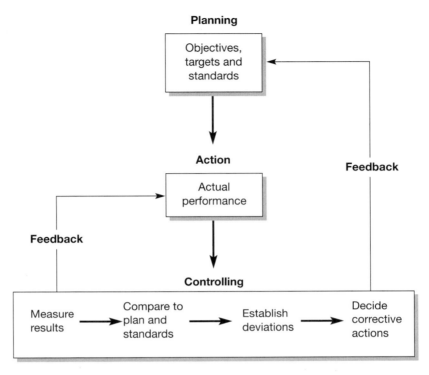

Fig 5.1 The planning, action, control, monitoring and feedback sequence

- helping managers to emphasise organisational strengths so as to allocate resources in the best possible way to meet company objectives
- helping managers to anticipate problems and deal with them
- clarifying what is required and how events can be controlled.

PLANNING TIMESCALES

Long-range plans are made by top-level management and may cover up to five years or more. Here, the managers can determine the longer-term needs and directions of the organisation and set the overall objectives and the strategies, structures and resources required to attain them. This may require a radical change in the way the whole business operates.

Medium-range plans are usually made by middle managers and cover one or two years. In this situation the general strategy and structure of the organisation has to be accepted, but manipulations of inputs, outputs, people, material and capital are possible.

Short-range plans cover one year or less and are made by lower-level management. Here, the strategy, structure and quantities are fixed but the resources, people and technology used can be scheduled as required in order to fulfil the medium-range plans. Figure 5.2 outlines the nature of plans for particular timescales.

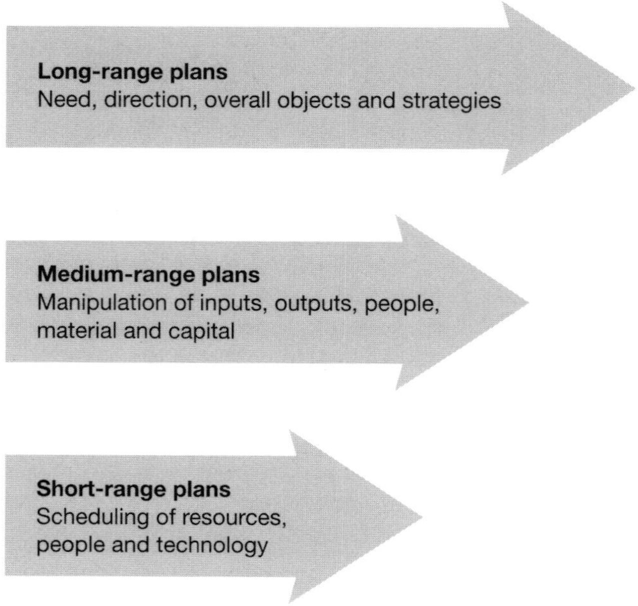

Long-range plans
Need, direction, overall objects and strategies

Medium-range plans
Manipulation of inputs, outputs, people,
material and capital

Short-range plans
Scheduling of resources,
people and technology

Fig 5.2 Nature of plans for particular timescales

WHAT ARE THE GOALS AND OBJECTIVES?

The goals

In the first place, the organisation needs to articulate what are the reasons for its existence. These are its goals. The activities of the organisation are directed towards the attainment of its goals. A goal is a future expectation or some desired future state. It is something that the organisation is striving to accomplish.

Defining the objectives

Having gone through the goal-setting process, sets of objectives then need to be devised which specify clearly how the particular goals are to be reached. Objectives should be realistic while stretching those involved. They should also be measurable and time-bounded. This can be achieved by agreeing with those involved what needs achieving, what particular priorities exist, and what needs to be done. Also, if people are to be stretched, they may require additional resources in order to complete tasks. For example, an objective may initially be formulated to conduct monthly training sessions for supervisors in quality control techniques with at least two teams prior to June next year. This objective can be reformulated in a measurable, time-bounded way as follows: have 50 per cent of supervisors using standard quality control techniques with at least two teams by May 15 next year.

Defining standards of performance

The objectives should contain standards which each management level can transmit down in an increasingly-detailed manner. Setting such standards is helpful in measuring performance, but of more importance is the process of the manager and subordinate discussing and mutually agreeing what the objectives and standards should be. By this means, hopefully, the standards should be realistically attainable and clearly stated and communicated. To enable control it is necessary to know how well the standards are being achieved. For this, measures are needed which can be expressed in quantitative terms.

Management by objectives (MBO)

Peter Drucker recognised that goal setting and planning were critical functions of management, and he introduced the concept of management by objectives (MBO) in 1954. Today, the value of setting goals and measuring performance is well accepted. Top management sets out yearly or quarterly organisation goals which take into account the organisation's longer-term strategy and capabilities. These goals are the future desired end results that the company should pursue.

Goal setting has the following benefits:

- Individuals know what is required of them and the ways in which they are held accountable. They have more control over their work.
- Individuals will be motivated to fulfil objectives they know will make them successful in the organisation.
- Individuals are more likely to work in a co-ordinated way if they have a set of common goals which they understand.

Accomplishing the objectives

In seeking to accomplish the objectives it is necessary to identify strengths and weaknesses in terms of the following areas:

1 **People**. It is often said that an organisation's most important asset is its people. It is important therefore that a review is made of how effective people are, how well trained they are, what skills they have, how well they are managed and motivated. This also applies to the use of outside contractors and consultants in terms of the expertise they bring.

2 **Resources**. Necessary technical competence is needed in terms of the quality and effectiveness of the company's plant, equipment, technology and systems. Important too is the availability of space and the conditions of the buildings and places in which people work.

3 **Management**. The experiences and skills of the managers need to be examined. In planning for change it is necessary to know who can take on greater responsibilities, provide leadership and be forward looking.

4 **Finance**. The financial health of the organisation is important to know in terms of how well it can fund or acquire funds to support any plans. This will ultimately determine the rate of the company's growth and development.

5 **Products and services**. Questions important to everyone are: Are our products in sufficient demand? What will their demand be like in the future? What new products should be introduced? Are our services adequate – for example, terms and conditions of sale, prices, availability, customer care etc?

6 **The organisation**. Here it needs to be ascertained how well the structure facilitates effective use of the organisation's resources.

7 **Management structures**. Organisational transition tends to be ambiguous and to need direction, and so special structures, such as project teams with an appropriate reporting relationship to senior management, need to be created to manage the change process.

Also the question needs to be asked, how well does the infrastructure, in terms of communications and systems, facilitate plans being achieved?

Overcoming barriers to the achievement of objectives

Problems managers experience

Planning takes up valuable time and may be viewed as being a distraction for busy senior managers. This may affect the amount of support they provide to middle managers. Even with support, middle managers may have difficulty converting the plans into operational ones and getting them implemented. This could be due to an inadequate analysis of what needs to be done at the operational level in order to support the higher-level objectives.

Other important detractors to change and reasons why barriers are formed can be through factors such as poor involvement, communications, resources and information.

Commitment planning

This activity involves identifying key people and groups whose commitment is needed for change to occur and deciding how to gain their support.

Participation

It is helpful to get people to participate in the goal-setting process. This ensures that objectives are more clearly understood, and increases the level of personal ownership of the objectives and hence commitment. Participative goal setting also helps to ensure that objectives are set at the best level for motivating performance; that is, the goals are challenging but realistically attainable.

Participative goal setting can be achieved by:

- requesting employees' input to make sure that the goals are clear and set at an appropriate level
- ensuring that goals are clearly understood with agreement on resources to be made available and deadlines to be met
- allowing some room for flexibility and mutually agreeing what difficulties may be encountered and what resources will be needed
- informing employees of how their work and goals contribute to the organisation's goals
- expressing confidence in the employees and assuring them of your continued support.

Top-down versus bottom-up goal setting

Goal setting can, however, lead to people having to fulfil certain prescribed tasks. For example, a top-down management approach can often engender resentment and stifle an individual's initiative and potential. At worst, people could try to beat the system. All this is detrimental to the organisation and, ultimately, to the individual. These problems can be overcome by not imposing goals but using them as a basis for dialogue. Rather than a top-down approach, employers should be encouraged to participate in goal setting and in establishing the yardsticks against which they are measured, as well as evaluating the results; that is, a combination of top-down and bottom-up goal setting and testing should be pursued.

Problems of pursuing objectives

- Outcomes that are easy to measure are often established wrongly as the objectives to pursue, even though they may contribute little to improved performance. For example, quality measures such as the amount of scrap and rework are focused on because their levels are known as areas that need improving. The trouble is that the cause of such poor quality may be due to low worker morale, which is difficult to measure.
- Easily-attainable targets may be set to guarantee good results.
- The administrative burden of collecting the information and crunching the numbers may preclude the process from being done frequently enough or taken seriously.
- The objectives, once set, may become tablets of stone. As conditions change, they may not be changed because of the work involved. The exercise then becomes ritualistic and irrelevant.
- In the pursuit of perfection, the redefining of objectives and task definitions may become the goal, instead of getting on with the work. Often, the best approach is to test things out as problems occur with the work and then make changes as and when they become necessary.

ACTION CHOICES

Defining the objectives provides the basis for decision making and *the courses of action to follow* in order to achieve the objectives. The feasibility of possible courses of action needs to be evaluated and a particular course of action needs to be chosen. Many alternatives may exist and these need reducing through analysis to consider which is the most promising. Alternatives may be examined as to how well they achieve the objective, and many variables may need to be taken into account, such as profit, costs, cash position, capital availability and so on. With so many variables to consider, the problem can become quite complex and the many tools of operations research, mathematics and computing may prove useful here.

Contingency planning

Contingency planning involves the identification of alternative courses of action that can be pursued if and when circumstances show the original plan needs modifying. Unexpected problems and events frequently occur and, rather than be caught by surprise, it is better to anticipate problems and be prepared with alternative action plans.

Contingency planning requires the identification of things that might block the success of the original plan, together with an estimation of the likelihood that each of these things will go wrong. It is then necessary to estimate the cost and inconvenience of developing plans to deal with them. Contingency planning requires good forward thinking and the ability to imagine worst-case scenarios. Looking ahead in this way facilitates taking quicker action if and when situations change to the extent that the existing plan is no longer useful.

The uncertainties of an ever-changing environment

It may also arise, due to the uncertainties that an ever-changing environment can bring, that little faith may be attached to plans which constantly need reviewing or have to be supported with contingency options. This may discourage emphasis on planning, which needs to be counteracted with a more proactive stance towards determining the future trends and how plans can be made and flexibly adapted to suit changing circumstances.

ACTION PLANS AND IMPLEMENTATION

Having established that change should take place and the form it should take, it is necessary to develop an action plan to show how the change will be achieved, and then to implement the plan. An action plan, as explained by Gilgeous (1995a), is developed as follows:

The actions needed

Activity planning involves constructing a schedule for the change programme, citing specific activities and events that must occur if the transition is to be successful.

Having made the plans, it is then necessary to state clearly what actions need to take place. An action plan can be developed by the manager and employee working together or by the employee alone, subject to the manager's approval.

Action plans address the following questions:

● **What** objectives are to be achieved?
● **How** will each objective be achieved? (What are the steps involved?)
● **Who** is responsible for each step?
● **Where** can each step be performed?
● **When** has each step to be performed?

As stated, the action plan requires a check to be made on progression towards the objectives. Figure 5.3 provides a format for an action plan.

Action planning is useful in that it provides a structure for considering alternative ways of pursuing particular objectives. If plans are then thwarted, such alternatives may be considered. Action planning also helps managers to track employees' progress, identify problems and provide resources, and co-ordinate effort to fulfil the objectives sought.

Implementation

Implementation should be considered as a structured process for managing the actions necessary to make the plans happen. Senior management can start this process

ACTION PLAN

Name: _____

Date: _____ Dept: _____

Objectives (What)	Steps (How)	Accountability (Who)	Deadlines (When)	Monitoring mechanisms (How's it going?)
1				
2				
3				
4				
5				
6				

Manager: _____ (Signature)

Fig 5.3 Action plan format

by the establishment of an implementation team. The implementation team should be headed by one who is given the responsibility and authority to ensure that all parties do their job to fulfil the activities set out in the plan. The team should include some, if not all, of those responsible for the original assessment of the need for change, including the assistance of an outside consultant or change facilitator. The team will need to assess the amount of disruption the change could cause. To achieve this it will be necessary to assess the current state and who will be affected by the change. It may also be necessary to review the history of the impact of previous plans for change.

Support from the sponsors

This, in turn, may give rise to questioning the extent of support by the sponsors, since the task could become very difficult, expensive and time consuming. Since change is also a situation where people vie for scarce resources, this could provide an ideal breeding ground for politics and infighting. Therefore, time may be needed to identify potential resistors and assess their strength in order to make decisions on how they are to be managed.

Implementation and consideration of resistance

An implementation programme should be drawn up to define what actions need to be taken and the types of changes this entails. This will require defining responsibilities at different levels from the top to the bottom in each area or function. Everyone at their own level must know clearly what is intended and required of them. It is also important that each level is in alignment with the one below and the one above in order to minimise overlap and indicate clearly who is responsible for what. The process of examining the problems of implementation by considering the forces for and against change and looking at ways of overcoming any resistance is presented by Gilgeous (1995b).

Feedback

Feedback is information which tells us what is going on, how well the standards are being met and to what extent the plans should be readjusted. Feedback can comprise typed statements, memos, letters etc., but the best form of feedback is face to face. In this way, a manager has the best chance of ascertaining if the message being conveyed is understood. Providing feedback, particularly on someone's performance, requires good communication skills on the part of the manager, along with a climate in which people do not feel threatened so that they will listen and act on what is said to them. To assist here, the management should see to it that the action plan contains detail on the type and level of resources that people need, as well as any training and assistance necessary for them to maintain and improve their performance.

Taking action

Obviously, a problem is encountered when actual performance is less than that desired. Corrective action may be necessary to restore performance. However, when actual performance is above standard, this signals the opportunity to ascertain why this is so, to recognise and reward good efforts, and to learn what can be done to maintain this good state of affairs.

PLANNING AND CONTROLLING OPERATIONS

To ensure that the operations satisfy customer demand and that they do so effectively, the operations require plans and require controlling. This is the purpose of planning and control. Essentially, the task of planning and control is to reconcile supply with demand to ensure that the available resources of the operation produce products and services in the appropriate *quantity* at the appropriate *time*, and at the appropriate level of *quality*.

This can be achieved in seven different ways as shown in Fig 5.4.

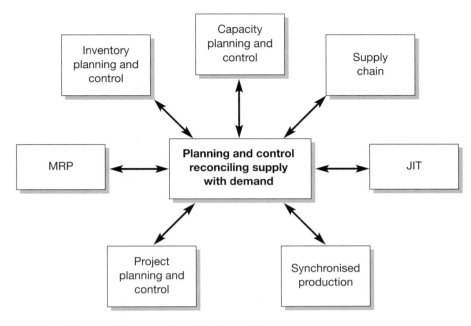

Fig 5.4 Ways of reconciling supply with demand

Capacity planning and control

Capacity planning and control (*see* Krajewski and Ritzman, 1993) is concerned with setting the effective capacity of the operation so that it can respond to the demands placed on it. Long-term capacity planning and control is concerned with choosing the optimum capacity of different facilities, balancing the capacity levels and the timing of capacity changes in the long term.

Short-term capacity planning and control, also referred to as aggregate planning, deals with how managers make decisions on how to adjust aggregated capacity of the operation to meet demand in the medium term, say 12 to 18 months ahead. Aggregate here means the combining of products or services to represent an overall capacity measure.

Inventory planning and control

Inventory planning and control (*see* Schroeder, 1993) is conducted to smooth the differences in timing between the supply and demand of materials. The main problem is maintaining the balance of having sufficient stocks of materials to satisfy demand, yet keeping the cost and difficulties of acquiring and holding these stocks to a minimum.

Supply chain planning and control

Supply chain planning and control (*see* Slack *et al.*, 1995) is concerned with co-ordinating the flow of information and materials through facilities. This involves the materials management and logistics of the whole supply chain, and the purchasing and supply and physical distribution to the first-tier suppliers and customers, respectively.

MRP

MRP (*see* Orlicky, 1975) can stand for material requirements planning or manufacturing resource planning. Both make use of the computer to plan and control the business's resources. They reconcile the supply and demand of resources by providing the means to make decisions concerning the volume and timing of materials flow in dependent demand conditions.

Just-in-time planning and control

Just-in-time planning and control (*see* Harrison, 1992) is concerned with the provision of products and services only when they are needed or 'just-in-time' for use by either internal or external customers.

Project planning and control

Project planning and control (*see* Meredith and Mantell, 1989) is often associated with the management of large-scale projects such as shipbuilding, bridges, aircraft, port construction etc. However, it can apply to one-off or small-volume activities, such as training projects, new designs, product introductions, teamwork projects etc., that have a defined start and end. First the project is defined and then the project activities are planned forward in time in a way that tries to ensure the most effective use of resources, money and time. The project is then controlled against the plan in an attempt to ensure that the project targets are met.

Synchronised production

Synchronised production (*see* Chase and Aquilano, 1995) refers to the entire production process working together in a synchronised way so that all resources are co-ordinated to achieve the goals of the firm. In this way, total system performance is sought, not localised performance measures such as labour or machine utilisation. The creator of this philosophy was Dr Eli Goldratt who devised a scheduling approach and associated software called *optimised production technology* (OPT). The OPT approach looked at what stopped production being synchronised in terms of the bottlenecks which disrupt the flow of production. The approach thus takes into account limited facilities, machines, personnel, tools, materials and any other constraints that could affect a firm's ability to maintain its schedules. The approach seeks to improve throughput rate and lower inventory and operating expenses. Goldratt presents nine rules which act as a guide to success with this approach.

PLANNING AND CONTROL ACTIVITIES

Whatever type of planning and control is taking place, certain basic activities are performed: *scheduling, loading* and *sequencing*. Scheduling is concerned with deciding on a start and finish time for the tasks that need to be completed. In determining the schedule, this imposes loads on different facilities, and the task of loading needs to be performed to consider how the facilities are to cope with the volume of work imposed on them. When decisions have been made as to the appropriate loading on facilities, then decisions need to be made as to the order in which the work scheduled for those facilities is to be done. This is called sequencing and involves determining the priority of tasks to be performed.

Scheduling operations

Scheduling decisions allocate available capacity or resources (equipment, labour and space) to jobs, activities, tasks or customers through time. In practice, scheduling results in a timetable or schedule of activities, showing at what time or date particular activities should start and when they should end. The schedule also indicates what is to be done, by whom and with what equipment.

Gantt charts

One of the oldest and most commonly-used devices for scheduling is the use of the Gantt chart. The work of Henry Gantt is interestingly dealt with in the historical context of the development of operations management in Chase and Aquilano. The Gantt chart is a simple device which represents time as a bar. Through the use of Gantt charts, it is possible to visualise what is happening against what should be happening in the operation. A Gantt chart for a machining centre is shown in Fig 5.5.

The complexity of scheduling

Scheduling is a complex task because it involves the simultaneous consideration of different processes and people, each of which has different capacities and capabilities. Also,

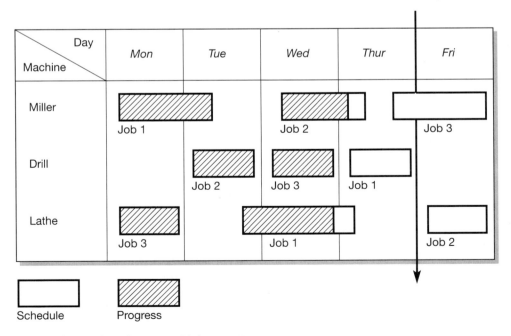

Fig 5.5 A Gantt chart for a machining centre

155

due to product changes, varying volumes required and product-mix changes, the schedule may need to be revised or dramatically altered quite frequently. In theory, scheduling is a mammoth task because the number of possible schedules increases rapidly as the number of activities and processes increases. For example, the number of different schedules that are possible for the way five different jobs can be processed on one machine is $5 \times 4 \times 3 \times 2 = 120$. For this reason, much use is made of proprietary scheduling devices, which are based on the Gantt chart principles, since they speed up the scheduling process and facilitate quicker evaluation of alternative schedules.

Johnson's Rule

Mathematical optimising approaches have been developed and are useful in certain situations. For example, where two or more jobs must be processed on two machines in common sequence, then 'Johnson's Rule' can be used to provide an optimum solution (*see* Schroeder, 1993, pp. 492–5). For more complex situations involving greater than three machines, other approaches can be utilised. A useful approach here is the Branch and Bound approach. The name derives from the ability to display the enumeration of the possible alternative schedules as a tree with many branches. This approach is described with other approaches in Bellman *et al*.

Scheduling trade-offs

In determining the schedule the objective is to achieve the best allocation of resources, and several conflicting objectives need to be considered. For example, in manufacturing efficiency may be achieved by a schedule which maintains high utilisation of labour, equipment and space. Of course, the schedule should also seek to maintain low inventories, which, unfortunately, may lead to low efficiency due to lack of available material or high set-up times. Thus, in this case, a trade-off decision in scheduling between efficiency and inventory levels is required. In the short-run, these trade-offs among conflicting objectives can be considered through the evaluation of different schedules. In the long-run, however, efficiency can be increased, customer service improved, and inventory simultaneously reduced by changing the production process itself through the planning and control approaches mentioned earlier, such as JIT, quality improvement efforts and OPT etc.

Forward and backward scheduling

With forward scheduling, work is planned to start as soon as it arrives and jobs are scheduled forwards in time. With backward scheduling, work is planned backwards from the due date for each job, and this means that jobs are started at the last possible moment. There are advantages and disadvantages associated with the use of each approach and these are shown in Table 5.1. In practice, the choice of backward or forward scheduling is dictated by the scheduling principle adopted by the scheduling system used. For example, both material requirements planning (MRP) and just-in-time (JIT) systems employ backwards scheduling, whereas project planning packages employ forward scheduling methods.

Table 5.1 Advantages of forward and backward scheduling

Advantages of forward scheduling	Advantages of backward scheduling
High labour utilisation – workers always start work to keep busy Flexible – the time slack in the system allows unexpected work to be loaded	Lower material costs – materials are not used until they have to be, therefore delaying added value until the last moment Less exposed to risk in case of schedule change by the customer Tends to focus the operation on customer due dates

Source: Slack, N. *et al*. *Operations Management*.

Push and pull scheduling

In many production operations the work is scheduled and allocated or pushed out to different areas in accordance with schedule start dates dictated by a production planning department or an MRP system. The trouble with this practice is that it does not realise quickly what the actual situation is and that certain areas may not yet need the work or in fact be able to cope with it. Therefore, the symptoms of a push system manifest themselves as queues occur, inventory rises and congestion occurs. (Pull systems are far less likely to result in inventory build-up.)

In contrast, work can be scheduled to start when a downstream work station (the customer) signals it is necessary. That is, the work is *pulled* from the upstream (supplier) work station. In effect, the customer acts as the 'trigger' for movement. In this situation, if nothing is required by the customer then no signal for work is given and no work is done or moved. The trouble with this type of scheduling is that, when demand changes, there may be a delay in the earlier upstream stages of the operations recognising this, and future throughput could be placed in jeopardy. Push and pull systems are depicted in Fig 5.6.

It is not possible to treat the scheduling of all types of operations as a single subject. One way of highlighting the different ways of scheduling is to classify scheduling by type of process: line, intermittent, and project.

Scheduling line processes

This refers to assembly lines and process industries. Here, the scheduling is done by the design of the process, and the main problems occur with multiple products when product changeovers are required. This necessitates the calculation of economic lot sizes and the determination of the best sequence of products on the line. Use can be made of mathematical models but, unfortunately, many do not consider demand uncertainty. If this is the case then there is a need to use a dynamic scheduling method. Exhibit 5.1 provides an illustration of calculating 'run-out time', which is a dynamic scheduling method that can be used for line processes.

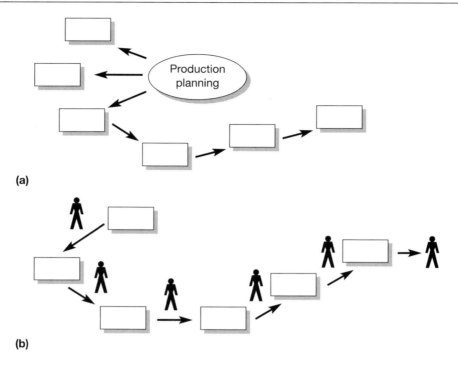

Fig 5.6 Push and pull systems
(a) Push system: Work is moved to the next stage according to the plan or when it has been processed
(b) Pull system: Work is moved when the next stage requires it

Scheduling intermittent processes

Intermittent processes (job shops, work centres) are characterised by unit flows through the process with many starts and stops through different work centres. Inevitably work queues build up and studies show that jobs or customers spend 95 per cent of their time in the system waiting. The job of scheduling is to manage the flows of customers/jobs so that this waiting time can be reduced. The scheduling of intermittent processes is closely related to the use of material requirements planning (MRP) systems.

Scheduling work patterns

Where the dominant resource in an operation is its staff, then the schedule of work times effectively determines the capacity of the operation itself. The main task of scheduling, therefore, is to make sure that sufficient numbers of people are working at any point to provide a capacity appropriate for the level of demand at that point in time. Operations such as postal delivery services, telephone operators, policing services, holiday couriers, shop workers, and hospital staff will all need to schedule the working hours of their staff with demand in mind. This is a direct consequence of these operations having a relatively high degree of customer contact. Such operations cannot store their output in inventories and so must respond directly to customer demand.

Exhibit 5.1

Run-out time calculations

If inventory for a particular product is low relative to its future demand then schedule it ahead of the other products which have larger relative inventories, i.e. schedule on the basis of lowest run-out time, that is lowest r;

where r = l/d

and   r = run-out time, weeks

      l = units of inventory

      d = units of weekly demand

An example of run-out time calculations

Demand data

Product	Weekly Inventory units (l)	Run-out demand units (d)	Time, weeks (r)
A	2100	200	10.5
B	550	100	5.5 *
C	1475	150	9.8
D	2850	300	9.5
E	1500	200	7.5
F	1700	200	8.5

Supply data

Production	Lot size, units	Production rate, units/week	Time, weeks
A	1500	1500	1.0
B	450	900	0.5
C	1000	500	2.0
D	500	1000	0.5
E	800	800	1.0
F	1200	800	1.5

* The lowest run-out time is 5.5 weeks, therefore product B should be scheduled first.

Source: Schroeder, R.G., *Operations Management: Decision making in the operations function* 4th edn, 1993, pp. 492–5. Reproduced with permission of The McGraw-Hill Companies.

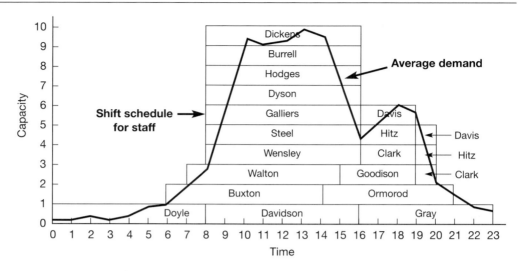

Fig 5.7 Shift scheduling on a home-banking enquiry service

Source: Slack, N., *et al.*, *Operations Management*.

For example, Fig 5.7 shows a scheduling system for a service operation. The scheduling task here is to allocate start and finish times to staff such that:

- capacity matches demand
- the length of each shift is neither excessively long nor too short to be attractive to staff
- working at unsocial hours is minimised.

Input–output control in intermittent processes

The purpose of input–output control is to manage the relationship between a work centre's inputs and outputs. The main characteristics involved in establishing a balance between input and output in a system are:

- input – the amount of work arriving per unit time in the system
- load – the level of work-in-progress (WIP) or back orders in the system
- output – the rate at which work can be completed in the system
- capacity – the maximum rate of output which can be produced by the system.

An hydraulic analogy of input–output control is presented in Fig 5.8.

The consequences of too little input are low resource and labour utilisation and high unit costs. With increased input, WIP and its associated costs increase as well as throughput time because of the queues and congestion that build up. As work builds up, expediting may be a popular way of trying to get out of the mess by identifying critical jobs and rushing them through, but this is a short-sighted solution and no substitute for proper planning, scheduling and control.

The relationship between utilisation and WIP

The results of work done by Colley *et al.* show the relationship between utilisation and WIP (*see* Fig 5.9). When utilisation is low, it is greatly improved by small increases in

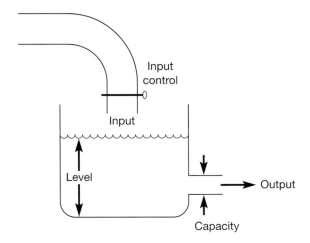

Fig 5.8 Hydraulic analogy of input–output control

WIP. This occurs because machines and people, not jobs, are waiting. When utilisation is high, say 90 per cent, only a large increase in WIP inventory can raise utilisation still higher. In practice, calculations need to be done to determine in each case how much money is saved by a reduction in WIP and the corresponding cost to the company in terms of reduced productivity through lower utilisation.

Effects of WIP on lead time and output rate

The effects of WIP on lead time and output rate are summarised in Fig 5.10. With low WIP, workers are waiting for work. In this case, increasing the level of WIP can help in increasing throughput to a point where WIP finally gets in the way. At the same time, increasing WIP can increase the average lead time because jobs spend more time in the

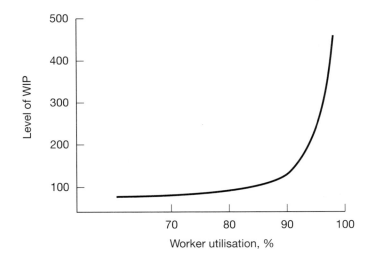

Fig 5.9 WIP inventory against labour utilisation
Source: Colley, J. L., Landel, R. and Fair, R., *Production Operations Planning and Control*, Holden-Day, 1977.

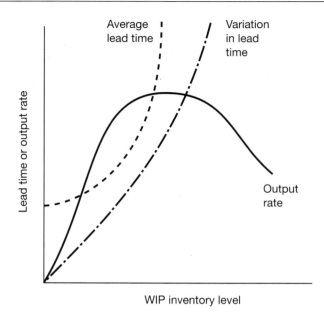

Fig 5.10 Effects of WIP on lead time and output rate

Source: Colley, J. L., Landel, R. and Fair, R., *Production Operations Planning and Control*, Holden-Day, 1977.

queues. Therefore, the key to controlling lead times, utilisation, and inventories is to control input to the intermittent process.

Analysis of input and output

Table 5.2 provides a typical analysis of input and output for a milling centre. If little attention is paid to input–output control, the result is high WIP inventories and long lead times. In this case, the work flow has to be managed. Ways of managing are to ensure that performance, facility size and level of input are correct. The level of input can be modified by scheduling work to or from other areas, and producing or subcontracting more or less.

Table 5.2 Analysis of input and output

Milling work centre (in standard hours) existing backlog 300 hours

Week ending	3/4	10/4	17/4	24/4
Planned input	300	300	300	300
Actual input	290	270	300	305
Cumulative deviation	−10	−40	−40	−35
Planned output	340	340	340	340
Actual output	290	290	290	290
Cumulative deviation	−50	−100	−150	−200
Cumulative change in backlog	0	−20	−10	5

Scheduling projects

Projects can range from large, one-off manufacturing activities, such as manufacturing ships and aircraft, to smaller, service activities, such as consultancy or training projects.

Two main scheduling methods can be used: Gantt charts and network methods. As mentioned, the Gantt chart method employs a bar or milestone format and is useful for small, less-complicated projects where the activities are not highly interrelated. The network method is described straightforwardly in Lockyer and Gordon and it is most suitable for complex project planning and control situations. Its advantage is that it uses a graph or network to show precedence relationships. The method also highlights some important scheduling considerations, such as critical path and slack. The method can also be used to consider time–cost trade-offs and probabilities of activities being achieved in a certain time.

Loading

Loading is the process of allocating work to a work centre. In doing this a 'load profile' is developed for a work centre. The number of hours or jobs loaded is used to determine when orders can be delivered or whether capacity will be exceeded. The time available for a work centre is often far below the maximum possible time available. This depletion of available time is due to many reasons, as Fig 5.11 shows.

There are two main approaches to loading operations: finite and infinite loading.

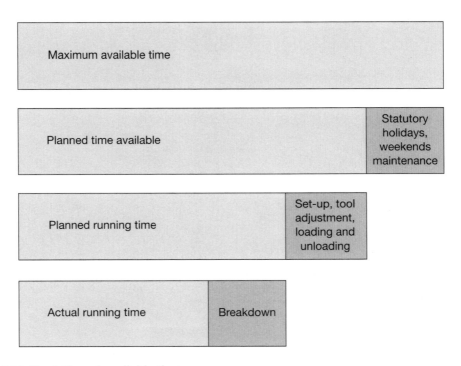

Fig 5.11 Depletion of available time

Finite and infinite loading

Finite loading means allocating work to a facility up to the limit of its capacity. Infinite loading means allocating work to a facility irrespective of its immediate capacity to deal with it.

The reasons for finite loading are numerous and include limits for safety, or where the success of the business is adversely affected by not limiting the load.

Infinite loading is used in the many situations where it is not possible to limit the load. For example, hospitals should not turn away arrivals needing attention. It may also be unrealistic to limit the load. For example, when a petrol station or store is busy, customers may have to wait their turn. The business, however, is taking the risk that customers might take their business elsewhere. Figure 5.12 illustrates finite and infinite loading patterns.

Sequencing

When the work that has been scheduled and loaded arrives at an area with other work, it becomes necessary to determine the *order* in which the work will be done.

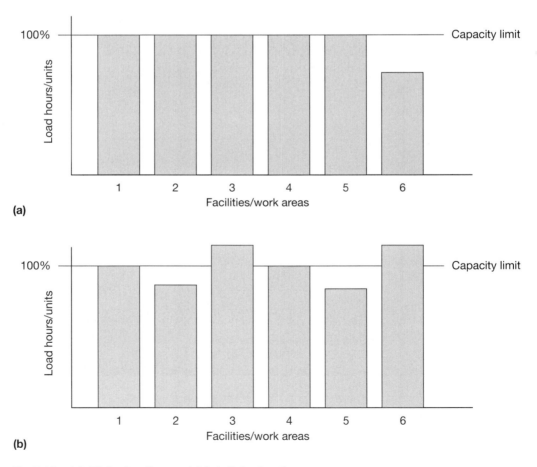

Fig 5.12   (a) Finite loading and (b) Infinite loading

This is the task of sequencing. The priorities for the work can be based on customer priority, the date it is due, or some other priority such as last-in-first-out (LIFO) or first-in-first-out (FIFO).

Dispatching rules

In practice, the established sequences are difficult, if not impossible, to maintain because of machine breakdowns, operator illness, materials not arriving etc. As a result, work can pile up at a facility and the question needs to be asked, 'What should be done next?' Use can be made of dispatch rules. A dispatch rule specifies which job from a queue of jobs should be selected next for work. Studies have been carried out at Hughes Aircraft (*see* Le Grande, 1963) and have considered the issues involved when a variety of orders arrive in a job shop. These being:

- manner in which jobs arrive
- number and variety of machines in the shop
- number of people in the shop
- flow pattern of jobs through the shop.

In allocating priorities to the jobs on particular machines, the rules that are commonly used in industry are:

- Assign highest priority to jobs with the earliest due dates.
- Assign highest priority to the job with the least slack (slack being the time remaining till due date).
- Assign highest priority to the job with the earliest due date at that machine. Allowable shop time is divided equally among the operations of the job to obtain the due date for each operation listed in the job route.
- Assign highest priority to the job which has the least slack per remaining operation.

In practice, many people tend to prefer the 'longest processing time rule', i.e. jobs with longer duration attach more importance. However, no one rule is best for every situation. The ultimate choice depends on how well a particular rule performs according to the criteria by which the schedule is evaluated.

Many studies have been concerned with the relative merits of the various priority rules. Exhibit 5.2 provides an illustration of minimising either mean job flow time or mean job lateness in a job shop.

Dispatching rules in services

It is interesting to note three practical examples of the effect of specialised priority rules in certain situations. Shearon studied the operation of a suite of operating rooms in a large general hospital and found that the most effective pattern of results on a day-by-day basis was achieved by sequencing the operations to be performed according to the 'longest operation first' rule. Practically, this served to 'get the most variable operations out of the way first', since the longest operating procedures tended to be the most variable. For instance, critical operations might take four to five hours, or the patient might expire soon after the procedure was started. This strategy led to the gradual attainment

Exhibit 5.2

Minimising either mean job flow time or mean job lateness in a job shop

Consider four jobs which must be processed on one machine:

Job	Due date	Processing time in days	Job slack (Due date – processing time)
A	4 days hence	3	1
B	9 days hence	6	3
C	5 days hence	5	0
D	9 days hence	7	2

The priority rules to be used are:

- Assign jobs according to their minimum slack time.
- Assign jobs according to shortest processing time.

The evaluation criteria to be used are:

(a) minimum mean flow time
(b) minimum mean lateness, where lateness is the difference between the job's due date and its flow time.

Solution 1

Using the minimum slack priority rule, the jobs would be performed in the order C, A, D, B, so that the flow of the jobs would be as follows:

Job	Flow time	Due date	Lateness (Flow time – due date)
A	8	4	4
B	21	9	12
C	5	5	0
D	15	9	6
	Total 49		Total 22

Mean flow time = 49/4 = 12.25 days
Mean lateness = 22/4 = 5.5 days

Solution 2

Using the shortest processing time rule, the order of jobs would be A, C, B, D, so that the flow of the jobs would be as follows:

Job	Flow time	Due date	Lateness (Flow time – due date)
A	3	4	0 (as early as
B	14	9	5 possible)
C	8	5	3
D	21	9	12
	——		——
	Total 46		Total 20

Mean flow time = 46/4 = 11.5 days
Mean lateness = 20/4 = 5 days

Thus, the shortest processing time rule (Solution 2) gave better results, and mathematically this rule in many situations has proved to be superior to others.

of stability in scheduling as the larger number of shorter and more predictable operations were tackled. Howell *et al.* found that the 'shortest operation' rule achieved the greatest number of operational helicopters (on average) in the simulation of a combat maintenance depot. That is, where a number of helicopters were always awaiting the attention of the limited maintenance personnel, giving priority to the helicopter estimated to require the least repair time would maximise the fleet of available machines. Likewise, Colley *et al.* found that the use of the 'shortest treatment time' discipline maximised the survivors of a saturated medical facility, such as a forward aid station in a combat zone. This resulted from the phenomenon that the shorter the expected treatment time, the higher the probability of survival. The rule thus led to getting the largest number of the most appropriate patients through the system.

PLANNING AND CONTROL SYSTEMS

A planning and control system should facilitate the development of good schedules, satisfactory loading and allocation of work, but should also ensure that schedules are implemented and corrected as needed. According to Schroeder (pp. 514–15), whichever methods of scheduling, loading and sequencing are in use, the systems they work within should answer the following:

1 **What delivery date do I promise?** Depends on both marketing and operations considerations, including available capacity, the customer's requirements, and the efficiency of the operations.

2 **When should I start on each particular activity or task?** Determined by the particular scheduling system used.

3 **How much capacity do I need?** Determined from examination of the loads imposed by the schedule.

4 **How do I make sure that the job is completed on time?** Dispatching rules can be used, and monitoring and feedback of activity progress is needed to ensure that delivery deadlines are met.

SUMMARY

- Planning is an important basic management function. Main planning considerations are the establishment of goals and objectives, the timescales, and the barriers to their achievement.

- Action plans provide detail on actions and events that need to take place and answer: What are the objectives? How are they to be achieved? Where and when can each step be performed and who is responsible?

- Feedback is information which tells us what is going on, how well the standards are being met, and to what extent the plans should be readjusted. If problems are encountered then corrective action is necessary to restore performance. When actual performance is above standard, this signals the opportunity to recognise and reward good efforts and learn what can be done to maintain this good state of affairs.

- The task of planning and control is to reconcile supply with demand to ensure that the available resources of the operation produce products and services in the appropriate quantity, at the appropriate time, and at the appropriate level of quality.

- Planning and control can be achieved in the following ways: capacity planning and control; inventory planning and control, supply chain planning and control, material requirements planning or manufacturing resource planning, just-in-time planning and control, project planning and control, and synchronised production.

- Planning and control of operations involves certain basic activities of scheduling, loading and sequencing.

- Scheduling is concerned with deciding on a start and finish time for the tasks that need to be completed. Scheduling involves considering issues of complexity, scheduling approaches, trade-offs, backward or forward scheduling, push and pull scheduling. A Gantt chart is one of the oldest and most commonly-used devices for scheduling. Scheduling can be classified by type of process – line, intermittent or project – and the considerations for each are different.

- Loading is the process of allocating work to a work centre. In doing this a 'load profile' is developed for a work centre. There are two main approaches to loading operations: finite and infinite loading.

- Sequencing is the task of determining the order in which the work will be done. The priorities for the work can be based on customer priority, the date it is due, or some other priority such as last-in-first-out (LIFO) or first-in-first-out (FIFO).

- In practice use can be made of dispatch rules to establish which job from a queue of jobs should be done next. Some of the rules that are commonly used in industry assign highest priority to jobs with the earliest due dates, the least slack, the shortest operation time or the longest processing time. The ultimate choice depends on how well a particular rule performs according to the criteria by which the schedule is evaluated.

- A planning and control system should answer the following questions: What delivery date do I promise? When should I start on each particular activity or task? How much capacity do I need? How do I make sure that the job is completed on time?

REVIEW AND DISCUSSION QUESTIONS

1 With respect to the establishment and fulfilling of planning objectives, explain the issues this raises, the means by which planning objectives may be defined, the organisational areas that need to be considered and the barriers that might exist.

2 Consider an area in your organisation (a typical organisation) which would benefit from improvements being made. Present the details of an action plan for pursuing these improvements and explain what steps could be taken to allay possible difficulties that might be experienced in implementing the action plan.

3 Regarding the scheduling of a line, intermittent or project process with which you are familiar, present your views on the complexity of the situation, the scheduling approach, the objectives being sought, and the trade-offs and the practical problems that might be experienced.

4 Discuss the value of using priority dispatching rules in either a service or a manufacturing situation and explain the different performance objectives that could be sought and the types of rules that might be employed.

ASSIGNMENTS

1 In the process of allocating work to a facility or area, discuss the implications of 'depletion of available time', 'finite and infinite loading', and worker utilisation.

2 Think or read up about some planning or scheduling systems that you know about or have encountered in your area or function. For one of these systems decide which are the four worst problem areas. Outline the nature of each of these and discuss what you think are the possible causes of each problem and what actions need to be taken to overcome them.

REFERENCES

Bellman, R., Esogbue, A.O. and Nabeshima, I., *Mathematical Aspects of Scheduling and Applications*, Pergamon, 1982.

Chase, R. B. and Aquilano, N.J., *Production and Operations Management: Manufacturing and services*, 7th edn, pp. 12–16 and 752–91, Richard D. Irwin Inc., London, 1995.

Colley Jr, J. L., 'A simulation model of a saturated medical system', Proceedings of the 18th Annual Institute Conference and Convention, American Institute of Industrial Engineers, Toronto, Canada, May 1967.

Colley, J. L., Landel, R. and Fair, R., *Production Operations Planning and Control*, Holden-Day, San Francisco, 1977.

Drucker, P. S., *The Practice of Management*, Harper & Row, New York, 1954.

Gilgeous, V. G.(a), *Structured Workshops for Improving Manufacturing Effectiveness*, Workshop 2, 'Developing action plans', pp. 21–36, Gower, Aldershot, 1995.

Gilgeous, V. G.(b), *Structured Workshops for Improving Manufacturing Effectiveness*, Workshop 3, 'Implementation', pp. 37–54.

Harrison, A., *Just-in-Time in Perspective*, Prentice Hall, London, 1992.

Howel, M. and Sienkiewicz, R., 'Simulation of a maintenance system for an assault helicopter company', Unpublished paper, Colgate Darden Graduate School of Business Administration, University of Virginia, 1975.

Johnson, S. M., 'Optimal two-stage and three-stage production schedules', *Naval Logistics Quarterly*, Vol. 1, No. 1, 1954.

Krajewski, L. J. and Ritzman, L. P., *Operations Management Strategy and Analysis*, 3rd edn, pp. 295–333, Addison-Wesley, Wokingham, 1993.

Le Grande, E., 'The development of a factory simulation system using actual operating data', *Management Technology*, Vol. 3, No. 1, pp. 1–18, 1963.

Lockyer, K. and Gordon, J., *Critical Path Analysis and other Project Network Techniques*, 5th edn, Pitman Publishing, London, 1991.

Meredith, J. R. and Mantell, S., *Project Management: A managerial approach*, 2nd edn, John Wiley & Sons, New York, 1989.

Orlicky, J., *Material Requirements Planning*, McGraw-Hill, New York, 1975.

Schroeder, R. G., *Operations Management: Decision making in the operations function*, 4th edn, McGraw-Hill, New York, 1993.

Shearon Jr, W. T., 'A study of hospital operating suite scheduling procedures', Thesis presented in partial fulfilment of the requirements for the degree of Master of Science in Industrial Engineering, North Carolina State University, 1969.

Slack, N., Chambers, S., Harland, C., Harrison, A. and Johnston, R., *Operations Management*, pp. 510–51, Pitman Publishing, London, 1995.

PART 3

The initiatives that make operations work

CHAPTER 6

The operations initiatives of TQM, MRP, JIT and OPT

OBJECTIVES

The objectives of this chapter are to:

- explain what total quality management (TQM) is, how it has evolved, what the experts in quality profess concerning its achievement and how quality is recognised both nationally and internationally

- become aware of the systems or files used in material requirements planning (MRP) and understand how MRP works and has developed, and to realise the use and benefits of MRP and what needs to be done in order to make it a success

- appreciate the philosophy and benefits of just-in-time (JIT), and to understand the in-company and inter-company activities needed to make JIT work, as well as the factors behind successful implementation of JIT

- examine what optimised production technology (OPT) seeks to achieve and appreciate how the features and rules of OPT are used to achieve synchronised manufacture.

TYPES OF INITIATIVES

There are many operations initiatives which can be used to support the performance of the activity areas in a company. Some initiatives that organisations employ are listed below.

- *total quality management (TQM)* – quality being a strategic issue involving everyone and every process in the organisation;
- *material requirements planning (MRP)* – a system for scheduling dependent demand items;
- *just-in-time (JIT)* – a philosophy of manufacturing, initially developed by the Japanese, and used to ensure that the right quantities are purchased and made at the right time with little or no waste;
- *optimised production technology (OPT)* – seeks to improve productivity through the use of an analytical technique which aims to synchronise production;
- *computer-integrated manufacture (CIM)* – planning and control of manufacture using computers and technology;
- *programme evaluation and review technique (PERT)* – a management tool for scheduling and controlling projects.

Questions concerning the use of initiatives

With respect to each initiative, three questions need to be asked concerning its use in a particular situation:

1 **Applicability to the situation.** For example, MRP could be used to schedule dependent demand items which lie within a medium-volume, medium-variety product category. If the items lie within a high-volume, low-variety product category then a JIT scheduling approach might well be more appropriate.

2 **Emphasis on features of initiative.** To be effective in managing operations it is necessary to know what features of the initiative need to be focused on and improved. For example, with respect to MRP, this could be the quality and integrity of the following features:

- master production schedule
- lead times
- batch sizes
- bill of materials
- stock file.

3 **Effectiveness of initiative.** How effective is each initiative at contributing to the achievement of the company's performance objectives?

The operations initiatives of TQM, MRP, JIT and OPT are outlined to provide the reader with a basic understanding of each.

TOTAL QUALITY MANAGEMENT (TQM)

Chase and Aquilano define TQM as:

> *managing the entire organisation so that it excels on all dimensions of products and services that are important to the customer.*

Markland, Vickery and Davies say that TQM is:

> *a philosophy and a set of guiding principles and tools for improving quality and a way to manage an organisation based on total customer satisfaction and a continuous process of improvement.*

According to them, experience has revealed several requirements that companies must meet in successfully implementing TQM. They are:

- strategic quality planning
- clear focus on customer satisfaction
- effective collecting and analysis of information
- effective use of teamwork and training
- effective design of products and services
- effective leadership.

Feigenbaum introduced the notion of total quality management in 1957. He defined TQM as:

an effective system for integrating the quality development, quality maintenance and quality improvement efforts of the various groups in an organisation, so as to enable production and service at the most economical levels which allow for full customer satisfaction.

In the West, other quality gurus such as Deming, Juran and Crosby have presented their contributions to the area of TQM. The concept of TQM is one that has evolved from the ideas and writings of a few American and Japanese individuals. A short, working definition of TQM from the Institute of Personnel Management, reads:

a cost-effective system for integrating the continuous quality improvement efforts of people at all levels in an organisation to deliver products and services which ensure customer satisfaction.

How TQM has evolved

Figure 6.1 shows the evolution of TQM through the following quality eras:

- **Inspection**, where the primary concern was product defect detection after production.
- **Statistical quality control,** where statistical tools and techniques were used to 'control in' quality.

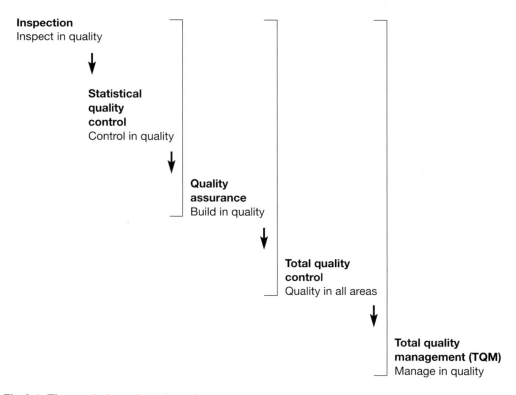

Fig 6.1 The evolution of total quality management

- **Quality assurance,** where the intention was to 'build in' quality through focus on programmes and systems to ensure product conformity to specification.

- **Total quality control,** where the intention was to expand the quality assurance philosophy from production to all areas of the organisation.

- **Total quality management,** where the view is that quality is a competitive opportunity and a strategic issue, and that through strategic planning and goal setting and developing a quality culture, i.e. 'managing in' quality, everyone and every process in the organisation is involved in improving quality.

A useful explanation of the various labels and approaches to quality is presented by Foster and Whittle.

THE QUALITY GURUS

Dr W. Edwards-Deming, Dr J. M. Juran, Philip B. Crosby, Dr Kaoru Ishikawa and Genichi Taguchi have all had considerable influence in matters of quality and are referred to as the 'quality gurus'.

The Deming approach

Deming lectured on quality management to Japanese companies in the 1950s. The Japanese consider him to be the father of quality control. Since then his messages of total quality management have become widespread. Deming's approach is to strive for reduction in the variation of processes. He points out that there can be both common and special causes of process variation and that it is management's task to identify and deal with the common causes. Deming thinks that all managers should be trained in statistical methods because their use should lead to quality improvement and effective management. He states that the elimination of common causes is a new job for management, but managers can only tackle these common causes within the process they control. The basic Deming principle is that no one should be blamed for performance they cannot govern. Deming sees four aspects of quality, namely:

1 innovation in products and service
2 innovation in processes
3 improvement of products and service
4 improvement of processes.

Deming believes managers must know what it is that they are committed to do. These obligations, which cannot be delegated, are incorporated into Deming's 14 points listed in Exhibit 6.1. In these points Deming emphasises the need for statistical control methods, participation, education, openness and purposeful improvement.

The Juran approach

Juran states that in Western companies quality problems are largely traceable to deficiencies in the methods used to plan for quality. Juran defines quality in terms of fitness for use and claims that this is properly determined from the customer's view-

Exhibit 6.1

Deming's 14 points

1 Create consistency of purpose.
2 Adopt new philosophy.
3 Cease dependence on inspection.
4 End awarding business on the basis of price alone.
5 Improve constantly the system of production and service.
6 Institute training on the job.
7 Institute leadership.
8 Drive out fear.
9 Break down barriers between departments.
10 Eliminate slogans and exhortations.
11 Eliminate quotas or work standards.
12 Give people pride in their job.
13 Institute education and the self-improvement programme.
14 Put everyone to work to accomplish it.

point and not the manufacturer's. Juran believes that top management must be involved, as producing quality products is a survival issue for the company. In particular, top management must take responsibility for:

● annual improvement in quality
● hands-on leadership
● extensive training in quality for all managers.

Juran thinks that attitudes will be changed as a consequence of changing behaviour. Hence, if a structure is created where people are forced to consider quality, then a change in attitude to quality will follow. Juran advocates the concept of 'zero defects' and states that it is founded on the assumptions that:

● the majority of defects are under the control of the workers
● human error is not inevitable
● a human error can be eliminated if proper motivation is applied.

The 'Juran Trilogy'

Juran states that objective researchers have regularly shown that 80 to 90 per cent of the causes of poor quality are directly traceable to managerial actions. However, he feels that it is not enough simply to get managers to give top priority to quality. They need to manage quality using a structured approach to quality planning, control and improvement. This has become known as the 'Juran Trilogy' and its aims are:

● **Quality planning**. Establish who are the customers and what are their needs. Develop products that reflect those needs. Create processes to produce those products. Put the plans into operation.

- **Quality improvement.** Create the organisational infrastructure to achieve annual quality improvement. Identify specific improvement projects; create a team for each project, giving a clear mandate; provide the resources, training and motivation for each team to enable them to remedy the true cause and sustain the gains.

- **Quality control.** Evaluate the actual performance, compare to the goals, and act on the differences.

The Crosby approach

Crosby, in his first book *Quality is Free*, created the concept of 'zero defects'. The main thrust of Crosby's approach is that nothing will improve in an organisation until its management begins to take quality as seriously as it does finance or production. In his book *Quality Without Tears*, Crosby presents his four absolutes of quality. They are:

1 The definition of quality is conformance to requirements.
2 The system of quality is prevention.
3 The performance standard is zero defects.
4 The measurement of quality is the price of non-conformance.

Crosby recommends that top managers need to find out where they are in terms of quality maturity to see to what extent they are ready to tackle a quality improvement programme. He also advocates extensive off-site training in quality for top managers. When they have done this, he recommends that other managers follow the same training programme, but with the addition of how to teach it to remaining managers and employees within the company. Crosby suggests the 14 points shown in Exhibit 6.2 should be followed. These should not be confused with Deming's 14 principles.

Exhibit 6.2

Crosby's 14 points

1 Gain management commitment.
2 Set up the quality improvement teams.
3 Measure quality.
4 Find the cost of quality.
5 Advocate quality awareness in the company.
6 Create systems for corrective action.
7 Instigate zero-defects planning.
8 Educate employees
9 Have a zero-defects day – a start point where management stands up and makes its commitment.
10 Set goals.
11 Create the error, cause, removal system.
12 Give recognition to good performers.
13 Set up quality councils.
14 Do it all again.

Source: Crosby, P.B., *Quality Without Tears*, McGraw-Hill, New York, 1984.

Kaoru Ishikawa's approach

Deming credits Ishikawa with the formalisation of quality circles in 1960. The Japanese journal, *Quality Control for the Foreman*, was established in 1960 by the Japanese union of scientists and engineers and edited by Ishikawa. It enabled quality circles all over Japan to learn from one another. In particular, Ishikawa considered worker participation to be important to successful implementation of TQM, and he believed that quality circles were an important way to achieve this. Ishikawa states that, from his experience, as much as 95 per cent of all company problems can be solved by elementary methods. In particular, he advocates the use of elementary, intermediate and advanced methods to assist in quality control. The elementary methods can be listed as seven tools:

1 Pareto charts
2 cause and effect diagrams, otherwise known as fishbone or Ishikawa diagrams
3 histograms
4 control charts
5 scatter diagrams
6 graphs
7 checksheets.

Genichi Taguchi

Taguchi is noted for statistically-designed experiments. Companies such as Ford and Xerox use his methods in the design of equipment. Taguchi defines quality in the following way:

> *A product imparts losses to society from the time the product is shipped ... better quality imparts less trouble to the consumer.*

Initially Taguchi was concerned with encouraging workers and managers, through team meetings, to improve product design. In considering the concept of the loss to society of the product or service, Taguchi developed a quality loss function (QLF) which deals with warranty costs, customer complaints and loss of customer goodwill etc. Taguchi uses the loss function to measure quality costs. The loss function suggests that the concept of zero defects, based on a conformance to specifications, does not always result in a quality product. The objective should be to reduce the variation on the ideal value of the desired functional characteristics. The reduction of this variation should be a measure of quality improvement. He states that it is the production department's duty to reduce variation while maintaining the required profit margins. Thus Taguchi's concept of reducing variation, even if the specifications have been met, is in line with the total quality management concept of continuous improvement.

The above shows that, although each guru stresses a different set of issues, each has made a significant contribution to TQM.

OTHER QUALITY INITIATIVES

Over the past decade there have been a number of attempts by organisations to improve quality. These attempts have been wide ranging and have often taken the form of campaigns or programmes. As part of their 1989 survey, consultants Devilin and Partners reported on a number of programmes, including:

- quality days
- customer first
- restructuring
- attitude surveys
- improvement projects
- customer needs surveys
- quality action teams
- overhead value analysis
- quality awareness
- human resource development
- just-in-time
- quality awards
- best practice incentives.

However, three efforts, when judged by the extent to which their titles have entered everyday business language, stand out. They are the introduction of the British Standard 5750 or the ISO 9000 series, quality circles and quality awards.

ISO 9000 and BS 5750

ISO 9000 is a worldwide standard to provide a framework for quality assurance. In the UK this standard is referred to as BS 5750. BS 5750 was introduced in 1979 as a national standard for quality management systems. It was harmonised in 1987 and is now equivalent to the international standard ISO 9000. The standard sets out procedures for the creation, documentation and maintenance of a quality management system. If a company adheres to the principles of the standard, which include specified standard elements relating to systems, then it is taking steps towards getting its product or service right first time. The British Standards Institution (BSI), the Department of Trade and Industry (DTI), and various management consultants and agencies have all attempted to get this message across.

A company may seek to achieve satisfactory assessment of ISO 9000 and BS 5750 for a number of reasons:

- customers will not buy from it unless it is registered as an ISO 9000 or BS 5750 company
- the BSI will not allow use of the kite mark without BS 5750
- for use as a marketing tool
- as a means whereby a quality manager hopes to improve quality standards
- because the top management feels it is necessary to help compete.

Quality circles

The widespread implementation of the technique of quality circles was carried out in Japan in the 1960s and '70s. The translation of the Japanese 'the gathering of the wisdom of the people' is *quality circles.*

The technique uses the theory that the person who can best identify and solve a work problem is the person who is actually doing the job. The National Society of Quality Circles, founded in 1982 to promote the healthy development of quality circles in the UK, describes the quality circle as follows:

> *It is a group of four to twelve people coming from the same work area, performing similar work, who voluntarily meet on a regular basis to identify, investigate, analyse and solve their own work-related problems.*

A quality circle presents solutions or proposals to management who decides whether or not to implement them. The circle team is usually involved in the implementation and monitoring of the proposal. Experience has shown that successful quality circle programmes in a company have a structure which nearly always includes some form of steering or overall management committee, at least one facilitator who has responsibility for the function of all or part of the programme and properly-trained circle leaders. Quality circles have shown that quality problems arise because someone somewhere cannot do their job properly, perhaps because of faulty equipment, inadequate systems, or even lack of training. Whatever the problem, quality circles are superb at finding it and recommending the remedy. The problems that circles tackle are not restricted to quality topics, but can include anything associated with work or its environment. Items such as pay and conditions and other negotiated items are, however, normally excluded. The general tone is that quality circles are important because of the motivation and involvement of the workforce.

Land Rover's manufacturing excellence

Exhibit 6.3 illustrates how Land Rover pursues manufacturing excellence through a strategy based on quality improvement, obtained by the involvement of every single person.

Quality Awards

The Deming Prize

Deming's influence on the Japanese was so great that today Japan's highest prize for quality is the Deming Prize. The Deming Prize can also be awarded to overseas companies which have successfully applied company-wide quality control based on statistical quality control. The companies are assessed in ten categories:

- policy and objectives
- organisation and its operation
- education and its extension
- assembling and disassembling of information
- analysis
- standardisation
- control
- quality assurance
- effects
- future plans.

Exhibit 6.3

Land Rover's quality improvement based on personal involvement

Land Rover, the specialist four-wheel drive manufacturer, represents the best in UK manufacturing practice. Part of the Rover Group which won the first UK Quality Award in November last year, the company is delighting its customers worldwide with its range of products. The latest offering is its all-new, luxury Range Rover, launched last September. Fruit of a clean-sheet design approach and a £300 million investment, the new model is assembled at the company's Solihull plant (as are the Discovery and the classic Land Rover).

Underlying the drive for manufacturing excellence is a strategy based on quality improvement. Explaining this strategy, Des Kelly, the quality and reliability manager, says, 'Rover now recognises that for quality improvement you have to get the involvement of every single person. . . What we have to do is to come out with a strategy that says "how do we make the bulk of the people understand about product quality and what is it they have to work on?"' ...

To do this the company is about to launch into its Quality Strategy 2000 to take it into the next millennium. It gets the message across through such mechanisms as personal development reviews which relate business objectives with departmental and personal roles to achieve company quality objectives.

Source: Adapted from Coyne, B., 'Land Rover – Heading in the right direction', *Quality Today*, pp. 10–12, March 1995. Published by Nexus Media Ltd.

The Malcolm Baldridge National Quality Award

Following the lead of Japan's Deming Prize, the US government established the Malcolm Baldridge National Quality Award in 1987, the intention being to promote improved quality management practices and quality in American industry. The Baldridge Award recognises quality efforts concerning:

- leadership
- information and analysis
- strategic quality planning
- human resource utilisation
- quality assurance of products and services
- quality results
- customer satisfaction.

The purpose of the award is to promote awareness of quality as an increasingly important element in competitiveness, improve understanding of the requirements for quality excellence, foster sharing of information on successful quality strategies, and show the benefits derived from implementation of these strategies.

For a comparison between the Deming Prize and the Baldridge Award see Bush and Dooley.

The European Quality Award

In 1992 the European Quality Award (EQA), Europe's most prestigious prize for total quality management, was launched. This award is given to the most successful exponent of total quality management in Western Europe each year. To win, the companies must demonstrate that they excel in the following areas:

- leadership
- policy and strategy
- people management
- resources
- processes
- customer satisfaction
- people satisfaction
- impact on society
- business results.

Exhibit 6.4 illustrates how D2D, ICL's contract electronics manufacturing subsidiary, beat the best to win the European Quality Award.

Exhibit 6.4

> ### D2D beat the best to win the European Quality Award
>
> Receiving the coveted award, Alastair Kelly, managing director of D2D, commented, 'Our total quality approach has been fundamental to our success at D2D in terms of improved sales, profitability and customer satisfaction. Three years ago we adopted the European Foundation for Quality Management (EFQM) self-assessment model as a strategic business planning tool to give us a better, all-round approach to quality. It now forms the backbone of our philosophy for continuous improvement.'
>
> Kelly also commented that many companies have tried and failed because they have selected parts of the process and not embraced the whole total quality management philosophy. TQM is not a quick fix, he warned, nor should it be seen in isolation.
>
> 'What attracted us to the EFQM model was its all-round approach to the total business.' And he also recommended that all companies should enter for the EFQM Award as 'It's the best bit of free consultancy you will ever get.'
>
> *Source*: Adapted from 'D2D – Beating the best', *Quality Today,* pp. 8–9, January 1995. Published by Nexus Media Ltd.

TOTAL QUALITY ORGANISATIONS

Firms both large and small can become successful total quality organisations. Three examples of Baldridge winners are presented in Exhibit 6.5.

Exhibit 6.5

Total Quality Award winners

Marlow Industries, a 1991 Baldridge winner that manufactures thermo-electric coolers, has created a Total Quality Management Council (TQMC) to oversee the entire quality process and to establish, review, and assess quality goals and implementation plans. This council, which has six senior executives as permanent members and seven other employees who rotate annually, has the authority to implement the quality system throughout the company. In addition, the TQMC, in co-operation with the board of directors and senior executives, plays an active role in developing the firm's strategic business plan. Thus, the quality plan and the business plan are integrated.

Westinghouse's Commercial Nuclear Fuel Division, winner of a 1988 Baldridge, has a quality council that sets goals for the division and then monitors and reports progress. The firm also uses eight key measures, called Pulse Points, to assess performance. Examples include fuel reliability, error-free documentation, and first-time-through yield of manufactured components.

Federal Express, a 1990 Baldridge winner, measures quality performance in terms of 12 service quality indicators (SQIs). Each SQI item is weighted on a scale of 1 to 10. Damaged packages, lost packages and missed pick-ups all have a weight of 10 because they have a greater impact on customer satisfaction than any of the other indicators. Packages that have lost their identifying labels are weighted at 5. The company tracks and reports each of the 12 SQIs, as well as overall performance, daily.

Source: Adapted from Luthans, F., Hodgetts, R. and Lee, S., 'New paradigm organizations: From total quality to learning to world class', *Organizational Dynamics*. Reprinted by permission of the publisher, from *Organizational Dynamics*, Winter 1994 © 1994. American Management Association, New York. All rights reserved.

MATERIAL REQUIREMENTS PLANNING (MRP)

Material requirements planning (MRP) is a computerised system for managing dependent-demand inventories, so called because they are dependent on demand for higher-level parts and components which comprise the end item or product required by the customer. Examples of dependent-demand inventories are raw materials and work-in-progress inventories, used in manufacturing companies to support the manufacturing process itself. Founders of the process of MRP are Oliver Wight and Joseph Orlicky.

SYSTEMS OR FILES USED IN MRP

For MRP to work, use is made of the following inputs, shown in Fig 6.2:

- forecast of demand
- order book
- master production schedule
- bill of materials
- inventory file.

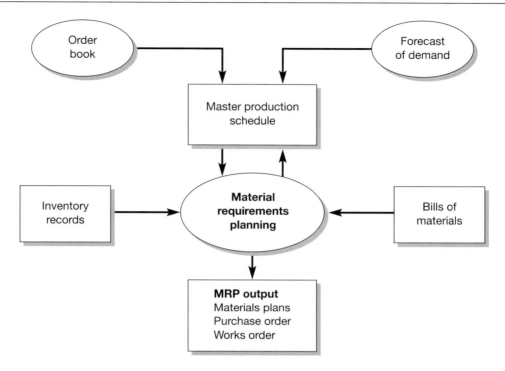

Fig 6.2 Inputs to MRP

Forecast of demand

The demand forecast is a forecast of the anticipated orders which the customer may place in the future but as yet has not made a firm commitment to do so. It is used to assist in the planning of production and provides an assessment of what the future production requirements are. This information is necessary as it provides information on anticipated demand throughout the planning period for which production is to be scheduled, whereas information on future production requirements obtained from the order book may only provide information about requirements in the near future. Obviously forecast of demand will be more error-prone in the further future.

Order book

The order book shows the firm orders placed by the customer that the company will need to fulfil.

Master production schedule

The MRP system is driven by the master production schedule (MPS) which specifies the quantity of 'end items' or output that it has been decided will be required from the production function in each time period. The decision as to what items or output to put in the MPS is made by the management referring to the order book, the forecast of demand and what it considers should be the company's priorities. All future demands for work-in-process and raw materials should be dependent on the master schedule and derived by the MRP system from the master schedule.

Bill of materials

The bill of materials (BOM) identifies the parts (the bill of materials), their quantities, and their relationship in the manufacturing hierarchy to all the other parts needed to manufacture the end item in the master schedule. The required parts may include assemblies, subassemblies, manufactured parts, and purchased parts. The BOM thus provides a 'parts explosion' to provide a complete list of the parts that must be either ordered or manufactured in accordance with a shop schedule. Figure 6.3 shows a desk, its simplified bill of materials, and the planned lead times for each item. This shows the total parts to be manufactured, including the top and modesty panel, and the parts to be purchased, which are the legs.

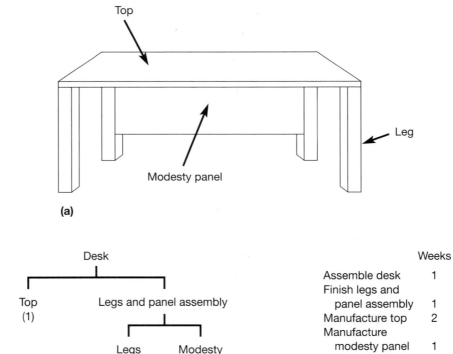

Fig 6.3 Bill of materials and planned lead time for a desk
(a) Drawing
(b) Bill of materials
(c) Planned lead times

Lead times

The lead time for each item is a specification of the time required either to make the item or to obtain it from a supplier. If the item is manufactured in-house, the planning lead time consists of estimates for the following time elements:

- set-up time
- process time
- material handling move time between operations
- waiting time in queue.

By combining each item's lead time and knowing the relationship or dependency between items, it is possible to determine when manufacture or purchase should be scheduled so that the end item can be made available when required. This information shows the amount of time needed to get the item into stock once the order is issued. If the planning lead time is longer than necessary, the item may arrive in inventory sooner than needed, thereby increasing inventory holding costs. If lead time is too short, stockouts, excessive expediting, or both may occur. If the item is purchased, the planning lead time is the time allowed to receive a shipment from the supplier once the order has been sent. Often the purchasing contract stipulates the delivery date.

Inventory file

Each of the parts shown in the BOM that is needed to fulfil the MPS should be shown on the inventory file. This file should be managed to show what is in stock, given the movement of materials and parts in and out of the stores. Accuracy of the information on this file is essential, and stock-taking or continuous auditing is necessary to update the file and ensure that the file data represent the actual physical stock.

HOW MRP WORKS

The MRP file accesses the master production schedule file to identify the quantity of end items that will be required in each time period. Using this information, the MRP file accesses the bill of materials file to identify the parts, materials, and their quantities, needed to manufacture the end item in the master production schedule. In order to schedule both manufacture and purchases, the MRP file needs to obtain two further pieces of information.

The first is information on when manufacture or purchase of each part should be scheduled so that the end item can be made available when it is required. To ensure that each component will be available in time to support the master schedule, each manufactured or purchased part needs to be offset (i.e. ordered earlier) by the amount of time it takes to get the part (the lead time). Each component's lead time is accessed from the BOM file and, through the file knowing from the MRP schedule when the item is required, the file then uses a scheduling process to *schedule backward* in time by the item's lead time. Thus the MRP file can determine when manufacture or purchase of each item should be scheduled. This process of backward scheduling is shown in Fig 6.4.

The second piece of information required is the amount needed of each manufactured or purchased item. To arrive at this figure, the MRP file accesses the inventory file to obtain information on the 'on-hand' quantities of parts and materials. It calculates the difference between this amount and the quantity of end items required, indicated by the BOM file as *gross requirements,* to arrive at a *net requirements* figure for the materials and parts. This process of determining the net requirements, from knowing what is on hand and what the gross requirements are, is also shown in Fig 6.4. The execution of the MRP program therefore results in a complete list of the parts and materials that need to be ordered, and a shop schedule showing what is required and when it is required to be manufactured.

Lot-sizing rules

The computer logic for MRP requires that a lot-sizing rule be preassigned to each item before the system can compute planned receipts and planned order releases. A lot-sizing rule determines the timing and size of order quantities. Although many types of rules may be used, they can be categorised as either static or dynamic. For a detailed explanation of these rules refer to Krajewski and Ritzman.

Safety stock

An important managerial issue is the quantity of safety stock required. Safety stock is more valuable when there is considerable uncertainty about future gross requirements or the timing or size of scheduled receipts. Consequently, the usual policy is to maintain safety stock for end items (at the master production scheduling level) and purchased items. This approach protects against fluctuating customer orders at the top of the BOM and unreliable suppliers at the bottom.

DEVELOPMENT OF MRP

Basic MRP

The system just discussed is a 'basic MRP' system in which the schedules determined are not compared with the capacities available on the shopfloor to ascertain where overloads or underloads may exist. The system will load the work onto the shop assuming infinite capacity is available. However, capacity planning is performed. First, the production plan is checked against aggregate capacity, and then a process called 'rough-cut capacity planning' is used where the MPS is checked against the capacity to see if it is achievable or if it needs adjusting.

Closed-loop MRP

Closed-loop MRP works in the same way as basic MRP but it also has the facility to plan for shopfloor capacities. In this system, the orders resulting from parts explosion are checked to see whether sufficient capacity is available. If there is not enough capacity, either the capacity or the master schedule is changed. The system has a feedback loop between the orders launched and the master schedule to adjust for capacity availability. As a result, this type of MRP system is called a closed-loop system; it controls both inventories and capacity.

If sufficient manufacturing and vendor capacity is available to meet the orders resulting from parts explosion, the MRP system will produce a valid plan for procurement

	WEEK 1	2	3	4	5	6
Desk						
Gross requirements	–	–	–	200	150	100
On-hand/scheduled receipts	50	–	–	–	–	–
Net requirements	–	–	–	150	150	100
Planned order releases	–	–	150	150	100	–
Top						
Gross requirements	–	–	150	150	100	–
On-hand/scheduled receipts	50	50	–	–	–	–
Net requirements	–	–	50	150	100	–
Planned order releases	50	150	100	–	–	–
Leg and panel assembly						
Gross requirements	–	–	150	150	100	–
On-hand/scheduled receipts	100	–	–	–	–	–
Net requirements	–	–	50	150	100	–
Planned order releases	–	50	150	100	–	–
Legs						
Gross requirements	–	200	600	400	–	–
On-hand/scheduled receipts	150	100	–	–	–	–
Net requirements	–	–	550	400	–	–
Planned order releases	–	550	400	–	–	–
Modesty panel						
Gross requirements	–	100	300	200	–	–
On-hand/scheduled receipts	50	–	–	–	–	–
Net requirements	–	50	300	200	–	–
Planned order releases	50	300	200	–	–	–

Fig 6.4 MRP backward scheduling and determination of net requirements

and manufacturing actions. If sufficient capacity is not available, it will be necessary to replan the master schedule or to change the capacity. In this way, the capacity-planning facility of closed-loop MRP provides accurate loading information and gives visibility of future load. Both the basic MRP and closed-loop MRP capacity management processes are depicted in Fig 6.5.

Manufacturing resource planning MRP or MRP II

Manufacturing resource planning (MRP), sometimes referred to as MRP II, a term coined by Wight, uses the MRP process just described to feed information to or drive other systems in the company, such systems being cash, personnel, facilities, and capital equipment, as shown in Fig 6.6.

The case for an MRP system manager

MRP II provides a valuable resource, that of information, which needs to be managed accordingly. According to Walter, modern, progressive companies doing business in an MRP environment should have an MRP system manager (MSM) position. This should be a full-time job and the manager should report at least to director level if not

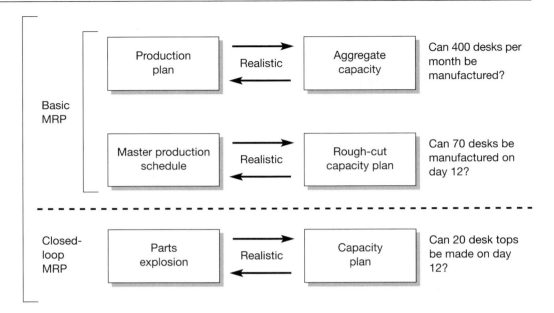

Fig 6.5 Basic MRP and closed-loop MRP

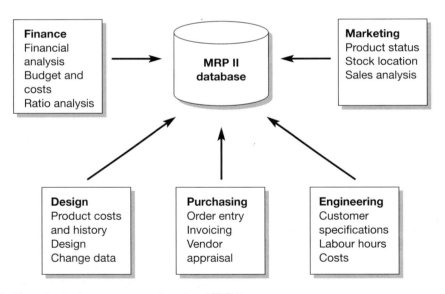

Fig 6.6 Manufacturing resource planning MRP II

to a vice president. The MSM should be independent of all operating departments in the manner of the quality assurance function. Exhibit 6.6 presents Walter's case for an MRP system manager.

Exhibit 6.6

The case for an MRP system manager

The MSM would be responsible for trouble-shooting the MRP II system itself, including isolating hardware, software, management process, policies, and procedures etc. As a major adjunct to this role, he or she would chair meetings at least once a month, if not weekly, on every product line with the representatives from every functional organisation involved present.

The MSM would evaluate the status (health monitor) of the MRP system in support of each program, employing meaningful criteria addressing key elements of the system itself. The analysis and solution to every serious MRP system operating problem aired at such meetings would be specifically assigned to individuals of the appropriate organisation(s), and progress towards solution reported on at each subsequent meeting until a solution is obtained. These meetings would service further as an early-warning system of emerging problems before they create a crisis.

The MSM would be responsible for staying current on the latest state-of-the-art in MRP II systems (hardware, software, management science etc.), making recommendations to senior management regarding system improvements. (This would include, when appropriate, examination of potential requirements for additional or alternative management systems such as JIT or synchronous manufacturing.) These recommendations should be followed regarding selection of outside MRP consulting and education organisations and services to be brought in on occasion. The MSM would be responsible for all MRP-related education and training programmes, including in-house continuing education programmes.

The MRP system manager would thus be a very important position, serving an extremely important role in assuring the initial and continuing success of the company MRP system. It would require an uniquely educated and experienced individual to do the job justice; someone who ideally would have sought to become a management generalist, comfortable with interfacing with engineering, marketing, sales, finance, production, materials management, procurement etc. Such a person would also have to be an expert in the MRP process and automated systems. It should be apparent that this role calls for a people-oriented individual – one skilled in the diplomatic approach of persuasion – rather than someone with a political or authoritarian-oriented personality.

The need for an MRP system manager is perhaps one of the most important lessons to have come out of the MRP 'school of hard knocks' in recent years. It is a lesson which should stimulate creation of this job position on the organisation chart of every company committed to doing business in an MRP environment.

Source: Adapted from Walter, W. C., 'Case for an MRP system manager', *Production and Inventory Management Journal*. Reprinted with permission of APICS – The Educational Society for Resource Management, Falls Church, Virginia. *Production and Inventory Management Journal*, 2nd Quarter, pp. 74–6, 1990.

MAKING A SUCCESS OF MRP

In order to make MRP successful, new responsibilities and roles will need to be realised by people both within and outside the manufacturing function. This will require much communication, education and training at all levels within the company.

According to Schroeder (1993), research indicates that five elements are required for success:

- implementation planning
- adequate computer support
- accurate data
- management support
- education and user knowledge.

Implementation planning

Implementation planning should be a prerequisite to any MRP effort. Unfortunately, too many companies jump in and start implementing MRP without adequate preparation. Later, confusion and misunderstanding occur as problems arise. Implementation planning can help smooth out implementation efforts by advance planning and problem-prevention efforts. Implementation planning should include education of senior management, selection of a project manager, appointment of an implementation team representing all parts of the company, preparation of objectives, identification of expected benefits and costs, and a detailed action plan. The plan should set production and system targets as well as responsibilities and measures of performance. Only after the plan is prepared should selection of hardware and software, improvement of data accuracy, and other implementation activities begin. By being thorough in this way, wrong expectations, such as lack of awareness of expected costs, benefits, changes and difficulties, may be avoided.

Adequate computer support

Adequate computer support is probably one of the easiest elements of MRP to implement, but inadequate computer support – inappropriate systems and unsatisfactory software and hardware – count high on the reasons for failure of MRP. Today, there are hundreds of MRP software packages on the market. Many companies use these standard packages rather than writing their own.

Accurate data

An MRP system requires accurate data, which can be very difficult to obtain. Many companies are accustomed to lax record keeping in manufacturing because the company has always been managed by the informal system, but accurate data are required when decisions are made from information supplied by the computer.

A company that does not have an MRP system will need to create accurate bills of material (BOMs) as a first step. In some cases, the BOMs are in such poor condition that the company literally has to start over from the beginning. In other cases, the BOMs may be relatively accurate and require only some updating. Once the BOMs are accurate, a system will be needed to keep them that way. This will require an engineering change co-ordinator who is in charge of all changes to the BOM.

Inventory records must also be accurate to support the MRP system. The initial accuracy of inventory records may be somewhat better than that of the BOMs, but inventory record keeping will need improvement too. The best way to improve and maintain the accuracy of inventory records is to install a system of cycle counting.

All other MRP system data, such as shop routings, shopfloor status and costs, must be initially screened for errors and then maintained in an acceptable state of accuracy. Keeping MRP data accurate for system integrity is one of the most important tasks in operating an MRP system.

Management support

The importance of management support to the successful MRP system can hardly be overemphasised. Many studies have shown that top management support is the key to successful implementation of systems.

Management support, however, requires more than lip service and passive support on the manager's part. 'Management participation' or 'leadership' would be a better phrase. Top managers must be actively involved in installing and operating the MRP system. They must give their time and they must change the way they operate the company. If top managers make changes, then the climate is set for other managers also to make the changes required by the MRP system. The ultimate change required by managers at all levels is to *use* the system and not to override it by using the informal system.

Education and user knowledge

Education should involve everyone up to and including the senior management. Emphasis should be on adequate user knowledge at all levels of the company. An MRP system requires an entirely new approach to manufacturing. All company employees must understand how they will be affected and grasp their new roles and responsibilities. In beginning the installation of MRP, only a few key managers need to be educated, but as the system begins to be used, all supervisors, middle managers and top managers need to understand MRP, including managers inside and outside of manufacturing. As the MRP system is broadened in scope, so too must the level of education within the company.

A favourable environment for MRP

Some companies do not adopt an MRP system, or are disappointed with its results, and according to Cerveny and Scott the manufacturing environment of some companies does not give MRP a distinct advantage over other systems. They identified four environmental characteristics which are particularly important:

1 **Number of BOM levels**. The greatest users of MRP are those industries which tend to have many BOM levels.
2 **Magnitude of lot sizes**. The relative superiority of MRP is greater with more BOM levels and larger lot sizes.
3 **Volatility**. A highly volatile manufacturing environment that management cannot stabilise is less likely to achieve large MRP savings.
4 **Manufacturing's positioning strategy.** MRP seems to be most attractive to firms that have positioned themselves with an intermediate strategy. They produce in batches, experience low- to medium-demand volumes, tend to offer a number of product options, and make products that have relatively short life cycles.

THE BENEFITS OF MRP

The benefits of MRP can be numerous and include:

- increased sales
- reduced sales prices
- reduced inventory
- better customer service and better response to market demands
- possibility of considering batch sizes, safety stock and lead times so as to make improvements
- advance notice so managers can see the planned schedule before actual release of orders
- ability to change the master schedule and to see the effect of changing the master schedule, therefore aiding capacity planning, prioritising orders, and expediting
- reduced set-up and tear-down costs
- increased productivity of labour
- increased productivity of plant
- reduced idle time
- reduced costs of quality
- reduced transport costs
- product structure clarity.

An illustration of two companies experiencing success through pursuing an MRP initiative is presented in Exhibit 6.7.

JUST-IN-TIME (JIT)

Just-in-time (JIT) is a philosophy concerned with the provision of products and services only when they are needed or 'just-in-time' for use by either internal or external customers. Initially developed by the Japanese, the aim is to ensure that the correct quantities are purchased and made at the right time with little or no waste. JIT started through the Japanese seeking ways of reducing the large set-up times involved in the manufacture of car body components. In solving this problem they found that batch sizes could be reduced, and that processes and the people within them could be linked closer together. This resulted in dramatic reductions in throughput time and inventory. It also meant that there was less margin for error, and weaknesses and problems in production, quality or equipment would surface quickly and would have to be solved quickly. This required a smarter, versatile workforce. In effect, by adopting the JIT philosophy, an improvement circle began with an improvement in one area facilitating and demanding improvement in another. The whole concept of JIT soon spread to incorporate the suppliers and led to the lean and efficient movement of material through the factory to the customers.

The aims of JIT

The aim of JIT is to improve overall productivity and reduce waste. It provides for the cost-effective production and delivery of only the necessary quality parts, in the right quantity, at

Exhibit 6.7

Company use of MRP

Example 1 Westair Reproductions Ltd[1]

Westair Reproductions Ltd makes and buys components which are assembled into products for the heritage and tourist trade. These are sold to many tourist sites in the UK and overseas.

In 1993, with sales expanding rapidly, the company operated out of two adjacent shop fronts on a hill in the Birmingham suburbs. The process can best be described as 'controlled chaos'. The willingness of the team overcame stresses of customer dissatisfaction with deliveries, quality problems, stock and space shortages and over-stocking. Cash flow and resources prevented an immediate move to more suitable premises.

The first task was to get sales and stocks in line. An MRP system was introduced and a short-term racking system for warehousing was designed internally to improve space utilisation. Training was instituted in MRP, JIT and quality techniques and a Kanban system introduced to supplement the MRP. The controls exercised allowed sales growth to continue, stock turns and customer services measures started to improve. It was realised they could not cope in these conditions for another peak season. Suitable new premises were located within two miles.

Results continue to be dramatic:

- Sales have more than doubled in two years
- Stock turns have doubled: there is less stock than two years ago
- Customers are openly complimentary on service and turn around times; one USA order was achieved by customising unit sizes to the customer's needs, without disruption to the Westair system; the US company has become a major customer
- The best change has been in the employees; from a sceptical start, they have gone to believing in the company
- Assembly productivity has improved 25% in one year
- Most lead times are being reduced steadily
- Commonality has been increased to make further savings.

Everyone realises that controls and parameters are still being tightened, the key being that customer service is improved. Suppliers are being brought into partnership, with forward visibility and Kanbans. Change is no longer seen in a fearful light, because employees can see how far they have travelled in two years.

Example 2 Landoll Corporation[2]

Landoll Corporation, operating in a job-shop environment is using MRP successfully.

The process of implementing MRP took place over a two-year period. The concepts utilised at the company to make MRP provide more accurate and timely information include:

- The development of reliable vendors who have the ability to deliver on time
- The reduction of vendor lead times through more active partnership participation
- A decrease of manufacturing lead times through reviewing move times and queue times
- The development of engineering that is integrated with the balance of the manufacturing system in such a way that engineering is aware of its impact
- The implementation of manufacturing self-inspection which improved our responsiveness to errors and error correction.

It is important to note, however, that the success of MRP in a job-shop environment is greatly dependent upon the attitudes of executive and middle-level management that operate in any company, especially job shops. Although a state of complete implementation of a closed-loop MRP II systems was not fully achieved, the company significantly accomplished what it started out to do, i.e. successfully implemented MRP and shop floor control in a job-shop environment.

[1] *Source*: Fredericks, M., 'MRP into the next century', *Logistics Focus*. Reprinted with permission of The Institute of Logistics.
[2] *Source*: Brucker, H. S. and Flowers, G.A., 'MRP shop-floor control in a job shop: Definitely works', *Production and Inventory Management Journal*. Reprinted with permission of APICS – The Educational Society for Resource Management, Falls Church, Virginia. *Production and Inventory Management Journal,* 2nd Quarter, pp. 43–6, 1992.

the right time and place, while using a minimum amount of facilities, equipment, materials and human resources. JIT is accomplished through the application of a range of approaches which require total employee involvement and teamwork.

Many companies use JIT but they may call it something else. For example, IBM and Philips have called their programmes 'Continuous Flow Manufacturing', which is an apt description of the aim of converting production to a continuous process from material receipt to despatch, and then from the supplier to the customer. A thorough consideration of the origins, nature and use of JIT is provided by Schonberger and Harrison.

The fundamental aims of JIT are:

- to produce instantaneously (only as needed)
- to emphasise quality
- to minimise waste
- to make continuous improvements.

Attacking the fundamental problems

The JIT approach of attacking waste and reducing inventories means there is less chance of problems remaining undetected. For example, smaller job batches mean that each production process will have a small amount of work to do before it expects the next job batch. If a process breaks down, then the expected work will not arrive at the next process and production will be halted. This means that any imbalances or problems with production are noticed sooner and have to be addressed so that production can continue. The nature of these problems is shown in Fig 6.7. Possible problems are a high level of work-in-progress causing queues, late deliveries which could turn out to be defective, machine downtime, unstable demand, inaccurate quantities, rework, off standards, untrained operators, poor floor layout, and scrap. Once identified, it becomes imperative to solve and eliminate these problems. In turn, this improves the utilisation of the organisation's main assets, which are its people, capital, inventory and space. This creates a 'virtuous improvement circle' which, as Fig 6.8 shows, is the essence of the JIT philosophy.

What are the wastes?

Kiyoshi Suzaki, in his book *The New Manufacturing Challenge: Techniques for continuous improvement*, discusses drains on effectiveness in operations and refers to the following seven types of waste, which Toyota identify as the most prominent:

1 **Waste from overproduction.** Waste from overproduction is most common. Overproduction waste is typically created by getting ahead of the work. Overproduction creates difficulties that often obscure more fundamental problems. It is necessary to realise that machines and operators do not have to be fully utilised, as long as market demands are met.

2 **Waste of waiting time.** Waiting should be exposed so that corrective action can be taken. Machines should be monitored so that corrective action can be taken quickly whenever a problem arises.

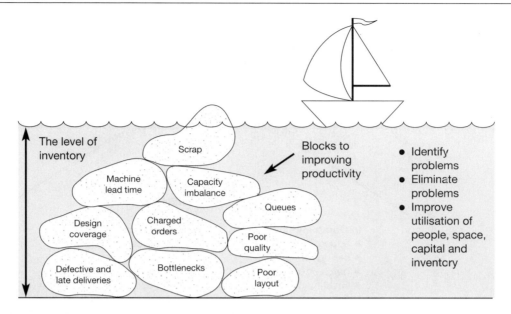

Fig 6.7 Reducing the level of inventory (water) exposes the blocks to productivity

3 **Transportation waste.** Double or triple handling can be a problem. For example, incoming material may be stored in the warehouse before it is brought to the line. Ill-planned layouts may make long-distance transportation necessary.

4 **Processing waste.** The processing method itself may be a source of problems which could be solved to make the job safer, easier and faster; for example, through the use of improved job and process design.

5 **Inventory waste**. As with waste of overproduction, excess inventory increases the cost of a product. It requires extra handling, extra space, extra interest charges, extra people, extra paperwork and so on.

6 **Waste of motion.** Time not spent in adding value to the product should be eliminated. It is necessary to bear in mind that 'move' does not necessarily equal 'work'.

7 **Waste from product defects.** When defects occur at one station, operators at subsequent stations waste time waiting. Also, rework may be necessary or the defective products may be scrapped. Other wastes here arise from sorting out bad parts from good parts, defects found after product delivery, and the warranty costs incurred which put future business at risk.

The non-obvious wastes

Schonberger, in his book *Building a Chain of Customers*, discusses the non-obvious wastes which also need to be addressed. They are:

- promotional waste
- waste of tracking the orders
- waste of tracking costs

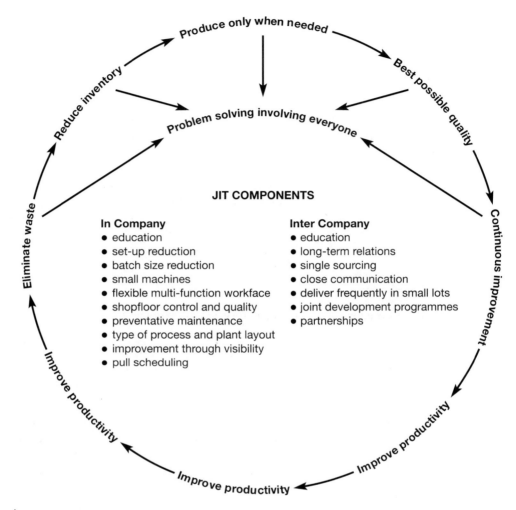

Fig 6.8 JIT virtuous improvement circle

- container-to-container waste
- waste of automating the waste
- waste of analysing the waste
- waste of costing the cost reductions
- waste of costing the bad quality
- waste of reporting on utilisation and efficiency
- unproductive efficiency.

THE COMPONENTS OF JIT

Organisations that practice JIT typically concern themselves with making improve-ments in the company and between companies.

JIT in the company

Here, the objective is to convert the business into a JIT-processing facility through the following areas:

Education

Education in JIT is necessary for employees to understand its value and meaning; also it is necessary to emphasise the benefits of JIT and encourage the employees to think how JIT affects their jobs and what the potential problems may be. Owing to the interlinked technical and people facets and the fact that JIT requires a fundamental change in employees' attitudes, the education process involved should be more comprehensive than that for MRP. Education should involve all employees and operate within and between companies. It should be ongoing, even after JIT implementation has been completed. This will reinforce the JIT philosophy and assist in its continual improvement.

Standardisation/product simplification

With regard to *design,* the focus is to rationalise the company's product lines. Having done this, the engineering for the selected winners would be simplified. The aim is to have a few products with a wide appeal. For *manufacturing,* the emphasis is on ease of manufacture, and this would be sought through moves towards becoming a focused factory or having more focused product lines.

Set-up reduction

Long set-ups are bad; they reduce efficiency and encourage increased batch sizes, which gives rise to high inventory levels, increasing the risk of obsolescence and reducing the flexibility in the process. Set-up time can be reduced by redesign to streamline or eliminate any set-up adjustment processes. It may be possible to separate the internal set-up from the external set-up and convert as much as possible of the former to the latter.

Batch size reduction and lower buffer stocks

Through set-up time reductions, process improvements, and waste reduction, it should be possible to reduce batch sizes and buffer stocks.

Small machines

The benefit of several small machines replacing one large machine is that they can be used to support focused product lines, thus improving flexibility. The aim in using these smaller machines is to reduce set-ups, handling, and WIP and to improve responsiveness.

Flexible, multi-function workforce

The objective here is to promote flexibility through having a flexible workforce. The Japanese refer to this as *shojinka* and, being flexible, the workers are free to move from low-demand to high-demand areas. This can be achieved by payment schemes, extensive cross-training and having a smaller number of job grades.

Shopfloor control with emphasis on quality and improvement

JIT seeks to change the shopfloor culture by putting the responsibility on the employee to solve problems and maintain quality at source. This can be facilitated through the use of suggestion schemes, using productivity circles, and reducing the number of command levels in the hierarchy.

Preventative maintenance

The reduction in waste – for example, reduction in buffer stocks and excess capacity – emphasises a greater need for preventative maintenance and improved reliability, which become important as a means of reducing the incidence of breakdowns and the level of downtime. Many companies have decentralised their maintenance and, as far as possible, have let the operators become responsible for routine work. To facilitate this, training is required, but the ownership of the care of their equipment has improved the operators' morale.

Type of process and plant layout

For many companies it is often possible to simplify their processes by moving from their traditional process layout to flow lines, each with a limited range on each line. In effect they become mini factories or focused product lines. This can be achieved through the use of group technology (GT) to identify product families, which will in turn facilitate cellular manufacture, i.e. the grouping of machines and workers by product family. A flexible workforce is necessary here so that the manning levels can rise and fall with product family demand. The use of U-shaped lines or manufacturing cells assists in the drive to reduce manufacturing process length, by bringing processes together and saving space. Finally, the way to make best use of people and to increase automation should be sought.

Improvement through visibility

Here, the objective is to make problems visible and so enforce improvement. This can be achieved through the use of charts, checksheets and an environment that fosters problem solving. Also, the reduced stocks and buffers with JIT allow less margin for errors and mistakes, and problems need to be rectified immediately. Features of JIT such as line-stop authority and undercapacity scheduling mean problems need to be addressed and sorted out quickly.

Process control changes – pull scheduling and level production

With JIT, a pull-type scheduling system is employed as described in Chapter 5. In contrast with a push-type system, the signal to produce parts or withdraw work is indicated by downstream local customer need. In Toyota this system is referred to as 'Kanban scheduling'. In contrast to push-type scheduling, typified by MRP systems,

Kanban scheduling reduces the level of WIP and speeds up the throughput rate, and so problems are soon identified.

Level production should be aimed at by setting the production levels across the sales range in proportion to the sales mix.

Inter-company JIT

This is an extension of the JIT philosophy to the relationships with customers and suppliers. Prominent features of inter-company JIT are:

- education
- long-term relationships
- single sourcing
- close communication
- delivery in small lots at frequent intervals
- joint development programmes
- partnerships.

JIT purchasing

The objective of JIT purchasing is to have parts and materials delivered just-in-time for assembly or processing. This can be achieved through JIT *supply contracts* which encourage *co-operation* between the customer and supplier and strive for more frequent, error-free deliveries with the minimum of paperwork. Cost and disruption are minimised if the *vendor delivers in smaller lots* and is local. This reduces stocks, transport costs, improves flexibility and lessens the risk of large defective deliveries. Purchasing staff are encouraged not to be reactive but to attempt to raise the standards of the vendors' components by careful *choice of vendor*, monitoring their performance and, if possible, assisting them to improve their performance. Since material costs form a large percentage of total costs, large savings can be made through improved purchasing. Companies experience economies of scale, less management problems, better relationships with sounder vendors by *reducing the variety of sources* of supply. A gradual move to *longer-term agreements* with vendors has been found to encourage better relationships, give vendors more security to invest in the company, and provide the best possible service.

Partnerships and improved communications

Partnership between customers and suppliers is an effective way of extending the JIT concept along the supply chain. This, together with the development of improved practices of data communication standards, such as electronic data interchange (EDI), training packages and related activities, can bring great benefits. Ultimately, the whole supply chain from the supplier, through the factory, to the customer should run on JIT principles.

Problems and differences between Japanese and UK parts suppliers to Toyota

Gilgeous and Yamada conducted an interview-based study to examine and rate the problems and differences between two United Kingdom and two Japanese companies which are suppliers to Toyota Motor Manufacturing UK Ltd in Derby. The results are summarised in Exhibit 6.8.

Exhibit 6.8

Problems and differences between Japanese and UK parts suppliers to Toyota

In comparing the practices of Japanese and UK parts suppliers, the fieldwork, the cases and the literature show that many significant differences, as well as similarities, exist. The importance of a JIT philosophy is manifest and in this respect the Japanese manufacturers are anxious that in the short term, as well as the long term, the UK suppliers may not perform as well as their Japanese counterparts.

With respect to the two UK and two Japanese companies studied, it was found that the UK suppliers need to improve their approaches to adding value and cost reduction. There were many similarities between both the Japanese and UK suppliers with regard to the meeting of particular supplier evaluation criteria and the performance of the sales personnel. In particular, the suppliers' good relations with the unions and their attitude towards applying the JIT philosophy bodes well for future relations. Also, since in many cases customers judge vendors by the performance of their sales personnel, both the Japanese and the UK suppliers would benefit by improving performance in this area. With regard to the respective performance of the supplier pyramids, flexibility and quality, then significant differences were observed which should be of concern to the UK suppliers. Also, the UK suppliers' expectation of profits through mutual trust could easily result in adversarial relationships with their customers if their expectations are not fulfilled.

Three propositions were posed as possible solutions to these problems:

1 technical assistance
2 education of subcontractors and lower management
3 more communication.

All three propositions are based on the idea of mutual trust, which Toyota has already established with its Japanese parts suppliers. Hopefully, these basic propositions can address these fundamental problems and, in the long-run, help to support Toyota's transplant operations in the UK.

Source: Adapted from Gilgeous, V. G. and Yamada, Y., 'An interview-based study of two United Kingdom and two Japanese suppliers to Toyota', *International Journal of Production Research*, Vol. 34, No. 6, pp. 1497–1515, 1996. Reproduced by permission of Taylor and Francis.

POTENTIAL BENEFITS OF JIT

There is clear evidence that JIT has been an important component of Japanese manufacturing success. JIT is used by Japanese companies in the UK, and many UK companies that have adopted JIT programmes have made spectacular gains in manufacturing performance. The potential benefits of JIT are numerous and can be classified as 'hard' and 'soft' cost benefits, as Table 6.1 shows.

Table 6.1 Hard and soft cost benefits of JIT

Hard cost benefits	Soft cost benefits
Inventory reduction	Increased sales
Work-in-progress reduction	Increased customer service
Increased productivity	Increased quality
Improved purchasing	Improved visibility
Reduced obsolescence	Multi-function workforce
Reduced transportation costs	Increased flexibility
More space	
Improved maintenance	
Improved layout	
Less scrap	
Standardisation	
Reduced lead times	

Examples of companies benefiting from pursuing JIT initiatives are presented in Exhibit 6.9.

Exhibit 6.9

Company use of JIT

To cope with monthly production mix variations of up to 30% while maintaining economic volumes, Dunlop Cox of Nottingham, car seat slide maker, implemented cellular manufacturing and JIT five years ago. Both techniques now underpin an ability to react flexibly to changes in demand.

As a supplier to another JIT practitioner, Ikeda Hoover, Washington, Tyne & Wear, Dunlop Cox sends seat fixings on nightly shipments. Ikeda has even a shorter call-off time – just 3 hours for supplying complete car seats to Nissan.

Just how vital a good computerised distribution package can be with total JIT is shown by Simmons' experience in America. As a JIT practitioner, Simmons, the mattress makers, come close to perfect JIT production and delivery. Before adopting JIT, the company's distribution was a 'maze and a mess', says Len Smolinski, Simmons' director of transportation and distribution. This make-to-order production and distribution technique has eliminated all 67 warehouses. The average size of the remaining 14 manufacturing plants has been cut from 300,000 ft^2 to 125,000 ft^2. Plant inventory typically consists of 1,000 mattresses being staged and loaded for delivery the next day, compared with 50,000 mattresses previously housed in the plants. As for the private fleet, Simmons now runs 85 tractors, down from 128.

Overall, the JIT programme has cut the freight bill from 6% of sales to only 4.7% and achieved a 99% on-time delivery performance. Market share increased by 4%. The number of tractors and trailers in its private fleet was reduced by more than a third.

Source: Adapted from Redmond, B., 'JIT implementation and support admired, suspected and abused'. *Materials Handling News*, pp. 38–40, April 1992.

IMPLEMENTATION OF JIT

Many companies fail to implement JIT properly because they do not understand what JIT is and what it can mean to them. In particular, they need to know what benefits it may bring and what needs to be done. Most importantly, they need to be aware of the tasks, the resources, the costs and the timescale. O'Grady details five steps to successful implementation of JIT.

Step 1: Getting the ball rolling

This step is depicted in Fig 6.9(a) and comprises the following stages:

- Acquire a basic understanding, make use of JIT champions and provide preliminary education.
- Undertake a cost/benefit analysis to determine both the hard and soft cost benefits.
- Gain top management commitment to authorise investments and appoint a high-quality JIT project team leader. Produce implementation budget, pilot plan and timescale.
- Identify and consider the factors that influence the 'Go' or 'No Go' decision.
- Select JIT project team with a full-time project leader, membership of key people, an aggressive implementation schedule, and regular meetings of all team members.
- Identify the pilot plant – relatively self-contained, representative of other plants, not geographically remote.

Step 2: Education

This needs to be more comprehensive than for MRP since it requires a fundamental change in attitudes. Education should be ongoing, even after JIT implementation is completed because reinforcement helps continual improvement. In- and out-of-company courses should be provided, involving all employees. Encourage employees to consider how JIT might affect their jobs; emphasise benefits and realise potential problems.

Step 3: Improving the process

Attack set-up time reduction; instigate a preventative maintenance programme by getting the shopfloor personnel involved; move further towards flow-line-type manufacture.

Step 4: Improving control

Develop a pull system; consider possible integration with an MRP system to feed information to the early process stages; change the shopfloor culture to obtain the right control; use suggestion schemes, productivity circles, and fewer levels of hierarchy.

Step 5: Supplier/customer links

Improve links with suppliers, monitor them, and improve their performance; gradually move towards single sourcing and longer-term agreements with suppliers;

concentrate on more local and frequent deliveries; cultivate customers to give earlier and firmer schedules of their requirements.

An implementation schedule for Steps 2 to 5 is shown in Figure 6.9(b).

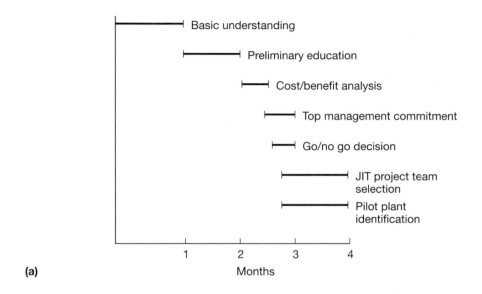

(a)

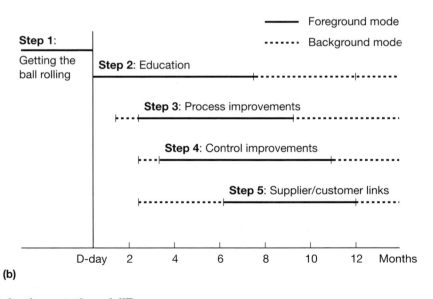

(b)

Fig 6.9 Implementation of JIT
(a) An ideal timescale for Step 1
(b) The proven path to successful JIT

Source: O'Grady, P., *Just-in-Time*, McGraw-Hill.

Potential implementation pitfalls

Implementation will not be possible without the full backing and the commitment of the top management. The move towards JIT will also fail if an adequate education programme is not provided. Process and control improvements, if not carefully planned, will also result in JIT not being realised. This will require dedication and time at the planning stage and may require the use of external assistance in the form of consultants. If all this is not also integrated with moves towards JIT purchasing, then again true JIT will not be accomplished. Finally JIT should not be viewed as a one-off scheme but as an ongoing continuous process.

Choice of JIT or MRP or combined JIT/MRP

Whether JIT is more applicable than MRP depends on the complexity of the product structure and routings, the volume and variety levels of the company's products, and the level of co-ordination and control of material and parts. Where the product structures are simpler and so is the complexity of the product flow paths, JIT is more applicable than MRP. This is illustrated in Fig 6.10. When the variety is high, the volume low, and the level of control high, an MRP system would be more applicable than a JIT system of planning and control. This is illustrated in Fig 6.11. When JIT and MRP are combined, sometimes referred to as 'synchro MRP', scheduling benefits arise. The delay in signalling customer demand changes to earlier upstream operations, that would normally be experienced through JIT pull-type scheduling, can be avoided through MRP pushing work out to them in accordance with the demand changes.

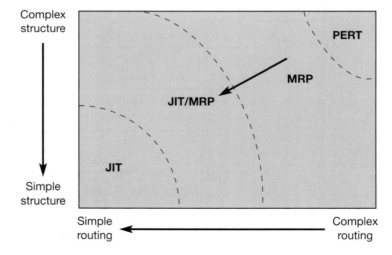

Fig 6.10 JIT and MRP in varying levels of product structure and routing complexity
Source: Voss, C. A. and Harrison, A., 'Strategies for implementing JIT' in Voss, C. A. (ed) *Just-in-time Manufacture*, 1978. Reprinted by permission of IFS International Ltd.

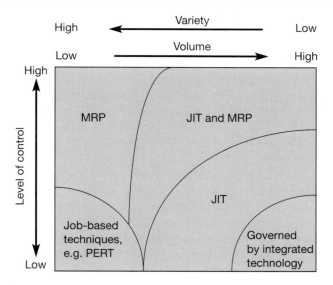

Fig 6.11 JIT and MRP in different volume, variety and control situations
Source: Slack, N., *The Manufacturing Advantage*.

OPTIMISED PRODUCTION TECHNOLOGY (OPT)

Optimised production technology (OPT) was initially developed in Israel by Dr Eli Goldratt during the 1970s. The OPT approach, explained through a fascinating story in a book entitled *The Goal* (written with J. Cox), is concerned with improving productivity to take a company closer to its goal of making money by increasing throughput and decreasing inventory and operating expenses. OPT seeks to do this through the use of an analytical technique which aims to synchronise production to work in accordance with realistic optimised schedules.

The success of OPT is assessed by measuring the three bottom-line financial aspects of shopfloor performance:

1 net profit
2 return on investment
3 cash flow.

Performance criteria

At the operations level, OPT defines three performance criteria which are important in evaluating OPT's progress towards the above financial goals. These criteria are throughput, inventory and operating expenses.

Throughput

In the OPT sense, throughput is the rate at which the manufacturing business generates money by selling finished goods or units. Obviously this is not necessarily a measure of production, since the rate of manufacture of components is not the same as the rate at which finished units are sold. For example, in the manufacture of cars many components are produced as throughput, but money is only generated, apart from spares etc., when finished cars are sold. Increases in throughput will result in a simultaneous increase in net profit, return on investments and cash flow. This is because the business will be selling more finished goods while maintaining a stable level of inventory and operating expenses. This obviously means a greater influx of money, larger profits and earlier recovery of investments.

Inventory

OPT defines inventory to be the raw materials, components and finished goods that have been paid for by the business but have not, as yet, been sold. To avoid confusion with other financial considerations of inventory, this does not include the added value of labour and overhead. For example, the wood and materials in the tops, sides, legs and drawers used to manufacture desks, plus the finished desks in stock at any moment, are all considered as inventory. These are materials that have been paid for and have not yet been converted back into money through the sale of finished desks.

A reduction in inventory directly impacts on return on investment and cash flow. Here, fewer costs are associated with a particular period since the inventory is lower. This improves the flow of money and helps recover investment. Profit is not changed, because the cost of raw material has not changed, and neither has the cost of transforming the raw material into a finished product.

Operating expenses

The costs involved in converting the inventory into the throughput are called 'operating expenses'. They include the cost of the direct and indirect labour, the heating, lighting and production facilities necessary to manufacture and assemble. These expenses need to be recovered by the sale of finished goods or units.

If operating costs are reduced while the inventory and the rate at which the finished products are sold remain unchanged, then increases in cash flow, net profit and return on investment will result.

FEATURES OF OPT

OPT considers activities on the shopfloor to be critical. Therefore, shopfloor issues, such as bottlenecks, set-ups, lot sizes, priorities, random fluctuations and performance measurements, are treated in great depth.

Bottleneck operations

A bottleneck is that operation which limits output in the production sequence. No matter how fast the other operations are, system output can be no faster than the bottleneck. Bottlenecks can occur because of equipment limitations or a shortage of materials, personnel or facilities.

Once a bottleneck is identified, production can be increased by a variety of possible actions:

1 Adding more necessary resources.
2 Using alternate equipment or routing.
3 Reducing set-up time.
4 Running larger lot sizes, thereby reducing the total amount of time spent in set-ups.
5 Clearing up or re-layout of the area.
6 Working overtime.
7 Subcontracting.
8 Delaying due date promises.
9 More investment in equipment and people.

Synchronising manufacture

As stated, no matter how fast the other operations are, system output can be no faster than the bottleneck. Therefore, OPT production is scheduled forward of each bottleneck to establish the end rate of requirement of parts, subassemblies and assemblies. This rate of production, allowing for some slack in the system, is applied to the initial feeding operations to ensure that the pace of upstream operations is the same as the initial operations. This ensures that work is not commenced before it needs to be, since it is in accordance with a realistic schedule. This co-ordinated forward and backward scheduling of production across the whole of the factory, in accordance with a realistic bottleneck schedule, provides 'synchronised manufacturing'. This process is fully explained in *The Race for a Competitive Edge*.

Measuring disruptions

As mentioned, it is important that bottlenecks are fully utilised. To ensure this, checks should be made to establish if there are any disruptions with manufacture which may delay the work planned to be done at a bottleneck. Disruptions to manufacture do occur, which means the actual work in front of the bottleneck is always less than planned, i.e. the work that should be there is not. This is a disruption in manufacture that needs to be filled by that work or some other work. OPT shows how this disruption can be measured in order to establish priorities for managing manufacture. Exhibit 6.10 summarises the experience of a single company which uses OPT software for production scheduling.

As is apparent, OPT challenges many conventional assumptions made about the operation of the shopfloor which OPT's developer, Eli Goldratt, considers are mainly responsible for the poor performance of manufacturing in the past. An excellent and detailed treatment of OPT is given by Chase and Aquilano in a chapter entitled 'Synchronised Manufacturing'.

Exhibit 6.10

Company benefits from the use of OPT production scheduling

Here the operation of OPT in a single company was studied. A product range of over 500 different sizes of a basic component is produced. Bought-out castings form the main raw material. There is no assembly process. Manufacturing facilities consist of a conventional machine shop of about 60 machines.

By applying the principles of OPT, management attention is focused on the two areas where the most significant improvements in productivity can be made – by increasing throughput at the bottleneck and by reducing the disruptions causing the biggest contribution to WIP.

Reduction in stock levels

Stock levels are significantly reduced in the OPT system compared with the manual system. Schedule performance is not directly measured, although the order backlog is monitored. In the case of OPT it is 0.5 days, which compares very favourably with the manual case of 7 days.

Improvement in working environment

It is interesting to observe the general working environment of those involved with the OPT system. There are no regular planning meetings – all the work is carried out by the detailed schedule generated by the OPT system, the phone does not ring incessantly (as witnessed by the author during extensive discussions about the system) and emergency purchase orders are rare.

It is also interesting to seek the opinion of shopfloor workers. From informal soundings it is apparent that a return to the previous manual methods would be unpopular. It is noteworthy that serious stress-related illness such as heart attacks reduced significantly after the introduction of OPT. A less dramatic, but nevertheless important, measure is absenteeism which is significantly less than that at the manually-scheduled shop.

Source: Adapted from Bond, T.C., 'An investigation into the use of OPT production scheduling', *Production Planning and Control*, Vol. 4, No. 4, pp. 399–406, 1993. Reproduced by permission of Taylor & Francis.

OPERATIONS INITIATIVES

Consideration of human resource issues

Exhibit 6.11 provides illustrations to show that companies cannot simply put in place the initiatives discussed without carefully attending to a number of human resource issues such as training and skills, co-operation and involvement, and overall work culture.

Exhibit 6.11

Consideration of human resource issues

The Australian companies studied below have attempted to improve manufacturing effectiveness via new systems. They must have, as part of the implementation, consultation with the workforce and the commitment and involvement of the whole workforce . . . Managers must work to dispel fear of redundancy and fear of change itself on the part of the shopfloor staff.

Dowell Remcraft employs around 200 people and manufactures wooden window and door frames.

An electrical engineering company employs about 400 people and is a major manufacturer of low-voltage electrical switchgear.

Trico (Australia) employs nearly 200 people and manufactures windscreen wiper assemblies for the automotive industry.

DeZurik of Australia Pty Ltd employs around 55 people and manufactures valves for process industries such as chemicals, mining, and petroleum refining.

W.A. Deutscher – Metal Products Group designs, manufactures and markets a range of speciality self-drilling and thread-forming screws.

Ramset Fasteners supplies a range of more than 3000 items to the non-dwelling construction industry and the home handyman. Products include fastening systems, drilling and anchoring systems, adhesives and sealants.

These studies show that there is an imbalance between the relative importance of system design and characterisation and the people/implementation issues. The content issues of these initiatives are now relatively well understood and the human performance and related cultural issues thus become the success factors or constraints requiring further understanding.

Source: Adapted from Samson, D., Sohal, A. and Ramsay, E., 'Human resource issues in manufacturing improvement initiatives: Case study experiences in Australia', *The International Journal of Human Factors in Manufacturing*, Vol. 3, No. 2, pp. 135–52, 1993. Reprinted by permission of John Wiley & Sons, Inc.

The choice of initiative: TQM, MRP, JIT or OPT?

Which is the best initiative to use: TQM, MRP, JIT or OPT? Managing operations and change successfully cannot depend on only one of them. An organisation must draw from the entire gamut to extract what makes particular sense for them. According to Ptak, as Exhibit 6.12 illustrates, there is no quick fix. The solution for one company is not necessarily the answer for all industries or even all companies within an industry.

Exhibit 6.12

Combinations of TQM, MRP, JIT and OPT as solutions

Some American manufacturers have recognised the urgency of the decline in the manufacturing base and have responded with their own home-grown, tailored combinations of these concepts. The efforts of Hewlett Packard, John Deere, and Harley-Davidson with JIT are well known. The Harris Corporation continues to refine and spread its own version of JIT through all its operations. Bausch and Lomb has refined the logistics of computerised stock replenishment and order picking of contact lenses with impressive efficiency. There is virtually no paperwork in existence until the final packing step. The computer even determines in what sequence and location the lenses are stocked, with consideration given to units sold, maximisation of available space, and rotation of stock. The Campbell Soup Company has implemented a form of OPT by flattening its organisational structure. It utilises its managers as long-term process-improvement facilitators by focusing on the bottlenecks of the process. They realised they could track to a micron how much everything costs while in the plant, but the time spent (four hours) was not the best use of talent. They have begun to construct smaller, regional manufacturing plants that are closer to major sources of supply or customers, thus increasing responsiveness to the customer while reducing carrying costs.

These companies compete in an aggressive world market and are succeeding. A common thread throughout these dramatic changes and improvements is that the changes came from inside. Some outside help was used at the start, but the final fit and structure came from within. The driving force to continue to improve and try new ideas is fostered as part of the company culture. These companies did not stop at the boundaries of one concept or philosophy, but crossed and mixed ideas until the blend was right for them.

TQM, MRP, JIT and OPT are not just the latest fad or a mix of meaningless letters.

Source: Adapted from Ptak, C.A., 'MRP, MRP II, OPT, JIT and CIM – Succession, evolution, or necessary combination', *Production and Inventory Management Journal*.

SUMMARY

- Total quality management (TQM) has evolved from the days of just inspecting the quality of products to quality now being a strategic issue where the culture of an organisation is that of everyone and every process in the organisation being involved in improving quality. The people, referred to as the 'quality gurus', who have influenced the area of quality are Dr W Edwards-Deming, Dr J M Juran, Philip B Crosby, Dr Kaoru Ishikawa and Genichi-Taguchi. The importance of quality is reflected by prestigious awards such as the Deming Prize, the Malcolm Baldridge National Quality Award and the European Quality Award.

- MRP can stand for material requirements planning or manufacturing resource planning. Both make use of the computer to plan and control the business's resources. Essentially, they reconcile the supply and demand of resources by providing the means to make decisions concerning the volume and timing of materials flow in dependent-demand conditions, i.e. where the materials are dependent on demand for higher-level parts and components which comprise the end item or product required by the customer. Founders of the process of MRP are Oliver Wight and Joseph Orlicky.

● Just-in-time (JIT) is a philosophy concerned with the provision of quality products and services only when they are needed or 'just-in-time' for use by either internal or external customers. Initially developed by the Japanese, the aim is to ensure that the correct quantities are purchased and made at the right time with little or no waste. By adopting the JIT philosophy, a 'virtuous improvement circle' can begin with an improvement in one area facilitating and demanding improvement in another. The whole concept of JIT soon spread to incorporate the suppliers and the lean and efficient movement of material through the factory to the customers.

● Optimised production technology (OPT) as a scheduling approach and associated software was initially developed in Israel by Dr Eli Goldratt during the 1970s. The OPT approach is concerned with improving productivity to take a company closer to its goal of making money by increasing throughput and decreasing inventory and operating expenses. The approach looks at what stops production being synchronised in terms of the bottlenecks which disrupt the flow of production. The intention is to get the entire production process working together in a synchronised way in accordance with realistic optimised schedules, so that all resources are co-ordinated to achieve the goals of the firm. In this way, total system performance is sought, not localised performance measures such as labour or machine utilisation.

REVIEW AND DISCUSSION QUESTIONS

1 Examine how total quality management (TQM) has evolved and the particular ways in which the 'quality gurus', namely, Dr W Edwards-Deming, Dr J M Juran, Philip B Crosby, Dr Kaoru Ishikawa and Genichi Taguchi, have influenced this process.

2 Outline the changes you think need to be made to particular processes, people, systems and structure in your organisation (a typical organisation) to make material requirements planning (MRP) a success.

3 Describe three in-company and three inter-company components of just-in-time (JIT) and explain how each can provide benefits to both the company and the customer.

4 Outline the main features of optimised production technology (OPT) that are used to synchronise manufacture and explain how the ten rules of OPT assist in this process.

ASSIGNMENTS

1 As director of quality in your organisation, the CEO intends to give you full backing for the development of a total quality management (TQM) initiative. He now expects you to explain the main things you plan to do to achieve this objective. What will you say to him?

2 As the head of a just-in-time (JIT) implementation team in your company, your job is to brief the new incumbents on the activities and changes that need to be made and explain to them what the main pitfalls to the programme could be. Discuss the details of your brief.

REFERENCES

Bond, T.C., 'An investigation into the use of OPT production scheduling', *Production Planning and Control*, Vol. 4, No. 4, pp. 399–406, 1993.

Brucker, H. S. and Flowers, G. A., 'MRP shop-floor control in a job shop: Definitely works', *Production and Inventory Management Journal*, pp. 43–6, 2nd Quarter 1992.

Bush, D. and Dooley, K., *The Deming Prize and Baldridge Award: How do they compare quality progress?*, American Society for Quality Control, pp. 28–30, January 1989.

Cerveny, R.P. and Scott, L.W., 'A survey of MRP implementation', *Production and Inventory Management Journal*, Vol. 13, No. 3, pp. 31–4, 1989.

Chase, R.B. and Aquilano, N.J., *Production and Operations Management: Manufacturing and services*, 7th edn, Richard D. Irwin Inc., London 1995.

Coyne, B., 'Land Rover – Heading in the right direction', *Quality Today*, pp. 10–12, March 1995.

Crosby, P.B., *Quality is Free*, McGraw-Hill, New York, 1979.

Crosby, P.B., *Quality Without Tears*, McGraw-Hill, New York, 1984.

'D2D – Beating the best', *Quality Today*, pp. 8–9, January 1995.

Deming, W.E., *Out of the Crisis*, MIT Centre for Advanced Engineering Study, Cambridge, Mass., 1986.

Deming, W.E., *Quality, Productivity and Competitive Position*, MIT Centre for Advanced Engineering Study, Cambridge, Mass., 1982.

Feigenbaum, A.V., *Total Quality Control*, 3rd edn, McGraw-Hill, New York, 1983.

Foster, M. and Whittle, S., 'The quality management maze', *TQM Magazine*, Vol.1, No.3, pp. 143–8, 1989.

Fredericks, M., 'MRP into the Next Century', *Logistics Focus*, pp. 36–7, June 1995.

Gilgeous, V.G. and Yamada, Y., 'An interview-based study of two United Kingdom and two Japanese suppliers to Toyota', *International Journal of Production Research*, Vol. 34, No. 6, pp. 1497–1515, 1996.

Goldratt, E.M. and Cox, J., *The Goal: Excellence in manufacturing*, 2nd revised edn, North River Press, Crotton on Hudson, New York, 1992.

Goldratt, E.M. and Cox, J., *The Race for a Competitive Edge,* Creative Output, Millford, CT, 1986.

Harrison, A., *Just-in-Time in Perspective*, Prentice Hall, London, 1992.

Institute of Personnel Management, 'Total quality management', Fact sheet 29, Institute of Personnel Management, London, May 1990.

Ishikawa, K., *Guide to Quality Control,* Asian Productivity Organisation, 1972.

Juran, J.M., *Juran on Planning for Quality*, The Free Press, New York, 1988.

Juran, J.M., *Quality Control Handbook*, 3rd edn, McGraw-Hill, New York, 1979.

Kiyoshi, S., *The New Manufacturing Challenge: Techniques for continuous improvement*, The Free Press, New York, 1987.

Krajewski, L.J. and Ritzman, L.P., *Operations Management: Strategy and analysis*, 3rd edn, pp. 655–8, Addison-Wesley, Wokingham, 1993.

Luthans, F., Hodgetts, R. and Lee, S., 'New paradigm organizations: From total quality to learning to world class', *Organizational Dynamics*, Vol. 22, No. 3, pp. 5–19, 1994.

Markland, R. E., Vickery, S. K. and Davis, R.A., *Operations Management: concepts in manufacturing and services*, West Publishing Company, St. Paul, Minn., 1995.

O'Grady, P., *Just-in-Time*, McGraw-Hill, New York, 1992.

Orlicky, J., *Material Requirements Planning*, McGraw-Hill, New York, 1975.

Ploughman, B. (Director and Partner), 'Quantifying total quality, Devilin and Partners Ltd', Paper presented at 'Administrating Total Quality: The Challenge for the 1990s', Conference at Bournemouth High Cliff Hotel, Bournemouth, 23–25 May 1990.

Ptak, C.A., 'MRP, MRP II, OPT, JIT and CIM – Succession, evolution, or necessary combination', *Production and Inventory Management Journal*, 2nd Quarter, pp. 7–11, 1993.

Redmond, B., 'JIT implementation and support admired, suspected and abused', *Materials Handling News*, pp. 38–40, April 1992.

Samson, D., Sohal, A. and Ramsay, E., 'Human resource issues in manufacturing improvement initiatives: Case study experiences in Australia', *The International Journal of Human Factors in Manufacturing*, Vol. 3, No. 2, pp. 135–52, 1993.

Schonberger, R., *Japanese Manufacturing Techniques*, The Free Press, New York, 1982.

Schonberger, R., *Building a Chain of Customers*, The Free Press, New York, 1990.

Schroeder, R.G., *Operations Management: Decision making in the operations function*, 4th edn, pp. 645–7, McGraw-Hill, New York, 1993.

Taguchi, G., *Introduction to Quality Engineering: Designing quality into products and process*, Asian Productivity Organisation, 1986.

Voss, C.A. and Harrison A., 'Strategies for implementing JIT' in Voss, C.A. (ed), *Just-in-time Manufacture*, IFS Springer-Verlag, 1978.

Walter, W. C., 'Case for an MRP system manager', *Production and Inventory Management Journal*, 2nd Quarter, pp. 74–6, 1990.

Wight, O., *Manufacturing Resource Planning: MRP II*, Oliver Wight Ltd, 1984.

PART 4

The people in the change process

CHAPTER 7

The people in the change process

OBJECTIVES

The objectives of this chapter are to:

- **examine how the sponsors, the change champions and the change players are involved in and can affect the successful achievement of change in an organisation**
- **appreciate styles of leadership, systems of management and management by objectives in order to understand the possible ways the sponsors and the change champions can effectively manage the change process**
- **gain an understanding of quality of working life programmes, job enrichment, the Investors in People initiative and principles of workforce management as systems of management practice that enable players to be effective.**

PEOPLE IN THE CHANGE PROCESS

The people who are involved or affected by the management of the operations and the associated changes made in the organisation are the sponsors, the change champions and the change players. The sponsors of change are those who have the authority and responsibility to command that certain changes be made. The change champions are those who plan and support these changes. The change players are those who in their daily lives have to experience and cope with the changes. The relationship between the sponsors, the change champions and the change players is depicted in Fig 7.1.

CHANGE SPONSORS

Change sponsors are those who have the authority to decide who should carry out the changes, and they bear the responsibility of seeing that the right people with the right skills are chosen and supported. Change sponsors are not just the most senior people in the organisation. They can exist at all levels in the organisation, provided the sponsors senior to them have adequately devolved responsibility and authority to them. In doing this they need to establish the framework or boundaries within which change is intended to take place. They should also ensure that the constraints within which the change champions are operating are understood. They then need to work on creating an environment of change and allow the people delegated with the responsibility for change the freedom to manage and develop with little interference. This requires the sponsors to set an example of their commitment to change programmes by providing their time and support and making efforts to ensure that the conditions and resources

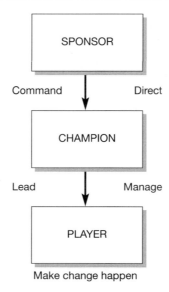

Fig 7.1 The relationship between the sponsors, the change champions and the change players

for change are made available. The sponsor should consider ways in which the change champion's personal development can be assisted, and reward and recognition should be given for any achievements. This should include feedback on the progress of the change programme and appraisal of the change champion.

The following is a summary of three key areas in which LaMarsh considers sponsors need to be effective:

Understanding the changes they are making

This means an in-depth and broad understanding of the intended future state, defining its boundaries and establishing where there is, or is not, room for flexibility. A clear picture of the change process should be presented, showing how the different changes integrate to achieve the future vision. This would show what changes need to be made in structure, process, people and culture; the skills and abilities people will need and the ways in which the managers will have to change.

Of particular importance is assessing the effects the intended actions will have on people, particularly the ways in which resistance might be marshalled to combat the changes.

Managing the resources required for the change

Change costs money and the sponsors need to understand the implications of not fully funding changes. Change also takes time, and in the planning process the consequences of adopting an aggressive change schedule, as against that of a more measured, cautionary approach, or somewhere in between, needs to be known. For example, how will the pace of change affect potential resistance? To what extent is the understanding, information and knowledge, necessary for the success of the change programme, compromised by a faster pace?

Sponsors must support the change champions by providing them with the necessary resources to make the changes. This will require providing training and adequate rewards. A crucial decision here is how much resource drain the organisation can tolerate for the benefits the change champions will bring.

Dealing with people involved in the change

The ability to deal with and work with people successfully is critical to a sponsor. This requires understanding what will happen to people in a change, communicating to them the intended changes, and providing time to listen to their reactions. Besides leading in terms of making decisions and being risk takers themselves, the sponsors also need to demonstrate that they have faith in others doing likewise. From failure, lessons need to be learnt and those involved should be counselled, given advice and encouraged to try again with, if necessary, the support of coaching. The sponsors should also know when to work as partners with the change champions and when to get out of the way.

CHANGE CHAMPIONS

The change sponsor needs to appoint a change champion with the right qualities to lead and manage the change programme. He or she must be able to influence and gain support from more senior managers and peers. In this sense, the change champions are also sponsors of change, since they may be expected to initiate change and also take responsibility. At the same time, they have to lead and motivate the players to ensure that the change programme is worked according to plan. Since they too will be affected by the change, they in turn will become players in the change process. The main duties of the change champion will include determining what needs to be changed with respect to culture, people, structures and processes in the company. The effect of the changes will need to be assessed and areas of resistance from the players will need to be tackled. This will require listening to people's concerns, counselling people, coaching people and developing teams and individuals to assist them to make the necessary changes. The champion will also need to be responsible for establishing a system which monitors progress.

The change champion may be appointed from within or outside the organisation:

Appointed from within the organisation

An organisation may appoint a change champion from within its ranks. Archetypal appointees are persons with a good track record who have been assessed by the change sponsor as having the right qualities to lead the envisaged change programme. The person chosen will probably know the business inside-out, which could be advantageous. The down side is that this person will be steeped in the existing ways, values and practices of the organisation, and their thinking on change may be constrained and they may lack the innovation which the organisation needs to move forward. Alternatively, a person lower down in the management hierarchy could present themselves as a potential change champion, and this can be particularly attractive if that person has a vision of why changes are necessary and an idea of how they can be made.

Exhibit 7.1 illustrates how the Eastman Chemical Company enlisted its own 'in-house champions at both ends' – a management-level project champion and a champion from within the maintenance ranks – to pursue its business vision.

Exhibit 7.1

Eastman Chemical Co. has in-house champions at both ends

The Stores and Supplies Organisation of the Eastman Chemical Co. knew that accomplishing its vision of being the preferred chemical company in the world would require co-operation from functions throughout the organisation, including but not limited to Stores, Maintenance, Information Systems, Engineering and Purchasing. The next step was to enlist commitment from top management to cut across those functional boundaries and provide a total business perspective.

Since Stores reported to Jim Hall, who was division head of Shops and Services, he was given the vision and enlisted as the management-level project champion. Hall put together and led a cross-functional team to help make the change take place.... Hall also recognised that the whole maintenance organisation would have to buy into the project as an equal partner.

The maintenance department head was asked to help select a second project champion, this time from within the maintenance ranks. This champion needed to be a first- or second-level supervisor who had come up through the ranks and who was well thought of by his peers and also by the mechanics. This person would carry the banner for maintenance, while serving as an internal change agent within maintenance because people believed him.

Driving, not driven

With a change champion in place at both levels, Eastman put together another cross-*functional* team to redesign the process.

Source: Adapted from Taylor, S., 'Business process re-engineering: Eastman Chemical strives for better than world class', *Industrial Engineering*, November, pp. 28–34, 1993.

Appointed from outside the organisation

This decision should reflect the politics of the situation and whether the existing managers have the requisite skills to lead and manage a change. An outside person should be chosen on the basis of their past experience and ability to lead and manage the company's particular change programme. Consideration should be given to their potential to inject a fresh approach to thinking and ideas into the business, and their ability to face any opposition they may encounter by being considered an outsider.

What can appear on the surface to be a straightforward change project, say the introduction of appraisal in a company, can go off-the-rails very quickly with disastrous long-term results if improperly managed. Unfortunately, not every manager has the necessary characteristics to be able successfully to lead and champion many apparently straightforward changes. Exhibit 7.2 provides a summary of what Wilson considers are the attributes which can be observed in successful change champions.

Exhibit 7.2

Attributes of successful change champions

- **Vision.** Champions leading large-scale change programmes must visualise the shape, style and philosophy of the organisation they are building. This will frequently involve overturning many existing practices and ways of doing things.

- **Clear values.** The values and beliefs of the change champion will determine how business is conducted and how people are treated and motivated to work effectively.

- **Energy and stamina.** Change projects can take several years and the workload and pressures on the champion can be enormous; therefore he or she has to be tough and both physically and mentally resilient.

- **Charisma.** The champion must have the presence and style to convince everyone of the value and benefits of the change programme. He or she has to be a missionary, conveying the vision.

- **Team builder.** Large and complex change programmes cannot be accomplished by one person alone. The champion has to build a team of like-minded managers who also fully support the values, vision and direction of the change and who then become missionaries.

- **Communicator.** The change champion has to be an excellent communicator and needs to ensure that effective communication is accomplished at every opportunity with consistency and fervour.

- **Persuader.** People do not abandon long-held beliefs easily and the champion should be a skilled persuader who can present the future direction and then discuss and argue the reasons for moving down that particular route.

- **Innovator.** Successful organisation change requires a great deal of innovative thinking and the change champion has to be the focus for this.

- **Achiever.** The change champion skills of achievement and accomplishment need to be instilled and developed in every person involved in the change process.

- **Delegator.** No one person is able to do everything on a complicated change programme and the champion therefore has to place a considerable amount of faith and trust in managers and project leaders.

Source: Wilson, T., *A Manual for Change*. Reproduced by permission of Gower Publishing Ltd.

The risks of being a change champion

Acceptance of being a change champion needs to be measured, and the role is a challenge because it can bring glory or failure, with the resultant pay-offs. If the change programme is a success, the organisation should ensure that the champion is rewarded and should publicise, for their own as well as the change champion's benefit, his or her achievements. This can be done via presentations and publications, both inside and outside the organisation, on what has been achieved and the associated benefits.

The change programme may initially have required a strong directive style to look for new methods and solutions to obstacles. To progress satisfactorily, the change programme may require a change in emphasis to one where there is more discussion and mutual agreement before decisions are taken. This may require a *change in champion*, from an inventive, hard-nosed type to one who adopts a more understanding and consensual style.

However, since change is a risky business, the change programme could fail to produce the intended results on time. Even worse, such failure could mean that people at all levels could suffer and jobs could be lost. In such cases the senior management may become blind to the real difficulties faced and hard work put in by the change champion. Besides being replaced, the change champion may be ridiculed and put out in the cold as far as career progression is concerned.

The change sponsor and the change champion working together

Both the change sponsor and the change champion have the authority and responsibility to command that certain changes be made. They are the ones who will be expected to plan and initiate change and they need to do this in ways that motivate and support people. This can be achieved through good leadership and working with people, getting them involved in establishing the change objectives and providing them with feedback and support.

The following sections develop an understanding of three issues, central to good management practice, that are important to the way the sponsors and change champions manage: namely, management by objectives (MBO), styles of management behaviour, and systems of management.

Exhibit 7.3 illustrates the importance Cambridge Consultants Ltd attach to having the right product champion who enjoys a good relationship with the development team and the resource enablers.

Exhibit 7.3

Cambridge Consultants Ltd's product champion

Cambridge Consultants Ltd employs 300 people and carries out new product and process development for manufacturing clients throughout Europe. Dr Chris Davies, director of CCL's product development practice, comments:

> *Large and small companies come to us for complete product developments and we get to recognise those that will succeed. CCL can help make a dramatic impact on the timescales and innovation for reduced cost or increased capability. The clients, however, make or break the product. Only with the right product champion can the product succeed.*

Success is a product that sells well and enhances the reputation of the supplier. It will have been delivered on time, at the right cost, be robust and attractive. The key to success is almost entirely in the hands of the product champion, enabled by his or her directors and development team ... The product champion is the focus of the development and will be more successful if a good relationship is built with the development team and the resource enablers. The resource enablers must trust the product champion to keep spending money right through to the low point of all cash flow charts – when all the development cost is spent and the income is yet to start.

Source: Adapted from Ruskin, C., 'The product champion tests his vision', *World Class Design to Manufacture.*

MANAGEMENT BY OBJECTIVES (MBO)

Management by objectives (MBO), first proposed by Drucker in 1954, is an approach which seeks to clarify and implement an organisation's hierarchy of objectives. In its simplest form, MBO is a process of joint objective setting between a supervisor and a subordinate. This involves establishing a formal agreement between the two to develop objectives which are timed, defined, understandable, measurable and challenging. These can then be used to monitor progress. The intention is to bring together individual actions ultimately to fulfil the organisation's business strategy.

The process of MBO deals with:

1 **The subordinate's performance objectives over time.** The subordinate proposes objectives to be achieved, usually over the next year. The supervisor and subordinate jointly discuss these and reach agreement.

2 **A statement of objectives in the time period.** This should be a written document that specifies the work objectives and the target dates for achieving them. Again, this should be agreed with the supervisor. The objectives should be made as specific and as quantifiable as possible. At all times the performance objectives, while presenting a challenge, should be realistic and attainable.

3 **What the measures will be.** These need to be established to assess whether or not the objectives have been achieved.

4 **Procedures for reviewing results**. What needs to be decided here is who checks the process and how frequently. Ideally, the subordinate should initiate the checks and keep the supervisor informed of progress. At the end of the programme the subordinate should report on the progress made.

5 **Repeating the cycle.** Lessons learnt should influence future objective setting and the way the process is planned and managed.

The MBO process is depicted in Fig 7.2.

This process seeks to enable the supervisor and subordinate to establish plans and control results jointly. The face-to-face communication between supervisor and subordinate should foster understanding and provide the subordinate with the opportunity to participate in decisions about the work programme. This full involvement of the subordinate should encourage self-control.

In the MBO process three types of objectives can be specified:

1 **Improvement objectives** show the need to improve a performance factor: for example, to reduce throughput time by 20 per cent.

2 **Personal development objectives** relate to personal growth activities: e.g. develop interviewing skills.

3 **Maintenance objectives** express intentions to continue with the current performance levels.

Important MBO issues

- **Compensation tied to MBO.** When MBO is tied to compensation this should motivate people to attain the objectives set. It is also an indication that the process of

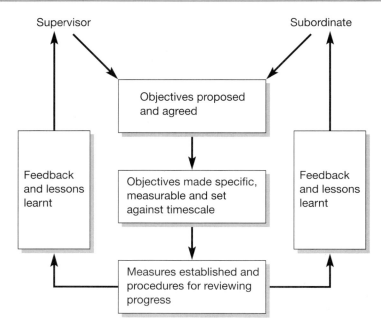

Fig 7.2 Management by objectives (MBO) process

MBO or the pursuit of organisation goals is being taken seriously. However, the objectives can become ends in themselves and people may focus solely on the objectives to the exclusion or downgrading of other everyday duties. This is especially so with easily-quantifiable objectives because they tend to focus efforts on limited achievements.

- **Excessive time and paperwork.** The strength of MBO lies in the formal process which encourages discussion with the intention of stating objectives and agreements in writing. This requires much time and paperwork, which many managers may resent.

- **Caution with consultants.** To use an MBO package proffered by an external consultant may require extensive modification to fit the actual work circumstances. The benefits of designing an MBO system to suit best the actual situation need to be considered.

- **The authoritarian view of MBO.** People may feel that upward as well as downward communication is not really occurring and that they are being told what their objectives are. A top-down approach goes against the participative concept which underpins MBO.

- **Difficulty in measuring objectives.** The MBO process does not provide guidance on how objectives may be measured. With easily-quantifiable objectives this may not be a difficult task. However, certain objectives may not lend themselves to measurement. Through experience, people should become more able to decide upon and establish useful measures.

- **Distrust of management.** People may not be enthusiastic about MBO if they see the management as being manipulative in terms of setting higher and higher targets and expecting more and more effort. This could lead to subordinates understating objectives and thereby restricting and not making explicit their capabilities.

- **Managers need to do MBO themselves.** MBO works most effectively when it is supported by managers from top to bottom in the organisation. Their commitment must be to reinforce the programmes through constant, direct person-to-person relationships with subordinates. This implies that managers should participate in MBO themselves, because it will not work as well if they abrogate their responsibility and let the personnel or human resource people in the organisation run the MBO programmes.

Bringing MBO up to date

As a management system, MBO was very popular in the 1960s and 1970s but may be perceived as being an unacceptable, top-down authoritarian style for today's workforce. However, many of the core aspects of MBO are embedded within the more sophisticated performance-setting and appraisal schemes for autonomous business units and self-managing teams that many of today's successful organisations use.

STYLES OF MANAGEMENT

Both the change sponsor and the change champion need to possess good leadership qualities. But what exactly does this mean? Blake and Mouton researched leadership and defined it in terms of a manager having concern for both production and people. They mapped these levels of concern in the form of a management grid, shown in Fig 7.3.

The concern for production is not about how much output is produced but the attitude of an individual to the quality of such things as research, processes, procedures, staff services and work output. People concern relates to the individual's attitudes and style of management with respect to working conditions, personal commitment, workers' self esteem, responsibility and trust.

The five main contrasting styles are depicted in Fig 7.3. Style 1.1, termed 'Impoverished Management,' depicts a management style where minimum effort is exerted with either production or people. Here the manager is acting simply as a messenger, relaying information from superiors to subordinates.

Style 9.1, termed 'Authoritarian Management', is where the human aspect is kept to a minimum so as not to interfere with work arrangements, and the manager is highly concerned for production.

Style 1.9, termed 'Country Club Management', is where people concerns are uppermost and satisfied by promoting a relaxed, friendly, unstressful environment. The manager has little concern for co-ordinating efforts to achieve targets.

Style 5.5, termed 'Middle-of-the-road Management', strikes a balance between the concerns for production and people, in that targets may not be too high and there are only satisfactory aspirations of morale.

Blake and Mouton argue that managers are capable of becoming, or can develop into, superior performance managers, or 9.9 managers. Style 9.9, termed 'Team

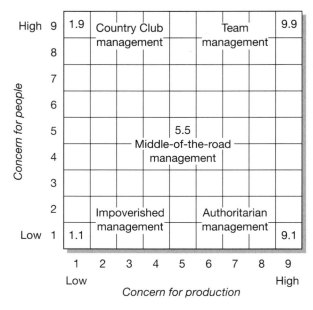

Fig 7.3 The management grid

Source: From *Leadership Dilemmas-Grid Solutions*, p. 29, by Robert R. Blake and Anne A. McCanse. Copyright © 1991 by Robert R. Blake and the Estate of Jane S. Mouton, Austin, Texas. Used with permission. All rights reserved.

Management', depicts a management style where superior performance is achieved through a high concern for production output as well as the needs of people.

Theoretically, it should be possible to discern 81 different managerial styles but, according to Blake and Mouton, the majority of managers would be placed somewhere near the diagonal running from 'country club management' to 'authoritarian management'. When times are good, managers adopt a country club style, but when things worsen, say through difficult markets or intense competition, they tend to adopt an authoritarian approach. Many managers, when faced with this situation, may take the middle-of-the road style in order to play safe. Managers react to changes and adjust their management styles to suit the circumstances. Unfortunately, the grid provides no indication of how managers could plan the adoption of specific styles of management to suit particular circumstances. Neither does the grid help us understand why a manager may adopt a particular style given a set of circumstances. This will depend on the situation, the personality of those involved and the working environment.

Systems of management

Rensis Likert distinguishes between four systems of management:

1 **Authoritative.** Here managers are autocratic and control people through fear and punishment. Communication is downward and little attention is paid to the ideas of subordinates.

2 **Benevolent authoritative.** Here people are motivated by rewards as well as the fear of punishment. Some upward communication is possible and some ideas from subordinates are sought, but the confidence and trust is more of a patronising nature. Delegation of decision making is limited and closely controlled.

3 **Consultative**. Here communications flow up as well as down the hierarchy and managers try to make use of subordinates' ideas and opinions. The level of confidence and trust is quite high but not complete. People are motivated by rewards but occasional punishments are made. Decision making on specific issues and consultation at the lower levels is allowed.

4 **Participative.** Likert identifies this as being the best management style and reported that companies using this style were most effective in setting and achieving their goals. It is characterised by complete confidence and trust between superiors and subordinates. Subordinates are free to discuss their job and their participation in the generation of new ideas is welcomed. Much communication and co-operative teamwork, as well as friendly relations, is sought. Feedback of information is used for the purpose of solving problems and not for punishment. Rewards are made on the basis of participation and the achievement of agreed goals.

CHANGE PLAYERS

LaMarsh, in her book *Changing the Way We Change*, refers to people who have to change as 'targets'. This has connotations of a passive set of people who are focused on, and who probably will not like, what is in store for them. In an optimal change environment the sponsors and change champions should make every effort to ensure that people do not feel like targets and that their co-operation as players in a total team effort to fulfil the change programmes is essential. Therefore, the author refers to these people as 'players'. The players are the people who make the change happen. They have to deal with the real and unforeseen problems that the planners have not articulated or are unaware of. They are the ones most personally affected in terms of changing work patterns, working with different colleagues in different areas, adapting to new practices and having to acquire new skills. They probably have the least say in what is about to happen. This could be due to a lack of training or of involvement. It could be because they resist the changes, are unaware of what is going on, or simply that they are new to the situation. Whatever the case, it is true that the players in the change process are the ones who are familiar with the real problems of the change.

Players and the present

Some players may wish to change the present system. It could be personal, in that they see their recognition and rewards as being poor in the current situation and hope for a change for the better. They may also perceive that the company's fortunes are dwindling because of the existing ways and wish that the situation could be reversed for everyone's benefit. In a more negative way, they might like change to signal the demise of somebody's empire or position – someone whom they despise.

Many players might wish to stay with the present situation because it suits them best. For example, the future may seem unattractive if it requires them moving to another location, or they may be planning on retirement in a year or two and would rather things remain settled. They may not appreciate the need for change as fully as the managers do. This can arise from lack of communication or understanding, or just that they feel that management is overreacting to the situation. It could be that past changes have not made improvements for the better, or simply that the players do not trust the management's ability to implement changes that will make life better for them.

Problems with the future

Players may feel uneasy or threatened if there is a possibility that the new ways mean them having to acquire new skills and knowledge, or working differently or harder at new locations with new people. These feelings can become exaggerated and unfounded, particularly if the future state is ill-defined or unknown to them. Players want to know what could happen and what is expected of them and others. According to LaMarsh, players have many foreboding questions about change. For example:

- How will we get from here to there?
- How will we manage all this extra work?
- Will we have to change all at once or in stages?
- What can I take with me from the present? What do I have to leave behind?
- Will the company go too fast? Too slow?
- Will I have a chance to say goodbye to what I leave behind?
- Do we have enough money to make this change?
- What will we do if things start to slip as we go through the change?
- What if they've made the wrong choice for the future; can we go back?

If such questions cannot be answered the players may hold back their co-operation and they may strongly resist any changes.

Managing the difficulties

The sponsors and change champions are there to manage the change process and assist the players to cope with and make the transition from old to new ways. The management needs to ask: How widespread is the perceived need for change? Who will be involved and in what ways? What level of support will be provided? The politics of the situation then need to be examined to determine the vital areas where it is important that support be gained and those where support is needed but may not be forthcoming. To do this, managers need to understand what the problems are, what the forms of resistance are and how they can be overcome. This process should not be seen as adversarial. That is, there is no need to adopt the attitude of 'let's overcome the forces against us'. Often, resistance to change is only human and so are the people who plan and initiate it. The feedback concerning resistance can be very useful to management because it makes them aware of serious problems or oversights, and they will often benefit greatly from modifying or altering the course of change.

Typical problems or concerns often expressed are:

- We will not get adequate rewards for this.
- It will just result in us having to work harder.
- The union will resist it anyway.
- The management does not understand what is really needed.
- The consultants involved lack understanding or experience of what we do.
- Past change has not improved matters.
- We have not been asked what we think.

- If it goes wrong we will be blamed or we will suffer.
- We get no support in the form of training or equipment.
- Previous changes have been mad-capped, hair-brained schemes.
- We do not trust their judgement on what is right.

To deal with these concerns in the best way, the management needs first to encourage the players to articulate their feelings, fears, concerns and what they see as being the problems. To achieve this, the environment needs to be one in which people feel safe to talk and criticise. They need to know the means they have to provide ideas and suggestions. This may require the use of discussion rooms, visual aids, facilitators, and training in problem solving and continuous improvement approaches. Management needs to create an environment where opposition by individuals or groups is not perceived as threatening, but as an opportunistic way to learn from others what could possibly be wrong with the proposed changes, and a way of diffusing anger through discussion and communicating and understanding how people feel.

Throughout this process the management may handle any resistance by getting the players to express their concerns, developing a mutual trust that support will be provided and, most importantly, getting involved by providing help to assist the players to face what is bothering them. It may be that, through this process, alterations to the change programme need to be made.

The above needs to be formalised into an approach for dealing with resistance to change. Kotter and Schlesinger have summarised this approach in six ways:

1 **Education and communication.** Use of one-on-one discussions, presentations to groups, memos, reports, and demonstrations to educate people beforehand about a change and to help them see the logic of the change.

2 **Participation and involvement.** Allowing others to help design and implement the change, asking individuals to contribute ideas and advice, or forming task forces or committees to work on the change.

3 **Facilitation and support.** Providing socio-emotional support for the hardships of change, actively listening to problems and complaints, providing training in the new ways, and helping overcome performance pressures.

4 **Negotiation and agreement.** Offering incentives to actual or potential resisters, working out trade-offs to provide special benefits in exchange for assurance that the change will not be blocked.

5 **Manipulation and co-optation.** Use of covert attempts to influence others, selectively providing information and consciously structuring events so that the desired change receives maximum support.

6 **Explicit and implicit coercion.** Use of force to get people to accept change, threatening resisters with a variety of undesirable consequences if they don't go along as planned.

MANAGING THE WORKFORCE

Much of what has been said about good practice regarding how to understand, work with, and enable players to be effective, stems from good workforce management approaches in the first place. The following sections consider some general principles and systems of workforce management, including quality of working life (QWL) programmes, job enrichment, Investors in People, and principles of workforce management.

QUALITY OF WORKING LIFE (QWL)

The concept of 'quality of working life' (QWL) became widely known in the 1970s and concerns job enrichment through improved job design as a means of motivating people. There is evidence that operational effectiveness is achieved in the main through people experiencing personal satisfaction with their work. To substantiate this, a Department of Employment report on the quality of working life studied people's experiences at work and (Wilson, 1973) showed that there is a link between satisfaction at work and efficiency at work. Also, employees and unions, according to an ACAS report ('Effective Organisations – The People Factor', September 1991) on the people factor in effective organisations, see QWL as a means of improving working conditions and as a means of employee productivity justifying higher pay. Management see QWL as one approach to dealing with stagnating productivity.

How to achieve good quality of working life

QWL recognises that since machines and processes need attention in order to work effectively, so do people. People should be seen not just as cost sinks but as assets which can be developed, and which can contribute knowledge, experience and skills for the benefit of the organisation. This means attention needs to be focused on working conditions and the way people are treated. Therefore, QWL programmes attempt to ensure that:

- pay is fair and adequate for the work done
- people have the chance to learn and practise new skills
- people's individual rights are protected
- people develop a sense of pride in the company and the work they do
- the working conditions are healthy and safe
- people have a chance to develop and progress in their jobs and careers.

A systematic attempt to define QWL explicitly in terms of its component elements was made in a study by Elizur. They were defined as being:

1 success in accomplishing aspirations and ideas in daily work
2 conditions to relax and refresh in work
3 feelings of calm and work is free from worry
4 self-confidence in work
5 involvement in activities which require physical force or dexterity
6 food considered to be suitable
7 feelings of physical well-being in work
8 feelings of security from violence and physical threats in work
9 feelings of respect from others
10 good relations with various institutions connected with work
11 feelings of closeness to other employees

12 feelings of confidence and togetherness with other employees
13 involvement in activities which express culture and beliefs
14 compatibility of culture and beliefs with work
15 feelings of satisfaction with work and with beliefs and opinions
16 loyalty to cultural beliefs or values.

Importance and benefits of QWL

QWL is important because it deals with people's changing social values and wider expectations of the quality of working life, and this is what motivates many people. What should attract managers and business people to adopt QWL as a type of management style, is the fact that it has been instrumental in reducing staff turnover, dissatisfaction and absenteeism.

QWL can improve organisational performance through jobs being more challenging and satisfying, through an improved working environment for everyone, and through more involvement and participation of people. In this way, a virtuous improvement circle is created where people experience more pride and satisfaction in the accomplishment of a good job.

Many best practice companies have benefited from adopting QWL programmes, examples being Procter & Gamble, Ford, General Electric, American Aluminum ALCOA, General Motors and AT&T (*see* Sherwood, 'Creating work cultures with competitive advantage', 1988).

Quality circles

Quality circles were popularised in Japan and have spread to many other countries. A quality circle usually includes members from the same functional area who meet regularly to discuss with supervisors work-related problems identified by themselves. The recommendations are often referred to a higher level for discussion, and when decisions to take action are made considerable employee involvement in implementation is used. The aim of quality circles is to increase productivity and worker morale.

Quality circles are reported to make work more interesting and challenging, as well as improving the awareness of employees regarding the work and feelings of colleagues. Effective use of quality circles can lead to increased confidence, pride, morale and motivation, as well as financial benefits. These benefits can only be achieved if management guidance and support exists – particularly during the implementation and establishment stages – along with a commitment to long-term training of employees in problem-solving skills.

Exhibit 7.4 summarises the results of a study, the major hypothesis of which was that participation in quality circles will be related to perception of increased QWL.

JOB ENRICHMENT

In 1959 research done by Herzberg and his colleagues showed that factors associated with work, such as achievement, challenge, responsibility and recognition, are potential satisfiers which motivate people. They therefore argued that jobs should be enriched in these ways, and in doing so job satisfaction would increase and so would productivity.

Exhibit 7.4

Quality circles lead to increased QWL: Higher use of abilities, more influence, autonomy and job satisfaction

The research was conducted in one of the manufacturing divisions of a large industrial corporation in Israel. The company had initiated the quality circle (QC) programme four years prior to the study. At the time of the investigation, about 100 quality circles were regularly active, predominantly in the manufacturing divisions.

A total of 160 employees in the manufacturing department were randomly selected and asked to participate in the study; half of them were active members of quality circles, and half were working in similar jobs in departments where quality circles had not yet been introduced. The response rate among QC members and non-members was similar. Eighty questionnaires were distributed in each group; 71 QC members and 72 non-members responded.

QC participants reported to have more influence, autonomy, opportunity to use ability, and opportunity to suggest changes and implement them than did non-participants. QC participants reported higher job satisfaction, more influence, more use of their initiative in their work and better relations with their supervisors than did non-participants.

QC participants may perceive QC activities as an extension and enrichment of their jobs. Quality circle activities seem to provide opportunities for increased use of talents and abilities in suggesting solutions to work-related problems. Implementation of suggested improvements may increase the perception of influence by participating individuals.

Source: Adapted from Elizur, D., 'Quality circles and quality of work life', *International Journal of Manpower*. Reprinted by permission of MCB University Press.

Job enrichment, therefore, is concerned with making the job more challenging and containing decision making, responsibility and autonomy. Job enrichment needs to be distinguished from *job enlargement* which is concerned with extending the scope of the job by adding similar tasks or by the rotation of jobs, but not extending the level of decision-making responsibility. Job enrichment entails redesigning jobs to give:

- greater responsibility
- greater autonomy
- better completion of the full job
- feedback.

The ways in which jobs can be enriched, shown in Fig 7.4, are as follows:

1 workers having a say in the way the work is done, e.g. work methods, sequence and pace
2 providing additional responsibility
3 increasing the degree of completion of jobs or making people aware of what part of what they do comprises the end result
4 increasing feedback on performance
5 involving people in considering how the work environment might be altered for the better, e.g. space, ventilation, heating, cleanliness, encouraging and facilitating participation with peers and superiors about all aspects of the job.

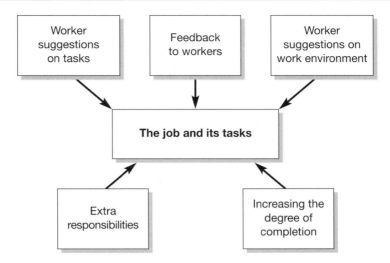

Fig 7.4 Ways of enriching jobs

Claims, limits and problems of job enrichment

There are numerous reports from companies such as Texas Instruments, Procter & Gamble and AT&T which show job enrichment as being important. These reports provide evidence of increased productivity and morale, and reduced costs and absenteeism. The main reservation about job enrichment is that it has limited application when jobs involving workers are highly automated. It can be slow as well as costly to make the necessary changes. It is also really only useful in situations where workers are and feel underutilised. Some workers, or those workers with jobs which require low skill levels, may not wish to have their jobs altered. Certainly the feeling nowadays, when companies are downsizing in order to remain competitive, is that people want to retain the job they have. Often, the redesign of jobs and processes includes automation, and this increases productivity with an ultimate drop in the need for people in the process. Therefore, before commencing a job enrichment programme, answers to these questions would be extremely useful:

1 To what extent will people appreciate their jobs becoming more challenging and responsible?

2 What do different people at different levels in the organisation with different skills want from their jobs?

3 Is job enrichment being imposed on people without their consent and involvement?

4 If productivity increases, how will the workers benefit?

5 To what extent will people be consulted and given the opportunity to make suggestions?

6 Will the workers be given feedback and will they be recognised? What is the level of support for job enrichment from the workers, their committees, their union leadership?

Overall, job enrichment is a powerful way to improve organisational effectiveness by focusing on people's jobs. How well it is received depends on individual needs and expectations. Although it is useful, it should not be treated as a substitute for effective management or leadership.

Job design for worker satisfaction (The Hackman and Oldham Framework)

Hackman and Oldham studied job enrichment to consider the personal and work outcomes that result from it. They considered that the issues to do with the job, such as skill variety, task identity, autonomy and feedback, lead to improved motivation, higher quality work performance, more satisfaction with the work and lower absenteeism and turnover. They developed a framework of job enrichment, showing how worker satisfaction arose from meaningfulness of the work, responsibility for the work and its outcomes, and receiving feedback, as shown in Fig 7.5.

Hackman and Oldham developed an overall measure of job enrichment called 'the motivating potential score' (MPS), which they expressed as:

$$\text{MPS} = (\text{skill variety} + \text{task identity} + \text{task significance}) \div 3 \times \text{autonomy} \times \text{feedback}$$

where the terms are defined as follows:

- **skill variety** – the use of different skills and talents
- **task identity** – more involvement in doing the job from start to finish
- **task significance** – how much the job impacts on others in the organisation or in the external environment

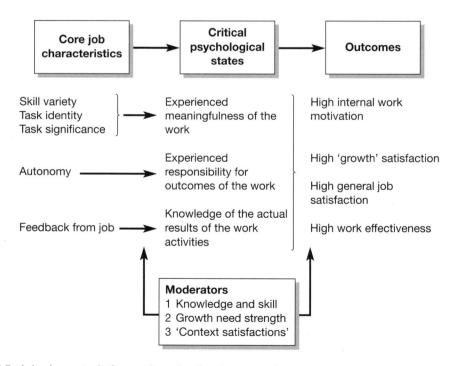

Fig 7.5 Job characteristics and motivation framework

Source: Hackman, J.R. and Oldham, G.R., *Work Redesign*. (Fig 4.6 from page 90). © 1980 by Addison-Wesley Publishing Co., Inc. Reprinted by permission of Addison-Wesley Longman Inc.

- **autonomy** – the amount of freedom, independence and discretion the individual has in performing the tasks
- **feedback from the job** – information on the results of performance.

They used the measure on a job diagnostics survey to analyse job dimension, giving a score between 1 and 7. A job that scores highly on the five core characteristics is considered to be enriched. The survey found that people with enriched jobs and higher score levels experienced more satisfaction and internal motivation. Also, jobs that scored high on the core dimensions had higher levels of personal and work outcomes.

As a result of their work, Hackman and Oldham recommended five ways to enrich jobs which are low in the core characteristics. These are:

1 Form natural units of work. Paid tasks logically relate to one another.
2 Combine tasks. This can expand the job responsibilities.
3 Establish client relationship, i.e. establish contact and maintain contact with people who use the results of the work both inside and outside the organisation.
4 Open feedback channels. People should receive feedback performance as they work to learn how they are doing over time.
5 Vertical loading. Give people more control over their work in terms of authority, planning and controlling things previously done by managers.

INVESTORS IN PEOPLE

The Investors in People (IiP) is the National Standard for effective investment in the training and development of all people to achieve business goals. The Investors in People Standard was developed in 1990. It draws on the experience of some of the UK's most successful organisations, both large and small, and has the support of both the TUC and CBI. It therefore provides a comprehensive benchmark of best practice against which an organisation can audit its policies and practice in the development of people. The intention is to provide a framework for improving business performance and competitiveness, through a planned approach to setting and communicating business objectives and developing people to meet these objectives.

Since 1990, tens of thousands of UK employers, employing millions of people, have become involved. The Standard has assisted in encouraging excellence in the field of human resource development (HRD) and making effective use of all resources, by developing a culture of continuous improvement. Overall it has improved business performance and enabled organisations to manage competitively in the face of change.

The Standard

The Investors in People Standard is a cyclical process based on four key principles:

1 **Commitment** to develop all employees to achieve business goals and targets.

2 **Reviewing** regularly training and development needs in the context of the business.

3 Taking relevant **action** to meet training and development needs throughout people's employment.

4 **Evaluating** outcomes of training and development for individuals and the organisation as a basis for continuous improvement.

These four key principles are broken down into 24 indicators and it is against these which organisations produce evidence for assessment.

How the process works

Five main stages are involved in achieving the Standard. They are depicted in Fig 7.6 and are:

1 Diagnosis and planning

- Carry out an initial review against the Standard to see how the organisation measures up and to identify any gaps in what is currently being done.
- Develop a plan of action to bridge the gaps, meet the Standard and improve the organisation.
- Make a commitment to achieve the plan to the Training and Enterprise Council (TEC) in England or Wales, Local Education Company (LEC) in Scotland, or the Training and Employment Agency (T&EA) in Northern Ireland.

2 Action

- Instigate the plan.
- Review the organisation's achievement against the plan and its progress towards meeting the Standard.
- Gather evidence to demonstrate how the organisation meets the Standard.

3 Assessment

- When the organisation feels it is ready, ask the local Assessment Unit for an external assessment.
- If the organisation does not yet meet the Standard, the assessor will provide information on what additional work is needed to achieve the Standard.

4 Achievement

- If the organisation meets the Standard, a recommendation for recognition as an Investor in People will be made to a panel of business people. The panel will ask for clarification on any issues of concern. Once the panel is satisfied with the recommendation, the organisation will be recognised and feedback will be provided.

The standard	FOUR PRINCIPLES 24 INDICATORS		THE BADGE		
The process	Diagnosis and planning	Action	Assessment	Achievement	Continuous Development

Fig 7.6 The Investors in People process

Source: © Investors in People, UK, 1996.

5 Continuous development

- Once the organisation has achieved the Standard, work should continue to ensure the organisation develops in line with the needs of both the business and its people.

Who is involved?

To become an Investor in People, everyone working for the organisation will need to be committed to achieving the Standard. Senior management, union representatives and all employee groups should take an active part in the journey towards becoming an Investor in People. Initially, senior management will need to approve and communicate the organisation's commitment to its employees and, crucially, to review the outcomes of working to the Standard to see how the business is benefiting. Experience shows that managers from operational, personnel, training or quality functions are well placed for managing the overall process and sustaining momentum.

National Vocational Qualifications (NVQs)

Targets should be set and national standards should be linked, where appropriate, leading to the achievement of National Vocational Qualifications (NVQs), or relevant units, or, in Scotland, Scottish Vocational Qualifications (SVQs).

How long does it take?

The length of time leading up to assessment ranges between six and 18 months. The actual time taken will depend, simply, on how much there is to do and how quickly the required changes in systems and attitudes can be affected.

The benefits

The practical and commercial benefits of working towards and achieving the Standard are many. A few examples include:

- **Public recognition and image**. The Investing in People status brings public recognition for real achievements measured against a rigorous national Standard. Being an Investor in People helps to attract the best quality job applicants. It may also provide a reason for customers to choose specific goods and services. For example, ICL is now a preferred employer, particularly for graduates. Boots the Chemists see the Investors in People badge as making a statement that they care about standards of excellence.

- **Enhanced quality**. Investing in people significantly improves the results of quality programmes by reinforcing continuous learning and improvement. Investors in People adds considerable value to BS 5750, ISO 9000 and other total quality initiatives. For example, at Lawson Mardon Plastics, customer returns are down 95 per cent from 1991.

- **Competitive advantage**. Through improved performance, Investor in People organisations develop a competitive edge which secures their future prosperity. For example, De Vere Hotels consider that the award of the Standard is a better indicator than the star rating in the eyes of some guests.

- **Sales**. Many Investors in People have increased their sales, fee income or turnover in recent years. For example, at Land Rover sales increased by 33 per cent between 1991 and 1993.

- **Improved motivation**. Through greater involvement, personal development and recognition of achievement, motivation is improved. This leads to higher morale, improved retention rates, reduced absenteeism, readier acceptance of change and identification with the organisation beyond the confines of the job.

PRINCIPLES OF WORKFORCE MANAGEMENT

The following is a broad set of workforce principles that in practice many managers follow instinctively. They have been devised by Schroeder and are derived from organisational theory and modern management thinking.

1 Match the worker and the job

This principle implies that people should be selected for jobs on the basis of their individual differences and preferences for work. It also implies that jobs should be designed for the workforce that is available. If the workforce is well educated, intelligent, and able to accept responsibility, broad jobs should be designed. Individuals should also be counselled to accept jobs which meet their personal needs.

This principle implies that jobs can be over-designed as well as under-designed. In other words, some people may be asked to accept too much responsibility, whereas others may be asked to accept too little.

2 Clearly define responsibilities of the worker

When job responsibilities are unclear or constantly changing, workers feel frustrated. The result can be poor quality, low productivity, and conflict between individuals. Therefore, one of the principles of good workforce management is to define job responsibilities clearly for all workers. This would normally be done via written job descriptions or statements of objectives which are kept up to date.

3 Set standards of performance

Standards of performance should be developed for all jobs. These specify what the worker is expected to accomplish and make it possible to decentralise more control to the worker on the basis of performance. When performance standards are not set, workers can become confused about their responsibilities and overly dependent on the supervisor for job direction. These standards should be subject to continuous improvement over time by the workforce and management.

4 Ensure communications and employee involvement

People need to be informed about company policies, and they need to feel that they can influence policies through participation in decision making. The idea of participative management (or employee involvement) has been widely supported by research studies as a way to gain improved performance. Performance is also improved when two-way communications are established between management and workers.

5 Provide training

Often training is viewed as a perk in organisations. When budgets are reduced, training is the first thing to be cut back. Ideally, training should begin the first day on the job to ensure that the employee is competent before beginning the work. Although this may sound like an obvious idea, trial-and-error learning on the job is widely practised. Employee development should be continued through training and education so that subsequent career advancement is possible. Training must be continuous in nature in today's world where knowledge is rapidly changing.

6 Ensure good supervision

As we have noted, there is nothing more fundamental to the worker than good supervision. A supervisor should be competent in both technology and management skills and should possess a sense of fairness in dealing with people. The supervisor should also be genuinely concerned with the welfare of each individual employee while also emphasising performance and results. According to behavioural theory, when the workers know what performance is expected and participate in developing those expectations, they will be motivated to perform. The supervisor should make sure that this type of performance climate exists.

7 Reward people for performance

When performance standards have been set, it is possible to reward people on the basis of performance. According to behavioural theory, this leads to further performance in expectation of further rewards. Since the workforce manager's primary responsibility is to obtain results, the giving of rewards for performance constitutes the prime method of motivating people toward goals. Rewards can include all forms of compensation (pay, promotion, status, a pat on the back etc.).

If these principles are followed, the workforce will be well managed. Continually improving performance and a satisfied workforce should result.

Exhibit 7.5 illustrates how the employees of Abbey National and Rank Xerox UK, like other UK workers, consider recognition from their employees for extra work effort to be a priority.

Exhibit 7.5

The importance of recognition for extra effort at Abbey National and Rank Xerox UK

Last year, Geraldine Manning, a senior customer services assistant with Abbey National, was working late on a regular basis. Three or four nights a week, she would stay back for a couple of hours a night, reading course notes to one of her colleagues, Graham Salmon, a blind mortgage adviser, who was working towards a promotion. It was an extraordinary act of service both to Salmon and to the company, and she didn't expect anything in return. 'I did it because he's a friend,' she says.

But Manning's efforts did not go unnoticed. A year ago, Abbey National introduced an employee recognition scheme called 'Bravo' and Manning was put up for – and won – its top-level gold award. 'I was really surprised,' she says, modestly. 'It's a brilliant award – you get 20 000 air miles (enough for one return trip to Australia, or two to the Seychelles) and a certificate.' Winners are made a fuss of and presented with their awards at a special ceremony in a hotel. 'I had to go up on stage; it was a bit embarrassing but I did like it,' she says.'You do feel really special.'

Manning is not alone in appreciating recognition. According to International Survey Research (ISR), a company specialising in employee attitude surveys, 'recognition for good performance' is the third job priority for UK workers after 'being treated with fairness and respect' and 'job security'. Interestingly, observes ISR managing director Roger Maitland, while 70 per cent of people say recognition is 'very important', just 37 per cent are satisfied with the recognition they are getting – the widest discrepancy among the 12 job priorities polled.

Nick Edmans, communications manager at Abbey National, says 'When people do things beyond the call of duty they are giving more of their time and effort and at the end of the day it's a commercial arrangement we have with our employees. You have to show that the company is prepared to give them something too.'

Paul Rutherford, communications and development manager at Rank Xerox UK, agrees. Rank Xerox has a series of recognition programmes, with graduated gifts and rewards, certificates and ceremonies. Although the company has been rewarding sales staff for years, three years ago it set up schemes to cover non-sales employees. 'We want to engender a culture of recognition. You have to put in a formal mechanism for that. But hopefully it helps people realise that it's the simple things that people appreciate most. At the most basic level a note to say "thank you, that was a job well done" is often enough', says Rutherford.

It is, however, not always easy to measure the success of a scheme. Rank Xerox says employee surveys have shown that people feel better with recognition and the company's score on recognition is eight per cent above the national norm. There is anecdotal evidence too, that people appreciate awards. 'You can see the awards adorning people's offices,' says Rutherford. 'There are little telltale signs; the excellence award will be standing on the bookcase just slightly tilted towards the door.'

Despite the difficulty of judging whether a scheme is working, most companies running them claim they are effective. It's not a cheap exercise, either in terms of management time or in the certificate and prizes. But most feel it is money well spent. 'How do you put a value on happy employees?' asks Edmans.

Source: Adapted from Syedain, H., 'The rewards of recognition', *Management Today*, May, pp. 72–4, 1995, Haymarket Publications.

SUMMARY

- The people who are involved in or affected by the management of the operations and the associated changes made in the organisation are the change sponsors, the change champions and the change players.

- The sponsors of change are those who have the authority and responsibility to command that certain changes be made. They need to have skills in deciding what changes are best, what the implications of the changes are and how to manage them. They will need to see that the right people, with the right skills, are chosen and supported. They should ensure that the environment supports change and that resources are sufficient. They should know how to delegate and manage with little interference while providing their commitment, their time and support.

- The change champion is a person who must have the necessary characteristics to be able to lead and champion a change process. This person will be expected to plan and initiate change and also to take responsibility for it. He or she will need to be adept at motivating people and working and managing them in terms of being a teamworker, assessor, trainer, and coach etc. Being a change champion is both a challenge and a risk because it can bring glory or failure, with the resultant pay-offs.

- Both the change sponsor and the change champion need to possess good leadership qualities. Research defines leadership in terms of a manager having concern for both production and people. Five main levels of concern have been identified, ranging from the 'impoverished manager' who exerts minimum effort with either production or people, to the 'team manager' who ensures that superior performance is achieved through a high concern for production output as well as the needs of people.

- Management by objectives (MBO) is an approach which seeks to clarify and implement an organisation's hierarchy of objectives. It is a process of joint objective setting between a superior and a subordinate that can be used to establish direction, motivate and assess progress towards the goals. Although MBO is a good planning tool it has its down sides which need to be understood and managed.

- Good management of both production and people is needed for effective change, and four systems of management have been identified: authoritative, benevolent authoritative, consultative, and participative. This last style is characterised by complete confidence and trust between superiors and subordinates and has been identified as being the best management style that companies can adopt when pursuing goals.

- The players are the people who have to make the change happen. They have to deal with the real and unforeseen problems that the planners have not articulated or are unaware of. Their co-operation to fulfil the change programmes is essential. Players can assist or strongly oppose any changes. The sponsors and change champions need to understand what the problems are, what the forms of resistance are, and how they can be overcome.

- Systems of management practice that enable players to be effective are quality of working life (QWL) programmes, job enrichment, Investors in People, and principles of workforce management.

  - quality of working life (QWL) concerns job enrichment through improved job design as a means of motivating people
  - job enrichment is concerned with making the job more challenging and containing decision making, responsibility and autonomy
  - Investors in People is the National Standard for effective investment in the training and development of all people to achieve business goals
  - effective workforce management principles are: match the worker and the job; clearly define responsibilities of the worker; set standards of performance; ensure communications and employee involvement; provide training; ensure good supervision and reward people for performance.

REVIEW AND DISCUSSION QUESTIONS

1 Your company is seeking to recruit a change champion, either from within or from outside, to lead a new and important change initiative. Consider yourself in the role of a senior manager in the change programme and present a report to your chief executive outlining the characteristics you think should form the basis of selection of this person.

2 As head of the works committee, the management has presented you with tentative change plans for your department. They have requested that you assess the views of and obtain suggestions from your co-workers regarding the plans. Discuss how you would go about this task and outline the main points that you would make in your reply.

3 You are a management trainer presenting a one-day seminar to senior managers, all of whom are anticipating embarking upon new change initiatives in their organisations. Discuss the content of your programme, given that you intend to place an emphasis on different management styles and management approaches.

4 Discuss the main features of two management approaches that aim to secure co-operation and get the most out of the 'partners' in the change process.

ASSIGNMENTS

1 As a senior manager with experience of implementing many change initiatives in the company, the personnel department has requested your assistance in the preparation of a training programme for managers, entitled 'Managing people in the change process'. The emphasis they suggest should be on how to pursue company objectives through participation, job enrichment, assessment, rewards and recognition. Discuss the main features of your advice to them.

2 An attitude survey indicates that the company you work for is poor at managing change. Apparently, the workforce does not trust the senior management, saying it lacks leadership qualities. Workers also feel that the managers who are supposed to champion the change are incompetent and cannot communicate properly. As a newly-appointed chief executive, the board of the company wants you to reply to this and outline a process which will remove these perceptions and enable change to be managed much more effectively in the company.

REFERENCES

Blake, R.R. and the Estate of Mouton, J.S., *Leadership Dilemmas-Grid Solutions*, Gulf Publishing, Houston, 1991.

Drucker, P.F., *The Practice of Management*, Harper & Row, New York, 1954.

'Effective organisations – The people factor,' *Advisory Booklet No. 16, ACAS*, September 1991.

Elizur, D., 'Quality circles and quality of work life', *International Journal of Manpower*, Vol. 11, No. 6, pp. 3–7, 1990.

Hackman, J.R. and Oldham, G.R., *Work Redesign*, Addison-Wesley, Reading, Mass., 1980.

Herzberg, F., Mausner, B. and Snyderman, B.B., *The Motivation to Work*, John Wiley & Sons, New York, 1959.

Investors in People, Chandos Street, London, 1996.

Kotter, J.P. and Schlesinger, L.A., 'Choosing strategies for change', *Harvard Business Review*, Vol. 57, pp. 109–12, Mar/Apr 1979.

LaMarsh, J., *Changing the Way We Change*, Addison-Wesley, Wokingham, 1995.

Likert, R., *The Human Organisation*, McGraw-Hill, New York, 1967.

Ruskin, C., 'The product champion tests his vision', *World Class Design to Manufacture*, Vol. 2, No. 5, pp. 11–15, 1995.

Schroeder, R.G., *Operations Management: Decision making in the operations function*, 4th edn, pp. 724–6, McGraw-Hill, New York, 1981.

Sherwood, J.J., 'Creating work cultures with competitive advantage', *Organisational Dynamics*, Vol. 16, pp. 5–26, 1988.

Syedain, H., 'The rewards of recognition', *Management Today*, pp. 72–4, May 1995.

Taylor, S., 'Business process re-engineering: Eastman Chemical strives for better than world class', *Industrial Engineering*, pp. 28–34, November 1993.

Wilson, N.A.B., 'On the quality of working life', Report prepared for the Department of Employment, Manpower Paper No. 7, HMSO, 1973.

Wilson, T., *A Manual for Change*, Gower Publications, Aldershot, 1994.

PART 5

The initiatives of change

CHAPTER 8

Teams

OBJECTIVES

The objectives of this chapter are to:

- understand what groups and teams are
- appreciate the reasons for forming teams and their various forms and characteristics
- appreciate the benefits and problems of teams
- know the issues and stages of team development
- be aware of the factors behind team success and strategies for team development.

WHAT IS A GROUP AND WHAT IS A TEAM?

It is rather unfortunate that organisations can adopt a teamwork philosophy without ever really understanding how to define a team or the conditions necessary for it to operate successfully. As the old adage goes, 'If you can't define it, you can't measure it'. Many arrangements of people which purport to be teams are in fact merely groups. There is a very large difference between groups and teams.

Groups

According to *Webster's Ninth New Collegiate Dictionary*, a group is:

> *a number of persons associated together in work or activity.*

According to Hunt, groups are:

> *any number of people who are able to interact with one another, are psychologically aware of one another, and who perceive and are perceived as being members of a team.*

Groups appear within organisations through the specialisation of functions, through the establishment of teams to handle projects, or naturally in order to satisfy social needs. They may be formally established by management or may informally arise amongst workers themselves. Management will establish formal groups in order to carry out specific tasks such as decision taking, project completion, problem solving, communication etc. Informal groups emerge as employees simply intermingle in working situations. Customs and social relations are established among the workers. Patterns of behaviour, informal rules, relations and working methods which are not typical of the organisation appear and become entrenched.

The importance of the group was first appreciated by the Human Relations school of thought. Notably, Elton Mayo and the Hawthorne Experiments brought to light the importance of groups, group values and norms, and the influence of groups on behaviour at work. Exponents of the systems approach brought to light the importance of groups within the socio-technical system, and the likes of the Longwall experiments highlighted the importance of groups in influencing behaviour at work.

Teams

The study of teams and teamwork originates from the study of groups, and interest and research into teams has been popularised by the likes of R. Meredith Belbin who developed a theory of successful team composition. The team is one of the main mechanisms for bringing about change in organisations. Many change initiatives are based on a teamwork philosophy in which the team becomes the central unit of the organisation.

Definitions of teams

Katzenbach and Smith make the following definition of a team, distinguishing it from a mere group of people with a common assignment:

> *A team is a small number of people with complementary skills who are committed to a common purpose, performance goals and approach, for which they hold themselves mutually accountable.*

Nolan states:

> *A team is a group of people working together to achieve common objectives and willing to forgo individual autonomy to the extent necessary to achieve those objectives.*

According to Bennett:

> *A team is a special sort of group.*

According to Bursic, teams have a general purpose which is

> *aimed at improving the overall efficiency and effectiveness of various organisational processes and/or improving the quality of work life within the organisation.*

One of the many similar differentiations between teams and small groups is that teams have well-defined positions and often tackle a variety of tasks over and above group problem-solving exercises and, broadly speaking, the difference between the two lies in the presence of teamwork (*see* Baker and Salas, 'Principles for measuring teamwork skills', 1992), which is, itself, somewhat difficult to define. However, in many instances, the terms 'team' and 'group' are used interchangeably. Another difference between groups and teams is that team members voluntarily co-operate and co-ordinate their work in order to achieve their objectives. Members of the team are interdependent and must, to some extent, interpret the nature of their particular role. Each team is led by someone who may or may not have been appointed by higher management and his/her authority is fully accepted by all team members. The leader represents the team and is formally answerable for the team's behaviour. Within each team there should be a high degree of group cohesion, interaction, mutual perception of issues and members who are willing to help and support each other.

REASONS FOR TEAMS

Wilson states that teams have their roots in socio-technical systems theory and support the socio-technical systems approach to good job design, and, as such, the overall aims of teams are similar to those of job design generally: *to enhance the personal satisfaction that people derive from their work* and *to make the best use of people as a valuable resource of the organisation and to help overcome obstacles to their effective performance* (Mullins, 1993). Many firms have seen teams as a possible medium for achieving these broad goals in the present climate of instability and rapid change.

Generally, teams are formed to increase employee involvement, commitment and participation. They allow and encourage individuals to get involved in the plans and activities of the organisation.

A team can produce much more than can the sum of the individuals, since they bring together a set of skills, talents and responsibilities so that the solution to a problem will have all available capacities applied to it. Tjosvold says of teams:

> Confronted with intense competition, shareholder and employee demands, and global possibilities, managers are reinventing their profession and transforming their companies. They involve employees through participative management and quality circles; circumvent the traditional hierarchy, push decision making deep down into the organisations, and make their organisations flatter; form partnerships with suppliers to reduce inventory costs and serve customers effectively ... Mechanical, bureaucratic, impersonal ways of working are giving way to lean entrepreneurial ones. Teamwork is needed to make these new ways of managing and organising effective.

Teams have been cited as the answer to many modern organisational issues and Schutz claims that teamwork *holds all the cachet of a corporate Aladdin's Lamp*. Certain reasons for organising work into teams, cited in Kezsbom, are presented in Exhibit 8.1.

Working together to achieve a common goal

For the team to be successful, the players in the team must work together towards a common goal – the success of the company. Organisations that do not use teamwork

Exhibit 8.1

Reasons for organising work into teams

- the increased need and emphasis on quality and the need for customer focus
- significant changes in the nature of the workforce away from homogenous skills towards a multitude of employee perspectives
- the trend towards participative rather than autocratic management styles and support for the idea that people support what they create
- changes in the psychological contract between employers and employees as workers expect a higher quality of working life (QWL)
- increased realisation of the complexity of work (particularly manufacturing) to the point where one person cannot possibly plan and control all contingencies.

Source: Kezsbom, D. S. 'Team-based organizations and the changing role of the project manager', *American Association of Cost Engineers International Transactions 1994*. Reprinted with the permission of AACE International, 209 Prairie Ave., Suite 100, Morgantown, WV, USA. Phone 800-859-COST/304-296-8444. Fax: 304-291-5728. E-mail: 74757.2636@compuserve.com.

see mistakes as an excuse for punishment, whereas in a teamworking organisation mistakes are seen as an opportunity to learn. With the implementation of teamwork, competition thrives as teams compete with each other and try to outperform and better each other in areas such as reducing lead times or increasing quality standards. Teamwork should hopefully eliminate the disruptive backbiting or dirty tricks that happen in many organisations which can lead to missed opportunities and loss of custom. People like to feel that they are working with others to achieve a common goal. Whether that goal is making a product, having fun, giving help or problem solving, teamwork can be exciting, satisfying and enjoyable. Compatibility of the group members grows in importance as the complexity of the task grows. The skills of the people in the group are important but the way in which they interact and work together dictates how strong the team will be.

The Hawthorne case study

The Hawthorne case study, in Exhibit 8.2, illustrates some of the problems and benefits of teamworking. This case study shows how groups can set their own standards and objectives which can often be opposed to the standards and objectives of the organisation if the groups are not closely monitored. To prevent teams from being a disruptive force, efforts must be made to ensure that the objectives and purposes of the individual, the team and the organisation all coincide.

America's best-run companies use teams

From their studies of America's best-run companies, Peters and Waterman received the message that small teams are 'beautiful' and they identified areas where teams can lead to gains. These are:

1 **Internal competition**. This is where the organisation becomes the market environment in which teams compete, such as in Procter & Gamble where brands compete with one another. This competition can also occur at managerial levels, so managers feel they must constantly strive to improve. The idea of the competition is to force managers and team leaders to drive out any inefficiencies within the system and also to be innovative, which in turn will drive down costs and create a feeling of loyalty and commitment within the team.

2 **Innovation through intense communication**. The team structure in these excellent companies needs effective communication systems to aid the innovative process it creates. The techniques being used have implications for managers at all levels, but they are especially applicable to the manufacturing function.

3 **Flexibility.** Once established, teams can be moved from project to project with much more ease than conventional structures, and this is the theme that Peters and Waterman noticed in excellent companies. For example, when discussing the Harris Corporation's ability to diffuse research funded by the government into commercially-viable operations, they noted that:

> *Harris's success is that the management regularly shifts chunks of engineers out of government projects and moves them, as a group, into new commercial venture divisions.*

Exhibit 8.2

The Hawthorne case study

The Hawthorne studies took place between 1924 and 1927 at the Hawthorne Works of the Western Electric Company in Chicago (*see* Roethlisberger and Dixon, 1966). These studies were conducted to determine how various levels of illumination affected output. Intensity of light for different work groups was varied, change in output measured, and the results analysed. The researchers were disappointed however. They failed to find any relationship between level of illumination and production. In some groups, output bobbed up and down at random; in others it increased. In one group it increased even though illumination was reduced to the level of moonlight. This amazed the experimenters. The output of the group had continued to improve and they had to look for other factors (rather than those which they had deliberately manipulated) which could explain the increase in output. The girls in this group had become extremely motivated to work hard and well, and the reasons for this were found to be: first, a good group atmosphere in the test room – the workers shared pleasant social relationships with one another and the desire to do a good job; second, supervision was more participatory – test room workers were made to feel important, were given a lot of information, and were frequently asked for their opinions. This was not the case in their normal work situation. Further studies were conducted to show that motivation to work, productivity and quality of work are all related to the nature of the social relations of the workers and between the workers and their boss.

In this study reported by Handy, two groups or 'cliques' of men were formed corresponding to those men working at the back of the room who thought their work was more challenging and were aware of a higher status, and the men working at the front of the room. The cliques had their own special habits and there was a lot of competition between them. There were a few people who did not belong to either clique. The group had developed some norms, these were what they thought were fair for the way in which processes and systems should operate. Some of these norms refer to production rates. They established a set figure that they could produce in a week. This figure satisfied the management but was way below the rate at which they could produce. At the end of the day the supervisor was supposed to report how much the group had produced. After a while this stopped and the group began to report their own figures. What the group actually reported was a standard figure for each day, no matter if they had produced more or less than that amount. This meant that if one day they worked hard and produced a lot of parts the next day they could be slack, as long as they reached the set figure for the week. Also, anyone who produced way above their set rate or indeed below their set rate was ostracised by the group until they got back into line.

Source: The Hawthorne studies are described in detail in Roethlisberger, F. J. and Dixon, W.J., *Management and the Worker*, Harvard University Press, Cambridge, Mass., 1966.

TYPES OF TEAMS

Teams come in various sizes, shapes and forms and their names are continually changing because they are usually categorised in terms of the tasks or areas to which they are being applied. For example, teams could include quality circles, employee participation groups, production teams, autonomous work groups, task forces, management teams, project management teams, product design teams etc. In each type of team the team aims can vary, from generation of cost-saving ideas to making and executing top-level decisions; from producing or designing products services, to solving organisational problems (*see* Bursic, 'Strategies and benefits of the successful use of teams in manufacturing organisations, 1992).

Three types of team-based systems

Much of the current interest in teams is driven by Japanese work practices. Cutcher-Gershenfeld *et al.* looked at eight Japanese factories in the US, so as to understand the nature and function of teams in Japanese factories. They identified three types of team-based systems within the eight Japanese factories. These are:

1 a lean production system team, as identified in the MIT automotive study report, 'The machine that changed the world' (Womack *et al.*, 1990)
2 an autonomous team structure which came from England and Sweden under the socio-technical system (STS) approach
3 a more traditional system, that resembles traditional US manufacturing plants at various stages of restructuring. These teams are of the off-line variety, for example quality circles, employee involvement groups, task forces and labour management committees.

Classification of teams

Teams can be applied to almost any work situation at different levels in the organisation. Stott and Walker categorise teams into top management, middle management, project (or task force), and working group teams. Two important and useful ways of categorising teams is by task or function and degree of empowerment. The types of teams in these two categories are shown in Table 8.1.

Table 8.1 Categorising teams by task/function and degree of empowerment

Categorisation of teams by	
Task or function	*Degree of empowerment*
Management teams Workplace teams, including quality circles Project teams Outside/inside teams Quality improvement teams User/supplier teams Employee/temporary worker teams	Problem-solving teams Special-purpose teams Self-directed work teams

CATEGORISING TEAMS BY TASK OR FUNCTION

Wilson summarises teams in terms of their task or function:

Management teams

A management team could be a board of directors, a group of departmental managers, or managers within a department who represent their functions and meet regularly to set policy and conduct the organisation's business.

Workplace teams

According to Stott and Walker, the basic team unit is the working group. Where a team approach is applied to a working group, the aim is usually to increase participation in an attempt to harness the creativity of the group. For this to occur, facilitation is needed rather than traditional management and leadership. A workplace team could comprise a group of production workers, office staff, telephone salespeople, accounts clerks or warehouse staff, with a team leader or supervisor, and the team would be responsible for performing a clear and defined aspect of the organisation's business. Working-group teams come in many forms, the most prominent of which are quality circles and variations or derivatives of quality circles, and self-managing work teams (also known as semi-autonomous work groups/teams, self-directed work teams etc.).

Unlike self-managing teams, quality circles do not delegate authority to make decisions and implement changes. Employees have an advisory role rather than a self-managing one. Many firms have adapted the concept of quality circles to meet their particular needs. An example of a quality circle derivative called STEP, Success Through Employee Participation, has been developed by a multi-national manufacturing company.

Project teams

A project team is a group of the organisation's experts selected and assembled to introduce a product, procedure, system or technique into the organisation. It lasts until the project is completed and is then disbanded. Project teams normally comprise personnel from different functional areas who meet regularly, but on a part-time basis, until their project is complete. Specific problems or issues are tackled and the team may be accountable for planning and implementing solutions. A project team may involve senior personnel as necessary and the team reports to senior management. The big advantage associated with project teams is that they enable complex issues to be addressed by specialists when such specialist skills are not economically viable as a permanent structure. Flexibility is therefore increased, but there is a trade-off between flexibility and loss of stability from more permanent structures. Human resource benefits, in terms of increased involvement and commitment, improved interdepartmental relations, improved interpersonal relations and decreased labour turnover, have all been accredited to project teams. However, one of the features of project teams is shared accountability, which can sometimes lead to no one taking responsibility for certain tasks. Other disadvantages include potentially wasted time due to too many meetings, and tension between different projects due to particular individual skills being in short supply.

An example of the application of a project team in a manufacturing firm is given in Exhibit 8.3.

Exhibit 8.3

Project team case study

Customer orders would come into Marketing which would pass on the information to Customer Services. This department would co-ordinate a number of activities, including purchasing, production and inventory control, and planning. There was usually a 48-hour delay before a response could be given to the customer, and then the Traffic department would book the shipping. Apart from the difficulties of co-ordinating this information, critical decisions had to be taken on which customers to satisfy and which orders had a higher priority. A task force was set up with the specific purpose of finding a way of dealing with enquiries and orders within 24 hours. The task force decided the only way to proceed was to bring together the various operations and look for solutions in each department to cut the time taken.

Source: George, W., 'Task teams for rapid growth,' *Harvard Business Review*.

Outside/inside teams

An outside/inside team is made up of both consultants or technical experts from another organisation and people from within the organisation. This kind of team is used when a new idea or technique is being brought into the business from outside. Again, the team will last for the lifetime of the project.

Quality improvement teams

Quality improvement teams can take many forms: workplace, management or cross-functional. They often have a very long life, and in organisations that have adopted a total quality management philosophy they produce cross-functional matrix management.

User/supplier teams

As the name suggests, a user/supplier team is a group of organisation people and suppliers which meets to refine and improve the service given by suppliers, at the same time transferring some of the organisation's standards and best practices into the supplier's organisation.

Employee/temporary worker teams

Organisations undergoing substantial change, involving a marked reduction in the number of employees, often have to bring in large numbers of temporary workers to make up for a shortfall. Some of these people can be employed for several years. Employee/temporary worker teams are led by a permanent supervisor or manager.

CATEGORISING TEAMS BY DEGREE OF EMPOWERMENT

Kezsbom classifies teams by their degree of autonomy along an 'empowerment continuum' which ranges from a traditional hierarchical structure on the one hand to self-directed teams on the other.

Three basic work team approaches which vary in terms of the degree of autonomy they allow are:

Problem-solving teams

For example, quality circles will typically consist of five to 12 volunteers, often from many departments across the organisation, and will meet several hours a week to solve some problem, in production for example. According to Larson and LaFasto, *the most important and necessary feature of this type of team is trust*. Each member of the team must expect and believe that interactions among members will be truthful and embody a high degree of integrity. There must be mutual respect between all the team members and each team member must be valued.

Special-purpose teams

These are an extended version of the problem-solving teams. These teams tackle problems which are of primary concern to management, labour, or both, and enable workers to have a say in higher-level decisions. These teams became popular in the US in the early 1980s and are becoming ever more popular. *A necessary feature of the structure of the team is 'autonomy'* (Larson and LaFasto, 1989). The difference in teams between the degree of discretion given can range from semi-autonomous to autonomous. The areas of autonomy are: goal and targets, methods, timing, criteria and evaluation, internal management and organisation, and external liaison. It is necessary to have an atmosphere of autonomy from systems and procedures in order to create a team where ideas are not quashed too early and to enable team members to explore possibilities and alternatives using their creativity.

Self-directed work teams (SDWTs)

SDWTs are attracting an increasing amount of interest and come under many different names, such as self-managing teams, superteams, or self-managing work teams, but they are all different names for the same thing. In SDWTs a small number of members are accountable for a clearly-defined area of work. It has been suggested by Barry that traditional management and leadership models are not adequate for self-managing teams and that leadership needs to come from within the team. SDWTs differ from less autonomous teams such as quality circles in that real authority to make changes is delegated and this requires *empowerment*. Stott and Walker state:

> *Empowerment in terms of teams means that members are seen as being innovative and able to contribute ideas, because they know the job better than others higher up in the organisation.*

Empowering employees and striving to obtain their maximum participation may require organisational restructuring. Also, the degree of authority and control delegated to the team can vary and may be increased, depending on the competence of the team.

The concept of the self-managing team is equally applicable to both project teams and work group teams. SDWTs have the ability to cut though the standard, hierarchical decision-making structures and respond quickly to environmental changes. Because today's global market demands high customer responsiveness, fast product development and innovation, SDWTs have become popular. Usually SDWTs are made up of two to 15 workers who produce a major portion, if not all, of a product or a service. The teams learn (are taught/trained) many, if not all, of the tasks which are needed to produce the product or service. Such teams conduct tasks and make decisions which were previously thought of as the role of the manager; tasks such as ordering the raw materials needed for their team's production, quality control, employing new workers to work in their teams, vacation scheduling and team discipline.

The teams will cut across old boundaries which means that the people within them must be carefully selected and well trained. Often team members will be expected to learn all of the jobs that fall within their work area. According to Larson and LaFasto, *In order for these teams to be successful the key ingredient is 'clarity'*. The team must be clear on what its goals and objectives are, what is expected from its members and what their performance measures are. According to the literature, the areas that need to be concentrated on for SDWTs to perform well are communications, organisational structure/culture, training, empowerment and leadership style.

Potential pros and cons of self-directed work teams

There are many pros and cons of SDWTs, and Zuidema and Kleiner describe some of the pros as *improved team involvement and performance, positive morale, and a sense of ownership and commitment to the team goals ... improved quality ... improved productivity and heightened employee morale*. Undoubtedly, where implemented effectively the advantages are immense in terms of higher quality jobs, improved interpersonal interactions and the knock-on improvements in performance. However, the cons are *workers' distrust of management, lack of job security for supervisors, manager unwillingness to relinquish control, personality conflicts between team members,* and employees who are reluctant to accept additional responsibility. Because of these potentially negative aspects, resistance may be experienced when trying to implement self-managing teams.

Problems for middle management

Waterman has suggested the need for management to give up control, which he explains gives rise to the self-managing team. Such teams can provide a platform for quick decision making by the lower-level worker without waiting for a decision from his/her supervisor and therefore bypassing the usual bureaucracy. To accommodate this, organisational restructuring is necessary due to the employee taking on the roles that were traditionally their supervisor's. In practice this means creating a 'flatter' organisation. This new-found worker freedom has led to greater job satisfaction for the lower-level workers but greater job insecurity for the middle management and supervisors. This can lead to a number of situations: namely, middle managers who are going to resist the introduction of SDWTs as they will not want to put themselves out of a job. There will also be fewer promotion opportunities for the lower ranks wanting to join the middle management.

Categorising teams by degree of permanence

Teams have also been usefully categorised by their degree of permanence. For example, from above, a working group team is relatively permanent whereas a project team is only functional for the duration of a project.

The choice of team type is complex

Exhibit 8.4 illustrates that the choice of team type is a complex decision, since each type has important advantages and disadvantages and limitations. The choice of a team type should, however, attempt to maximise the strengths of the firm's production technology and employees.

Exhibit 8.4

Japanese team-based work systems in North America: Explaining the diversity

Many US employers seeking to establish team-based systems are surprised by the diversity of meanings they find for the term 'teams'. Workplaces are filled with off-line teams, lean production teams, and socio-technical systems teams – as well as training teams, task force teams, sales teams, and softball teams. Although many consultants, and much of the literature, do not distinguish between alternative types of team systems, it should be clear that each has important advantages and disadvantages and limitations. The choice of a team system is more complex than many people believe. Type of product, technology, organisational structure and culture, and physical layout are only a few of the most important considerations in the matching of a team system to a company. A lean system optimises flow-through manufacturing but reduces the amount of worker autonomy. A socio-technical system achieves worker autonomy by optimising the balance between social and technical subsystems, but may do so at the expense of efficiency or operating costs. The off-line team optimises the application of problem-solving tools to specific issues, but does not address daily work operations. In other words, firms must not only pick the system that will maximise the strengths of the firm's production technology and employees, but they must also understand the trade-offs in the present and for the future.

Source: Adapted from Cutcher-Gershenfeld, J. *et al.*, 'Japanese team-based work systems in North America: Explaining the diversity', *California Management Review*. Copyright © 1994, by The Regents of the University of California. Reprinted from the *California Management Review*, Vol. 37, No. 1. By permission of The Regents.

TEAM CHARACTERISTICS

One of the most important characteristics a team must possess is a common purpose and a clear understanding of the team's objectives and goals. The people in a team must have mutual respect for each other, both on a personal basis and on the basis of the contribution that each member makes to the team.

A team must have the authority to be able to bring together any resources needed to complete the task in hand. It is also important that team members are not picked for seniority or any other status-related reasons. A team member must be chosen solely by the nature of the expertise the task requires. The team itself must operate without regard to status, since teams are essentially non-hierarchical.

Size of teams

The size of the team to be formed is obviously an important consideration. Nolan suggests the team size should be less than eight if effective working is to be guaranteed. Nolan has the feeling that:

> the larger the team, the greater the diversity of talent, skills and knowledge ... however ... there is less chance of an individual participating ... large work groups (20 or over) tend to have more absenteeism and lower morale.

Studies in Slack show that:

> For best participation, for highest all around involvement, ... teams with ... five and seven seems to be the optimum.

According to Nolan:

> optimal group size in most studies is about seven.

Managers must therefore look at the level of knowledge required within the team and also the level of member participation, taking care to keep the size down.

According to Peters, the structure of teams will vary considerably between organisations, but findings from a study into America's best run companies, by Peters and Waterman, conclude that effective product teams:

> usually range from five to ten in size ...consist of volunteers, are of limited duration, and set their own goals.

Member characteristics

The main consideration in this area is whether the individuals have the necessary skills and capabilities to accomplish the task in hand. Peters and Waterman say that when looking at a group:

> ...the seniority of its members is proportional to the importance of the problem,

showing that managers must assign people to groups who have the necessary experience or seniority to cope with the importance of the decision to be made. Also, the personalities of the group members can have a profound effect on the effectiveness of the group. Handy comments that choosing people with similar attitudes, values and beliefs tends to form *stable enduring groups,* whereas heterogeneous groups with conflicting personalities, *tend to exhibit more conflict, but most studies do show them to be more productive than homogeneous groups.*

Team roles

The people within a team need to have a variety of characteristics in order for that team to perform well. A team of able people does not necessarily produce favourable results, but a balanced group of able individuals will. Too many leaders is bad for a team, but teams with a mixture of assertive and independent people are effective. These groups lead to variety, but variety that can be organised.

Teams fail if the team members cannot work together effectively. Therefore, Belbin proposed that it is the composition of the teams which is of vital importance. Although people show infinite variety in their behaviour, the range of useful behaviour for a successful team is finite. This finite range of behaviour can be defined as *team roles*. Although the most effective structure or mix of members cannot be definitively laid out, Dr Meredith Belbin conducted a study of the best mix of characteristics in a team and suggested the eight team roles shown in Exhibit 8.5. The ideal team would have someone in each of these roles, but in some situations certain types would be unnecessary, and in small teams one person may have to fill more than one position.

Exhibit 8.5

Team roles

The Chairperson. In a manufacturing situation this would be the team leader, who may be a worker elevated to this position or a manager presiding over the team. This person would be disciplined, focused and balanced, and is someone who works well through other people and who has the respect of others.

The Shaper. This person is the *task leader* who is outgoing and dominant and in the absence of the *Chairperson* would fill that role. The Shaper is needed in the team to spur the other members into action.

The Plant. This is the person who provides the most intellectual input into the team, coming up with ideas and imaginative proposals.

The Monitor-Evaluator. This person provides an analytical side to the team, detecting flaws in arguments and carefully considering ideas. The monitor-evaluator is most likely to be the quality inspector in a manufacturing situation.

The Resource Investigator. This member brings new ideas and developments to the group, contributing greatly in meetings. However the rest of the team is needed to do the follow-up work on the resource investigator's input.

The Company Worker. This member holds the administrative post, making sure everything is correct and manageable.

The Team Worker. This person holds the team together in a certain respect, supporting others and helping to resolve any conflict or problems.

The Finisher. This member checks details and makes sure that deadlines are met, following everything through, often with a sense of urgency.

Source: Belbin, R. M., *Management Teams: Why they succeed or fail*. Reproduced by permission of Butterworth-Heinemann, Oxford.

Belbin managed to identify one particular characteristic that was present in all successful teams; this was the role of *The Implementer*, but teams made up entirely of implementers did not succeed and suffered from a lack of ideas and inflexibility. Belbin went on to identify two other types of team members which are of particular use:

Co-ordinators and *plants.* This is reflected in what Alan Fowler wrote in *People Management.* Putting these two types together with the plant, that is the plant, implementer and co-ordinator, gives a combination of bright ideas, practicality and direction.

THE BENEFITS OF TEAMS

Most writers on teams have developed lists of perceived benefits associated with successful teams. Some characteristics can be more easily justified with hard data than others, but this does not mean that they are necessarily more important than other, more subjective, benefits. Amongst the many perceived benefits of teams are:

- improved performance in terms of quality, productivity, flexibility, speed and customer service
- reduced costs
- fewer and simpler job classifications
- better job design (hence increased motivation and performance)
- enhanced ability of an organisation to attract and retain the best people
- increased learning
- reduced duplication of effort
- increased co-operation
- an increase in innovative ideas produced
- better decisions made
- easier adaptation to change
- increased commitment
- reduced destructive conflict
- improved intergroup and interpersonal relationships and communication
- opportunity for employees to perform to the best of their abilities.

Exhibit 8.6 illustrates the benefit to Duffy Tool and Stamping of using teams.
Particular benefits of teams are discussed in the following sections, and are summarised below:

- They make up the building blocks of the organic organisation.
- They do more than individuals can.
- They improve performance, personal growth and work products.
- They improve job satisfaction, quality and service.
- They improve morale, cohesiveness and enjoyment.
- They have a positive effect on culture.
- They result in advantages for the organisation.
- They result in benefits to operations.
- They have advantages for individual workers.

Teams make up the building blocks of the organic organisation

According to the Reser Miller Group:

> *Teams in and of themselves are almost never the entire solution to the challenges faced by modern business. Instead, teams make up the building blocks of the organic organisation.*

So, if teams are to form the cells of the business, what can they provide?

Exhibit 8.6

Excellence Teams in action at Duffy Tool and Stamping

Duffy Tool and Stamping manufactures a wide variety of products, many of which are automotive related. The company employs approximately 300 people and operates out of two manufacturing locations. The company asked the question, how does a company increase efficiency and quality, cut costs, and become more responsive to customer needs? Duffy Tool chose the Excellence Team (ET) approach. A steering committee, chaired by the vice president of finance and composed of top management personnel, was organised to oversee the entire effort. The committee's specific responsibilities included selecting individuals for the initial teams and ensuring that company funds were available for the programme. The teams meet on a regular basis, usually weekly, in a room designated exclusively for the Excellence Team programme. They use a very structured problem-solving methodology and begin by identifying job-related problems in their work area.

Benefits of the programme

The Excellence Team programme has made a significant impact at the company that has resulted in important financial savings. During the six-year period from 1988 to 1993, sales decreased for the first three years, then increased at an average rate of approximately 14 per cent over the next three years. During that same six-year period, pre-tax profits increased significantly every year, even those years when sales revenues went down. Managers are convinced that the Excellence Team programme made an important contribution toward the cost reductions and resulting profits.

An important overall impact of the Excellence Team programme at Duffy Tool and Stamping has been the development of personal and interpersonal skills of the team members. The process of learning a well-defined problem-solving process and applying it within a group of co-workers has instilled an increase sense of competence and cooperation among participants.

Can the Excellence Team process work for your company? Because the Excellence Team simply are applying a problem-solving methodology, it should apply to any size or type of company. The chances of success, however, probably are best in companies that have a reasonably good working relationship between management and line employees. At Duffy Tool and Stamping, there was a history of trust within the company that allowed the programme to take root and grow through the difficult beginning stages. Perhaps the more critical factor for successful implementation is top management support. If the programme is initiated and endorsed strongly by the top management, the prospects for success are great, and the rewards, financial and non-financial, are likely to be far-reaching.

Source: Hanks, G.F., 'Excellence Teams in action', *Management Accounting*. Reprinted with permission from *Management Accounting*, February 1995. Copyright by the Institute of Management Accountants.

Teams do more than individuals can

According to Hill (*see* Tjosvold, 1991) managers use a wide variety of teams for highly practical reasons; mainly because they get things done. Not ordinary things, for most of these can be accomplished by individuals working alone. Teams get extraordinary things done; they are a practical way to foster communication and involve stakeholders:

> *Team members can combine their strengths and efforts to complete tasks that individuals working alone could not efficiently do. Through discussion, they challenge and correct*

one another's errors and biases in reasoning, present a variety of information that no one person has or can adequately remember, and combine perspectives into new solutions not previously considered.

Teams improve performance, personal growth and work products

Katzenbach and Smith argue that teams bring performance results, personal growth and collective work products:

In any situation requiring the real-time combination of multiple skills, experiences, and judgements, a team inevitably gets better results than a collection of individuals operating within confined job roles and responsibilities. Teams are more flexible than larger organisational groupings because they can be more quickly assembled, deployed, refocused and disbanded, usually in ways that enhance rather than disrupt more permanent structures and processes. Teams are more productive than groups that have no clear performance objectives because their members are committed to deliver tangible performance results. Teams and performance are an unbeatable combination.

Teams improve job satisfaction, quality and service

Wall *et al.* used self-report surveys to measure qualitative variables, for example job satisfaction and worker motivation, under different conditions such as autonomous teams and conventional work designs (*see* Bursic, 1992). These surveys found that teamworking led to increases in job satisfaction, but improvements in motivation or worker performance were not found. Other organisational improvements were in quality and service, both due to the use of teams.

Exhibit 8.7 illustrates the use of teams in meeting customer needs at ITW Paslode.

Teams improve morale, cohesiveness and enjoyment

When a team successfully achieves a goal, a sense of group identity is built. According to Adair, *the moment of victory closes the psychological gaps between people,* which leads to rising morale. If a team succeeds, team spirit will develop naturally, which, in combination with good internal communications, makes the group much more likely to perform well. This will also lead to a better working environment for the individual. If the needs of individuals are recognised and they feel as if they can make a worthwhile and characteristic contribution to both the task and the group, their results will be much improved. Group cohesiveness and enjoyment are increased via achievement of tasks, as well as corporate and individual morale. If members of the group get on well and can work closely as a team, their work performance will be increased and their needs will be met, such as self-esteem. Adair believes the three areas of task, team and individual interlink, each area exerting an influence on the other two. This model is shown in Fig 8.1.

Teams have a positive effect on culture

There are many cultural factors which may influence the effects of using teams. In manufacturing, organisational culture is an important aspect of the use of teams. Bursic states that positive effects on organisational culture include:

Exhibit 8.7

Teamwork: A real story in meeting customer needs at ITW Paslode

The Illinois Tool Works (ITW) of Chicago is the most competitive company in the US, according to *Money* magazine. It, along with three other leading domestic performers with top quality products (i.e. Xerox, AMP and Harley-Davidson), is hammering the Japanese and other competitors at home and abroad.

Gean Stalcup, the operations manager for ITW Paslode, explains that about five years ago, Illinois Tool Works acquired Paslode and empowered its people – not just the staff, but all the people. 'We developed common goals and missions. Working together as a team, we established the values and direction of our company as if we owned it. Our core common goal was very simple, but more powerful than you can imagine: to be the best at meeting customer needs.

'To achieve that elusive moving target, we decided that the culture of the organisation must first be changed. The process began with people and the desire to serve our customers better than anyone else in the world. The change we made is about real teamwork, trust, respect, involvement and accountability – about the business of empowering people to be the best they can be and then expecting the best. It is about having pride in what it is we do. We recognise that we are not perfect, never will be, and that we will never be finished.

'The response of our people to a recent business crisis dramatically illustrates the empowerment process in action. We had a very large customer who was considering doing business with one of our competitors. In fact, representatives from this customer had toured the competitor's facilities. They were impressed with what they found.

'We decided that we were to keep this important customer. To get a clear understanding of what happened next, you must first consider a typical corporate structure. Imagine for a moment a pyramid. At the top of that pyramid you find the highest-ranking official of that company. At the bottom you find those who make the products. The direct link to the customer is only by way of the top.

'At ITW Paslode the pyramid has been inverted. The people who actually make the products for the customer have a direct link to the customer. After all, we said, how can you be the best at meeting the needs of your company when information is filtered through layers of organisational bureaucracy?

Now it was time to practise what we had been preaching no matter how high the risk. The management team decided to get out of the way, support the fastener production team and let them take care of the plant tour.

There are many memorable things about this event, but I would like to share with you a particular conversation that shows the genuine emotions that were present. When one person was asked if they would like to participate in this customer visit, the response came in tears.

Much to my surprise, this was not a reaction of fear, but one of great honour and pride that we would trust this individual with something so important – a customer!

What could have been the biggest disaster in customer relations history turned out to be the biggest win that I have ever seen. Our customer learned who we really are, and I believe they felt better than ever before about ITW Paslode because of all the people they met. In addition, we got to know this customer better by doing something that had most likely never been done before.'

Source: Cusimano, J.M., 'Creating leaders by training managers as leadership trainers', *Industrial Engineering*, pp. 58–60, November 1993.

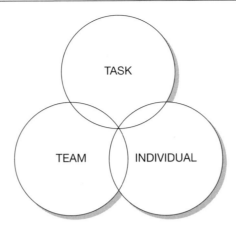

Fig 8.1 Interlinking of task, team and individual
Source: Adair, J., *Understanding Motivation*, 1990. The Talbot-Adair Press, Guildford.

- increasing co-operation between departments
- improving communications
- changing outdated traditional procedures and processes
- increasing employee involvement at various levels.

It is known that many of these factors contribute to an individual's motivation, and changes involving them fulfil some employee needs, such as recognition and responsibility, and will ultimately increase job satisfaction. Bursic believes that changes introduced by team programmes may have a positive influence on job satisfaction and motivation among the organisation's employees. Wall *et al*'s survey asked the open-ended question 'What, in your opinion, are some of the advantages and disadvantages of working in teams?', which provided them with an idea as to the positive cultural changes, otherwise known as benefits, of teamworking. Some of the responses were:

> *Great for communications among employees ... Better co-operation among workers ... Promotes better relationships ... Teams communicate problems and needs more effectively ... Working in teams gives you more of a chance to interface with people needed to help with problems who you wouldn't normally be able to contact.*

Teams result in advantages for the organisation

There are many reasons for the formation of teams within organisations, which may account for their apparent success.

Handy notes the uses for organisations as being:

- **For the distribution of work:** enables particular duties to be allocated to those workers with the necessary skills or talents.
- **For the management and control of work:** to allow work to be organised and controlled by appropriate workers with responsibility for a certain range of work.
- **For problem solving and decision making:** the more people considering a problem or decision then the more likely that the solution will be to everyone's liking, as it will have been arrived at using the various skills and talents of those involved.

- **For information processing:** for the freer flow of information to those who need to know.
- **For information and idea collection:** for the ease of information collection from ideas or suggestions.
- **For testing and ratifying decisions:** group discussions can be held to test the validity of decisions.
- **For co-ordination and liaison:** helps co-ordination between divisions.
- **For increased commitment and involvement:** as people feel that they are part of a team they will be more willing to get involved in future plans and activities taking place within the organisation.
- **For negotiation or conflict resolution:** team discussions can help arrive at satisfactory solutions, which may not otherwise have been possible.
- **For inquest or inquiry into the past.**

These are the reasons organisations may benefit from team structure and they can be applied at all levels, from boardroom to shopfloor. The system of working in teams would not produce the desired effect if it was only the organisation which benefited; however, there are many reasons why teams are beneficial to the individuals involved.

Teams result in benefits to operations

In Bursic's paper 'Strategies and benefits of the successful use of teams in manufacturing organisations', the following are stated as being the benefits of using teams:

- productivity improvements
- increased worker morale
- better union–management relations
- improved product quality
- a more flexible organisation
- more effective decision making and execution
- increased job satisfaction
- increased motivation
- lower absenteeism.

Exhibit 8.8 provides an example of the benefits of mixed teams to operations in a successful brewing company.

Teams have advantages for individual workers

Again, Handy offers a summary of the advantages of teams for individuals, which he has gathered from his own personal experience, as well as his conclusions from the work of others on this subject:

- A means of satisfying individuals' social or affiliation needs – the desire to belong to something or share in something.
- A means of establishing a self-concept. Most people find it easier to define themselves in terms of their relationship to others, as members of a role set with a role in that set.
- A means of gaining help and support to carry out their particular objectives, which may or may not be the same as the organisation's objectives.

Exhibit 8.8

The benefits of mixed teams to operations at The Whitbread Beer Company

The Whitbread Beer Company was voted the Commended Factory in Wales in the 1994 *Management Today* Britain's Best Factory Awards for Manufacturing Excellence. The company's task is the low-cost supply of canned and kegged lagers and ales. *Their outstanding features are mixed teams*. From the company's outset, a lot of attention was given to industrial relations. In 1978, single-status employment conditions, a single-unit agreement and no separate craft negation rights were considered very innovative. Today, thanks to a very thorough benchmarking exercise, Chris Hughs, the general manager, knows for sure that these, plus state-of-the-art brewing equipment, have enabled the plant to achieve its objectives of being the lowest-cost producer of beer in Whitbread – and very possibly within the UK too. Mixed teams of operators have been set up with merged responsibilities for production, quality and engineering. The plant now works six-and-a-half days with rostered shifts instead of five days on three shifts. These changes account for a 26 per cent increase in product capacity and a 24 per cent fall in middle management. 'Forget the image of the master brewer', says technical manager Robin Cooper, 'with mixed teams, we now have beer brewed by former engineering supervisors.'

Source: Wheatley, M. and New, C., 'Britain's Best Factory Awards for Manufacturing Excellence', *Management Today*, Haymarket Publications.

- A means of sharing and helping in a common activity or purpose, which may be making a product or carrying out a job. This can be related to the motivational factor of the need for a sense of belonging and love which Maslow identifies in his 'Hierarchy of Needs' model as being important in the life of an individual. Individuals need to feel that they belong, and being part of a team at work can satisfy this.

PROBLEMS WITH TEAMS

There is some evidence by Saarel to suggest that teams have not always delivered what has been promised in terms of benefits. A good example of this was found by Wall *et al.* when carrying out a long-term investigation into the implementation of autonomous work groups in a manufacturing firm. The conclusions of this well-designed study were that, contrary to expectation, productivity increases were mainly due to the elimination of supervisors, and labour turnover actually increased. However, long-term benefits to job satisfaction were found.

Sources of people's reluctance for teams

For teams to work there must be a positive mental attitude towards them within the company, from the managing director to the person doing the most menial task. Katzenbach and Smith suggest three primary sources of people's reluctance to be involved with teams:

1 **Lack of conviction.** Some people think teams cause more trouble than they are worth. They generate more complaints than results and waste time in endless discussions. Some believe they are a useful human relations exercise but have no real gains. Others believe they erode the discipline and performance of specific small groups. These concerns can be brought about by a misconception of the word 'teams'.

2 **Personal discomfort and risk.** Some people will always be loners. Others find the team approach too time-consuming, too uncertain or too risky. They may be uncomfortable speaking up, participating or being conspicuous. They may not like having to depend on others or to assimilate contrary points of view. This can be linked to the idea of 'if you want something doing, do it yourself'.

3 **Weak organisational performance ethics.** The organisation may be more concerned with internal politics or external public relations than a commitment to a clear set of goals.

Conflict

According to Tjosvold, the largest problem associated with teamworking is conflict, both within the team and between teams. More than 20 per cent of a manager's time is concerned with dealing with conflicts. Conflict usually occurs within teams when the attitudes, motives, values, expectations or activities of team members are incompatible, and if members perceive themselves to be in disagreement.

Hunt states that the majority of conflicts occur within groups because of differences among members in terms of attitudes, goals and feelings. It becomes very difficult to resolve this conflict if people are greatly involved with these attitudes, goals and feelings, as it is difficult to change people's perceptions of these. It is usually personal goals and attitudes about power that are at the root of conflict; however, they are not always the cause. Conflicts often occur over goals, unclear task assignments, unfair evaluations, insults and criticism, unrealistic workloads, unfair distribution of rewards, refusal to interact, and a lack of feedback, challenges and efficiency.

Intergroup conflict is the most frequent form of conflict, such as sales versus production, according to Hunt. He believes this occurs quite simply because people are separated into functions. Another reason for intergroup conflict is that different people with differing attitudes, goals and perceptions are attracted to different functional groups.

Some forms of conflict are said to be constructive (Hunt, 1986). They are said to be beneficial to the group because they may:

- introduce different solutions to the problem
- clearly define the power relationships within the group
- encourage creativity and brainstorming
- focus on individual contributions rather than group decisions
- bring emotive, non-rational arguments into the open
- provide for catharsis.

However, more often, conflict is considered to be destructive. In these cases, conflict may:

- prevent members from 'seeing' the task at all
- dislocate the entire group
- undermine the objectives in favour of subgoals

- lead people to use defensive and obstructing behaviour
- result in the disintegration of the entire group
- stimulate win–lose conflicts.

Too much conflict is detrimental for a group, but too much co-operation may cause the enjoyment of the interpersonal processes that evolve with teamworking to come before actual completion of the task. It is often very useful to avoid conflict to enable tasks to be completed in the short term. However, ongoing processing and reflecting is critical in order to enhance the team's capabilities, identify and reduce frustrations and strengthen trust and emotional bonds.

CREATING AND DEVELOPING TEAMS

Although it is possible to focus on the characteristics that are displayed by successful teams, it should be remembered that teams are dynamic and they do not acquire the necessary characteristics to be successful overnight, whatever those characteristics may be. Instead, teams develop different characteristics naturally over time. Intervention strategies can be used to speed up this process, to guide teams towards developing desirable characteristics and help them to move from one development stage to the next.

Changing to a teamwork culture

According to Wilson, any organisation wanting to change to a culture based on teamwork needs first to acquire or develop change champions who are in favour of teamwork, and second to promote teamwork as one of its values, supported and continually reinforced by senior management. It may also be necessary to make structural changes to the groups of people in the organisation so that they are able to operate as teams.

Team leaders and members should be selected on the basis of two main criteria. The first is the technical or commercial skills required by the team to perform its function. If the team is required to perform an accounting function, for example, then it must have the correct blend of technical skills to do the job. The second criterion is teamwork skills. There should be a blend of team skills and abilities so that members co-operate and work to make the best use of technical skills for the benefit of the team, its members and the organisation as a whole.

After the teams have been defined and selected, teamwork has to be developed by gradually training and educating everyone in the organisation. This must form part of a carefully-constructed strategy which should contain the following elements: the cascade principle, team training and team leader training.

Team development

Katzenbach and Smith set forth a number of team basics to help develop teams. There are three disciplines: skills, commitment and accountability. The skills are problem solving, technical/functional and interpersonal. Commitment is brought about by specific goals, a common approach and meaningful purpose. Accountability must balance the mutual with the individual, and lends to the idea of having a small number of people in a group. Teams must focus on performance and team basics rather than on trying to 'become a team':

> Most people simply do not apply what they already know about teams in any disciplined way and thereby miss the performance potential within existing teams, much less seek out new potential team opportunities.

The key lessons Katzenbach and Smith put forward are:

1 Significant performance challenges energise teams regardless of where they are in an organisation.
2 Organisational leaders can best foster team performance by building a strong performance ethic rather than by establishing a team-promoting environment alone.
3 Biases towards individualism exist but need not get in the way of team performance.
4 Discipline, both within the team and across the organisation, creates the conditions for team performance.

They talk of a common, meaningful purpose setting the tone and aspirations of the team. It is normal that a demand is set by management and the team shapes its own purpose.

Peters and Waterman refer to this as 'solution space', where management defines the boundaries and scope of authority clearly enough to indicate direction, yet allows flexibility for the modification required to develop commitment.

Stages of team development

The Human Resource Group at the Cranfield School of Management investigated the problem of developing and stimulating effective teams. They developed a team development wheel as a means of training workers, in particular managers, to work in teams and perform as team members. Other writers have developed similar models, notably Bass and Ryterband, and Woodcock. Tuckman's conclusion was that a team experiences four distinct learning stages of development, beginning with a group of individuals and developing into a cohesive unit, as shown in Fig 8.2.

Stage 1: Forming

The first stage in development involves the team getting to know one another, understanding one another's views, expectations, ideas and objectives. People will be testing one another out and creating their personal identity within the group. They will be guarded in the issues they raise and the opinions they give.

Stage 2: Storming

As members develop a better understanding of others, they will begin to put forward their views more openly and forcefully. Group leadership may be questioned at this stage. Some infighting may occur as allegiances are questioned and the nature of the tasks and programme are challenged. As a result some members feel demotivated and leave.

Stage 3 : Norming

> The sooner the group attempts to fulfil certain task goals, the sooner it will break out of the infighting stage.

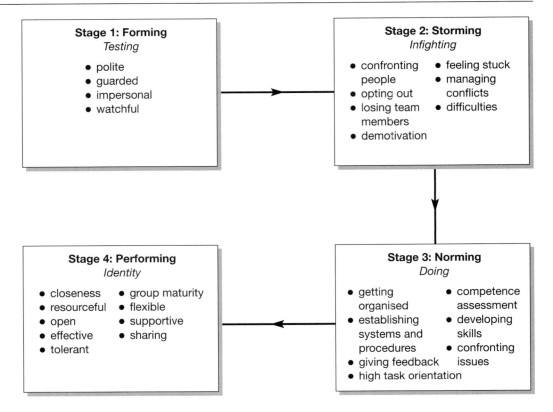

Fig 8.2 Four stages of team development
Source: Tuckman, B. W., 'Development sequence in small groups', *Psychological Bulletin*, 63, pp. 384–99, 1965.
Copyright 1965 by the American Psychological Association. Reprinted with permission.

During this stage the group becomes more organised and establishes systems and procedures to achieve particular goals. The skills level, competence and norms of behaviour of each member become apparent. Interpersonal barriers tend to fall into the background as members begin to co-operate and exchange their views, ideas and experiences on work-related problems.

Stage 4 : Performing

How quickly the group progresses to this stage depends on the leader's skills in reconciling differences and developing cohesion, and in assisting group members to identify with one another. In this stage, the group has matured and is acting as a real team. It is much more cohesive, with members supporting one another, sharing information and ideas and tolerating one another's differences. Through the group's ability to marshal its full resources to pursue common goals, it is likely to be at its most effective.

Teams naturally progress from one stage to the next, although the speed at which this is done varies for each team, and teams may become stuck at any stage of development for a variety of reasons. If teams are left to develop naturally they may develop norms that are not beneficial to performance.

Tips for the development of teams

Katzenbach and Smith have put together eight tips for the development of teams, which are:

1 Establish urgency and direction.
2 Select members based on skills and skill potential, not personalities.
3 Pay particular attention to first meetings and actions.
4 Set some clear rules of behaviour.
5 Set and seize upon a few immediate performance-orientated tasks and goals.
6 Challenge the group regularly with fresh facts and information.
7 Spend lots of time together.
8 Exploit the power of positive feedback, recognition and reward.

In doing any or all of this they admit that there will be intra-team conflict, but this is good. Without this, members will not come to respect the others. Conflict is a strong point for good teams.

In essence Katzenbach and Smith push three points:

- The team must have a common purpose – no amount of creating the right conditions will induce teamwork if the team has nothing to focus on.
- The team must have a common approach. It must know how it is going about its task, and again it must be agreed on the issue.
- The team must accept mutual accountability. This is all about commitment and trust.

The cascade principle

One design, presented by Wilson, which allows teamwork to flourish, is based on a series of interlocking teams from the top to the bottom of the organisation. This is illustrated in Fig 8.3.

In this kind of arrangement each team leader is also a member of a higher-level team; for example the warehouse team leader would also be a member of the distribution team. Following the same principle, the distribution team leader would be a member of the executive team. These links ensure that each team overlaps with those above and below, helping information to flow quickly from the top to the bottom of the organisation and vice versa.

Following the cascade principle, first the executive team is trained in team-building and teamwork principles. The distribution team leader is a member of the team, so he or she attends the training event. The training then cascades down the organisation as the distribution team leader attends a training event with their own team. Each team leader thus attends two training events and the process continues all the way down the organisation. In this way important links and relationships are forged between teams, and every person in the organisation learns about teamwork and the behaviours necessary for teams to operate effectively.

FACTORS BEHIND TEAM SUCCESS

The factors behind team success according to the perspectives of four different experts are shown in Exhibit 8.9. Kazemek lists ten general effectiveness criteria which are

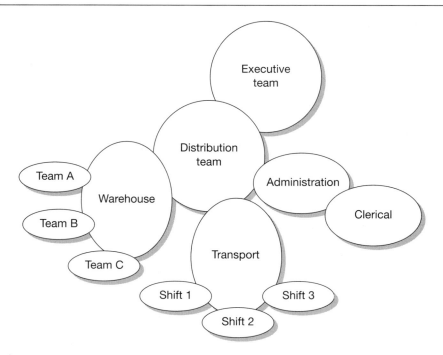

Fig 8.3 Interlocking teams

Source: Wilson, T., *A Manual for Change*. Reproduced by permission of Gower Publishing Ltd.

similar to Hitt's ten attributes of a productive team. Huszczo's list of seven broad characteristics has a slightly different emphasis and is related to a model for team analysis. Logan identifies eight key ingredients needed in a winning team. Her list is the product of research from teams in many environments based on insights into outcomes, attributes and features of successful team projects (i.e. it relates specifically to project teams), and it pertains to reliance on executive leadership and decisions. Finally, Bursic presents a broader view and believes that, in order for teams to be successful, several organisational factors, both external as well as internal to the team, need to be present.

Belbin's success factors

Belbin approaches the subject from a research perspective based on his experiments with teams. His examinations of teams under laboratory conditions reveal several factors that are conducive to success and other factors that lead to teams failing to operate effectively. Belbin's work is based on team roles, which are described in more detail when considering the finer, behavioural aspects of teams.

Belbin found the majority of winning teams to be strong in terms of personal qualities relevant to eight team roles which he identified, and diverse enough to make up for weak or missing roles. Belbin also found three other types of teams that tended to win or do well at least some of the time. First, a team of 'co-operative stable extroverts' are, on occasions, able to make up for their lack of diverse team roles by their flexibil-

Exhibit 8.9

Factors behind team success

Kazemek's ten general effectiveness criteria

1 Goals and objectives are understood and agreed.
2 Conflict is dealt with constructively.
3 Members share the leadership role.
4 People's abilities are used.
5 Communication is open and participatory and members know what is going on.
6 Members support the team's controls and procedures.
7 They have well-established problem-solving and decision-making approaches.
8 Experimentation and creativity are encouraged.
9 They evaluate their functions and processes regularly.
10 Members understand their roles, responsibilities and authority limitations.

Huszczo's seven characteristics

1 Goals should be clear and related to the wider organisation, and members should be committed to the goals.
2 Teams should have sufficient *talent* to accomplish tasks and development of talent should be encouraged.
3 Members need to be clear about their *roles* in the team and what they should contribute.
4 *Procedures* need to be in place that allow effective interaction, problem-solving and decision-making.
5 *Interpersonal relations* skills need to be developed so that team members communicate and relate well and resolve conflict.

6 There is a need to *reinforce* effective behaviour through recognition at the personal and organisational levels.
7 Care must be taken to build *external relationships* with other groups outside of the team, but which form part of the team's environment.

Logan's eight key ingredients needed in a winning team

1 Top management championship
2 The right product selected for focus
3 A five- to eight-member team representing *all* involved functions
4 Management-team alignment on purpose and expectations
5 Management provided resources
6 Results-oriented team technologies
7 Management implementation of team recommendations
8 A customer-centred culture that rewards teamwork.

Bursic's broader view of what makes teams successful

1 Top management support
2 Definition of leadership
3 A facilitator
4 Clear objectives and goals
5 Early planning
6 Interdisciplinary teams
7 Definition of the team structure
8 Use of team building
9 The training of team members in problem solving, measuring results etc.

ity in adapting their behaviour. Second, teams that have a 'superstar' who is also the chairperson can sometimes come out on top, due in the main to a coherent strategy driven by the chairperson. Finally, what Belbin calls 'Apollo teams' occasionally win. These teams are made up of individuals of high mental ability, who contribute little in the way of team roles (i.e. like those used in the Apollo space programme). Apollo teams are normally plagued with conflict, but if they can overcome their self-destructive nature they are potentially successful.

The use of team leaders, team facilitators, rewards and empowerment

The writers in the area of teamwork do not all use the same terms or even the same ideas on how to improve teams, but there are areas they agree are important. These include:

- team leaders
- team facilitators
- rewards
- empowerment.

Team leaders

The team leader must be the ultimate team player, listening to others and willing to let the team make its own decisions. He/she must acknowledge they are not the fount of all wisdom and should not force the team to produce its own answers. However, the team leader must give up decision space only when the group is ready to accept and use it, and so he/she must accept that the team-leading role will change as the group develops:

> Team leaders act to clarify purpose and goals, build commitment and self-confidence, strengthen the team's collective skills and approach, remove externally-imposed obstacles, and create opportunities for others. Most important, like all members of the team, team leaders do real work themselves.

Team facilitators

As mentioned, the role of a team leader and the effects of the leader on the performance of the team and its importance in achieving team success cannot be overstated. However, the traditional 'leading' role is not appropriate in a semi-autonomous team environment and it has been discarded in favour of new values. The 'leading' role in a self-managing team (where the leadership is distributed between team members) is one of facilitation, which involves co-ordinating the factors that allow the team to be successful. This means viewing employees as experts with unique skills and knowledge, only imposing selective control over the work of others, encouraging employees to participate in goal setting and in defining how work should be accomplished. In effect, the team facilitator should draw out the characteristics that successful teams must possess, and if this is not done well, a team has little chance of success.

Kezsbom suggests the following characteristics for a team leader of the 1990s:

- a facilitator
- skilled at group dynamics
- encouraging others to participate in plans and decisions
- understanding how to coach, inspire, and motivate
- no longer the 'expert'
- working to get resources for the team ('boundary spanner')
- comfortable relying on the expertise of others.

It is important that the 'facilitator' assumes the role without being 'over-responsible', which may stunt the commitment, input and ownership of other team members. To overcome this tendency requires a significant shift in mind from a traditional supervisor approach to that of a facilitator.

Rewards

Many writers, including Nolan, Katzenbach, Drucker, Deming and Tjosvold, all stress the need to reward as a group if team coherence is to be gained. It not, morale, commitment and respect will be lost, while jealousies and individualism will rise.

Tjosvold expresses it well, in using the word 'justice':

> *Fairness and justice are prerequisites for commitment. Employees want their work life to be rich and fulfilling, but they must also see that rewards are just.*

Empowerment

Empowerment means the people in the team have authority and control to make the changes they decide on. This embodies the concept of self-managing teams. The degree of authority and control with which the team is empowered can vary and may be increased depending on the competence of the team. However, it is appreciated that the team members know the job better than others higher up in the organisation, and the process of empowerment is seen as a mechanism to facilitate innovation, contribution of ideas and responsibility for outcomes in members of the team.

Ingredients for success with teams

Basic ingredients for success with teams include senior management direction, learning, and self-sufficiency.

Senior management direction

Senior management should provide the policy and direction and make efforts to create the environment in which teams can be formed and flourish within the company. They should be held accountable for their use of resources; overall results, however, will remain in the hands of those who contribute to policy and resource dissemination.

Learning to become a team

Developing the skills necessary for people to work as a team takes time. People need to learn how to work together to fulfil the team objectives, and the team leaders need to learn how to facilitate this process.

Self-sufficiency

By multi-skilling the team members, and including all the knowledge and skills necessary for the team to accomplish its tasks, control its processes and succeed, the team can become largely self-sufficient. In this way the team can develop the confidence to look after its own affairs and work within its own resources, but also have the confidence to ask when it requires help.

Examples of team learning and self-sufficiency, provided by Choppin, are shown in Exhibit 8.10.

Exhibit 8.10

Team learning and self-sufficiency

Self-sufficiency

A company working in an area of high unemployment suffered high absenteeism amongst its young workforce. They worked shifts and many out with friends the night before an early shift would be persuaded to indulge in another beer, rather than going to bed early. The company formed the workforce into teams, putting an extra operator in each team of eight or nine, but expecting the team to cover natural breaks and the occasional absentee. Quickly absenteeism diminished as the peer group exerted greater pressure than management had ever been able to.

Team learning

The senior management group of a service sector organisation, wishing to develop a total quality culture, decided to put all TQM developments on ice for three months while they learnt to become a team. They then led by example, allowing true teamwork to permeate the entire organisation.

Source: Adapted from Choppin, J., 'TQM: Teamwork and total quality', *The Plant Engineer.*

TEAM DEVELOPMENT APPROACHES

There are a number of possible intervention strategies that can be used to manipulate team development with the aim of improving the team's effectiveness. Many of these stem from organisational development approaches related to organisational change. Stott and Walker say that examples of these are quality circles, teambuilding, sensitivity training and quality of working life. Prominent in these approaches is teambuilding.

Teambuilding

Teambuilding is similar to Senge's 'team learning discipline', *the process of aligning and developing the capacity of a team to create the results its members truly desire*. Teambuilding has been defined by Kazemek as:

> *a method under which groups experientially learn to increase their skills for effective teamwork by examining their structures, purposes, setting, procedures and interpersonal dynamics.*

Several models exist that advocate different approaches to teambuilding. The most prominent of these are presented in Stott and Walker:

- **The Goal-setting Model:** largely based on Locke's 'Goal-setting Theory of Motivation' and Drucker's 'Management by Objectives'
- **The Interpersonal Model:** evolved from the organisation development 'sensitivity training' and T-groups (This model is similar to Senge's 'Shared Vision'.)
- **The Role Model:** uses principles derived from the work of Belbin.

A strategy for teambuilding

Woodcock and Francis consider that there are five main considerations that organisations need to make regarding the use of teams to improve effectiveness:

1 Is poor teamwork a significant organisational problem?
2 Does the organisation require a team approach?
3 Is the team ready for teambuilding?
4 Does the organisation have competent teambuilding resources?
5 Does the organisation need a teambuilding consultant?

The eleven building blocks of effective teamwork

Woodcock and Francis studied hundreds of teams in many organisations and analysed those which have been particularly successful. From their experience over the last 30 years they consider that successful teams are usually those which have undergone a process of formal or informal teambuilding and which have dealt with 11 key aspects of function and performance. If one, or more, of these key aspects is missing or under-developed, the team will fail to achieve its full potential. They call them the 'eleven building blocks of team effectiveness', and they are presented in Exhibit 8.11.

Exhibit 8.11

The eleven building blocks of effective teamwork

1 Balanced roles
2 Clear objectives and agreed goals
3 Openness and confrontation
4 Support and trust
5 Co-operation and conflict
6 Sound procedures
7 Appropriate leadership
8 Regular review
9 Individual development
10 Sound intergroup relations
11 Good communications.

Source: Woodcock, M. and Francis, D., *Teambuilding Strategy*. Reproduced by permission of Gower Publishing Ltd.

1 Balanced roles

Truly effective teams are able to use different personalities to suit a wide range of situations, but they can only do this if the mix of team membership is balanced. Too often work teams are formed without any conscious effort to ensure that membership is balanced.

2 Clear objectives and agreed goals

Only when the objective of an activity becomes clear is it possible for people to pull together constructively and decide what is relevant and important. Until objectives are agreed they have little force. It is a vain hope to imagine that every member of a team can be fully committed to identical objectives. Differences of opinion and conflicting interests will always exist, and the most significant requirement is to develop mechanisms for exploring viewpoints, finding common ground and learning to live with differences.

3 Openness and confrontation

Teams which work well together are capable of coping with confrontation and encourage a high level of openness between team members. This quality of relationship needs to be built and reinforced by genuine feelings of support between team members. If a team is to be effective, its members need to feel able to state views, opinions, judgements, rational and irrational feelings, facts and hunches without fear of being belittled or embarrassed.

4 Support and trust

Support and trust are extremely valuable characteristics of human relationships. One of the reasons why historically so much business has been done between family relatives or within ethnic groups is that a high level of trust has been built up. Trust becomes a valuable commodity which enables risks to be taken that would otherwise be avoided.

5 Co-operation and conflict

Co-operation can be expressed as 'working together for common gain'. This is an essential characteristic of a team approach, where the individuals put the team's objectives before their own and share in the gains and rewards from their joint activities.

Traditionally, conflict has been seen as a negative characteristic promoted by trouble makers who are seeking personal acclaim at the expense of the team. Of course, destructive conflict is present in many relationships. However, the potential benefit from constructive conflict is great because it promotes more realistic and effective problem solving. Skills of conflict resolution can be learned and the procedures which follow are generally applicable.

A developed team has accomplished a high degree of co-operation which enables the resources of the group to be used for the benefit of all. When relationships do conflict, such differences are welcomed positively as they help bring creativity and realism to the group.

6 Sound procedures

Most teams consist of individuals who have different functional or specialist responsibilities. The behaviour of each team member affects the others and procedures for clarifying roles, channelling communications and managing meetings need to be effective. It is helpful for members to discuss the team's basic organisation and assess whether their existing procedures are meeting the needs of the situation.

7 Appropriate leadership

Studies of leadership have determined that leaders perform two vital functions: influencing people and controlling situations, while developing good relationships and encouraging participation.

It has been shown that people need different kinds of leadership according to their ability and attitude. When there is low ability or low willingness to perform a task, it is necessary for the leader to spend a lot of time in controlling and directing. However, where there is greater ability and willingness to perform, a leader will encourage individuals by increasing participation and involvement.

8 Regular review

Regular review of performance is essential to the development of competence. The most valuable reviews incorporate objective and impartial data. A team will gain from periodic reflection on its performance and a dispassionate enquiry into missed opportunities and inadequate performance.

9 Individual development

Observers have noticed that the most effective individuals and the least effective individuals almost invariably display two different sets of characteristics. The less effective seem to have a passive approach to life, wishing to be as undisturbed as possible. They find challenge frightening and avoid it whenever possible. Successful people, by contrast, seem to have an active approach to life. They are the people who make things happen and are constantly seeking new challenges for themselves and the groups which they represent.

Often, those individuals who predominantly exhibit the high-effectiveness characteristics are uncomfortable people to work with – their drive and dynamism at first sight appearing to inhibit the common good of the team. The really effective teams, however, learn to capitalise on these good qualities and encourage their less effective members to move towards them.

10 Sound intergroup relations

Interteam relations often need to be consciously developed, particularly where daily routines fail to provide sufficient contact to establish a rapport. Many managers fail to perceive the need for deliberate 'bridge-building' between groups, but usually much can be done to improve co-operation.

Interteam relations are an important area because almost always teams need to co-operate to achieve common objectives. Although it often seems that there is a natural force pulling a team together, it also appears that there is an equally natural force which polarises teams. Indeed, some teams develop increased coherence by demonstrating their superiority to other groups.

11 Good communications

Effective communication is necessary at and between every level in an organisation, between its constituent parts and with many groups which comprise the external environment. Each needs to communicate to some extent with the other, and depending upon the role, most need to communicate with the external environment.

Effectiveness of different intervention approaches

The relative success of the different intervention approaches is difficult to assess due to the lack of consensus in this field and the absence of sufficient, well-designed research. Stott and Walker suggest that the various approaches can be combined, and that effectiveness can be assessed by viewing their contributions towards influencing behaviour at four levels (dimensions). These dimensions measure:

- effects at the individual level
- effects at the task level
- effects at the team level
- effects at the organisational level.

SUMMARY

- Groups are a number of persons associated together in work or activity. Informal groups emerge as employees simply intermingle in working situations. Management will establish formal groups in order to carry out specific tasks such as decision taking, project completion, problem solving, and communication. A team is a special sort of group which has well-defined positions and often tackles a variety of tasks over and above group problem-solving exercises; and broadly speaking the difference between the two lies in the presence of teamwork.

- Generally teams are formed to increase employee involvement, commitment and participation and thereby make the best use of people as a valuable resource of the organisation and help overcome obstacles to their effective performance. Teams should bring together a set of skills, talents and responsibilities so that the solution to any problem will have all available capacities applied to it.

- Since the Hawthorne case study, cases have abounded of companies illustrating the benefits of teamworking. Both the UK and America's best run companies make use of teams.

- Teams come in various sizes, shapes and forms and their names are continually changing because they are usually categorised in terms of the tasks or areas to which they are being applied. Teams can be classified by task or function as management teams, workplace teams (including quality circles), project teams, outside/inside teams, quality improvement teams, user/supplier teams and employee/temporary worker teams. Classification can be by level of empowerment, and three basic work-team approaches, which vary in terms of the degree of autonomy they allow, are problem-solving teams, special-purpose teams and self-directed work teams.

- In finding the balance between large and small teams, managers need to look at the level of knowledge, skills and capabilities needed to accomplish the task in hand, taking care to keep the size down. For best participation, for highest all-round involvement, a team with five to seven members seems to be the optimum.

- The people within a team need to have a variety of characteristics for that team to perform well. Belbin proposed that it is the composition of the teams which is of vital importance. He conducted a study of the best mix of characteristics in a team and suggested eight team roles: the chairperson, the shaper, the plant, the monitor-evaluator, the resource investigator, the company worker, the team worker and the finisher. The one particular characteristic present in all successful teams is the implementer, and members which are of particular use are the co-ordinators and the plants.

- Teams provide advantages for the organisation, its operations and individual workers. The benefits of teams are that they make up the building blocks of the organic organisation. They do more than individuals can. They improve performance, personal growth and work products, job satisfaction, quality and service, morale, cohesiveness and enjoyment, and have a positive effect on culture.

- The primary reasons for people's reluctance to be involved with teams are lack of conviction, personal discomfort and risk, and weak organisational performance ethics. The largest problem associated with teamworking is conflict, both within the team and between teams.

- To create and develop teams it is necessary to create a culture based on teamwork needs. To help develop teams the three disciplines of skills, accountability and commitment need to be considered.

- Four distinct stages of team development have been identified. They are forming, storming, norming, and performing.

- The cascade principle of teams is that of a series of interlocking teams from the top to the bottom of the organisation. These links ensure that each team overlaps with those above and below, helping information to flow quickly from the top to the bottom of the organisation and vice versa.

- Factors or characteristics that lie behind team success are being strong in terms of personal qualities relevant to Belbin's eight team roles; a broader understanding of the big picture; recognition; management commitment and support; a team process that is fun, educational and which stimulates improved relationships; leadership; facilitators; mutual caring and bonding; unity of purpose; rewards and empowerment.

- Intervention strategies that can be used to assist the development of teams are quality circles, teambuilding, sensitivity training and quality of working life.

- A strategy for teambuilding makes use of eleven building blocks. They are: balanced roles, clear objectives and agreed goals, openness and confrontation, support and trust, co-operation and conflict, sound procedures, appropriate leadership, regular review, individual development, sound intergroup relations and good communications.

REVIEW AND DISCUSSION QUESTIONS

1 Differentiate between a group and a team and explain why it could be beneficial for an organisation to have teams.

2 Teams can be classified by their level of empowerment or by their task or function. Explain the usefulness of categorising teams in these ways and outline the nature of a team in each category.

3 Discuss the characteristics of organisations, teams and individuals which enable teams to perform well.

4 Describe how teams develop and the approaches that could be used to assist this process.

ASSIGNMENTS

1 As an executive director, the chief executive has asked you to prepare a team development programme for the organisation. Outline your proposals, making special reference to strategy, culture, training and types of team.

2 It has been said that teams which are empowered and have autonomy are beneficial to an organisation – more so than ordinary teams. Discuss your level of agreement with this statement in the context of your organisation. Explain the purpose and problems of fostering such teams in your organisation.

REFERENCES

Adair, J., *Understanding Motivation*, The Talbot-Adair Press, Guildford, 1990.

Baker, P. and Salas, E., 'Principles for measuring teamwork skills', *Human Factors*, Vol. 34, No. 4, pp. 469–75, 1992.

Barry, D., 'Managing the boss-less team: Lessons in distributed leadership', *Organisational Dynamics*, pp. 31–47, Summer 1991.

Bass, B. M. and Ryterband, E. C., *Organisational Psychology*, 2nd edn, Allyn and Bacon, London, 1979.

Belbin, R.M., *Management Teams: Why they succeed or fail*, Butterworth-Heinemann, Oxford, 1996.

Bennett, R., *Personal Effectiveness*, 2nd edn, Kogan Page, London, 1994.

Bursic, K.M., 'Strategies and benefits of the successful use of teams in manufacturing organisations', *IEEE Transactions on Engineering Management*, Vol. 39, No. 3, pp. 277–89, 1992.

Choppin, J., 'TQM: Teamwork and total quality', *The Plant Engineer*, pp. 34–5, Mar/Apr 1993.

Cusimano, J.M., 'Creating leaders by training managers as leadership trainers', *Industrial Engineering*, pp. 58–60, November, 1993.

Cutcher-Gershenfeld, J. *et al.*, 'Japanese team-based work systems in North America: Explaining the diversity', *California Management Review*, Vol. 37, No. 1, 1994.

Fowler, A., 'How to build effective teams', *People Management*, pp. 40 & 41, 23 February 1995.

George, W., 'Task teams for rapid growth', *Harvard Business Review*, p. 71, Mar/Apr 1977.

Handy, C., *Understanding Organisations*, Penguin, London, 1976.

Handy, C., *Understanding Organisations*, 4th edn, pp. 156–8, Penguin, London, 1993.

Hanks, G.F., 'Excellence Teams in action', *Management Accounting*, pp. 33–6, February 1995.

Hitt, W., *The Leader-Manager: Guidelines for action*, Battelle, Ohio, pp. 41–71, 1988.

Hunt, J.W., *Managing People at Work*, Institute of Personnel Management, 2nd edn, London, 1986.

Huszczo, G., 'Training for team building', *Training and Development Journal*, Vol. 44, No. 2, pp. 37–43, 1990.

Katzenbach, J. and Smith, D., *The Wisdom of Teams*, McKinsey and Co. Inc., New York, USA, 1993.

Kazemek, E., 'Ten criteria for effective team building', *Healthcare Financial Management*, Vol. 45, No. 9, 1991.

Kezsbom, D.S., 'Team-based organizations and the changing role of the project manager', *American Association of Cost Engineers Transactions*, Transactions (HF11-HF15), 1994.

Larson, C.E. and LaFasto, F.M.J., *Teamwork: What must go right/What can go wrong*, series in interpersonal communications, Vol. 10, Newbury Park, CA, Sage Publications, 1989.

Logan, L.R., 'Team members identify key ingredients for team-building success', *National Productivity Review*, Vol. 12, No. 2, pp. 209–23, 1979.

Maslow, A., *Motivation and Personality*, Harper & Row, New York, 1954.

Mullins, L.J., *Management and Organisational Behaviour*, 3rd edn, p. 489, Pitman Publishing, London, 1993.

Nolan, V., *The Innovator's Handbook: Problem solving, communication and teamwork*, Sphere Books Ltd, London, 1989.

Peters, T., *Thriving on Chaos*, Pan Books, Basingstoke, 1988.

Peters, T. and Waterman, R., *In Search of Excellence*, Harper & Row, New York, 1982.

The Reser Miller Group, USA. Taken from its advertising on the internet, 1994.

Roethlisberger, F. J. and Dixon, W. J., *Management and the Worker*, Harvard University Press, Cambridge, Mass., 1966.

Saarel, D., 'Triads: Self-organising structures that create value', *Planning Review*, Vol. 23, No. 4, 1995.

Schutz, W., 'Real teamwork', *Executive Excellence*, Vol. 6, No. 10, pp. 7–9, 1989.

Senge, P., *The Fifth Discipline*, Doubleday, New York, 1990.

Slack, N., *The Manufacturing Advantage: Achieving competitive manufacturing operations*, Mercury Books, London, 1991.

Stott, T. and Walker, A., *Teams, Teamwork and Teambuilding: The manager's complete guide to teams in organisations*, Prentice Hall, 1995.

Tjosvold, D., *Team Organisation: An enduring competitive advantage*, John Wiley & Sons Ltd, Chichester, 1991.

Tuckman, B. W., 'Development sequence in small groups', *Psychological Bulletin*, 63, pp. 384–99, 1965.

Wall, T., *et al.*, 'Outcomes of autonomous workgroups: A long-term field experiment', *Academy of Management Journal*, Vol. 29, No. 2, pp. 208–304, 1986.

Waterman, R., *The Frontiers of Excellence*, Nicholas Brearley Publishing, London, 1994.

Wheatley, M. and New, C., 'Britain's Best Factory Awards for Manufacturing Excellence', The Whitbread Beer Company company report, *Management Today*, p. 133, 1994.

Wilson, J.R. and Taylor, S.M., 'Simultaneous engineering for self-directed work teams implementation: A case study in the electronics industry', *International Journal of Industrial Ergonomics*, Vol. 16, Nos. 4–6, pp. 1–13, 1995.

Wilson, T., *A Manual for Change*, Gower, Aldershot, 1994.

Womack, J., Jones, D.T. and Roos, D., *The Machine that Changed the World*, Rawson Associates, New York, 1990.

Woodcock, M., *Team Development Manual*, 2nd edn, Gower, Aldershot, 1989.

Woodcock, M. and Francis, D., *Teambuilding Strategy*, Gower, Aldershot, 1994.

Zuidema, K.R. and Kleiner, B.H., 'New developments in developing self-directed work groups', *Management Decisions*, Vol. 32, No. 8, pp. 57–63, 1994.

CHAPTER 9

Empowerment

OBJECTIVES

The objectives of this chapter are to:

- develop an understanding of what empowerment is and how it affects people and the organisation
- illustrate some of the benefits of empowerment
- explain how people can be empowered, particularly by encouraging them to work in teams
- explain the various ways of empowering teams
- outline the steps a manager should take in order to empower people
- present an 'empowerment process management model' which identifies six key steps that should be followed to empower an organisation
- discuss the implications of empowerment regarding structures, managers, workers and some unions
- highlight the dangers of misuse and misinterpretation of empowerment
- recognise and understand the many and varied factors that are necessary to achieve maximum empowerment
- present a method of assessing the extent of empowerment in an organisation
- present a method by which people can assess to what extent they feel empowered in their job.

WHAT IS EMPOWERMENT?

Empowerment is a relatively new idea in the business environment. It involves devolving the level of responsibility all the way down the organisational hierarchy to those individuals who have the relevant understanding to make the best decisions. The intention is to give employees greater responsibility and control for the tasks they carry out. This creates a sense of ownership and thus increases their self-esteem.

The literature abounds with definitions of empowerment and some are presented in Exhibit 9.1.

According to Foy, empowering people is as important today as involving them was in the 1980s, or getting them to participate was in the 1970s.

Cook describes empowerment as a process which has evolved in response to trends towards a greater degree of responsibility and involvement amongst employees in the running of their organisations. This trend has emerged as organisations have recognised the capacity of their employees to improve and enhance business performance

9 · Empowerment

Exhibit 9.1

Definitions of empowerment

... a feeling of job ownership and commitment brought about through the ability to make decisions, be responsible, be measured by results, and be recognised as a thoughtful, contributing human being rather than a pair of hands doing what others say (Byham, 1992).

Empowerment is simply gaining the power to make your voice heard, to contribute to plans on decisions that affect you, to use your expertise at work to improve your performance and with it the performance of your whole organisation (Foy, 1994).

Empowerment is leadership that increases the authority and responsibility of those closest to our products and customers. By actively pushing responsibility, trust and recognition into the organisation we can harness and release the capabilities of all our people (Waterman, 1994).

Empowerment is the term used to describe the philosophy for running a business which permits an organisation's employees the authority and responsibility for those decisions which affect their jobs (Cook, 1994).

when they are informed and involved, when their skills and experience are recognised, and when they are encouraged to be creative, to innovate and to take risks. The sceptics would say that this trend is due to less people being left to do the work.

Guy Wallace believes empowerment is often mistaken as a powerful tool and technique on its own, when in fact it exists as a management component of total quality management (TQM). He considers that empowerment requires that the systems of TQM be in place to support its efforts/teaming, leadership, reward systems and communication systems.

An empowered structure

In *The Financial Times*, November 1993, Lorenz describes his version of an empowered structure:

> *Instead of a series of levels which command or control the one immediately beneath them, power and information on many issues must be delegated, decentralised and diffused. Trust must be established between bosses, peers and subordinates. Individual effort within narrow departmental boundaries must be replaced by cross-functional teams. Instead of information being withheld in each successive level in the hierarchy, it must become shared, or at least accessible through networking. The new structure invariably means fewer managers, each with wider responsibilities.*

THE HOW AND WHY OF EMPOWERMENT

Empowerment has grown out of a number of trends which have evolved in the development of the organisational environment. According to Cook, as depicted in Fig 9.1, these are:

- employee involvement
- the quality of working life
- total quality management
- continuous improvement
- teamworking
- the learning organisation.

According to Eccles, empowerment is ordinary common sense activity and simply resurrects recognisable past fashions in a new guise (*see* Table 9.1). The *suggestion schemes* which were favoured 30 years ago have been revived as a way of tapping workers' direct experience at the sharp end of the organisation where products and services are made and delivered. Similarly, *job enrichment*, touted some 25 years ago as the route to capturing workers' latent skills in the service of the organisation, and then sidelined as having insufficient productive effect, is now recommended again as another aspect of empowerment. Eccles comments that those who advocated *worker participation* 15 years ago as the route to harmony and productivity at work, only to see the appeal of mutuality – as power sharing was christened – crumble under the impact of free market economics and the unremitting hostility of Anglo-Saxon managements, can be permitted a wry smile. Now, as a branch of empowerment, it is deemed to be a prospective salvation for companies which are struggling to compete with fierce international competition.

Eccles continues:

> *The best new thing about empowerment is itself, the word empowerment, which is so positive that it has enabled managers to embrace old, well-known, more productive ways of managing which had previously languished. The process is fascinatingly inward-looking.*

> *Before they can market empowerment to their employees, managements have a more introverted task. They have to market it to themselves. Having flocked to the banner of empowerment, Western managements are now beginning to do what sensible Japanese managements have been quietly doing for decades. But what a fuss some Western companies make about it. No wonder that there are now firms which are too embarrassed to use the word empowerment – even when they begin to practise it.*

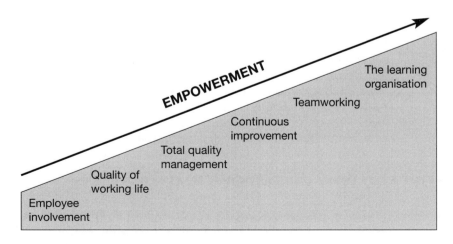

Fig 9.1 The evolution of empowerment

Table 9.1 The history of empowerment

Aspect of empowerment	Equivalent historical aspect
• Suggestion involvement	Suggestion schemes (30 years)
• Job involvement	Job enrichment (25 years)
• High involvement	Worker participation (15 years) (but no Industrial Democracy)

Empowerment has arisen from the following needs:

- **To meet the new challenges**. It would appear that, as organisations face increasing market place and economic pressures, they see empowerment as a means of enhancing their business performance by devolving responsibility to unleash fully the capabilities of their people. In particular, the new challenges of the rapidly-changing business environment are, for example: customer demands, new technologies, global economies, redefined workforce values, and increasingly tough competitors (Byham, 1992).

- **To streamline**. Successful organisations are competing by redefining their organisational values, cutting costs and streamlining to remove all the things that get in the way of their focus, such as bureaucracy, hierarchy, overheads and functionalism. This has resulted in a reduction in the number of layers of management. The idea is to reduce the organisation to as few levels as is possible. Some organisations have been cut to three levels: *directors, managers and people* (DTI, 1994). The result is a reduction in the number of people employed; i.e. downsizing is taking place.

- **To restructure to give control**. Such restructuring to produce more with less has inevitably required that people become empowered. Because of these changes, responsibility and accountability are pushed more to the fore and, increasingly, the people working in the organisation are recognised as an asset to the company and encouraged to fulfil their potential while at work. This results in empowerment of the individual, which is a dramatic change from the old style of management where managers thought their job was to control others. Waterman believes that managers and leaders now need to understand that they have to give up control, i.e. empower others, in order to get results. Certainly, empowerment assists in giving people what they want: *people want to feel as if they have some control over their lives*; it makes them feel healthier and happier, and they tend to be more effective in the jobs they perform.

- **To empower employees**. The results of the 1993 Employment in Britain Survey suggest that, in some areas at least, employees are feeling more empowered than they were even a few years ago. Sixty-three per cent of employees surveyed reported that the level of skills they use in their jobs had increased in the last five years, while 70 per cent said they influenced routine decisions regarding the amount and the quality of their work. Substantially more than in 1984 said that they were involved in decision making about their work tasks. However, this new-found influence does not seem to have extended as far as workers would like. Only 32 per cent of employees responding to the survey felt they could exert influence over broad changes in the way their work was organised; 49 per cent thought that they should have more say in these kind of decisions.

THE IMPLICATIONS OF EMPOWERMENT ON PEOPLE

Empowerment has implications on the way we are treated, the way we work and the way we treat others. These implications, depicted in Fig 9.2, are:

Changing roles

According to Peters, the middle manager can become the most important player in the newly-conceived structure, but his/her role must be wholly changed from the traditional one. Clutterbuck and Kernaghan say that empowerment can be a frightening prospect for managers at all levels. But if they worry about their job security and satisfaction in an empowered organisation, they may have more to worry about in an unempowered one. Not only are empowered organisations arguably more competitive, and thus more likely to survive in the long term, but the job of a manager in an empowered organisation can be immensely more satisfying than in a comparable command and control role. Clutterbuck and Kernaghan state:

> *Instead of playing policeman, empowered managers can share ideas with and learn from their employees. They are also freed of much of the routine work involving and running the company and are thus themselves empowered to get on with the job of strategy formulation, planning and leadership.*

Changing the way we reward

To obtain results in this new order, it will be necessary to break down functional barriers and alter the way people are rewarded. Peters' prescription is to:

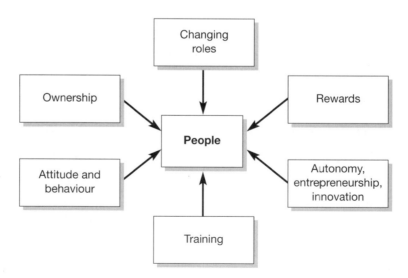

Fig 9.2 The implications of empowerment on people

dramatically shift reward (formal and informal) and evaluation systems for middle managers in order to emphasise 'making things happen' across formerly sacred functional boundaries.

Transferring ownership

At every level in the organisation leaders must transfer ownership of work to those who execute it and create an environment for ownership in which each person wants to be responsible for his or her performance. As Belasco and Stayer state:

Under the new paradigm, leaders lead and employees manage.

The antithesis of this, according to Oren Harari, is that if employees are given the message that the right decision is the manager's decision, this is a sure fire way to diminish their creativity, accountability and morale.

Pamela Johnson uses 'The Wizard of Oz' as a simile for an empowered workforce comprising scarecrows, tinmen and cowardly lions. The three qualities to empowerment are brains, a heart and courage. Without these, a workforce is composed of people who are passive and unmotivated.

Changes in attitude and behaviour

For individuals whom the organisation wishes to empower, the process can also cause initial fears. According to Cook, many of us are conditioned to look to authority figures to make the decisions which direct the pattern of our working lives. Empowered individuals, often working with other team members, set their own agenda and determine the quality of their own working lives. This may demand the development of alternative skills as well as attitude and behavioural changes.

For empowerment to be truly effective throughout an organisation, responsibility for action needs to be passed down as far as possible to those people who have the relevant understanding to make the best decisions.

Autonomy, entrepreneurship and innovation

People who have a sense of being in control often perform better and are more motivated than workers who are dictated instructions on every aspect of their day-to-day, routine jobs. This point is further illustrated by Peters and Waterman who describe eight attributes which they believe a successful company must have. They call their eighth attribute 'simultaneous loose-tight properties'. What this says is that individual members of the company are given freedom and are encouraged to innovate, but they also know that their actions will be scrutinised and judged. Peters and Waterman consider that, for empowerment to work, the rank and file must be allowed 'autonomy, entrepreneurship and innovation', which again are the features of this eighth attribute for success.

Training needs

Training is a key component of empowerment, with empowered employees spending up to 'ten per cent of their time on training courses' and training being the 'epicentre of empowerment', according to the DTI. The knowledge and education gained from the training can often be used to gain a competitive advantage.

STEPS IN THE EMPOWERMENT PROCESS

It helps if everyone in the organisation has a clear understanding of what they are trying to achieve by empowerment and what they must do to achieve their purpose. To assist with this process, Kinlaw has provided an 'empowerment process management model' which identifies the six key steps that should be followed in the planning, initiating, and evaluating of a company's empowerment policy. These steps, shown in Fig 9.3, are as follows:

1 **Define and communicate** the meaning of empowerment to every member of the organisation.

2 **Set goals and strategies** that become the organising framework for people at every organisational level as they extend and strengthen empowerment by their own efforts.

3 **Train** people to fulfil their new roles and perform functions in ways that are consistent with the company's goals for extending and strengthening empowerment.

4 **Adjust the organisation's structure** so that it demands lean management, reduces bureaucracy, and forces the creation of greater autonomy and freedom to act.

5 **Adjust the organisation's systems** (such as planning, rewarding, promoting, training, hiring etc.) to support the empowerment of people.

6 **Evaluate and improve** the process of empowerment by measuring improvement and the perceptions of the organisation's members.

Critical to the operation of this process is that people understand the meaning of empowerment and the payoffs that can be expected. It is essential that targets for empowerment should be identified, and planning and control systems specific to empowerment be developed in order to achieve them.

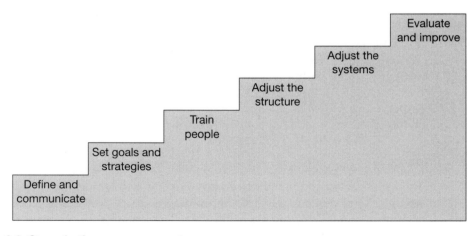

Fig 9.3 Steps in the empowerment process

EMPOWERMENT THROUGH TEAMS

The most common way, at present, of empowering employees is to encourage them to work in teams. This creates a virtuous improvement circle, since teams become more successful if the employees in an organisation are empowered.

Tjosvold believes there are various ways of empowering teams:

1 **Relate the team's vision to the organisation**. Employees must discuss how the team's goals will further the business strategy and teamwork of the organisation. The executives indicate how they see the team's role in the company and discuss their common direction with the team.

2 **Allocate resources**. To be effective, teams require access to the resources necessary to achieve their aim. They also need the support and permission of management. The team needs a budget and people assigned to the team to enable them to complete their task.

3 **Include skilled, relevant people**. To achieve its goals, a team needs specialists in technical areas, facilitating groups and linking the team with management.

4 **Structure opportunities to work together**. This may include regular meetings, locating offices close together, or members communicating via electronic mail.

5 **Hold individuals accountable**. Each member of the team is responsible for a particular activity or set of activities and must report to the rest of the group on what they have achieved.

EMPOWERING PEOPLE

For empowerment to be successful, managers must give their subordinates enough confidence to take on their new responsibilities and contribute openly to ways of improving their own work schedules and standards.

What should be left behind is the 'management says, workers do' attitude, so that the workers can exercise control over their own work and make decisions regarding it without having to ask the permission of management.

Byham and Cox suggested three steps managers must take to empower their people. These steps, the authors say, lead to the soul of empowerment, which is to offer help without taking responsibility:

1 **Maintain self-esteem**. This step refers to the manager/supervisor maintaining the self-esteem of the employee. A manager can do this by finding positive things to say about the employee's work and never putting people down, even if they have made mistakes.

2 **Listen and respond with empathy**. This involves the manager listening to what is being said by the employee when talking about the problems he/she has encountered. After listening to the employee the manager should give a quick resumé of what has been said so that the employee knows that the manager was listening. Then the manager should respond positively by telling the employee what he/she can or cannot do about the situation. This will make the employee feel as though they have been heard and considered, not just ignored.

3 **Ask for help in solving problems**. This is perhaps the hardest point for managers to accept, since they may ask what good they are if they cannot solve the departmental problems. If some of the people in the department are asked to help in solving a problem, the problem will be overcome quicker, and the employees will feel as though they are an asset to both the department and the organisation. The remaining people in the department should not feel as though they are being left out: the manager should explain to them about the problems being experienced and ask them to get involved by covering the work of the people solving the problem.

THE BENEFITS OF EMPOWERMENT

Lower absenteeism and turnover

With the implementation of empowerment it is reported that levels of absenteeism are reduced as employees begin enjoying their work role more. Clutterbuck and Kernaghan comment on the positive effects of empowerment on job security and turnover:

> *Employees who worry about their job security and satisfaction in an empowered organisation may have more to worry about in an unempowered one ... There seems to be solid evidence that labour turnover is higher in unempowered jobs than in empowered.*

Sense of ownership

Empowerment involves giving the core workers a sense of ownership so that they feel that they belong in the company rather than just working there. Workers gain a sense of ownership when they are able to decide how the job should best be done, their ideas are listened to, and, more importantly, their ideas are acted upon. Overall, the workers feel more in control as the management give up the tight control over their everyday jobs.

Taking responsibility

Byham says that the 'soul' of empowerment is offering help without taking responsibility. This means giving the employees problem ownership – letting them take on the responsibility of finding a solution to a problem, testing whether or not the solution will work, and implementing the solution when it has been found.

> *Employees who are empowered are less risk-aversive, more creative, and more willing to suggest bolder solutions.* (Johnson, 1994)

A good feature of this degree of empowerment is that, if practised properly, it should share the load:

> *If it worked, we'd all be better off. If nothing else, I'd sleep better at night from not feeling so damned lonely. My employees will share my profits, but they will also share my anxieties.*
> Robert Frey, owner and president of the Cin-Made Corporation, Cincinnati, Ohio.

This illustrates a problem found with some quality circles, where the employee is expected to find a problem with the system or process, but it is then handed over for someone else to fix. Thus the original team loses ownership of the problem and hence any enthusiasm for the proposed solution.

Motivation

If people are given control, i.e. empowered, over some or all of their work tasks, they will feel more satisfied and therefore their motivation to achieve their and the organisation's objectives will increase. Increased responsibility and feedback on their achievements will increase their job satisfaction, which will, in turn, increase their motivation to achieve more. This increase in motivation and satisfaction will also lead to increased worker performance.

The case study presented in Exhibit 9.2 illustrates how the owner of a small company which was experiencing severe difficulties made a startling turnaround through employee empowerment.

PROBLEMS WITH EMPOWERMENT

Loss of control and insecurity

Empowerment implies a transfer of power and control from one group of individuals to another, which may mean that line managers – often those at the middle level – must relinquish their authority. According to Cook:

Middle managers are frequently the people who feel the least powerful within an organisation. They frequently perceive themselves as sandwiched between senior management who create company policy and the workforce who may resist the changes which senior managers wish to make.

Giving up power and control can cause middle managers to feel increasingly insecure and anxious about their positions. According to the Industrial Society (*see* Exhibit 9.3), empowerment is most likely to be unpopular with middle managers. It takes courage to learn that devolving power does not mean a loss of control. By giving up power managers can gain control.

More responsibility, more stress, no more pay

Worker participation and empowerment may be seen as a way to increase productivity, reduce lead times or increase throughput, but not everyone agrees with the idea. Some people find it too stressful being expected to find new ways of performing their jobs more efficiently, or having continually to come up with their own solutions to problems they have found. According to Cook, increased responsibility can bring additional stresses and strain to individuals. Also, some unions view worker empowerment as just another ploy to motivate employees to work harder for the same pay. They think that it is just a further way to undermine the authority of the unions. Some companies experience high employee turnover rates as self-directed work teams (SDWTs) are introduced. This is because these teams need to work on the basis of individuals being empowered and taking extra responsibilities, which they may not be happy with.

Clutterbuck and Kernaghan offer the down side to empowerment:

Exhibit 9.2

Empowerment or else

Robert Frey, owner and president of The Cin-Made Corporation in Cincinnati, Ohio, writes:

'Almost ten years ago, a partner and I bought a small, troubled company in Cincinnati that made mailing tubes and composite cans – sturdy paper containers with metal ends. The product line had not changed in 20 years. Profits were marginal. Labour costs were out of control, job definitions were rigid, and union relations were poor.

Today we make a new mix of highly differentiated, specially protected, environmentally responsible composite cans; our workforce is flexible and deeply involved in our success; strict job descriptions are a thing of the past; we have not raised the contract wage for eight years; and our relations with the union are excellent. What's more, the company is doing well in a demanding market and making a lot of money.

How did we achieve this startling turnaround? Employee empowerment is one part of the answer. Profit sharing is another.

But the kind of change we experienced doesn't come simply from treating people well. People hate change. Change of *any* kind is a struggle with fear, anger and uncertainty, a war against old habits, hidebound thinking and entrenched interests. No company can change any faster than it can change the hearts and minds of its people, and the people who change faster and best are the people who have no choice. I had no choice because the company was close to failure, and I was overwhelmed and exhausted. At my wit's end, I decided to share my problems and profits with my employees. And why did they have no choice? Because I gave them none. I forced empowerment and profit sharing on them pretty much against their will.

Despite their bitterness, the employees could also see that we'd reached an impossible dead end. Although they suspected my motives and disliked my style, we both realized that to save the company, we had to work together. Like it or not, we had a marriage and there was no good way to get a divorce.

I wanted to share this company with my employees. In the beginning, it was the pain I wanted to share as much as the profit. I wanted the workers to worry. Did any one of them ever spend a moment on a weekend wondering how the company was doing, asking if the right decisions had been made? Maybe I was unrealistic, but I wanted that level of involvement.

The payment scheme never paid out much money. And my idea was to pay out *lots* of money, enough to create a tangible connection between the way people worked and the profits they shared, enough to get everyone passionately involved in the effort to cut costs, increase sales and make money.

I did a bunch of calculations and decided it would work. I even believed it would be attractive, at least to the workforce. As for my partner, my creditors, and my family, they would probably think I was crazy to offer so much. But what the hell, I thought. If this works, we'll all be better off. If nothing else, I'll sleep better at night from not feeling so damned lonely. My employees will share my profits, but they will also share my anxieties.

"That's not my job," they'd say. "Why not?" I'd say. "Well, it just isn't," they'd say. "But I need your input," I'd say. "How in the world can we have participative management if you won't participate?" I don't know," they'd say. "Because that's not my job either. That's *your* job." And I'd lose my temper.

In the beginning, I really did lose my temper every time I heard the words, "It's not my job." Later on, when I discovered my outbursts were having some effect, I started faking them a bit. Whenever anyone said, "It's not my job," I'd go beserk. Sometimes I didn't know myself if I was really mad or simply playacting, but people had to understand that those words they weren't allowed to utter.

Gradually, I induced my managers to share more information with employees I also got them to learn how to share power or to quit and let me replace them with managers who would.

Gradually I began giving my best people new responsibilities. For example, I expanded the duties of the union steward, a woman named Ocelia Williams, from sheet-metal cutting to inventory planning to materials ordering to head of the metals department.

Gradually, hourly workers in general began to take on some of the work of problem solving and cost control. I pushed and prodded and *required* people to help solve problems related to their own jobs. Sometimes I felt like a fool, albeit a very pleased fool, when they came up with simple solutions to problems that had persistently stumped me and my managers'.

Exhibit 9.3

Employee power worries managers

Giving frontline employees more responsibility, resources and authority – known as empowerment – is most likely to be unpopular with middle managers, according to a survey by the Industrial Society, the advisory and training organisation.

Senior managers were the most enthusiastic about the process, which the survey predicted would become increasingly important. More than half of the 580 managers who responded said they would soon expect to be empowering their employees.

The south and north of England are the two regions with more employers expected to stick to the old ways. The areas with the strongest shift to empowerment are Northern Ireland (74 per cent) and Scotland (64 per cent).

The main motive for increasing empowerment was to make better use of people's skills. This was cited by more than 66 per cent of respondents, compared with just over half who mentioned better customer service.

In nearly one in three cases an increase in empowerment followed the appointment of a new chief executive. It was also associated with a cut in management layers. Some 54 per cent agreed that empowerment reduced layers of management. More than one in three reported cuts in the number of middle managers.

Even though one in three respondents saw managers having less involvement in day-to-day matters, the scope of their jobs may be broadening. Some 40 per cent referred to middle managers having a wider span of control. One in four were taking on more personnel functions. There was also an increasing emphasis on supporting rather than controlling staff.

Mr Bob Dixon, of the Industrial Society, said, 'Empowered staff are better able to maximise their potential an so increase the competitive advantage of their organisation.

'Empowerment is far more than delegation. It means harnessing the creativity and brainpower of all employees – not just a few managers. There must be a "no-blame" culture in which mistakes are seen as learning opportunities.'

Source: Bolger, A., 'Employee power worries managers', *The Financial Times*, 27 Feb 1995. From *Best Practice*, *Issue No. 8, Industrial Society*.

> *All too often empowerment can simply mean shouldering more responsibility for less reward. In these cases, employees rarely find themselves empowered to say 'No'. Many employees are not prepared to take on more work and responsibilities simply for the pleasure of feeling more in control. Indeed, it may not be too fanciful to wonder whether the victims of empowerment outnumber the beneficiaries.*

What empowerment should attempt to do is harness the energy that people spend moaning about a situation and channel it into making their jobs better. People do have a fundamental interest in their own jobs.

The benefits and problems of empowerment are contrasted in Fig 9.4.

Misconceptions and dangers

The deceptive allure of empowerment

According to Eccles, despite its appeal, empowerment can be trivial. One well-known retail chain encourages its store teams to show initiative and responsibility, but the

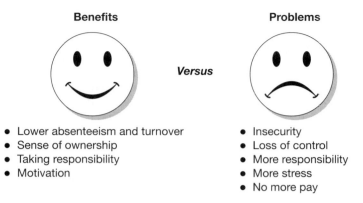

Benefits		Problems

Versus

- Lower absenteeism and turnover
- Sense of ownership
- Taking responsibility
- Motivation

- Insecurity
- Loss of control
- More responsibility
- More stress
- No more pay

Fig 9.4 The benefits and problems of empowerment

teams cannot alter prices, product specifications, decor or fittings at store levels and have virtually no say over the product range or which items are stocked in the store. What initiative means is that, if, for example, they see hot weather approaching, they should order more sandals, sandwiches and soft drinks. All that they are empowered to do is carry out the closely-specified task with maximum responsiveness. They simply have to keep things going – pacifying complaining customers and tweaking store operations ever more efficiently. Exhibit 9.4 illustrates the degree of caution General Electric (GE) exercises when it comes to empowerment.

Exhibit 9.4

Caution with empowerment

Similarly, the much vaunted 'Workout' programme at GE results in such supposedly noteworthy items as the moving of factory pipes so that the product no longer spilt onto the floor and the persuading of a manager to open closed windows to ventilate an over-hot workspace. In neither case could the employees do those things without managerial authority. More interesting were suggestions to adopt a cheaper in-house design of a protective shield, to source paint from one not two suppliers to reduce inconsistency, and to connect cash registers to speed up the opening of new customers' accounts. Again, the employees were not empowered to do anything – only to recommend. *Decision and resource power remained firmly with management.* The only alteration was that, with 'Workout', the responsibility for the burden of proof shifted, so that rather than the employees needing to prove their case, the onus of decision lay on the manager, who could only kill the idea by explicit rejection. Yet it was still the manager's decision and the employees remained supplicants.

Source: Fortune. © 1991 Time Inc. All rights reserved.

Empowerment is not delegation

There are some common misconceptions of empowerment, one of which is that empowerment means delegation. The distinction between delegation and empowerment is that delegation is action by the manager, and empowerment, if it works well, is action by the subordinate. All too often delegation equals dumping, and although it is sometimes more positive and consists of a balance between direction and autonomy, it still usually lacks the element of support which empowerment involves. According to Richard Boren, empowerment unleashes within each person their own power to make a difference, power that cannot be taken away by some outside force. According to him, delegation is acting on others' behalf; definitely empowerment does not begin with delegation.

Empowerment is not responsibility without authority

Empowerment is not responsibility and responsibility alone is not empowerment. Empowerment is not just a matter of pushing more responsibility down an organisation. It is stupid and crazy to do so if people do not have the skills and competences to take control of their work. In a similar vein, John Nevin says that if you want to drive a

Exhibit 9.5

The problems of empowerment

A summary of the results of a survey in which 65 per cent of the middle and junior manufacturing managers in an international avionics company responded:

Perhaps the most disappointing non-respondent was the Production Director. Neither he nor his two direct subordinates replied. Although the management at the company have produced a mission statement that mentions empowerment they have not in practice empowered the middle managers and they have not encouraged the middle managers to empower their subordinates. In fact the organisation operates in exactly the same way as it always has. That is adopting a controlling, rule bound, reactive and punitive environment.

The employees' general attitude is that they are not made to feel essential and are not assured of their importance to the organisation. The organisation has lost touch with the human side of running a business, and the employees are becoming demoralised and disenchanted with the company, even though the order books are full for the next two years. They consider that the feel-good factor has been removed and the job satisfaction is almost non-existent. Employees believe that minimum standards of performance are in force and minimum levels of pay are the norm. Therefore nobody is prepared to raise their level of performance above the minimum as they believe it won't be recognised and almost certainly won't be rewarded. The general feeling within the company is that of 'why should we shoulder more responsibility simply for the pleasure of having more control over our tasks?' The employees are not prepared to take any risk, as the whole organisation is dominated by a blame-orientated culture with the constant threat of redundancy hanging over their heads. They know that at the first sign of trouble, perhaps only a slight hiccup, the management will be pointing fingers. The employees are more concerned with self-preservation than with the company's goals. The manufacturing managers in general think the senior management is neither visible nor approachable and the majority of people in the company have little confidence in their management's abilities. Overall this is having a 'morale sapping' effect on the workforce.

Source: Lovett, J.F., 'The resources, skills and support available to manufacturing managers', B.Eng. Dissertation.

person crazy, the easiest way to do it is to give him/her a deep sense of responsibility and no authority (*see* Clutterbuck and Kernaghan, 1994, p. 19).

Mismanaging empowerment

The danger of introducing empowerment to an organisation, unless the process is properly managed, is that it will be seen as a threat and cause confusion as traditional roles and responsibilities are challenged. Karen Matthes questions the benefit of empowerment and states that some employers are beginning to wonder if empowerment programmes which promise improved quality, productivity, employee morale and motivation really deliver what they promise. Marilyn Kennedy agrees, and says that it is clear from talking to employees and middle managers that the idea of empowerment – pushing responsibility down – has lost much of its appeal. Both their observations show that empowerment was oversold, the political realities ignored, workplace values changed radically and the workloads increased dramatically.

The case study in Exhibit 9.5 illustrates the problems one international company has had with respect to empowerment.

PITFALLS AND SUCCESS FACTORS

The pitfalls to avoid and success factors to look for in developing an empowered organisation are shown in Table 9.2.

Pitfalls

Mistakes will be made in the process of developing an empowered organisation. There are, however, a number of typical pitfalls that can be avoided. From his experience, Kinlaw lists these as:

1 Failure to create the conditions for beginning and continuing the process of empowerment.
2 Discounting or reducing the potential of empowerment.
3 Making empowerment a matter of individual taste and initiative.
4 Failure to test and learn.
5 Failure to equip people with the necessary competences to perform in an empowered organisation.

Success factors

There are various factors that Byham believes are necessary to achieve maximum empowerment. They can be seen as goals which organisations should strive to achieve, and are as follows:

1 **Understanding empowerment and how to achieve it.** As empowerment is a value or belief system, an understanding must be gained of how it can meet personal and business needs, and what needs to be done to achieve it. Peters believes that listening

Table 9.2 Empowerment pitfalls and success factors

Pitfalls	Success factors
Wrong conditions	Developing understanding
Discounting potential	A vision and set of values
Left to individual taste	Expectations and feedback
No testing	Job design
No competency development	Communications
	Rewards and recognition
	Organisational system
	Training
	Teams

is the key to empowerment because it allows people to put forward and give answers and to take risks by trying new approaches, which are bound to fail at times. The key is taking people seriously by listening, and making it clear that you are taking them seriously by acting on what they say.

2 **Understanding and accepting the vision and values of the organisation.** Empowered organisations support decision making at lower levels within the organisation. For appropriate decisions to be made, a clear understanding of the organisation's vision is needed, as well as each employee knowing how they personally contribute to it. Knowing the organisation's basic values also aids in decision making.

3 **Expectations and feedback on performance.** Together, leaders and their empowered employees develop a clear understanding of responsibility, authority and methods for measuring success. Individuals need to know the performance expectations of the organisation, linked to the objectives of the team, department and the organisation's overall business strategy. Employees are also more likely to achieve optimum performance if they receive continuous feedback on their performance and suggestions about how they can improve.

4 **Jobs designed for empowerment.** Byham considers that empowerment must be built into jobs. Tasks must be defined, giving individuals responsibility for a meaningful process or output, and allowing them to make decisions, for example about committing resources to projects. Individuals should also be able continually to measure their successes. According to Byham, *empowered employees have the time, knowledge, and resources to achieve success.*

5 **Continuous communication.** Continuous communication is believed to be an essential part of empowerment and continuous improvement. Communication is a two-way process and takes place in many directions within the organisation: between peers, and between superiors and subordinates. Communication channels should flow upwards, downwards and horizontally within the organisation. Most leaders in empowered organisations encourage feedback and ideas from their subordinates. Communication may take the form of regular meetings, internal newsletters and regular contact with customers. Managers may also spend time walking around the organisation meeting

and talking to employees, trying to encourage the team concept rather than the 'them and us' concept. Communicating the organisation's position and its vision to its employees makes it easier for them to identify with the organisation. It will also encourage employees to support actively the organisation's actions and contribute to its success.

6 **Reward and recognition systems.** As empowered employees tend to be inherently proud of their accomplishments and contributions, reward programmes, both psychological and tangible, enhance these feelings. Reward systems have to be geared to the values of the empowered organisation. This may require them to be more team-orientated when recognising performance and specific accomplishments.

Exhibit 9.6

Empowerment brings success at the Illinois Tool Works of Chicago

The Illinois Tool Works (ITW) of Chicago is the most competitive company in the US, according to *Money* magazine. It, along with three other leading domestic performers with top quality products (i.e. Xerox, AMP and Harley-Davidson), is hammering the Japanese and other competitors at home and abroad.

In explaining ITW's success, *Money* magazine cites the company's R&D prowess and its degree of decentralisation and empowerment. Each division of ITW is autonomous with the freedom to chart its own course to success. This emphasis on autonomy and responsibility runs through the organisation from the boardroom to the factory floor. Such autonomy encourages employee empowerment, participation and leadership.

Empowerment has played a dramatic role in the success of ITW's Paslode division. With over 600 employees, Paslode is in the business of joining wood. Paslode manufactures fasteners – nails and staples – and the pneumatic tools that drive them. It manufactures the world's only cordless, airless power nailer/stapler.

A lesson in manufacturing

Paslode's success shows the key role employee empowerment can play in manufacturing today. The empowerment process began in 1989, fuelled by a management vision based on a commitment to developing leadership throughout the organisation, team building, culture change and a passionate commitment to being the best at meeting customer needs. Today the hallmark of Paslode is the autonomy of its employees.

Perhaps the most dramatic example of the results of the process if the division's new manufacturing facility in Arkansas. It is a self-directed work plant where the workers set the policies that govern themselves. This is a step well beyond the self-directed work teams that have made such an impact on modern manufacturing.

With workers establishing their own work rules, the new plant has been tremendously productive. For example, working together, the three shifts established their own absentee policy. The results have been striking. In 1992 the absentee rate at the Arkansas plant was 0.0008 per cent compared to the national average of 1.8 per cent. This kind of performance is emblematic of the change at Paslode.

Source: Adapted from Cusimano, J.M., 'Creating leaders by training managers as leadership trainers', *Industrial Engineering*, pp. 58–60, November 1993.

7 **Organisational systems.** Systems such as information systems, travel reimbursement policies, career-planning procedures, discipline, personnel policies, quality circles and suggestion systems often give a sense of power. In other circumstances, they can lead to workers feeling as if they have no power.

8 **Training.** *Training is seen as a key component in achieving empowerment of the individual and in maintaining focus on the customer in order to remain competitive* (DTI, 1994). Training can be seen as being at the centre of empowerment, as about ten per cent of an employee's time is spent on it, and successful companies use it as another way of gaining competitive advantage. Education and training provide employees with the skills necessary to enable them to achieve their tasks and satisfy the customer.

Leaders have the ability both to encourage empowerment and to build employee confidence by the control they exercise, the initiative they encourage, the feedback they provide and by delegating certain tasks. If leaders coach for success and help employees feel ownership for their ideas, they will ensure employees are dedicated and committed to their work.

It is common in empowered organisations for employees to rotate jobs. To be able to do this, they need to understand how all the jobs within the team are carried out. Byham believes there is nothing more empowering for employees than being able to train in all the skills necessary to carry out their jobs well.

9 **Teams.** A common way to empower employees is to encourage teamwork. Byham believes this to be an excellent way of empowering individuals whose current jobs are limited in scope.

Exhibit 9.6 illustrates how the Illinois Tool Works of Chicago adopted many of the above success factors to become possibly the most successful company in the US.

ASSESSING THE LEVEL OF EMPOWERMENT

Having made efforts to understand and develop an organisation that empowers, it is important to check to see if, as it were, 'the medicine is working'. This can be done by assessing the extent of cultural changes that contribute towards empowerment. This extent can be established by examining how the organisation's culture fosters a traditional environment as against an empowered environment (Cook, 1994)(*see* Table 9.3).

Extent of empowerment

According to Wilson, the extent of empowerment in an organisation can be assessed in terms of the factors shown in Exhibit 9.7.

THE EMPOWERMENT HIERARCHY

Wilson also talks about the need for a person to develop an understanding of how empowered they are in their job. At the one extreme people are unlikely to be empowered if they feel that their job is repetitive, unchallenging, uninteresting and pointless. Such people would not be motivated to make changes and improvements. At the

Table 9.3 Changes from a traditional to an empowered environment

From	To
Traditional Environment	*Empowered Environment*
Hierarchical	Flat
Controlling	Informing
Directive	Inspiring
Reactive	Proactive
Rule-bound	Knowledge-orientated
Compliance-orientated	Co-operative
Autocratic	Democratic
Compartmentalised	Open-plan
Rigid	Flexible
Task-orientated	People-orientated
Inward-focused	Customer-focused

Source: Cook. S, *Training for Empowerment*. Reproduced by permission of Gower Publishing Ltd.

Exhibit 9.7

Factors that contribute to empowerment

- **Reputation**: The degree to which the organisation is rated by stakeholders, customers, competition, managers, employers and the informed public as empowering all its staff.
- **Management focus**: The degree to which senior management values, encourages, supports and practises empowerment.
- **The management of empowerment**: The degree to which managers understand empowerment and correctly manage it.
- **Atmosphere**: The degree to which there is an atmosphere of empowerment in the organisation.
- **Leadership**:The degree to which the leadership of the managers' initiatives encourages and supports empowerment.
- **Releasing human potential**: The degree to which every person's latent talents and skills are released and used.
- **Recognition and rewards**: The degree to which the organisation formally and informally recognises and rewards empowerment.
- **Innovation**: The degree to which the organisation is innovative.
- **Trust**: The degree to which there is a level of trust and openness in the organisation that enables people to become empowered and take risks.
- **Teamwork**: The degree to which the talents of empowered teams are used.
- **Decision making and control**: The degree to which decision making and control has been pushed to its lowest level in the organisation.
- **Communications**: The degree to which there is open and regular communication within the organisation.
- **Customers**: The degree to which empowerment initiatives are directed towards customer satisfaction, be they internal or external to the organisation.
- **Structure and procedures**: The degree to which the organisation has made changes in its structure and procedures to support empowerment.
- **Organisation aims**: The degree to which empowerment initiatives contribute to the achievement of the aims of the organisation.

Source: Wilson, T., *The Empowerment Manual.* Reproduced by permission of Gower Publishing Ltd.

other extreme there are people who literally love their job. They find it stimulating, challenging and satisfying. As a result they are highly motivated and committed to what they do. They want to be empowered and will usually set examples of empowerment for others to follow. The seven levels of job empowerment presented in Fig 9.5 were developed by Wilson and can be used in two ways:

- for a person to consider the extent to which they feel empowered in their job
- to assist them to plan for greater empowerment in their job.

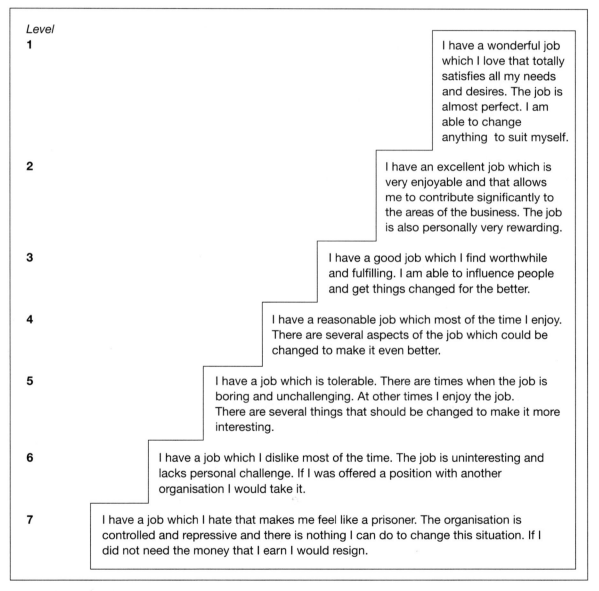

Level

1   I have a wonderful job which I love that totally satisfies all my needs and desires. The job is almost perfect. I am able to change anything to suit myself.

2   I have an excellent job which is very enjoyable and that allows me to contribute significantly to the areas of the business. The job is also personally very rewarding.

3   I have a good job which I find worthwhile and fulfilling. I am able to influence people and get things changed for the better.

4   I have a reasonable job which most of the time I enjoy. There are several aspects of the job which could be changed to make it even better.

5   I have a job which is tolerable. There are times when the job is boring and unchallenging. At other times I enjoy the job. There are several things that should be changed to make it more interesting.

6   I have a job which I dislike most of the time. The job is uninteresting and lacks personal challenge. If I was offered a position with another organisation I would take it.

7   I have a job which I hate that makes me feel like a prisoner. The organisation is controlled and repressive and there is nothing I can do to change this situation. If I did not need the money that I earn I would resign.

Fig 9.5 Seven levels of job empowerment

Source: Wilson, T., *The Empowerment Manual*. Reproduced by permission of Gower Publishing Ltd.

As a means of planning for greater empowerment, people should consider how their job rates on the scale and make plans to put themselves into a position or future job where they will have more, or a greater chance of experiencing more, of the positive feelings of the higher levels.

SUMMARY

- Empowerment is leadership that devolves responsibility and control to employees to take personal responsibility for the way they do their jobs. People are recognised as an asset to the company and encouraged to fulfil their potential while at work.

- Some of the benefits of empowerment include reduced routine work for managers, reduced absenteeism, turnover and risk aversion. The improvements are job security, personal control, job satisfaction, motivation, achievement of personal and organisational objectives, sense of ownership, autonomy, entrepreneurship and innovation, responsibility to find solutions to problems and sharing of the load.

- The most common way of empowering employees is to encourage them to work in teams. There are various ways of empowering teams: relate the team's vision to the organisation; allocate resources; include skilled, relevant people; structure opportunities to work together; hold individuals accountable.

- The steps managers should take to empower their people are: maintain self-esteem; listen and respond with empathy; ask for help in solving problems.

- The 'empowerment process management model' identifies six key steps that should be followed to empower an organisation: define and communicate; set goals and strategies; train people; adjust the organisation's structure; adjust the organisation's systems; evaluate and improve.

- Empowerment can result in new structures with fewer layers of management, which invariably means fewer managers, each with wider responsibilities. The middle managers, in devolving their power and control, may feel increasingly insecure and anxious about their positions. Some people find the increased responsibility of being empowered is stressful; some unions view empowerment as a ploy to motivate employees to shoulder more responsibility and work harder for the same pay.

- The dangers of empowerment are that it can be misinterpreted as delegation and it could be used to give people a deep sense of responsibility but with no authority. It can be seen as a threat and cause confusion as traditional roles and responsibilities are challenged. It will not work if it is oversold, the political realities ignored, the workplace values changed radically or the workloads increased dramatically.

- Factors that are necessary to achieve maximum empowerment include: understanding the meaning of empowerment and how to achieve it; having the vision and values to guide decision making; understanding job responsibilities and methods for measuring success; designing jobs to provide ownership and responsibility; having effective communication on plans, successes and failures; instigating reward and recognition systems, organisational systems, training, and the use of teams.

- The extent of empowerment in an organisation can be assessed in terms of reputation, strategy, leadership, management capabilities, culture, structure, systems and procedures, and customers.

- People can assess themselves against seven levels of job empowerment to consider the extent to which they feel empowered in their job and to assist them to plan for greater future empowerment.

REVIEW AND DISCUSSION QUESTIONS

1 Explain what empowerment is and outline the benefits you would expect to result, for both the organisation and its people, from successful empowerment.

2 Explain what you think are the different ways people can be empowered, particularly by encouraging them to work in teams.

3 What do you understand to be the dangers of misuse and misinterpretation of empowerment?

4 In the role of a general manager, provide details of how you would assess the extent to which your organisation and the operatives are empowered.

ASSIGNMENTS

Consider a process of empowerment in the organisation in which you work or at some other, and:

1 examine the extent to which the various factors that are necessary to achieve maximum empowerment exist;

2 explain how well your managers perform the three steps considered necessary to empower people.

REFERENCES

Belasco, J.A. and Stayer, R.C., 'Why empowerment doesn't empower: The bankruptcy of current paradigms', *Business Horizons,* Vol. 37, No. 2, pp. 29–41, 1994.

Bolger, A., 'Employee power worries managers', *The Financial Times,* 27 Feb 1995. From *Managing Best Practice,* Issue No. 8, Industrial Society, Birmingham, Tel 0121 454 6767.

Boren, R., 'Don't delegate – empower', *Supervisory Management,* Vol. 39, No. 10, p.10, 1994.

Byham, W.C., 'Would you recognise an empowered organisation if you saw one?', *Tapping the Network Journal,* Vol. 3, No. 2, pp. 10–13, 1992.

Byham, W.C. and Cox, J., *Zapp! The Lightning of Empowerment,* Century, London, 1991.

Clutterbuck, D. and Kernaghan, S., *The Power of Empowerment,* Kogan Page, London, 1994.

Cook, S., *Training for Empowerment,* Gower, Aldershot, 1994.

Cusimano, J.M., 'Creating leaders by training managers as leadership trainers', *Industrial Engineering,* pp. 58–60, November 1993.

Department of Trade and Industry, *Competitiveness: How the Best Companies are Winning,* report published jointly by the DTI and the CBI, designed and produced by CGI London Limited, 1994.

Eccles, T., 'The deceptive allure of empowerment', *Long Range Planning,* Vol. 26, No. 6, pp. 13–21, 1993.

Fortune, p. 19, 12 August 1991.

Foy, N., *Empowering People at Work*, Gower, Aldershot, 1994.

Frey, R., 'Empowerment or else', *Harvard Business Review*, pp. 80–94, Sept/Oct 1993.

Harari, O., 'Stop empowering your people', *Small Business Reports*, Vol. 19, No. 3, pp. 53–5, 1994.

Johnson, R.P., 'Brains, heart and courage: Keys to empowerment and self-directed leadership', *Journal of Managerial Psychology*, Vol. 9, No. 2, pp. 17–21, 1994.

Kennedy, M.M., 'Empowered or overempowered?', *Across the Board,* Vol. 31, No. 4, pp. 11–12, 1994.

Kinlaw, D.C., *The Practice of Empowerment*, Gower, Aldershot, 1995.

Lorenz, C., 'Uphill struggle to become horizontal', *The Financial Times*, 5 November 1993.

Lovett, J.F., 'The resources, skills and support available to manufacturing managers', B.Eng. Dissertation, Department of Manufacturing Engineering and Operations Management, University of Nottingham, 1995.

Matthes, K., 'Empowerment: Fact or fiction?', *HR Focus*, Vol. 69, No. 3, pp. 1–6, 1992.

Peters, T., *Thriving on Chaos*, Macmillan, London, 1988.

Peters, T.J. and Waterman, R.H., *In Search of Excellence*, Harper & Row, New York, 1982.

Tjosvold, D., *Team Organisation: An enduring competitive advantage*, John Wiley & Sons, Chichester, 1991.

Wallace, G.W., 'Empowerment is work, not magic', *Journal for Quality and Participation*, Vol. 16, No. 5, pp. 10–14, 1993.

Waterman, R.H., *The Frontiers of Excellence*, Nicholas Brealey Publishing, London, 1994.

Wilson, T., *The Empowerment Manual*, Gower, Aldershot, 1996.

CHAPTER 10

The learning organisation

OBJECTIVES

The objectives of this chapter are to:

- introduce the concept of the learning organisation (TLO) and highlight the need for learning
- review the characteristics of learning organisations
- consider how an organisation learns and summarise the building blocks of learning organisations
- consider the barriers to learning
- show how an organisation can utilise learning to overcome the blocks to effectiveness in key operational areas
- show the main steps necessary to create an action plan for learning
- illustrate some of the practical issues and problems of becoming a learning organisation.

WHAT IS A LEARNING ORGANISATION?

Learning has been identified by many management gurus as the essential characteristic an organisation needs in order to progress effectively. This is due to the need of companies to create and manage the organisational cultures that foster commitment, responsibility and the development of individual potential for the corporate good. In other words, a learning organisation is needed to respond flexibly to the current business environment. Bottoms notes that those who first recognise the new world of global business, and learn to exploit change, will capitalise on the millions of opportunities that accompany it.

Some definitions

There are many definitions of the learning organisation and some disagreement between people. Straightforwardly Pedler *et al.* describe a learning organisation as:

> *an organisation that facilitates the learning of all its members and continuously transforms itself.*

Peter Senge, who popularised learning organisations in his book *The Fifth Discipline*, described learning organisations as:

> *places where people continually expand their capacity to create the results they truly desire, where new and expansive patterns of thinking are nurtured, where collective aspiration is set free, and where people are continually learning how to learn together.*

Obviously, the learning organisation places a great emphasis on the development of the individual and the organisation together. It is important to develop the people in the organisation so that they want to, and have the ability to, learn, change and improve. In turn this will enable the organisation itself to learn, change and improve.

The importance of learning indicates the need for a much closer look at the human side of the organisation. In the process of changing an organisation, especially a manufacturing organisation, there is a tendency to let the hardware, the system, and the procedures dominate one's thinking and analysis. But when it comes to achieving improvement in performance, it is the people in the organisation and the way they link with these technical, inanimate factors that will determine the success of the change. That is why emphasis needs to be placed on the learning element of people and the organisation itself.

Clearing up the confusion over learning

Unfortunately, the literature shows that there is considerable disagreement on what a learning organisation is. Nonetheless, most scholars believe that organisational learning is a process that unfolds over time, and link it with knowledge acquisition and improved performance. However, as Garvin adds:

> new ideas are essential if learning is to take place and ... a learning organisation is an organisation skilled at creating, acquiring and transferring knowledge, and at modifying its behaviour to reflect new knowledge and insights.

He warns however that although ideas are the trigger for improvement, they cannot by themselves create a learning organisation and that, without accompanying changes in the way the work gets done, only the potential for improvement exists. In this sense there are organisations that pass the definitional test. For example, Honda and General Electric have become adept at translating new knowledge into new ways of behaving. These companies actively manage the learning process to ensure that it occurs by design rather than by chance. Distinctive policies and practices are responsible for their success, forming the building blocks of learning organisations.

Exhibit 10.1 illustrates how Rover created the Rover Learning Business (RLB) as an attempt to set individual learning in a framework that values all learning and adds additional value to the individual learning that takes place in the company.

The European Consortium for Learning Organisations (ECLO)

Shirley Daniels comments that because the learning concept is new, it has to be promoted and explained. An organisation has been set up to do just that. The European Consortium for Learning Organisations (ECLO) is a new organisation (formed in 1993) and is essentially a forum for discussion on the concept of the learning organisation. It has, so far, run a number of workshops to promote learning organisations and to assist in the process of establishing a shared understanding of the concept and how it might be delivered. It hopes in the future to produce materials which will assist in the conversion of organisations to learning organisations.

Exhibit 10.1

The learning organisation: A Rover perspective

For a number of years the company has conducted employee attitude surveys. These consistently revealed that our employees did not feel that best use was being made of their talents and that they were prepared to rise to greater challenges than we put in front of them. They felt that they were not well enough informed about opportunities for involvement, development and progression within the business. In responding to those very serious and clearly-articulated statements, several thrusts for progress have been undertaken. The first has seen the establishment of the Rover Learning Business (RLB). Rover Learning Business is a 'business within a business'. It has its own chairperson, managing director, executive committee and board of governors. Its primary aim is to provide a top quality learning and development service to all employees as customers, regardless of geography and with equal opportunity. It is committed to providing assistance to everyone wishing to develop themselves. It attempts to change the emphasis from 'training', which most people still regard as having something done to them, to 'learning' – doing something for themselves.

Clearly, the learning opportunities within any business are widespread. The emphasis within RLB's title on the word 'learning' was intentional, designed to bring about that switch of emphasis such that self-development and acceptance of responsibility by the individuals and their line manager should be the way forward, rather than the traditional route. Rover Learning Business provides learning packages and consultancy within the company. Its first product, launched in May 1990, was the 'REAL' programme (Rover Employees Assisted Learning), under which any employee is entitled to received up to £100 a year for pursuing virtually any kind of learning programme. The emphasis has been very much on saying 'Yes' to proposals put forward by employees rather than having a list of restrictions, although in order to ensure compliance with tax regulations there have had to be a number of rules and policies put in place. But these have been very much to a necessary minimum. Courses in 'in-shore navigation', sheep husbandry, outward-bound team events, Japanese, swimming, have all been approved. The criterion is only that it is a legitimate learning experience, receipted and delivered by a recognised body.

Language training and system/software appreciation have proved most popular. In the second year of operation some who undertook personal interest courses have switched to more academically demanding programmes. The learning culture is starting to take hold.

The intent has been to establish a more populist approach to learning and development, emphasizing that careers can be something pursued, not only by a relatively small band of professional and managerial employees, but also by any one of our employees who feel so motivated to take up the challenge. The personnel mission statement sets out the objectives for Rover to create that kind of learning environment.

Source: Bower, D.G., 'The learning organisation: a Rover perspective', *Executive Development*. Reproduced by kind permission of the author, David Bower, Personnel Director, Rover Group Ltd.

Single- and double-loop learning

Bateson mentions that most organisations have a capability which helps them to cope with change in the environment and calls this *single-loop learning*; that is, developing corrective actions without changing existing strategies. This means that the organisation itself has not changed, so there is no organisational learning. According to Argyris and

Exhibit 10.2

Manufacture of multi-valve engines

Multi-valve engines have been around since the 1920s. European car manufacturers decided not to use this concept very widely because of its high cost due to the complexity of the technology. Referring to the types of loop learning, this is single-loop learning: the corrective action taken was not to use the system, because it did not fit the existing strategies.

In the late 1970s Japanese car manufacturers faced a dilemma. They developed small, low-consumption, four-cylinder engines to lessen the high cost of petrol due to the energy crisis. However, fuel prices fell. This meant consumers could afford more powerful engines again, making the small engines unfashionable. It was decided to improve the performance of the existing engine range, since developing a new range of larger engines would take too long.

By this time, Japanese car manufacturers were already lean manufacturers. They managed to develop multi-valve engines in a cheap way. Frustrated Western car manufacturers had to adopt Japanese approaches to develop multi-valve engines too. That corrective action can be seen as double-loop learning: by changing strategies, improvements could be made.

Source: Reprinted with the permission of Rawson Associates/Scribner, a Division of Simon & Schuster, from *The Machine that Changed the World* by James P. Womack, Daniel T. Jones, Daniel Rocs. Copyright © 1990 by James P. Womack, Daniel T. Jones, Daniel Roos and Donna Sammons Carpenter.

Schön, organisational learning is *double-loop learning*, where corrective actions are taken but also strategies are modified if necessary. A modified strategy means learning has taken place at an organisational level.

An example of organisational learning in the sense of double-loop learning is given in Exhibit 10.2.

THE NEED FOR LEARNING

Organisations unable to sustain innovation – not able to 'learn' – are in great danger of failure. As Ray Stata, Chairman of Analog Devices Inc., observed:

> *I would argue that the rate at which individuals and organisations learn may become the only sustainable competitive advantage, especially in knowledge-intensive industries.*

According to Mills and Friesen, all organisations learn, but some do not learn fast enough to survive. In today's world, in which knowledge workers are becoming a key ingredient of success, the ability of a firm to keep up to date by learning is more important than ever. Furthermore, just as firms were required to create a particular business model (a combination of organisation structure, management practices and internal support systems) to utilise mass production techniques, so will they need to build a business model effectively to encourage learning and utilise the outputs of innovation in their operations.

As can be seen, the learning organisation is becoming more and more of a necessity. Leaders, besides managing the resources of an organisation, must in the future engage themselves and their workforce in a commitment to improve through learning.

CHARACTERISTICS OF LEARNING ORGANISATIONS

To understand better the forms of organisational learning, several interpretations can be given.

Senge, recognises three characteristics of a learning organisation: it expands its capacity to create results, there is a collective aspiration, and people learn to learn.

Jashapara recognises learning at several levels in the organisation:

- organisational learning
- team learning
- individual learning.

Some of the above characteristics are quite self-explanatory, but the term 'learning' still remains vague. Rheem describes several types of learning, which give more meaning:

- competence acquisition
- experimentation
- continuous improvement
- boundary spanning (collecting data from outside).

Mills and Friesen offer a similar variation of the above in the shape of three characteristics of an organisation which equip it for learning.

First, it must make a *commitment* to knowledge. A very important aspect of this commitment involves the selection of people. Another aspect of commitment to learning involves the development of learning internally through a variety of means.

Second, a learning organisation must have a *mechanism for renewal* within itself. Departments and other units of firms continually fall into bureaucratic rigidity. They cease to adapt, to learn. They become impediments to the success of the firm. A learning organisation must be able to intervene in such situations to renew and revitalise them.

Third, a learning organisation possesses an *openness* to the outside world so that it may be responsive to what is occurring there. For the firm's staff as a whole, an openness to the changing needs of customers and suppliers is required.

The eleven characteristics model

The 'eleven characteristics model', as described by Pedler *et al.,* provides a detailed and complete view of the characteristics of what they call a 'learning company'. The main advantage of this model is its practical nature; that is it makes explicit the requirements of a learning company.

The eleven characteristics are discussed in the following sections:

1 The learning approach to strategy

This means that company policy and strategy formation, together with implementation, evaluation and improvement, are consciously structured as a learning process. It allows business plans to be developed, formulated and revised as one goes along. Managerial acts are thus seen as conscious experiments rather than set solutions. Deliberate small-scale experiments and feedback loops are built into the planning process to enable continuous improvement in the light of experience.

2 Participative policy making

This characteristic refers to the sharing of involvement in the policy and the strategy-forming process; that is all the members of the company have a chance to take part, to discuss and contribute to major policy decisions. There is a deliberate fostering and encouragement of contributions and a recognition that successful debate involves working with tensions, or even conflicts, between different values, positions and views. There is a commitment to airing differences and working through conflicts as the way to reaching business decisions that all members are likely to support. These members include different groupings of employees, customers, suppliers, owners and neighbours, including the community and the environment.

Participative policy making requires three fundamental attitudes towards this diversity of groups, namely that:

- all diverse groups have the right to take part, and their values and so on be taken into account (this is the ethical or moral dimension of the learning company)
- such diversity, although complicated, is, in fact, valuable in that it leads to creativity, to better ideas and solutions
- only by striving to delight customers and meet the requirements of other stakeholders will the company be successful in the long-term achievement of its purpose.

3 Informating

This describes the state of affairs in which information technology is used to inform and empower people rather than, as so often is the case, disempower them. This involves three major shifts in attitude or perspective about:

- to whom information is made available – make it as widely available as possible
- the use to which the information is put – not to reward (or punish) or have control over, or report on, or keep in storage just in case, but, rather, to understand what is happening in the company's systems and processes
- understanding the nature of data – in particular, that all systems and processes have some natural or inherent variation in their output. Therefore, when interpreting data it is essential to find out if it is simply representative of the inherent variation. If so, the system is said to be 'in control' and the only way to improve the output is by carefully and scientifically working on the system. Alternatively, something unusual is happening in the system, such that the output cannot be explained by the inherent variation. In this case, the system is said to be 'out of control' and, before one can say or do anything about its capability, the special causes of abnormal variation need to be investigated.

4 Formative accounting and control

Formative accounting ensures that the systems of accounting, budgeting and reporting are structured to assist learning and hence 'delight' the internal customers. This is the way in which such systems add value to the company. In fact, although this sounds simple, it represents a huge change in perspective. Asking those who run a control system who their customers are and what would delight them is a radical shift.

5 Internal exchange

Internal exchange involves all internal units and departments seeing themselves as customers and suppliers, and contracting with one another in a partly-regulated market economy. The purpose of a department is thus to 'delight' its internal customers. To do so, individuals, groups, departments and divisions engage in constant dialogue – exchanging information on expectations, negotiating, contracting and giving feedback on goods and services received. At the same time, internal customers recognise that their suppliers have rights and needs too and treat them with respect. In any case, it is fully understood that the way to deliver quality is to receive it; hence we need good relationships with our suppliers in order to develop good relationships with our customers.

6 Reward flexibility

In tune with ideas about increasing degrees of participation, there is a need to start to explore new, alternative ways of rewarding people in a learning company. First, there is a need to recognise that money need not be the sole reward and that, for many people, a whole range of approaches might be considered 'rewarding'. Often the underlying assumptions in a payment/reward system are unstated, hidden, unrecognised. In a learning company, these will be brought out into the open, shared, examined and alternatives will be discussed and tried out.

According to Pedler *et al.*, this is probably the most difficult of the 11 characteristics on which to make progress, since it is likely to change, not only the distribution of reward, but also the distribution of power.

7 Enabling structures

Enabling structures create opportunities for individual and business development. Roles are loosely structured, in line with the established and contracted needs of internal customers and suppliers, in such a way as to allow for personal growth and experiment. Thus, departmental and other boundaries are seen as temporary structures that can flex in response to changes. The aim is to create an organisational architecture that gives space and headroom for meeting current needs and responding to future changes.

8 Boundary workers as environmental scanners

Just as informating takes place within a company, so data are collected from outside. Although there may be people or departments who specialise in this process, in a learning company such scanning is carried out by all members who have contact with external customers, clients, suppliers, neighbours and so on. These boundary workers deliver goods and services, receive supplies and orders *and* systematically collect and carry back information that is collected and disseminated.

9 Intercompany learning

Since a learning company seeks to delight its customers, it will engage in a number of mutually advantageous learning activities. Joint training, sharing in investment, sharing in research and development etc. – these are just some of the ways in which this mutual learning takes place. The corollary is that the company also joins with its suppliers in these activities. It is also possible to learn from companies in other industries using benchmarking practice. For example, Rank Xerox set out to learn from Caterpillar, considered to be the world's best company (i.e. the benchmark) at delivering heavy equipment.

More surprisingly, perhaps, competitors get together for mutual learning. They do not fight each other (win–lose), which in the long-run always leads to suboptimisation (lose–lose), but engage in successful (win–win) learning. They both recognise that their interests will be served by increasing the market, bringing in technological advances, establishing joint industry standards and so on. Rank Xerox has a slogan 'come and steal shamelessly from us'.

10 Learning climate

In a learning company, managers see their primary task as facilitating members' experimentation and learning from experience. It is normal to take time out to seek feedback, to obtain data to aid understanding. Senior managers give a lead in questioning their own ideas, attitudes and actions. Mistakes are allowed – if not actively encouraged – for it is recognised that we will never learn if we never try out new ideas or new ways of doing things, and these will not always work. We need to recognise that there is no such thing as a failed experiment – as long as we learn from it.

Importance is attached to the idea of continuous improvement. We can always learn and do better, no matter how well we think we are doing at present.

11 Self-development opportunities for all

Resources and facilities for self-development are made available to all members of the company – employees at all levels and, ideally, external stakeholders too. With appropriate guidance, including systems for feeding back data, people are encouraged to take responsibility for their own learning and development.

The 11 characteristics of the learning organisation comprise five main elements, namely:

- strategy
- looking in
- structures
- looking out
- learning opportunities.

Figure 10.1 depicts the characteristics of a learning organisation.

Exhibit 10.3 illustrates some of the key learning characteristics and values adopted by Motorola and Zytec.

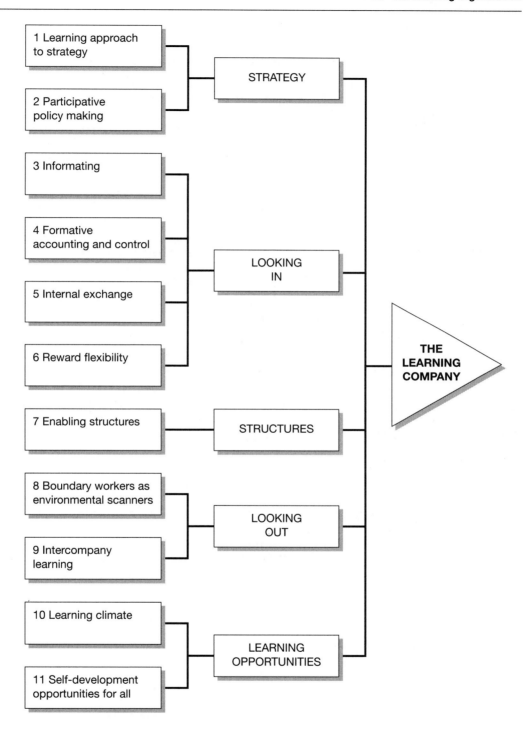

Fig 10.1 Characteristics of the learning organisation
Source: Pedler *et al.*, *The Learning Company: A strategy for sustainable development.*

Exhibit 10.3

Key learning characteristics at Motorola and Zytec

By definition, the overriding characteristic in a learning organisation is the intense desire to learn. For example, when Motorola set out to improve its delivery schedules, it examined the current level of performance and the degree to which this level could be raised if the employees performed their jobs well. Motorola then designed a strategy for closing the gap between current performance and attainable performance.

Another closely-related characteristic is a strong commitment to generating and transferring new knowledge and technology. This is facilitated by information gathering and training programmes (offered by both internal and external sources).

Still another key characteristic is an openness to the external environment. The learning organisation is responsive to, and is trying to learn what is going on in, the outside world. Learning organisations rely heavily on periodicals, research reports, briefings from key personnel, and talks and seminars by outside experts.

At Zytec, for example, the company receives a wealth of information each day from published sources. Zytec employees constantly interact with the external environment by attending technical and management development meetings and seminars, and by benchmarking the practices of competitors and other firms that can provide insights on how to do things better and faster.

Source: Adapted from Luthans, F., Hodgetts, R. and Lee, S., 'New paradigm organizations: From total quality to learning to world class', *Organizational Dynamics*. Reprinted by permission of the publisher, from *Organizational Dynamics Winter 1994*. © 1994. American Management Association, New York. All rights reserved.

HOW AN ORGANISATION LEARNS

An organisation learns in several ways. Primarily, it learns through the individuals who are part of it. It can achieve this by absorbing other organisations with desired knowledge, or by recruiting people who have the required competences and knowledge. Also, people learn through experience on the job or through formal training. The trouble with individual learning is that it can remain only individual. That is, if the individual does not use the learning for the benefit of the company, or they leave, then the organisation has learned nothing. Therefore, it is important that organisations adopt the learning principles and develop mechanisms which transfer learning from an individual to the group. Equally important is the ability of the organisation to systematise knowledge into practices, processes and procedures.

According to Palframan, as Exhibit 10.4 illustrates, continuous learning occurs in a learning organisation, which manufacturers such as Rover, Unipart, Brooke Bond Foods and Lucas all aspire to become.

Learning how to change

How do people in the organisation, especially the managers, learn to do very difficult things? This is the question people always ask. Burgoyne believes that there are three levels of learning in most organisations.

The first one is very simple learning. The firm learns how to introduce and manage processes. These processes are then turned into a set of procedures which establish the

Exhibit 10.4

Smarter companies learn out of habit

The argument in favour of a learning organisation is that it can provide the competitive advantage that companies in rapidly-changing markets are seeking. 'It is becoming increasingly difficult to have a competitive edge from product performance, cost or technology, because companies can copy you very quickly. But there may be an edge in having an organisation than learns and improves faster than the competition,' says Peter Beddowes, Dean of Ashridge Management College.

'Managers in a learning organisation are coaches and facilitators of learning. They have a responsibility to develop others, in addition to meeting their business objectives,' Beddowes adds.

Companies also need to consider the different learning styles of their people. The Industrial Society, for example, runs workshops on the number of ways in which to develop staff. To date, it has identified 48 different ways, which range from reading a book to someone representing the company on an external committee.

People have to be encouraged to learn and to share their learning. Not everyone is a natural mentor, for example, but the skill can be acquired.

There is also the possibility that some people will be reluctant to learn. The answer according to Dr Ian Cunningham, chair of the Centre for Self-Managed Learning, is to offer rewards for learning. He maintains: 'If people are learning, they should be rewarded in all ways. They should be given praise, recognition, money and promotion.'

In a learning organisation, evaluation is essential but the results are not instant. Forrest, the human resources director at the Industrial Society, cites Brooke Bond Foods, which set a five-year plan to become a learning organisation. Within the plan were certain milestones. One indicated that, after two years, line managers should take more responsibility for developing people, a task that had previously been in the hands of the training department.

Hirman Walker, part of the Allied–Lyons food and drinks organisation, has spent three years cascading the idea of mentoring and self-managed learning through the workforce. The process started with the board and has now reached the sales people. Essentially, the company believes that as a learning organisation it will be more profitable because it will have smarter people, especially sales people, than the competition.

Source: Adapted from Palframan, D., 'Smarter companies learn out of habit', *Works Management*, pp. 43–5, August 1994.

ongoing required method of operation or method of working. Learning at this stage assumes that the environment is stable and is not concerned with change.

The second level of learning is when an organisation can adapt to its environment. It recognises when markets are changing or have changed and alters itself to meet these new demands. Often, this alteration takes the form of improving performance in order to survive.

The third level of learning is more complex and sophisticated. Managers now try to exert an influence on the environment so that they can exist more comfortably and be ready for major crises. They try to improve not only their own organisation but also their suppliers, while attempting to give their customers more satisfaction through better quality goods and services. Attempting to control the environment in these ways requires clear values, a high level of knowledge and the ability to persuade and help others to change their ways. If the organisation is successful, this should result in a more stable and predictable environment for everyone.

Learning takes time

Organisations that successfully make use of learning principles need time to develop: time carefully to cultivate attitudes and commitments, to establish direction, develop strategic plans and develop supporting management processes. To begin with it is necessary to develop an environment that is conducive to learning. This is a more planned, measured, less 'macho' approach, where time is allowed for reflection and analysis concerning the customer needs, the product, the competition and current methods. At the shopfloor level, management needs also to free-up employees' time so that they can learn by developing their skills, brainstorming and problem solving.

HOW TO CREATE A LEARNING ORGANISATION

A necessary prerequisite is understanding what a learning organisation is and being able to define it in practical terms. There need to exist clear, actionable guidelines that are communicated to everyone, on how to put the learning organisation into practice. The managers as well as the workforce should be prepared for what lies ahead. Questions should be asked such as: Is everyone sufficiently trained? Are people being imbued with the appropriate knowledge? Are non-traditional thinking patterns and new ways of approaching and solving problems being encouraged? If learning is taking place then it is a requirement to know that it is and that it is having the desired effects. This requires having the right tools for measuring such learning and measuring the expected quantifiable improvement in performance. Once these issues are addressed, the management will have a solid base for developing a learning organisation.

Measuring learning

There is an old management saying that 'if you can't measure it, you can't manage it', and there is a felt need to measure learning like any other business objective. Traditionally, use has been made of 'learning curves' or 'experience curves', where costs and prices fall by predictable amounts as total production is increased. With respect to organisational learning of the type described here, these measures are incomplete. They focus on only one single measure of output (cost or price) and hence only on how output levels are improved through learning. This ignores the way learning can affect other competitive criteria, such as quality, flexibility, new product introductions or customer service. More importantly, it tells us little about the sources of learning and the effects of it on improving effectiveness.

Another measure of learning is that of the 'half-life curve'. This measures the time it takes to achieve a 50 per cent improvement in a specified performance measure. Here, performance measures such as speed, dependability, defect rates and so on are plotted on a logarithmic vertical axis, with the timescale plotted horizontally on an ordinal scale. Visually, steeper slopes indicate faster learning.

The faults with this approach are twofold. First, the instrument of measurement is too blunt. The respective rates of improvement are compared one against the other without any consideration of the difficulty one area of improvement may have over another. Also, the differences in importance that management may attribute to different areas of improvement are not explicitly considered. Second, some learning improvements can take years to manifest themselves, and such improvements are unlikely to be highlighted by half-life curves. Further, besides measuring the effects of learning, effort should be made to measure the approaches that facilitate learning, such as the quality of formal training and hiring; learning from other organisations, customers and within; development programmes for developing management and functional skills, personal attribute awareness, and problem-solving skills; schemes to facilitate learning such as benchmarking, continuous improvement, experimentation, on-the-job experience, job rotation; rewards and incentives to learn; processes for information/knowledge acquisition and transfer.

Most important is the problem with all measuring devices: they focus solely on the results of processes that can be more easily measured or quantified themselves.

The right atmosphere

When trying to achieve the right atmosphere for learning in an organisation, several critical success factors should be considered. Peters mentions a number of factors important in creating a learning organisation. First of all, people should feel some kind of ownership concerning the outcomes of actions taken. Challenges should be taken, not in competition, but in co-operation with colleagues. Learning should fit in with the company's policy on strategy, reward systems and culture.

Kline's prescribed path towards becoming a learning organisation should promote this type of atmosphere:

- Assess your learning culture.
- Promote the positive.
- Make the workplace safe for thinking.
- Reward risk-taking.
- Help people become resources for one another.
- Put learning power to work.
- Map out the vision.
- Bring the vision to life.
- Connect the systems.
- Get the show on the road.

Exhibit 10.5 provides a practical example of a company adopting the concept of the learning organisation.

Building on a total quality approach

According to Hodgetts *et al.,* companies such as Motorola, Zytec, and Toyota have moved from a total quality approach to a learning approach because they not only *adapt* to change, they *learn and stay ahead* of change. They are not content simply to build products to meet quality expectations; they are continually increasing quality in order to *exceed* and *anticipate* customer demands. This requires a learning climate in which employees find new, creative ways of doing the work. At Zytec, for example, group members are empowered to call a meeting any time they feel it is necessary to analyse a problem and formulate a solution. They then have follow-up meetings to review progress, note additional problems, and formulate follow-on solutions.

Exhibit 10.5

The learning organisation at Life Sciences International

Life Sciences International wanted to promote the need for continuous improvement in its managers. Therefore the company started using the concept of the learning organisation. One of the most important issues to cover for this company was communication. This had to be improved to ensure success with the new approach of coaching people with problems. The coaching concept basically meant asking people for their opinion when they asked a supervisor for help with a problem. In this way, people felt more involved and more able to do their work. An additional effect of the learning organisation approach for this company was the decrease in labour turnover from 10 per cent to 6 per cent and a decrease in absenteeism from 3.5 per cent to 3 per cent.

A common problem with training people is that, after a period, awareness concerning the topics taught decreases. The communication training programme was designed to overcome this problem. The programme was held one day per month. In between course days, people were asked to practise some of the techniques discussed in the training programme, and then to provide feedback at the following session.

Source: Arkin, A., 'Formula for a learning organisation', *Personnel Management*.

Empowered employees and teams, of course, are closely associated with total quality management (TQM). However, there is a difference between empowerment in TQM and in learning organisations. In a TQM setting, empowerment gives employees a means to serve customers better. In a learning organisation, empowerment stimulates learning and creativity. For example, in describing empowerment at Motorola, Robert Galvin noted:

> *Creative teams of people keep saying, 'Oh, but there's a variation or an addition or a new trend,' or 'I just learned that this would be related to that.' Again, teams of people each contribute some piece, and once in a while, your brilliant idea, mine, or somebody else's may be the stimulating force. Somebody says, 'Let's now create a new rose,' and then we start all over.*

Superior capability in new product and process development

Exhibit 10.6 considers how superior capability in new product and process development can be achieved through learning and outlines seven elements that enable a company to make learning a reality.

POLICIES AND PROGRAMMES FOR LEARNING

It is necessary for the management to define the policies and programmes which will enable the organisation to progress to becoming a learning organisation, and to specify the type of changes in behaviour that are required. To assist this process, Garvin proposes the following five building blocks of learning organisations*.

*Adapted and printed by permission of *Harvard Business Review*. From 'Building a learning organization', July/August 1993. Copyright © 1993 by the President and Fellows of Harvard College; all rights reserved.

Exhibit 10.6

Superior capability in new product and process development through learning

There are various tools and techniques, many of which are now well established, that can enable a manufacturing company to create a distinctive and superior capability in new product and process development. However, as Steven Wheelwright of Harvard University stressed, 'The key to achieving this', he submitted, 'is to make organisational learning a reality.'

One company that seems to have proved itself very capable of coping successfully with today's market place, by anticipating market trends and providing quick response to changing customer needs, is W.A. Baxter & Sons Ltd. Known internationally for its 'family of fine foods', the company also has its own way of organisational learning: that of remaining a family-owned and family-managed business.

This vital need for organisations to enhance significantly their learning ability has been highlighted by research undertaken in the USA by the Manufacturing Vision Group ... First, it was recognised that, in the manufacturing world of the 1990s, the key to success is to excel in both learning and converting that learning into commercial products and processes ... The research also defined seven elements that enable a company to excel in this kind of learning. These elements are:

1 *Core capabilities*. The attributes of a company that enable it to serve customers in a unique way, distinguishing it from its competitors.
2 *Guiding vision*. A clear picture of the future, that acts as a focal point for daily work.
3 *Organisation and leadership*. Companies need customised systems for promoting teamwork and supplying managers to head projects who have a clear concept of what a given product should be, can provide direction, and have decision-making authority.
4 *Ownership and commitment*. The sense of devotion that team members feel towards a project defines their ownership and commitment.
5 *Pushing the envelope*. The practice of constantly making improvements to a company's products, processes and capabilities on a broad front.
6 *Prototypes*. Models, mock-ups, and computer simulations of the product or process, used at strategic junctures in development projects, create a common language and help employees solve problems faster and better.
7 *Integration*. To optimise work, companies need a system to promote joint decision making among all functions involved in the project.

Source: Adapted from Lee-Mortimer, A., 'Competing through new product delivery', *World Class Design to Manufacture*, Vol. 2, No. 2, pp. 37–40, 1995.

- learning from systematic problem solving
- learning from experimentation
- learning from own experience
- learning from others' experience
- transferring knowledge through the organisation.

More specific examples of learning approaches are:

- learning from past failure
- learning from close relationship with the customer
- learning from linking with other organisations such as research institutes and universities
- learning from training
- learning from individual motivation
- learning from continuous improvement programmes
- learning from technology and management transfer.

The following sections outline some of the important learning approaches.

Systematic problem solving

This approach makes use of the lessons learned in the quality movement where a scientific method, rather than guesswork, is used for diagnosing problems – what Deming calls the 'Plan, Do, Check, Act' cycle; insisting on data, rather than assumptions, as the background for decision making; and using simple statistical tools such as histograms, Pareto charts and cause-and-effect diagrams to organise data and draw inferences. Adopting these methods enables employees to become more disciplined in their thinking and more attentive to details. They must continually question why things are the way they are and seek to improve. If there is no improvement they should inquire into the reason and learn from what they observe.

Experimentation

The experimentation approach is when new knowledge is sought, as a means to expand existing horizons and seize new opportunities through experimentation, which requires systematic searches and tests. Employees who in the main are concerned with current difficulties must feel that the benefits of experimentation exceed the costs, otherwise they will not participate. This creates a difficult challenge for managers who are trapped between two perilous extremes. They must maintain accountability and control over experiments, without stifling creativity by unduly penalising employees for failures. This environment requires an incentive system that favours risk-taking.

Learning from past experience

The organisation learns from what works. Past experiences and memories form part of the organisation learning mechanism. Hendry and Hope state that we can add to our experience, but we cannot subtract from it, and that is why we have to learn the positive effects of those past experiences.

Therefore, companies need to review their successes and failures, assess them systematically, and record the lessons in a form that employees find open and accessible. By failing to reflect upon the past, much valuable knowledge is escaping and mistakes may be repeated. Modesto and Zirger's study of more than 150 new products concluded:

> *The knowledge gained from failures is often instrumental in achieving subsequent successes... In the simplest terms, failure is the ultimate teacher.*

Thus a company needs people with a mindset that recognises that through failure is borne insight and understanding. In contrast, things can go well, but nobody knows how or why.

This is not a new story, and many companies are only successful today because they have had to build on, and learn from, their own experiences over many years. Hayes *et al.* concluded that:

> *We found no magic answer; as in the golden years of American manufacturing, high performance today is built on the solid foundation of effective capital investment, thoughtful product and process design, and operating clarity and precision. There is one other common denominator in high-performance plants: an ability to learn – to achieve sustained improvement in performance over a long period of time. When assessing a manufacturing organisation, learning is the bottom line.*

Learning from training programmes

The fundamentals of learning can be pursued using training programmes as a vehicle. Every organisation would be wise to pursue some sort of training programme for their employees, especially for those who are new to the company. Some companies train their staff internally, whereas others use external training agencies. Whichever method is chosen, the message is clear. It is important to tune the people into the organisation and assist them to contribute effectively to their role in the organisation.

Realising the importance of training and human resource development, most developing countries are now providing incentives for companies to send their workers on training programmes. For example, it was reported in *Berita Harian* (a Malaysian newspaper) on 20 October 1995 that the government had put aside grants amounting to $5 million to subsidise companies in Malaysia to train their staff to be more efficient in producing products and services that compete in the world market.

The importance of staff training is also reflected in Exhibit 10.7.

Learning from others

Not all learning comes from inward-focused analysis and reflection. It is necessary to look outside one's immediate environment to gain a new perspective. Companies in completely different areas of business can be fertile sources of ideas and catalysts for creative thinking. In the early days of Japanese industrialisation, people all over the world had the impression that Japanese products were cheap, abundant and of very low quality. Since World War 2, the Japanese have become obsessive about acquiring information and learning from it. They introduced benchmarking, which most people at that time referred to as 'copying'. When we look at Japanese products today, they are synonymous with quality and value and they are successful worldwide.

By adopting benchmarking, best practice organisations can be studied as a means of improving one's own practices and performance. Learning can also occur through obtaining information from customers about how they view the product, what their preferences are and what they feel about the service provided. People in learning organisations at all levels need to be aware of and learn from what others do.

Many companies are adopting this approach in their attempts to become world competitive. Specifically, a number of American companies have come to grips with this realisation. Hayes *et al.* concluded that:

Exhibit 10.7

Becoming a learning organisation through staff development

The following descriptions relate to staff development at the Procter & Gamble Plant in Lima, Ohio:

Operator B

Every employee that starts work for the company will work as an Operator B until they have acquired a level of skill. The person starts off as part of a control-room work team and in essence learns how to make Downy.

Operator A

After a year or so, once the technician is able to demonstrate to their fellow team members that they have a thorough knowledge of and ability in making Downy, they can progress to the level of Operator A.

General Technician

The operator has to demonstrate knowledge and competence in making Downy, but this time at a much higher level. The operator also needs to demonstrate knowledge and skills outside of the day-to-day business of the team.

On-line, Off-line Technician

This is the top qualification level and the highest pay level. Usually, the technicians can work both 'on-line' and 'off-line'. On-line work means anything directly connected to making the product, packing it, and shipping it. Off-line work means everything else. Usually the off-line work will involve working in self-directed teams within the company. In this way the worker becomes involved in decision making through team participation and in doing so learns to become part of the organisations management.

Source: From *Frontiers of Excellence: Learning from companies that put people first* by Robert Waterman; 1994; published by Nicholas Brealey Publishing, 36 John Street, London WC1N 2AT @ £9.99.

American managers eventually learnt that all that infighting and pointing of fingers was a luxury they couldn't afford. Fortunately, they now had the opportunity to study what their competitors were doing and learn from them. For a long while Americans didn't think they could learn much from others, but that has changed. The bad news is that it will take time to put those ideas – and some of the ones Americans have developed themselves – into practice. The good news is that it can be done.

Transferring knowledge

To achieve the maximum impact of learning, knowledge should not be held locally; it must be spread quickly and efficiently throughout the organisation. There are many ways of transmitting ideas and knowledge. They include written, oral, and visual reports, site visits and tours both inside and outside the organisation, personnel rotation programmes and action learning programmes. Actively experiencing something is considerably more valuable than having it described, and for this reason, personnel rotation programmes and action learning (studying other organisations) are some of the most powerful methods of transferring knowledge.

Essentially, the organisation that can learn is the one that will have a high probability of success. Peters and Waterman suggest that the control provided by a strong learning culture is seen as the critical enabler of change. This idea was again supported by Hayes *et al.* who concluded that:

> *Making significant commitments to new equipment and new systems may be perfectly appropriate, even essential, for some companies... But our research has taught us that there are many things that ought to be done first to prepare one's organisation for these new technologies. Managers ought to begin by attempting to reduce confusion, and by motivating and managing the learning process in their organisation.*

For all of the above to occur a particular mindset and pattern of behaviour is needed. Systems and processes that can support these activities and integrate them into the fabric of daily operations need to be in place. In this way companies can manage their learning more effectively.

BARRIERS TO LEARNING

It is necessary to identify the barriers to learning. For example, one barrier may be a lack of strategy that gives substance to the ways learning should be pursued in the organisation. This can manifest itself through a lack of top management support and the responsibility for learning not being allocated to key people. Other barriers include:

- inappropriate organisation structure
- poorly-structured or weak management
- poor quality of processes for information/knowledge acquisition and transfer
- a lack of schemes to facilitate learning, such as benchmarking, continuous improvement, experimentation, on-the-job experience and job rotation
- insufficient resources afforded to competence acquisition through formal training, hiring, from other organisations, customers and within
- a lack of the measurement of learning
- no means of allocating rewards or providing incentives to learn.

CASE STUDY: THE USE OF LEARNING

The following is a case study by Van Delft, conducted in a successful international company, to show the reader a method of determining the extent to which this company, or any other, makes use of the learning organisation (TLO) and how it can be used to overcome the blocks to effectiveness in operational areas which the company deems to be critical.

Background of Company A

Company A is part of an international shoe design, manufacturing and retailing group. It is located in Plymouth. The group is active in the manufacturing, retailing and wholesaling of shoes and bags. It currently employs around 18 000 people worldwide and owns 22 factories and 968 shops. In 1994, the group sold 41 million pairs of shoes. The outline of Company A is as follows:

Turnover:	£784m (Group 1994)
Capacity:	1.6 million pairs of shoes per year
Number of employees:	360
Location:	Devon, UK
Nature of business:	Producing formal ladies' shoes.

Current state of TLO in the company

To determine whether or not to adopt TLO in the company, the factory manager, design manager, production manager, components manager, personnel manager and accountant were interviewed, and the following questions were asked:

The learning strategy

1 How are plans made?
2 To what extent are people involved?
3 Do plans include movements in new directions?
4 Do management values reflect the real situation?

The learning climate

(Related to individuals)

5 In what ways are incentives given to people; is there a reward flexibility?
6 Are differences in people's background used to learn from one another?
7 In what ways are careers planned?
8 Is material for learning provided?

(Related to groups)

9 Do you view other departments as customers and suppliers?
10 Is it easy to get people together in a group for problem solving/improvement plans?
11 Are you aware of the knowledge of other groups? (i.e. do you know what their problems and solutions are?)

(Related to the organisation)

12 Are organisational structures fixed?
13 Are people empowered; i.e. who makes decisions?
14 Do people learn something if things go wrong?

Learning information

(Related to people)

15 Do people share information about performance (i.e. in meetings)?

(Related to own performance)

16 Is it possible to find out how you are doing?
17 Is it possible to collect information (like cost) for experiments?

(Related to others' performance)

18 In what ways do you collect information about the competition?
19 Do you use benchmarking?

The interviews with these managers revealed both strong and weak 'learning capabilities' in the company.

Strong learning capabilities

The learning strategy
- People are involved and listened to.
- Management plans actions in new directions.

The learning climate
- An important point is that departments see one another as customers and suppliers.
- If actions have to be taken, it is easy to organise people and use their specific skills.
- Organisation structures are not seen as fixed.

Learning information
- Information is shared in meetings.
- Feedback information concerning current activities and experiments is easy to obtain.

Weak learning capabilities

The learning strategy
- Currently, there is no written strategic plan stating both quantitative and qualitative goals.

The learning climate
- Concerning employment, there is no career planning (planned for next year), no reward flexibility and no structured plan to train people.
- There is no dedication to learn from failures.
- People are not fully aware of what other people are doing because of the informal organisation.

Learning information
- There is a lack of structured benchmarking and external information collection.

In summary it cannot be said that the company is a true learning organisation. However, the purpose here was to identify where improvements could be made and how TLO can be used to the company's benefit.

Assessing the blocks to operational effectiveness
Using Slack's importance–performance matrix and method of analysis, the criteria in Table 10.1 were ranked according to their urgency to the company's operational effectiveness (the highest urgency factor being the most important).

Blocks to 'on-time delivery' and their strength
For example, the criterion of 'on-time delivery' has been chosen since it is one of the criteria with a high urgency factor for which there are no current improvement plans. The main blocks to it, together with a weight (WT) relating to how easy it would be to remove each of the blocks (WT = 1 = easy, WT = 5 = difficult), were identified by the managers as follows:

- There is no written strategic plan to follow to provide direction on how to solve this problem. WT=2

Table 10.1 Urgency of operational effectiveness criteria

Ranked criteria	Urgency factor
1 Fast delivery	36
2 On-time delivery	27
3 New products	18
4 Design change	9
5 Volume change	6
6 Cost	6

- There is no benchmarking information on which goals might be based. WT=4
- Time pressures preclude the current situation being adequately understood, or further improvements being considered. WT=4
- Lack of historical data makes identification of causes difficult. WT=5
- There is a lack of active response from shopfloor personnel to develop countermeasures. WT=5
- The informality of the organisation prevents the sharing of learned lessons to adopt countermeasures. WT=2

Removing the blocks through being a learning organisation

The final step of the fieldwork considered whether the blocks could be removed by using the concept of the learning organisation. Because of its practical nature, the learning framework containing 11 characteristics, as described by Pedler *et al.* and summarised earlier, was used as a reference to the perfect learning organisation. The results obtained are presented in Table 10.2. This shows the removing effect it is estimated each characteristic of the learning organisation will have on each of the blocks. A removing value (A) is assigned on a scale from 1 to 5, where 1 represents no removing effect and 5 represents a large removing effect. Column B represents the weights of the blocks.

The values in column C of the table are a product of the removing effect of the learning on the block and the weight of the block, and so represent the management emphasis that needs to be placed on each learning characteristic.

Total weighted removing effect of learning on the blocks

The sum of the C values is found for each of the learning characteristics. These are listed in Table 10.3. They are ranked according to their total effect; with the characteristic with the highest total removing effect being ranked on top.

Results

With respect to Company A benefiting from becoming a learning organisation, the analysis shows that pursuing a 'learning climate' will have the greatest effect on removing blocks to one of their main areas of operational concern, that of 'on-time delivery'. This is followed by 'internal exchange' (departments seeing one another as customers and suppliers) and 'informating' (information systems which provide support to assess new activities and empower people).

Table 10.2 Effect of removing blocks using TLO approach

Learning characteristic	Block 1: No Strategic plan			Block 2: No benchmarking information		
	Value (A)	Weight (B)	Effect (C = A × B)	Value (A)	Weight (B)	Effect (C = A × B)
1 The learning approach to strategy	4	2	8	1	4	4
2 Participative policy making	3	2	6	1	4	4
3 Informating	1	2	2	1	4	4
4 Formative accounting and control	1	2	2	1	4	4
5 Internal exchange	2	2	4	3	4	12
6 Reward flexibility	1	2	2	1	4	4
7 Enabling structures	1	2	2	1	4	4
8 Boundary workers as environmental scanners	1	2	2	5	4	20
9 Intercompany learning	1	2	2	5	4	20
10 Learning climate	1	2	2	1	4	4
11 Self-development for all	1	2	2	1	4	4

Learning characteristic	Block 3: Time pressure			Block 4: Lack of historical data		
	Value (A)	Weight (B)	Effect (C = A × B)	Value (A)	Weight (B)	Effect (C = A × B)
1 The learning approach to strategy	1	4	4	2	5	10
2 Participative policy making	2	4	8	1	5	5
3 Informating	1	4	4	4	5	20
4 Formative accounting and control	1	4	4	3	5	15
5 Internal exchange	3	4	12	2	5	10
6 Reward flexibility	1	4	4	1	5	5
7 Enabling structures	1	4	4	3	5	15
8 Boundary workers as environmental scanners	1	4	4	1	5	5
9 Intercompany learning	1	4	4	2	5	10
10 Learning climate	1	4	4	5	5	25
11 Self-development for all	1	4	4	2	5	10

Learning characteristic	Block 5: Response of shopfloor personnel			Block 6: Informality of the organisation		
	Value (A)	Weight (B)	Effect (C = A × B)	Value (A)	Weight (B)	Effect (C = A × B)
1 The learning approach to strategy	1	5	5	4	2	8
2 Participative policy making	3	5	15	5	2	10
3 Informating	3	5	15	3	2	6
4 Formative accounting and control	3	5	15	2	2	4
5 Internal exchange	2	5	10	3	2	6
6 Reward flexibility	4	5	20	1	2	2
7 Enabling structures	3	5	15	2	2	4
8 Boundary workers as environmental scanners	2	5	10	1	2	2
9 Intercompany learning	2	5	10	1	2	2
10 Learning climate	4	5	20	2	2	4
11 Self-development for all	5	5	25	1	2	2

Table 10.3 Total removing effect of learning characteristics

Characteristic	Total effect
10 Learning climate	59
5 Internal exchange	54
3 Informating	51
2 Participative policy making	48
9 Intercompany learning	48
11 Self-development for all	47
4 Formative accounting and control	44
7 Enabling structures	44
8 Boundary workers as environmental scanners	43
1 The learning approach to strategy	39
6 Reward flexibility	37

ACTION PLANNING FOR LEARNING

It is important that managers agree on what actions are necessary to create or further develop a learning organisation. It is important too that students understand the nature of the actions that are necessary to create or further develop a learning organisation. The points referred to in Table 10.4 will assist this process, and managers should be encouraged to make use of it and develop it further to suit their particular circumstances. Students should make their own notes in the spaces provided as a means of revising this important subject area.

CASE STUDY: THE CLEARVIEW COMPANY

We should have started to learn sooner

Fiona had visited her opposite number in a company that had taken on board the principles of 'The Learning Organisation' (TLO). The company was doing extremely well and in each of the last two years had been cited in the DTI's best practice company awards. This successful company, in the form of Roger, the company's Personnel Director, who liked Fiona, was willing to assist Fiona and let her use its company training plan for TLO. What had impressed her was that it was a vehicle within which her training and development programme could be structured more strategically than at present. Also, it could form the backbone of changing the behaviour and developing the necessary competences for change at Clearview.

Fiona thought Nick, the IT and Communications Manager, who was standing in for Andrew Brown, the IT and Communications Director, would be a good ally on this one, since for months now he had been saying that his IT area could be used more for the purposes of learning. She asked Nick for his thoughts.

'It's a great idea, Fiona,' said Nick. 'From what I know, this learning organisation stuff puts great store on the use of IT for obtaining and distributing information. This would help us communicate quicker with our suppliers as well as internally to meet

Table 10.4 Action planning for learning

What is meant by the term 'The Learning Organisation' (TLO)?	
In what ways, if any, does the company's strategic plan incorporate TLO as an integral factor in its development? You may wish to consider some of the following aspects of TLO to make a judgement: ● competence acquisition through formal training, hiring, other organisations, customers and from within ● development programmes for developing management and functional skills, personal attribute awareness, problem-solving skills ● schemes to facilitate learning, such as benchmarking, continuous improvement, experimentation, on-the job-experience, job rotation ● rewards and incentives to learn ● supporting organisation structure. For example flat structures, flexible boundaries and the use of teams ● quality of processes for information/knowledge acquisition and transfer ● the use of IT and networked systems needs considering here.	
To what extent are you a learning organisation?	
What are your learning objectives and policies?	
What are the components of the framework or a structured approach you intend to follow?	
What are the main actions that must be taken?	
Who would be responsible?	
When will each action take place?	
How would you go about measuring learning?	

the changing demands placed upon us by our customers. Let's also not forget,' said Nick, winking at Fiona, 'If we can use this as a vehicle for development in our respective areas, it will be a feather in both our caps.'

However, they felt they needed a greater understanding of TLO and the benefits it could bring to the company. Over the next five weeks they tracked down and visited another two companies that were using TLO, read up on the subject and attended a course on it, which was presented at the first company Fiona had visited.

At the next meeting of the change team they put forward their thoughts.

Mike, who was in attendance, was furious about the whole thing being suggested, as it was without any forewarning or mention on the agenda. Moreover, he said that he thought their suggestions were too vague and if they did have any merit, why had they not been proposed earlier. He felt they were wasting everyone's time.

Mike said, 'The things you are talking about would require major changes in the way we operate. If you consider this to be so important, why didn't you present it for consideration at the initial operations and change strategy planning meetings? If we were thinking of adopting TLO, that's when it should have been considered. Now you come here with some "pie in the sky" idea, you don't make it clear what it all means, what needs to be done, what it is supposed to achieve and what it would cost. You're acting like amateurs and wasting everyone's time.'

Don muttered, 'Sounds more like a case of "not invented here syndrome" to me!'

Mike turned on him, 'If I were you Don I'd get my sales figures up further before I started shouting the odds.'

The meeting fell silent. Then George spoke up, 'Look, Mike, if there is anything in this, I know it should have been considered earlier, but we could be missing out on an opportunity to strengthen the process of changing our operations. So far the skills training that has been provided has boosted productivity and has paid off. If this learning organisation stuff is going to be similar but company-wide then it should pay for itself. Also, Fiona and Nick have spent some time considering this and I think you ought at least to give them the chance to meet again and discuss this all in a more informed way.'

Mike replied, 'I'll only consider this when I know what it could involve and what it could cost. Put the details on my desk as soon as you can.'

Mike could not attend the next meeting but he had asked Eric, the Finance Manager, to break the bad news that he thought the timescale of the programme was too ambitious. The programme Fiona and Nick had proposed would involve the company going 35 per cent over its training and development budget and that could not be afforded.

The extra costs were mainly due to the proposed training programmes, the extra monies required for learning-related payments and the costs involved in the proposed IT development; the latter being for networked systems, training schemes in the use of additional software packages, and the introduction of an electronic data interchange (EDI) link with the main suppliers.

Many of these comments had been anticipated by Fiona and Nick. First, Fiona said that the timescale for full implementation could be extended. In any case, it would take time to revamp the strategic plan to incorporate TLO. It was agreed that, in time, the training costs would pay for themselves but, since the last meeting, she had found these costs could be greatly reduced to be near budget. She identified details on local authority and DTI grants; that a teaching company scheme could provide the company with one or two good graduates to work on the change programme; that two of the company's main suppliers had agreed to enrol, for free, groups of Clearview's people on their in-house purchasing and supplies management course. After negotiations, the local college had consented to put on management development seminars, as well as a series of workshops on how to improve manufacturing effectiveness, at half its regular tuition rate.

Nick added that the company's computer equipment and software supplier would put on a course on IT, word-processing and spreadsheets, as well as one on the use of Windows, free of charge if Clearview agreed to stay with them for the next two years. Since this was in the plan, he thought this all made good sense.

Eric listened intently. 'I'll get back to you,' he said, 'but I still think the costs for any proposed learning-related payments and for networked systems and an EDI link will prove to be prohibitive.'

'No you won't,' said Fiona. 'We'll all meet on this one. I think we can all see the value of this, and we need everyone's agreement – and especially the full backing of Mike.'

They met again two weeks later. Mike was present and he had set the agenda. He said that he had attended a seminar on TLO at the local training agency. At the seminar he had met other managers involved with TLO and he commented that it had cleared up his mind on some matters. He said he had booked the executive on the course in two weeks' time. Other managers would then follow suit if it was considered to be useful. He wished to postpone deliberations until they had also attended the course, but he asked for another meeting to clarify what Clearview's objectives were to be if they were to pursue TLO. He also asked the whole team to clarify, in their respective areas, what they expected to achieve on the learning side and what the resultant benefits, in terms of productivity and customer service, would be.

After they had all attended the TLO course they met again. Mike asked Nick for details on how IT and communications could foster learning; Eric for plans for a revamped payment and rewards system based around learning; Fiona for ideas on how learning could be improved through hiring new people, retraining and job rotation; Don for plans on how to interface with the customers and suppliers in order to learn more about the business; and George for details on how to benchmark against the best competition and the site visits that could be made to look at 'best practice' processes.

'Well, this is a turn around on your part, isn't it Mike?' goaded Don, who added, 'but what about the costs for learning-related payments, networked systems and all that EDI stuff?'

'Well, sonny,' snapped Mike, 'if you did your homework and knew more about the finances around here you would know that all of the IT stuff had been costed in to the budget for the next year. Besides, I make the big decisions around here, not you!' Mike continued, 'I consider that TLO can be a major enabler to our programme for managing operations and change. However, before we start doing anything out there I want certain things done. Let everyone know what this is all about and obtain their views. In each of your respective areas find out to what extent we are a learning organisation. Draw up action plans in your areas and meet in the next few weeks to develop a co-ordinated action plan for Clearview to become a learning organisation. Finally, let me know how we can monitor the progress of all this and get a feel for how well we are achieving our targets of learning and effectiveness in our operations and service to the customer.'

George commented, 'I think we all welcome your ideas on this and the very strong support that you are offering.'

Mike replied, 'I like to think I'm progressive.'

They all nodded at Mike and smiled at one another.

Fiona and Nick smiled at each other. Their hard work had paid off; something they believed in was about to take off. They now, with the rest, had to make it work; but at the moment they could reflect on how their interventions had made improvements and how overall things were moving further in the right direction.

SUMMARY

- A learning organisation can be described as one that facilitates the learning of everyone within it, and is skilled at creating, acquiring and transferring knowledge. It makes use of a knowledge-based approach to managing operations and change in order to compete effectively.

- The characteristics of a learning organisation are that it should: adopt a strategy for learning; assess internally where there are opportunities to improve performance; adopt a structure to improve performance; look outside to see and learn how things might be done better; monitor the existing situation and identify learning opportunities.

- An organisation learns by knowing what a learning organisation is and having clear guidelines on how to put it into practice. People need to be sufficiently trained and imparted with new knowledge, new ideas and non-traditional thinking patterns. Systematic problem solving and experimentation should be encouraged. An atmosphere where people learn from their past experiences and from each other should prevail. People should feel some kind of ownership concerning the outcomes of actions taken. Challenges should be taken, not in competition, but in co-operation with colleagues. Mechanisms for transferring knowledge should be in place. Learning and the expected quantifiable improvement in performance should be measured.

- It is necessary to identify the barriers to learning; for example a lack of strategy structure or rewards for learning.

- A company should adopt a process by which it can utilise learning to overcome its blocks to operational effectiveness. For example, the company should identify the areas in its operations which are of concern. The barriers to improvement in these areas, together with their strength, should be identified to establish how each aspect of the learning policy can overcome them.

- An action plan for learning should include competence acquisition, development programmes and schemes to facilitate learning, rewards and incentives to learn, a supporting organisation structure and processes for information/knowledge acquisition and transfer. It should also ask: To what extent are you a learning organisation? What are your learning objectives and policies? What framework or structured approach do you intend to follow? What are the main actions that must be taken? Who would be responsible? When will each action take place? How would you go about measuring learning?

REVIEW AND DISCUSSION QUESTIONS

1 Assume that you are employed as a warden in the prison service. In what ways do you think your particular prison could benefit from adopting the principles of the learning organisation?

2 Discuss four particular ways in which a management consultancy business could pursue learning.

3 Describe the characteristics of a true learning organisation.

4 Explain how a general hospital could make use of Pedler *et al.'s* Eleven Characteristics Model.

ASSIGNMENTS

1 Put yourself in the shoes of a manager whose managing director has called a meeting to consider how the company could become a learning organisation. The MD has chosen you to lead a discussion on this and requires you to brief him/her on the main issues on which you intend to focus on and the practical means you would propose for the adoption of learning at the company.

2 Prepare a summary for presentation to the other senior managers in your company on the benefits the company might realise from becoming a learning organisation. Also, spend some time detailing a process for determining the main obstacles to progress and the steps the company could take to overcome them.

REFERENCES

Argyris, C. and Schön, D. A., *Organizational Learning: A theory of action perspective*, Addison-Wesley, Wokingham, 1978.

Arkin, A., 'Formula for a learning organisation', *Personnel Management*, pp. 48 & 49, July 1993.

Bateson, G., *Steps to an Ecology of Mind*, Ballantine, New York, 1972.

Bottoms, D., 'Facing change or changing face?', *Industrial Week*, pp. 17 & 18, 1 May 1995.

Bower, D.G., 'The learning organisation: a Rover perspective', *Executive Development*, Vol. 6, No. 2, pp. 3–6, 1993.

Burgoyne, J., 'Creating a learning organisation', *RSA Journal*, pp. 321–30, April 1992.

Daniels, S., 'The learning organisation', *Work Study*, Vol. 43, No. 8, pp. 5 & 6, 1994.

Deming, W. E., *Quality, Productivity, and Competitive Position*, MIT Centre for Advanced Engineering Study, Cambridge, Mass., 1982.

Galvin, R., *Organisational Dynamics*, Vol. 20, Issue 4, pp. 56–69, Spring 1992.

Garvin, D.A., 'Building a learning organisation', *Harvard Business Review*, pp. 78–91, July/Aug 1993.

Hayes, R. H., Wheelwright, S.C. and Clark, K. B., *Dynamic Manufacturing: Creating the learning organisation*, The Free Press, New York, 1988.

Hendry, J. and Hope, V., 'Culture change and competitive performance', *European Management Journal*, pp. 401–6, December 1994.

Jashapara, A., 'The competitive learning organisation: A quest for the holy grail', *Management Decision*, Vol. 31, No. 8, pp. 52–62, 1993.

Kline, P. and Saunders, B. L., 'Ten steps to a learning organisation', *Executive Excellence*, Vol. 12, No. 4, p. 20, April 1995.

Lee-Mortimer, A., 'Competing through new product delivery', *World Class Design to Manufacture*, Vol. 2, No. 2, pp. 37–40, 1995.

Luthans, F., Hodgetts, R. and Lee, S., 'New paradigm organizations: From total quality to learning to world class', *Organizational Dynamics*, Vol. 22, No. 3, pp. 5–19, 1994.

Mills, D. Q. and Friesen, B., 'The learning organisation', *European Management Journal*, Vol. 10, No. 2, 1992.

Modesto, A. M. and Zirger B. J., 'The new product learning cycle', *Research Policy*, Vol. 14, No. 6, pp. 299–309, 1985.

Palframan, D., 'Smarter companies learn out of habit', *Works Management*, pp. 43–5, August 1994.

Pedler, M., Burgoyne, J. and Boydell, T., *The Learning Company: A strategy for sustainable development*, McGraw-Hill, Maidenhead, 1991.

Peters, J. 'On learning', *Management Decision*, Vol. 31, No. 6, pp. 62–5, 1993.

Peters, T., and Waterman, R.H., *In Search of Excellence*, Harper & Row, New York, 1982.

Rheem, H., 'The learning organisation', *Harvard Business Review*, p. 10, Mar/Apr 1995.

Senge, P., *The Fifth Discipline: The art and practice of the learning organisation*, Doubleday Dell, New York, 1990.

Slack, N., 'The importance-performance matrix as a determinant of improvement priority', *International Journal of Operations & Production Management*, Vol. 14, No. 5, pp. 59–75, 1994.

Stata, R., 'Organisation learning: the key to management innovation', *Sloan Management Review*, pp. 63–73, Spring 1989.

Van Delft, M., 'Improving the competitive level at the CLKS Company', MSc Dissertation, Department of Manufacturing Engineering and Operations Management, University of Nottingham, 1995.

Waterman, R.H., *Frontiers of Excellence*, Nicholas Brealey, London, 1994.

Womack, J.P., Jones, D.T. and Roos, D., *The Machine that Changed the World*, Rawson Associates/Scribner, New York, 1990.

CHAPTER 11

Business process re-engineering

OBJECTIVES

The objectives of this chapter are to:

- explain how business process re-engineering (BPR) came about and what it is
- illustrate why BPR is popular and, conversely, present what are considered to be the risks associated with it
- show how BPR can be approached and present and critique a number of available methodologies
- contrast BPR with other management philosophies and approaches
- provide an action plan for BPR
- illustrate some of the practical issues and problems associated with a company considering the uptake of BPR.

WHAT IS BUSINESS PROCESS RE-ENGINEERING?

The term 'business process re-engineering', or BPR, was first coined in 1988 by Michael Hammer, an information technology (IT) consultant. He wrote an article in the *Harvard Business Review* exhorting managers to rethink their business processes rather that simply investing in huge amounts of IT to automate them. He urged business people to 'obliterate, don't automate'. His argument was that IT and total quality management (TQM) needed to stop fighting and work together. In practice this meant tightening processes and eliminating unnecessary and redundant steps, rather than supporting the present process systems with complex IT systems.

Some definitions

Business process re-engineering is a controversial management technique, since there is no definitive guide as to what business process re-engineering, or BPR, or re-engineering as it is sometimes called, stands for.

Manganelli and Klein viewed re-engineering as:

> *The rapid and radical redesign of strategic, value-added business processes, and the systems, policies and organisational structures that support them, to optimise work flows and productivity in the organisation.*

This focuses on the strategic value of re-engineering and associated systems, whereas the most widely known definition, from Hammer and Champy is broader and includes all processes within the definition:

The fundamental rethinking and redesign of business processes to achieve dramatic improvements in critical contemporary measures of performance, such as cost, quality, service, and speed.

This, and the quick definition provided by Hammer, associated with 'starting over', highlight the clean-sheet approach to process redesign, i.e. not simply tinkering with what already exists or making incremental changes that leave basic structures intact. It means abandoning long-established procedures and looking afresh at the work required to create a company's product or service and deliver value to the customer. The question to be answered now is: If the company were to be recreated today, given what is known and the current technology, what would it look like?

Talwar however prefers an alternative definition of BPR:

Changing mindset, attitudes, and behaviour to allow the fundamental rethinking and redesign of business activities, structures and working relationships in order to maximise value added and achieve radical and sustainable improvements in all aspects of business performance.

This takes the definition one stage back from the actual change, highlighting the necessary prerequisites of change management, people's perceptions and willingness to be changed.

From these definitions and the many others available, it is possible to discern certain main themes which form the essence of BPR, these being:

● its strategic aspect
● disagreements over whether it is a project, a process, or a philosophy
● disagreements over whether or not the present systems should be used as a basis for improvement
● the necessary changes in culture which accompany BPR, and how the company can be positioned best to achieve a successful re-engineering initiative
● the influence of customer service, and what drives BPR
● some of the effects of re-engineering, most notably the flat, team-based structures, and productivity
● the measures against which performance should be assessed
● whether the initiative should produce radical and dramatic results or just improvements.

The above points show there is some confusion about what BPR is. What does not help is that there is no defined standard for BPR as there is for quality systems (ISO 9000), and as yet there is no proliferation of gurus providing definitive versions of the subject, as has been the case with TQM and JIT.

Two BPR camps seem to have emerged: one based around Hammer's original definition concerning a strategic approach aiming for dramatic improvement through radical changes in business process design; the other, often referred to as 'process re-engineering', offering the opportunity to rethink and streamline individual processes. In the latter, the emphasis is on identifying one or more 'core processes', analysing them and then radically rethinking and redesigning their execution. Although such initiatives may be supported by the chief executive, they are typically 'owned' by a senior manager.

The need to challenge the status quo

The concepts of BPR provide a source for many useful ideas, chief among these being the idea that organisations may not increase competitiveness if they follow traditional rule books. Managers need to challenge the way things are as well as their own mind-set. They need to realise that the existing ways are not fixed in stone; they are limitations to what could be. The opportunities are there for organisations to consider themselves from an holistic perspective and radically transform processes in order to achieve dramatic improvements.

THE ORIGINS AND EVOLUTION OF RE-ENGINEERING

Manganelli and Klein suggest that there are no specific origins to re-engineering; rather it has emerged as a natural response to intense competition.

Pendlebury *et al.* also refer to international competition as a driving force behind this brand of process management. They argue that even though many organisations, particularly manufacturing ones, have been using a process orientation for a number of years, they have been using it in a tactical sense to improve their own operations, rather than applying the philosophy in a strategic sense to gain competitive advantage.

Carr and Johansson see the development of BPR coming from the TQM movement in the form of a reworking of TQM principles to suit the Western management style for quick-fix solutions (*see* Fig 11.1).

However, from the sources reviewed, the roots of the modern BPR movement could be attributed to two major sources, as well as a number of other subsidiary influences:

● intense market competition
● a development of TQM and practical problems with its implementation.

What is clear is that BPR is not a totally new phenomenon, but the bringing together of various strands of modern, and not so modern, management theory in an attempt

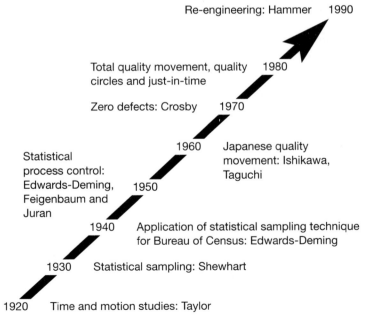

Fig 11.1 TQM and BPR in an historical context

Source: Carr, D.K. and Johansson, H.J., *Best Practices in Re-engineering*, McGraw-Hill 1995. Reproduced by kind permission of The McGraw-Hill Companies.

Exhibit 11.1

BPR as a vehicle to serve customer demands

In 1991, as part of an ongoing performance improvement effort, San Francisco-based Schlage Lock Co. initiated a business process re-engineering programme. In particular, Schlage, which is part of Ingersoll-Rand Worldwide, wanted to accommodate the needs of the high-volume 'value' retailers, such as K-mart, Wal-Mart, Home Depot and Builders Square.

The company defined its primary re-engineering goals as increasing throughput and productivity, reducing operations costs and improving customer relations. To achieve these Schlage was led by a Strategic Information Systems Plan (SISP) team.

As interpreted by Schlage, business process re-engineering entails defining, understanding, simplifying and documenting business and manufacturing processes in order to make them candidates for automation or other change. The aim was the development and implementation of superior-order management and manufacturing processes, systems and technologies that would delight the customer and support Schlage's strategic goals. Attempting such changes was expected to have a major impact on company culture, as it would involve alteration in day-to-day operations, introduction of multi-functional processes and emphasis on teamwork. While the company's TQM philosophy provided an attitudinal foundation for this plan, implementation of the SISP provided the operational foundation.

Source: Adapted from McCloud, J., 'Changing customer demands serve as impetus for BPR at Schlage Lock Co.', *Industrial Engineering*, June, pp. 30–4, 1994.

to solve the problems faced by today's business executives. These same problems Hammer and Champy neatly sum up as the three Cs:

1 **customers** becoming more demanding
2 **competition** becoming stronger
3 **change** becoming the only thing that is constant.

Exhibit 11.1 illustrates how changing customer demands served as an impetus for BPR at the Schlage Lock Co.

The driving force behind BPR

It would appear that, in common with most major change programmes, re-engineering is driven by crisis, caused by intense competition shifting power from suppliers to customers. What this suggests is that the problems encountered by modern organisations are not caused by lazy workers or poor managers, but more often by poor systems, design, structure and processes.

THE POPULARITY OF BPR

BPR's popularity is marked, especially in the US. One survey for the National Council for Manufacturing Sciences in the US found that 80 per cent of large manufacturers were either well into BPR efforts or were starting them up in 1994 (Carr and Johansson, 1995).

Carr and Johansson see the problems with TQM and the growing market pressures relating to customer service, response time, design time to market, quality, cost, and flexibility as having a big impact on the take-up of BPR. Many manufacturers have found that their traditional structures, customer-service philosophies and business methods are no longer competitive. The result is that managers have become receptive to new ideas, but they have yet to find a simple means (as if they ever could) of dramatically improving their profitability and competitive position. This has allowed management consultants to devise more initiatives, which when phrased and promoted correctly have been very enticing to organisations.

From the survey carried out, via in-depth interviews with 47 companies, Carr and Johansson found that many different types of target goals had been set for BPR initiatives, suggesting that framing BPR as a wide-ranging panacea for modern business problems had enhanced its acceptability among business leaders (*see* Fig 11.2).

Information about the popularity of BPR in the US from 1992 to 1994 comes from surveys by management consultants, Gateway (*see* Manganelli and Klein, 1994). The results show that BPR is a popular initiative undertaken by senior executives to achieve their strategic goals.

Exhibit 11.2 outlines the results of a survey to identify the use of business process re-engineering within different industries in the UK.

The largest study of BPR was undertaken by the CSC Index (*see* Carr and Johansson, 1995). The latest CSC survey does indicate some of the differences between American and European efforts. Most North American re-engineering efforts are aimed at points of direct customer contact:

- 25 per cent of re-engineering activity in the customer service process
- 16 per cent in order fulfilment
- 11 per cent in customer acquisition activities such as sales and marketing.

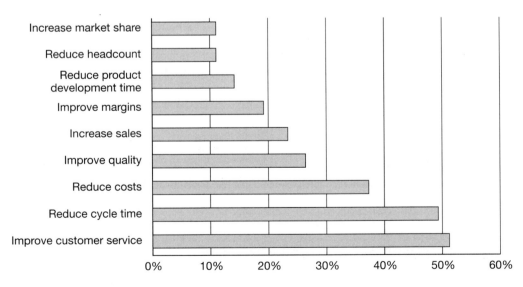

Fig 11.2 Target goals often set for BPR

Source: Carr, D.K. and Johansson, H.J., *Best Practices in Re-engineering*, McGraw-Hill 1995. Reproduced by kind permission of The McGraw-Hill Companies.

Exhibit 11.2

Survey of business process re-engineering

Aims of the survey

The aims of the survey were to identify the use of business process re-engineering within different industries in the UK.

Sampling criteria

Questionnaires were sent to managers at organisations identified to be manufacturers, services, public sector organisations (including local and national governmental bodies), and National Health Service Trusts (hospitals). In total, 125 questionnaires were sent to managers in each sector; 65 responses were received, giving an overall response rate of 13 per cent.

Respondents were asked to suggest which factors have inhibited and which have facilitated BPR in their organisation. The majority of factors were perceived to be facilitators more often than inhibitors by the majority of respondents. Only two factors, existing information systems and management systems, were defined as inhibitors more often than facilitators. Available IT expertise, project time frames, and organisation structure and culture were found to be quite frequently mentioned as inhibitors, although they were more often classed as facilitators.

Few differences stand out in analysing responses by industrial sector. However, manufacturing organisations reported project time scales to inhibit BPR less frequently than other sectors; services felt organisation structure inhibited BPR more often than other sectors; and public sector respondents suggested organisation culture was less often an inhibitor than other sectors.

When the importance of the factors affecting BPR is considered, the analysis is more reassuring. The most important factors (leadership, customer focus, training, team make-up and communication of objectives) were all reported to facilitate BPR much more often than inhibit.

Respondents were finally asked to compare the actual and expected benefits from BPR. The expected benefits in terms of performance improvements generally exceeded the actual benefits of BPR. The greatest benefits were expected in terms of improved financial performance, quality, customer satisfaction, process and organisational flexibility, and increased competitiveness. Of these measures, only improvements in financial performance and organisational flexibility ranked significantly lower than expected. Increased competitiveness, on the other hand, ranked higher in terms of actual benefit.

Source: Adapted from Zairi, M. and Sinclair, D., 'Business process re-engineering and process management: A survey of current practice and future trends in integrated management', *Management Decision*, Vol. 33, No. 3, pp. 3–16, 1995.

CSC found that in Europe:

- 23 per cent of re-engineering activity is taking place in manufacturing processes, or internal processes in service companies
- 15 per cent in customer service
- 15 per cent in distribution.

Peppard and Rowland suggest that, if successfully implemented in an organisation, the BPR-related benefits will include:

- lower stocks
- shorter lead times
- reduced costs
- higher productivity.

In contrast with the aforementioned customer focus, these are all universal goals for many organisations, which may explain the popularity of the concept.

Exhibit 11.3 illustrates how Osram Sylvania's time-based continuous improvement approach to BPR has resulted in lead-time reduction, productivity increase, scrap/rework decrease, materials cost reduction, inventory reduction, set-up reduction and space savings.

THE RISKS ASSOCIATED WITH BPR

Research by Carr and Johansson showed that two-thirds of BPR efforts fail, and given that US companies spent $32 billion in 1994 on re-engineering, this is a lot of wasted resource – just the type of resource which BPR sets out to allocate more effectively and efficiently. The CSC index, however, found that 25 per cent failed, far lower than anecdotal estimates which had ranged as high as 85 per cent in the US press. Much of the difference between the figures is due to the definition of success and the timescale allowed. Nonetheless, there are still a considerable number of failures reported.

Research by Hall, Rosenthal and Wade showed that most BPR projects result in little overall improvement in financial performance, even if they appear to have changed the operational system out of all recognition.

Coulson states that in many cases the existing workforce is likely to be unhappy with the new vision. There is evidence to show that organisations:

- have lost a number of staff at once who had no desire to be part of such an approach
- have a significant minority of 20 to 40 per cent who would strongly prefer to return to the traditional ways.

It could be argued, as Peppard and Rowland do, that the above type of problems are due to a lack of consideration of the behavioural aspects of change. This may explain a large proportion of early failures.

For Morris and Brandon the main risks are concerned with the inability of organisations to complete the implementation of BPR rather than any inherent weaknesses concerning its principles. According to them:

- Re-engineering cannot be done halfheartedly.
- Executive management should be involved from start to finish.

Concerns about BPR

Even if organisations are able to take these ideas as a mechanism for change in order to increase their efficiency and competitiveness, serious concerns about BPR still prevail for these reasons:

1 It is not grounded in any strong theoretical base.
2 It seems to offer a panacea for many problems within organisations, but proof of success is hard to quantify.

Exhibit 11.3

Osram Sylvania's time-based continuous improvement approach to BPR

Osram Sylvania is America's second largest manufacturer of incandescent, fluorescent and high-intensity discharge lighting products. The company employs 12 500 people in 25 manufacturing facilities in the United States, Canada, Puerto Rico, Mexico and its headquarters in Danvers, Mass. The word 'Osram' appearing before the familiar Sylvania name refers to the Munich-based company, OSRAM GmbH (a subsidiary of Siemens A.G.), that purchased Sylvania's lighting products group from GTE Corp. in January 1993.

Osram Sylvania's productivity and quality department (formerly the industrial engineering department) has fashioned a framework for BPR that also encompasses the company's continuous improvement and employee involvement efforts. Dubbed the Time-Based Continuous Improvement Approach (TBCIA), the programme incorporates engineering and employee involvement with more traditional industrial engineering (IE) tools and techniques to create an umbrella for 'self-sufficient quality', or the transfer of change-related improvement skills to plant employees.

Now, under the aegis of TBCIA, the IE team goes into a facility 'to tackle an entire business cycle that goes on under that plant's roof – typically from order entry to shipment,' explains Steve Soffron, lead industrial engineer.

To elicit employee input in the initial research phase, the IE team conducts interviews, asking, 'If this were your candy store, how would you run it?'

The information gleaned from interviews forms the foundation for composing a process map, or breaking down the whole cycle into steps. Typically, a business cycle within a plant extends from order entry to scheduling, procurement, receiving, storage, production, inspection, warehousing and distribution.

Next in the TBCIA cycle, the IE teams analyse the results of the process map to determine which of the steps are 'value-added', or essential to the desires of the customer – the idea being that re-engineering emphasises ultimate outcomes rather than initial tasks, with the desires of the customer paramount. 'In our experience,' Soffron says, 'the great majority of a process's steps – maybe even 80 per cent of them – do not add value to the customer's eyes. If you were to ask a customer, "If we were to do this in the making of the product, would you be willing to pay for that step that costs $1.25 as a part of the (product's) price?", most often the answer would be "No".' As part of the mapping, the non-value-added steps are marked for elimination, if possible.

Following the analysis of value-added versus non-value-added, teams are formed, comprising those employees who actually do the work in question and who possess some degree of autonomy. The team devises a plan for re-engineering the process to maximise the value-added steps and minimise the non-value-added ones.

After the team re-engineers the process, it gauges the results of the new operation. Kevin Watts, director of productivity and quality, insists that measurement is fundamental to any successful BPR project, with determining baselines and discerning first-pass yield (the percentage of products of services acceptably completed on the first attempt without rework) serving as prime yardsticks, along with pinpointing barriers and identifying value-added versus non-value-added activities. Once satisfactory, the newly-re-engineered process is standardised using a programme for continuous improvement that takes advantage of systems such as ISO 9000's regimen of quality surveys and internal audits, and relies on a culture of sustained employee involvement.

The forecasts for TBCIA's eventual benefits are substantial: 30–70 per cent lead-time reduction, 5–25 per cent productivity increase, 15–40 per cent scrap/rework decrease, 6–45 per cent materials cost reduction, 5–60 per cent inventory reduction, 60–90 per cent set-up reduction, 10–35 per cent space savings. IE teams realise that re-engineering creates new means for better ends, generating more holistic benefits than simple cost reduction or improved labour efficiency. Enhanced employees commitment, increased internal communication and improved customer service are projected as immediate strategic benefits of TBCIA.

'Re-engineering forces you to look at the big picture,' Soffron says. 'To be a world-class competitor, we need to think that way in order to satisfy our customers faster and with higher quality than the competition. We see it, really, as the only way to survive in the global economy of the future.'

Source: Adapted from Bambarger, B., 'Osram Sylvania's time-based continuous improvement approach to BPR', *Industrial Engineering*, December, pp. 14–18, 1993.

3 There appears to be no unique selling point or particular type of organisation it is demonstrated can be certain to gain from these ideas.

Given these concerns, the dubiousness of the success rate of BPR, the plethora of methods and views on BPR and the availability of alternative management ideas and approaches, it is difficult to see how companies can generally achieve success with BPR. It may be that, without substantial guidance from consultants or personnel experienced in BPR, failures will abound. As a consequence, BPR may become another management technique that fails the test of time.

CHOICE OF METHODOLOGY FOR BPR

Methodology or clean sheet

Having selected which process or processes are to be transformed it needs to be known which methodology for BPR should be followed. The alternative is to adopt a clean-sheet approach.

Manganelli and Klein argue in favour of a methodology rather than visionary thinking. However, this may be linked with the fact that they have their own methodology called 'Rapid Re', standing for Rapid Re-engineering. Interestingly, they also argue that consultants are not required if a methodology is followed during BPR.

Coulson believes the clean-sheet approach should be used by those who view methodologies as inhibitors of original thought.

Exhibit 11.4 illustrates how Eastman Chemical Co. improved its competitive edge by taking a clean-sheet approach to the use of business process re-engineering.

The elements of a BPR methodology

In summary, this and other literature shows there to be mixed views on whether a methodology or a clean-sheet approach to BPR is essential for success. To help decide whether a methodology is suitable, Manganelli and Klein list the following key elements that the BPR structure should contain:

1 Develop a clear statement of corporate goals and strategies.
2 Consider the customer as the driving force.
3 Address business processes.
4 Identify value-added processes.
5 Make proven use of available management techniques and tools.
6 Provide analysis of current operations.
7 Provide for the development of breakthrough visions rather than incremental change.
8 Consider solutions in which employee empowerment and technology are the basis.
9 Develop an actionable implementation plan.

The following section gives a summary and critique of particular BPR methodologies.

Exhibit 11.4

Eastman Chemical Co. embraces business process re-engineering and increases its maintenance productivity

At Eastman Chemical Co. being world class is just not good enough. The company has set its sights on being the preferred chemical company in the world – a goal that requires a level of operating performance in a class by itself.

When an internal survey revealed that maintenance staff were spending as much as 50 per cent of their time finding and ordering equipment parts, Eastman knew the time had come for radical change. After a massive re-engineering effort that took nearly three years, Eastman has cut by 80 per cent the time needed to find and order materials. As a result, maintenance productivity has risen sharply, equipment uptime has increased and the company is saving more than $1 million every year in duplicate inventories costs.

Since that first project was completed, Eastman has embraced business process re-engineering (BPR) as a key strategy to give the company a significant competitive edge. The company has in place a top-level BPR strategy team and an active internal training programme. Specific BPR projects, using Michael Hammer's 'clean-sheet' approach and starting from scratch, are now underway and aimed at those areas, such as pricing policies, customer interfaces, order management systems and product development cycles, that Eastman believes will make it the world's preferred chemical company.

Says Bob Savell, the senior management engineer, 'There are two things you have to do to achieve effective BPR. You must have a vision of where you are going, and you need a case for action.'

Source: Adapted from Taylor, S., 'Business process re-engineering: Eastman Chemical strives for better than world class', *Industrial Engineering*, November, pp. 28–34, 1993.

A SELECTION OF BPR METHODOLOGIES

The original view of BPR

Hammer and Champy's BPR process presents a number of stages, which follow a traditional change management pattern, as follows:

Stage 1: The first stage is to determine where the re-engineering opportunities are within the organisation.
Stage 2: The re-engineering team needs to understand the process.
Stage 3: This is the redesign stage where new ideas are brought into the picture and new processes mapped out.
Stage 4: Once a new process has been planned, it can then be piloted to refine the design, then implemented.

On occasions, Hammer's work, although he is credited as the founder of the modern BPR movement, is full of superlatives and dramatic impact. Many would say it lacks sufficient detail to be used as a blueprint for change in their organisation.

The Rapid Re methodology

Manganelli and Klein, who prescribe a complete methodology for BPR, as would be expected, also come up with a comprehensive and detailed guide to BPR for managers. This methodology, called the 'Rapid Re', includes 54 separately identifiable steps in five stages. The stages are:

1 Preparation
2 Identification
3 Vision
4 Solution
   a technical design
   b social design
5 Transformation.

The 'Rapid Re' is most useful for those organisations without change management experience. It is best used as an ideas book, picking and choosing rather than slavishly following the whole 54 steps.

Carr and Johansson: The technical and behavioural view

Carr and Johansson structure their methodology in two parts: a *technical* one and a *behavioural* one. This reflects their experience that failures are more likely to be caused by lack of attention to the behavioural aspects of BPR.

The steps in the technical effort are limited to:

1 Identify the processes throughout the business.
2 Select from these the core business processes that directly add value for the company.
3 Redesign one or more of those processes to tighten connections with the customers, streamline operations, and eliminate wasteful, non-value-added steps in the identified processes.

The other focus on the behavioural change aspects is less well defined, but urges management to concentrate on the need to:

• overcome employee resistance to change

• empower employees

• consider employees working in natural teams

• set up, where appropriate, self-managed teams

• engage every single worker in the improvement process.

In this way, BPR can and should be used to extend the gains of employee empowerment and teamwork created under any TQM effort.

A European framework for BPR

Another complex methodology, provided in Coulson, provides more details at each stage of the implementation and comes from COBRA, a methodology manual for the

Commission of the European Communities. The particular emphasis of this plan is on the goal setting and planning, which needs to take place at the start of the project.

The key elements of the COBRA methodology are:

1 Consider the impact of BPR
2 Unfreeze
3 Understand
4 Reshape
5 Embed change
6 Review and monitor.

This structure appears to be based on the Lewin model of change – that of unfreeze, change, freeze – which has formed the basis of many change management approaches. The intention is to provide a generic framework for BPR by including many elements within a graphical form to be able to show the links and therefore make independent ideas appear to fit into one plan. However, in attempting to include everything, it can lack the detail that many practical implementers of BPR would be seeking.

A UK perspective on re-engineering

Peppard and Rowland also provide a great deal of detail regarding BPR planning and implementation. They provide a split, on the basis of the size of BPR project, suggesting that smaller projects should not undertake full BPR; instead they should use an existing change management framework and benchmark. A benchmarking framework they could adopt is:

• identify the process
• assess size of the BPR process and the corresponding team
• map, understand and analyse process
• refine process: change the obvious
• design benchmarking study
• collect information
• analyse study results
• design and implement the approved BPR programme.

The approach to BPR they recommend encompasses five stages:

1 Create the environment
2 Realise strategy
3 Pilot and conduct the changes
4 Restructure the organisation
5 Analyse, diagnose and redesign processes.

This offers a flexible approach to BPR, being more of a philosophy than a change method. This is useful because companies should be able to adapt their methods to suit the situation. However, it poses the problem of the time commitment and resources needed to fulfil it.

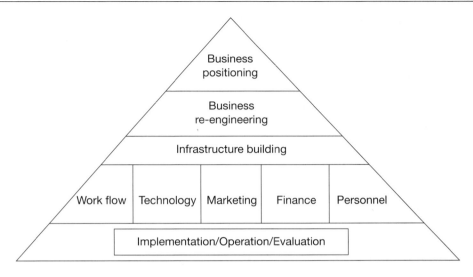

Fig 11.3 The Dynamic Business Process Re-engineering Model

Source: Morris, D.C. and Brandon, J.S., *Re-engineering your Business*, McGraw-Hill 1994. Reproduced by kind permission of The McGraw-Hill Companies.

Re-engineering through business positioning

Morris and Brandon develop their own context in which BPR should take place, which they term the 'Dynamic Business Process Re-engineering Change Model'. Using the model, Morris and Brandon go beyond BPR to discuss the context in which these changes should take place. They are also more specific in their understanding of how BPR fits into the change process. Their model can be broken down into a number of distinct stages and levels, as shown in Fig 11.3.

Positioning involves placing the company in the market place, by gathering information about the organisation and comparing where it is now to where it wants to be. This stage is needed because positioning is outside the framework of the re-engineering process. Re-engineering is about making changes in the company. In this sense, BPR is viewed as one stage of a change management programme. The overall questions, actions and outcomes required for each of the stages, including re-engineering, are shown in Table 11.1.

What is provided is a comprehensive package designed to guide businesses from initial thoughts about change to the end result. It should prove useful for those organisations less experienced in change management.

Using BPR for radical breakthroughs

Pendlebury *et al.* provide a different angle on BPR projects. Their BPR objective is breakthrough rather than simply improvement. In this case companies must first consider how to improve their processes before the more radical work of re-engineering core business processes. Companies thus need to have completed more tactical process-orientated techniques such as JIT or TQM. Consequently, the company should have learned most of the following important lessons:

Table 11.1 BPR questions, actions and outcomes

Stage	Questions	Actions	Outcomes
Business positioning	• What are we today? • What can we do to improve? • How can we best use the competition? • What are our best investments? • What is our best strategy?	• Competitive and market analysis • Business baseline definition	• Opportunities • Objectives • Strategy • High-level work flow map
Business re-engineering	• How do we change? • What will be the impact of our plans? • How will the new plans fit into the current operations?	• Map the current business processes • Model new, re-engineered work flows • Analyse impacts • Design new organisation work flows	• New processes and work flows • New organisation, work flows, systems definitions • Cost and benefit figures
Infrastructure building	• What changes need to be made in the way we do business? • How do we manage the impact on staff? • How do we co-ordinate all the changes?	• Financial arrangements • Technology systems development • Organisational development • Detailed implementation planning	• Technology infrastructure • Human resources and organisational structure • Adequate budget • Initial marketing plan and goals
Implementation, operation and evaluation	• Are we doing as well as we can? • What can we do with new ideas?	• Starting up the new operation • Running the business • Evaluating the business	• Profit • Experience • Satisfaction

Source: Morris, D.C. and Brandon, J.S., *Re-engineering your Business,* McGraw-Hill 1994. Reproduced by kind permission of The McGraw-Hill Companies.

- rigorous analysis of operations to eliminate waste
- elimination of non-value-added steps
- teambuilding
- cross-functional teamwork
- employee empowerment
- doing it right first time.

The basic approach to re-engineering a process, according to Pendlebury *et al.*, consists of three phases:

1 **Discover**. The company creates a strategic vision for dominance or renewed competitiveness in the market place, and determines what can be done to its processes to help achieve the strategy.
2 **Redesign**. The re-engineered process is detailed, planned and engineered.
3 **Realised**. The redesign is implemented to effect the strategy.

The steps in each of these phases are clearly indicated and easy to follow. However, there is less emphasis on the technical/behavioural split than in some other methods.

In summary, the approach provides a rather limited perspective of BPR but it is possibly closer to the original intentions of the concept.

Review

The range of methodologies simply reflects the wide spectrum of interpretations of what BPR is and how it should be implemented. Therefore, comparing the methodologies is a difficult if not futile exercise. Choice will depend on how radical the BPR project should be, how formalised it should be, how long it should take and how much of the business it should affect. This being said, there are a number of common themes that can be found within BPR and these seem to follow a typical change management process of:

1 preparation and understanding of the principles and methods
2 planning of the project
3 redesigning a process or processes
4 implementing the redesign, via a pilot scheme initially
5 feedback.

Here emphasis should be placed on the initial planning and decision stages. Also, it is important that the plans should reflect a socio-technical view of change, in which the people are as important as the technical aspects in the change process.

Finally, it must be said that, given the wide variety of situations in which BPR can be applied, professional and experienced input in the form of previous developers or consultants of BPR is essential. Without such guidance many organisations risk choosing an unsuitable method and put their chances of achieving success in jeopardy.

COMPARISON OF BPR WITH OTHER MANAGEMENT PHILOSOPHIES

As can be appreciated, the strengths and weaknesses of BPR compared to other management philosophies depend a great deal on the definition attached to BPR and how other management philosophies are represented.

Carr and Johansson feel that BPR has emerged by overcoming limitations inherent in other management concepts and approaches. The main alternative approaches they mention are:

1 Downsizing, which they feel is cost compression, which over time will begin to break down.

Table 11.2 Comparison of BPR with other programmes

	BPR	Rightsizing	Restructuring	TQM	Automation
Assumptions questioned	Fundamental	Staffing	Reporting relationships	Customer wants and needs	Technology applications
Scope of change	Radical	Staffing, job responsibilities	Organisation	Bottom-up	Systems
Orientation	Processes	Functional	Processes	Processes	Procedures
Improvement goals	Dramatic	Incremental	Incremental	Incremental	Incremental

2 Technology, which should be used as an enabler rather than a driver of change.

3 Functional performance improvement initiatives such as manufacturing excellence and just-in-time, which fall far short of the radical change necessary.

4 Material requirements planning (MRP), which focuses only on corrective problems within the existing structure.

5 Total quality management (TQM), which in many companies has been too narrowly focused and often functionally based, rather than process orientated.

Manganelli and Klein highlight the differences between improvement programmes and BPR programmes, as shown in Table 11.2.

TQM versus BPR

For Coulson, the main source of comparison for BPR is taken as TQM. As Table 11.3 shows, the two ideas are similar in many respects.

Table 11.3 Similarities between TQM and BPR

BPR	TQM
Process focus	Process focus
Emphasis on teams and shared values	Emphasis on teams and shared values
Redefine process boundaries then radically improve the few strategic ones	Improvement of processes within functional boundaries

Source: Coulson, C. T. (ed), *Business Process Engineering: Myth and reality*, Kogan Page, 1994.

Carr and Johansson see the main differences between the two techniques, TQM and BPR, as shown in Table 11.4.

Table 11.4 Differences between TQM and BPR

Factors	TQM	BPR
Type of change	Evolutionary – a better way to compete Adds value to existing processes	Revolutionary – a new way of doing business Challenges process fundamentals and their very existence
Scope	Encompasses whole organisation	Focuses on core business processes
Role of technology	Traditional support, e.g. MIS	Use as enabler

Source: Carr, D. K. and Johansson, H. J., *Best Practices in Engineering: What works and what doesn't in the re-engineering process*, McGraw-Hill 1995. Reproduced by kind permission of The McGraw-Hill Companies.

However, it is noted that TQM and BPR also have a lot in common, such as:

- people
- management and leadership
- organisational culture
- functional expertise
- stockpiling – new advances
- instantaneous reaction
- new assets and their management
- performance indicators: quality, lead time, cost, service.

BPR acts to make radical improvements from challenging traditional assumptions, breaking down barriers, making innovative use of technology, introducing new ways of working, changing relationships and redrawing traditional boundaries. TQM however is more short term and works within an agreed framework to improve continuously. Here, activities may be examined from a departmental perspective rather than considering the total processes in the organisation and how they serve the customer.

BPR is better in total quality organisations

According to the results of a survey conducted by McCloud to identify the use of business process re-engineering within different industries in the UK, the only significant difference in perception between total quality (TQ) and non-TQ organisations was that non-TQ organisations found organisation culture and structure to inhibit BPR more frequently than did TQ organisations.

The Peppard and Rowland comparison matrix

Peppard and Rowland compare BPR with modern management techniques to demonstrate the areas and approaches in which BPR takes a different perspective *(see*

Table 11.5 Business philosophy comparisons

Element	TQM	JIT	Simultaneous engineering	Time compression management/ Fast cycle response	BPR
Focus	Quality Attitudes to customers	Reduced inventory Raised throughput	Reduced time to market Increased quality	Reduced time (time = cost)	Processes Minimise non-value-added
Improvement scale	Continuous incremental	Continuous incremental	Radical	Radical	Radical
Organisation	Common goals across functions	Cells and team working	R&D and production work as single team	Process based	Process based
Customer focus	Internal and internal satisfaction	Initiator of action 'pulls' production	Internal partnerships	Quick response	'Outcomes' driven
Process focus	Simplify Improve Measure and control	Work flow/ throughput efficiency	Simultaneous R&D and production development	Eliminate time in all processes	'Idea' or streamlined
Techniques	Process maps Benchmarking Self-assessment SPC diagrams	Visibility Kanban Small batches Quick set-up	Programme teams CAD/CAM	Process maps Benchmarking	Process maps Benchmarking Self-assessment IS/IT Creativity

Source: Peppard, J. and Rowland, P., *The Essence of Business Process Re-engineering*, Prentice Hall 1995.

Table 11.5). (Note that comparing these different management philosophies is rather like comparing apples and pears.)

TQM, JIT and simultaneous engineering all prescribe the way organisations should work from day to day; fast cycle response (FCR) and BPR are concerned simply with how organisations can shift performance based on one way of working to another.

BPR relative to other change programmes on a management grid

Obolensky sees business re-engineering as one of a number of change programmes which can be represented in a change management grid, as shown in Fig 11.4.

The grid shows the status of BPR as being a significant change programme which affects the whole organisation and can be used to bring about dramatic changes in performance.

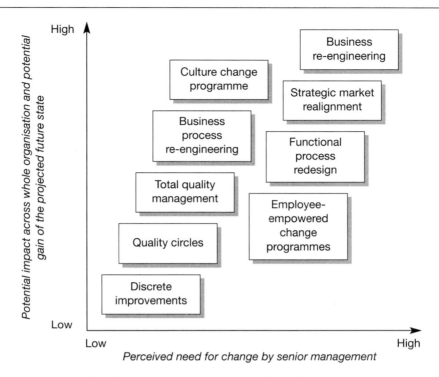

Fig 11.4 Position of business re-engineering and BPR relative to other change programmes in management grid

Source: Obolensky, N., *Practical Business Re-engineering*, Kogan Page 1994.

Summary

The theory shows there are distinct differences between BPR and other management philosophies. JIT and TQM are viewed as tactical process-orientated techniques, which, even if successful, may not bring companies to international standards. In practice the differences are less and are due mainly to interpretation.

WILL BPR LAST?

It is interesting to note that some proponents of BPR are already predicting its downfall. Lawrence applies the concept of the life cycle to new management philosophies. In doing so, he postulates that BPR, like other management philosophies, will fall into disuse. Perhaps this is a sign of our business times in which information, approaches and technology start to have an increasingly short life cycle. Nonetheless, BPR appears to be a potentially powerful approach and therefore sufficiently important to warrant its inclusion, along with other modern techniques, in the list of management philosophies.

Table 11.6 illustrates the achievements of process re-engineering at Western Provident Association.

A practical case example, provided in Exhibit 11.5, presents some of the many successes as well as failures that can arise from implementing BPR.

Table 11.6 Process re-engineering at Western Provident Association

Approach	Change	Achievement
• target of best service in the industry • relocate to Taunton – higher calibre of people • training investment three times the UK average • use document image processing to automate mundane procedures • develop 'systems for experts' not 'expert systems' • adopt open systems – easy access, supporting all business activities	• created customer-orientated business units; devolved authority/direct contact • document image processing provides access to two years' worth of paperwork in 40 seconds • case workers now handle all new business processing activities • eliminated bulk of interfunction communications • automatic access to all customer correspondence and activity log	• new business processing reduced from seven people taking 45 minutes over 28 days to one person taking four minutes over less than four days • working time on new business cases reduced from 40 minutes to four • staff reduced from 400 to 260 • salaries up 8 per cent in real terms in three years • 30 per cent service improvement • staff turnover cut from 66 per cent to 8 per cent • lapse rates down from 25 per cent to 10 per cent • productivity doubled over two years

Source: Reprinted from *Long Range Planning*, Vol. 26, No. 6, R. Talwar, 'Business re-engineering: A strategy-driven approach', pp. 22–40, Copyright © 1993, with kind permission from Elsevier Science Ltd, The Boulevard, Langford Lane, Kidlington, OX5 1GB, UK.

IS BPR A VIABLE PRACTICAL TECHNIQUE?

BPR has shown itself in the literature to be capable of producing some dramatic turn-arounds of corporate fortunes. Although it is not possible to scientifically isolate the BPR contribution in these cases, it is possible to say that, with the right culture, support of top management and careful planning, there is no reason why most companies would not benefit from implementing a BPR initiative.

Since BPR is designed to operate on processes, it will be more suitable for organisations which operate in a traditional hierarchical structure, and less beneficial to those companies which operate less rigidly.

Exhibit 11.5

Business process re-engineering at ISS

The ISS Company

ISS UK is part of a large conglomerate multinational manufacturing organisation, with a Global turnover of approximately $4 billion p.a. The prime focus of the European companies within the ISS Europe subgroup is the manufacture of building products and related consumer goods. ISS UK is part of this group, operating from three manufacturing sites in the UK, making a range of ceramic products.

The practical implementation of BPR at ISS

The BPR initiative at ISS had, at the time of the interviews, only been in progress for some six months. Therefore it was not going to be possible to assess whether the project had been a complete success or failure. Rather, the aim was to find out what had been happening, what progress had been made, and what the prospects for success were, as envisaged by the management. The view from the top of the organisation was that a new initiative was needed in order to increase the corporation's competitiveness. From this point of view the organisation considered BPR carefully and bought into the idea that it was more important to get the right processes than it was to improve existing processes.

The corporation's reason for starting BPR also ties in with the majority of other successful applications of BPR – to improve customer service.

In the initial stages, the company also recognised the importance of the human resource (HR) aspect to this change programme, with the appointment of senior HR personnel to prominent positions in the change programme's management structure.

However, in ISS the project did not start so well. A co-ordinator was appointed who has less than six months to go to retirement, and new process owners were put in place before the company has already started deciding which were the best options. The processes were decided on a European-wide basis, which may not have fitted in with individual company's preferences or styles.

ISS did appear ready for the change, and given the successes of other change management initiatives in the fields of quality and teamworking, it would have been expected the process would run smoothly.

Within ISS the reasons for the change were quite clearly spelled out, enhancing competitiveness through improved customer service, so that as more people became involved in the project they were well aware of the expectations the corporation had of them. Although the way in which the objectives were agreed, without much involvement or participation from management in general, meant that a certain level of resistance was already being formed.

Before getting down to the details of the project, some senior managers went to an ICI plant to discover what undertaking BPR meant in a practical sense. This visit and ensuing discussions allowed a few senior people to see BPR in a new light, as a complete programme which could enhance company performance. But at the same time, they saw that the time commitments and support needed from management to get the results were significant, and that in order to maintain the success, management needed to empower the employees and implement whichever solutions were presented, otherwise all commitment to the project vanished.

Further problems were apparent in the setting up of the steering committee which, in the end, appeared to be the whole of the management team. Given that no people were asked to support the project full time (apart from the co-ordinator who was close to retirement), it was clear that a low priority was initially attached to the initiative. As the process progressed managers became more uneasy about the intentions of the corporation and uncertain about how much commitment they should put into the project, given that most of them also had full commitments from their normal functional positions.

(continued)

Teams were started and within a few weeks they were grinding to a halt. Resources appeared thin on the ground, support was diminishing, there was no cover provided for people's core functional jobs, and problems became unresolved. The enthusiasm started to wane and people lost interest. But during this brief period, many new ideas had emerged, some of which were put into practice and others were under consideration. This shows that if the project had received more support and resources the company could have been well on the way to achieving some successes. One particular process team which had performed well was the one considering the plastic manufacturing and internal supply process.

From this brief insight into practical BPR, the successes of the company were:

1 The process at corporate level had been well planned and thought through.
2 Senior managers had been involved in training and development sessions about BPR, so were well aware of some of the techniques.
3 The goals and vision were well known: improved competitiveness through better customer service.
4 People had gained some useful experience of team problem solving, even though there had been less than full commitment of members through the initial period of the project.
5 Some useful ideas has been generated, which when implemented increased the efficiency of operations, proving that the system does work when applied correctly.

However there were a number of failures, which caused the initiative to grind to a halt:

1 The process did not appear voluntary; people were co-opted onto teams.

2 The overall direction and objectives of the project teams were set without the involvement of team members, which reduced many people's motivation.
3 There was a lack of support from top management within the company.
4 People involved in the project had to combine busy daily schedules with the increased workload generated by the project, without additional help.

Conclusions: Was ISS right to start out on a BPR initiative?

The conclusions, from the evidence, are that BPR was a rational choice of change management programme in the circumstances. The corporation had planned the initiative fairly thoroughly, and involved some senior managers at an early stage in training and preparation. However, the implementation of the project at company level within ISS was poor. The lack of top-management support, the lack of resources for training and assistance for all those involved in the project proved that BPR cannot be implemented without 100 per cent commitment from all those involved. Whether the project will be a success in stimulating radical change and dramatic improvement in process efficiency in the future will depend on the determination of the new senior management at corporate and group level resurrecting the teams and giving more resources and support to those actually involved. Without these changes it is logical to assume that the best that can be hoped for in the circumstances is for a system of continuous improvement to be established, albeit at a lower intensity. Any such scheme involving only those people who are prepared to take on the extra responsibility and time commitments without the full support of senior management is risking the possibility of failure.

Source: Hoy, A.H., 'An evaluation of the theory and practice of business process re-engineering', MBA Dissertation.

However, from the evidence of the practical case at ISS (Exhibit 11.5), it is clear that BPR is a high-risk venture, and that many companies have had, and are likely to have, false starts and failures with BPR efforts.

To illustrate this point, in *Information Week* it was stated that:

> *American companies will spend an estimated $32 billion on business re-engineering projects and nearly two-thirds of these, on current evidence, will fail.*

Companies can fail to meet the high expectations that BPR sets for itself, although this may not be true failure. In truth, the absolute measure of success is very dependent on setting appropriate initial objectives.

Other failures are likely because companies fail to appreciate all the risk factors, to communicate and attempt to get everyone involved in the process. Without top-management support at local level people will not be committed to the project; after all whatever is important to the boss is by nature important to his/her subordinates.

In conclusion, it would appear that BPR is a powerful management tool which, when used under the right conditions, can lead to dramatic improvement in company performance. However, you can never get something for nothing, and the same is true of BPR, as it requires a considerable commitment in time and resources from the company before it can even start. It requires determination over a long period, of up to two years, to let teams work away at problems with freedom and flexibility. Overall, it is in essence the unleashing of knowledge and experience which employees have gained over their years of service being put to good use to improve company performance. But many companies cannot handle this new culture, and so until they can adapt to this new environment, they may be wise not to undertake BPR as an initial change initiative, but start by developing team-based problem solving under other initiatives such as empowerment and learning.

ACTION PLANNING FOR BPR

It is important that managers understand what BPR is and agree on what actions are necessary to re-engineer their organisations. It is also important that students have a similar understanding. The points referred to in Table 11.7 will assist this process. Managers are encouraged to make use of it and develop it further to suit their particular circumstances. Students should make their own notes in the spaces provided as an aid to revising this new and important subject area.

CASE STUDY: THE CLEARVIEW COMPANY

The possibility of adopting BPR

Mike reflected on the learning company initiatives and other changes that the operations change team had introduced over the past year. He was pleased with the progress made, and this was being reflected in the sales, expanded markets and improved contribution through improved efficiency and subsequent lower costs.

He was, however, seriously concerned about one important thing – well, two. The first was that some of the suggested changes, certainly the most recent one on the learning organisation, had shown the company strategy to be incomplete. It was being revamped but he knew this was only a sign that many things in the company now had to be rationalised, and this would mean starting over with a new strategy. The second

Table 11.7 Action plan for business process re-engineering

Achieve an understanding of what BPR is.	
Obtain involvement of executive management from start to finish.	
Choose the approach – clean-sheet approach to process redesign or standard methodology for BPR. Consider the need for professional and experienced input on BPR and the need to acquire expertise in the form of previous developers or consultants of BPR.	
Determine what is driving BPR, e.g. the customer service process, order fulfilment, customer acquisition activities such as sales and marketing, the manufacturing processes, service processes, distribution.	
Position the company in the market place and compare where the organisation is now to where it wants to be. Develop a clear statement of corporate goals and strategies.	
Decide how holistic and radical the initiative should be and the timescale, e.g. should the present processes and systems be used as a basis for improvement or should a fundamental rethink and redesign take place?	
Identify the processes throughout the business. Select the strategic core business processes that directly add value for the company. Understand the processes. Redesign one or more of those processes and the associated organisation structure in order to tighten connections with the customers, streamline operations, and eliminate wasteful, non-value-added steps. Make use of benchmarking.	
Redesign the systems, policies and organisational structures that support the strategic core business processes.	
Consider the behavioural aspects of change. Concentrate on areas such as changing culture, mindset, attitudes, behaviour; employee resistance to change; empowered employees; employees working in natural teams – self-managed teams; engaging every worker in the improvement process.	
Determine the measures against which performance should be assessed.	
Develop an actionable implementation plan.	
Review and monitor.	

matter was that the company's improved service and market penetration now meant that it traded internationally. Clearview was now competing globally with the best. If it were to maintain its market share and expand, it would need to keep the customer needs foremost and excel continually in this respect over the competition. Since marketing had shown that Clearview's closest rivals were hot on its heels, this company needed to move up a gear, in fact up several gears. For this to occur there would need to be radical changes in the organisation's operations.

Under the management development initiative, Mike had attended three or four seminars on improving organisational effectiveness. One seminar was about Business Process Re-engineering, BPR for short, which he thought might be the best way of approaching the problems he considered Clearview now faced. All these ideas needed to be thrashed out, and so he called a meeting of the executive board to do just that.

At the meeting all the executives were present and everyone was positive about the need for a new wave of change – particularly one which would rationalise existing changes and introduce new ones to position the company better in the future. Don was the only dissenter when it came down to BPR as being the best vehicle for change.

On this point Mike said, 'We need to understand more about what BPR is, so I've invited an expert on BPR from the University to talk about it. But, at this point, Don, I would like to hear why you think it could be the wrong thing to do.'

Don said, 'As you know, before I came to Clearview I worked at ISS. In the last year I was there, the company embarked on a BPR project. It failed, leaving people fed up and the senior people having to do a PR job to smooth things over.'

Mike asked, 'What went wrong?'

'Well', replied Don, 'first they tried a clean-sheet approach to BPR and then realised that they lacked proper guidance on what to do. Also, the objective to fulfil customer needs was not properly considered by the senior executives and, basically, they handed down a 'wish list' to the BPR team. The team resented this, as well as the fact that they had not been consulted. The trouble was that the senior executives were not committed or really that competent and half of them were due for retirement anyway. Consequently, the BPR team was not led properly and was allowed to drift. No one in the BPR team took command or ownership, and they didn't get involved enough or push to get things done. As a result, certain initiatives were implemented at the operations level halfheartedly. They failed.

'The senior executives blamed the team; the team blamed the workforce, and the workforce became teed off with the whole thing. This took a year, a wasted year where nothing got done, time was wasted, money was spent and everyone became disillusioned. In the meantime, the efficiencies at ISS dropped and their sales also started to drop. In my opinion BPR is difficult, futile and dangerous.'

On that note Mike said, 'No wonder you left! It may be that we decide to embark on BPR; it will be a risk, but if we are to do it we will do it right. Anyway, let's see what the experts have to say at the next meeting.'

At the next meeting, John, from the City University, explained that he lectured on BPR to postgraduates and had been involved in a number of BPR developments through student projects as well as the consulting work that he undertook. He explained what BPR was and the different ways of approaching it. Essentially, he said that for BPR to be successful it was necessary that the senior management of a company assign it top priority and be actively involved from the start. He outlined some of the different BPR methodologies and summarised the process of BPR as 'redesigning selected strategic core business processes with the intention of tightening connections with the customers, streamlining operations and eliminating wasteful non-value-added steps'. He spent some time talking about the importance of the behavioural aspects involved, measuring the performance of BPR, developing an actionable implementation plan and monitoring progress. He then went on to explain the benefits and pitfalls of BPR. After his talk Mike asked the executive group to ask John questions about BPR, particularly in the context of any problems with it at Clearview. Mike then thanked John for his input and expert advice

After John had left, Mike spoke to the executives. 'Well, there you have it. As I see it there are some very difficult questions to be answered concerning BPR. First, if we are to adopt BPR, how radical should we be? Are we to revamp all our major business processes or just some? Second, we need to decide whether to use a clean-sheet approach to BPR or a standard methodology. Either way I think we will need continued guidance from an experienced expert in this area, and therefore we need to decide on whether to recruit or hire a consultant. One thing is certain – a lot of hard work will be needed.'

Mike asked each of the executive team in turn what they thought about BPR and whether they thought it should be adopted at Clearview. This took some time, and coffee and sandwiches had to be sent for. That night they all went home late, but decisions had been made.

Over the next three weeks two more similar meetings took place. At the final meeting it was concluded that BPR was to be adopted at Clearview in the following way: Clearview's future positioning in the market place was to be determined, with the aim of being the best at satisfying both existing and new customers. A detailed analysis was to be made of Clearview's current position compared to its projected future position. From this, a clear statement of corporate goals and strategies would be developed. Then decisions would be made to determine how holistic and radical the initiative should be, i.e. should present processes, structures and systems be modified and improved or should a fundamental rethink and redesign take place? Thus the actions would be dependent upon the decisions made at that point as to the extent and nature of the changes to be made. To carry out all this a new team would be formed.

Mike and the other executives thought the operations change team had done a good job and agreed to reward the team financially and put Fiona, Eric and Nick onto the executive board. Mike then suggested that they throw a party for the team and asked for an open day to be organised, as well as a social event for all the employees at Clearview, with an open bar and merit presentations to be made. George and Don thanked Mike on behalf of the team. Mike then announced that, in the light of company development and improved business, everyone else, from the executive team to the shopfloor, was to be rewarded in the form of additional bonuses split equally from the year's profits.

He asked the executive to meet again with the aim of jointly envisioning Clearview in the future and to thrash out what the new business objectives should be and what the new core business structures should look like. Mike asked George and Don to convene a meeting with the rest of the operations change team in order to provide feedback on the use of teams, the problems they had experienced and the lessons they had learned. Their remit was to build on their experience and select a new team which would operate under a new title. The team should have about seven people of which two or three would be from the existing team. The rest would form a steering committee to oversee their progress and to advise. Mike then added, 'We must face that the new business and structure is going to be vastly different; tasks and duties will be different, and certain people may need to be moved. This may require retraining and development. But whatever happens, everyone will be invited to remain with their salaries protected. Certainly the benefits to everyone, as a result of taking a structured approach to managing operations and change, are evident. No one at Clearview should fear the changes needed to face the future.'

SUMMARY

- The term 'business process re-engineering', or BPR, was first coined in 1988 by Michael Hammer, an IT consultant. He exhorted managers to rethink their business processes and, rather than support them with complex IT systems, to redesign them completely to eliminate unnecessary and redundant steps.

- There has been a proliferation of views as to what BPR is, and this has caused confusion. There seem to be two BPR camps: one based on Hammer's original definition concerning dramatic improvement through radical changes in business process design; the other based on a reworking of the BPR concept applied to other change management problems.

- The process of BPR can be defined as redesigning selected strategic core business processes with the intention of tightening connections with the customers, streamlining operations and eliminating wasteful non-value-added steps. This assumes the prior process of the positioning of the business in the market place and identifying the strategic core business processes that directly add value to the company.

- It is believed that, through BPR, organisations can direct their processes, structures and systems to best meet the customers' needs.

- Studies show that BPR can have a positive impact on a wide range of business goals, predominant amongst these being improved customer service and order fulfilment.

- Some research shows that BPR efforts fail or result in little financial gain. Often staff are unhappy with the approach, and this could be due to a lack of behavioural considerations in the change process involved.

- A clean-sheet approach to BPR or a standard methodology can be used. Either way, it would be wise to ensure continued guidance from an experienced expert in this area.

- A wide range of methodologies for BPR exist. Choice is dependent on how radical the BPR project should be, how formalised it should be, how long it should take and how much of the business it should affect.

- Some see BPR as a development of TQM. The theory shows there are distinct differences between BPR and other management philosophies and approaches. Overall, JIT and TQM are viewed as tactical process-orientated techniques, which, even if successful, may not bring companies to international standards. In practice the differences are less marked and are due mainly to interpretation of the definitions attributed to BPR and the other management approaches.

● An action plan for BPR should be worked out, containing the following elements: BPR should be understood and senior management should be actively involved from start to finish. The business should be positioned in the market place so as to develop statements of corporate goals and strategies. The strategic core business processes that directly add value to the company should be determined. Decisions should be made as to how holistic and radical the BPR initiative should be. The selected strategic core business processes should be redesigned taking into account the behavioural aspects of the intended changes. The measures against which performance can be assessed should be decided on, and an actionable implementation plan should be developed. Finally, the process should be monitored and reviewed.

REVIEW AND DISCUSSION QUESTIONS

1 Explain why you think business process re-engineering (BPR) has become a popular management initiative and provide some examples of how an organisation might benefit from its adoption.

2 Discuss the differences between BPR and other management approaches and philosophies such as total quality management (TQM) and just-in-time (JIT) and explain what you think are merits and drawbacks of BPR.

3 Describe the main stages a typical manufacturing organisation might go through when it sets about re-engineering its business.

4 In pursuing BPR an organisation is likely to experience a variety of problems. List what you think they may be and, in the role of a senior executive, explain what actions you would take to overcome them.

ASSIGNMENTS

1 You have been recruited by a company which is considering undertaking a complete overhaul of its structures, systems, procedures, and ways of working. You have been appointed to lead a working group to consider the use of BPR as a means of achieving this. For the first meeting of the working group prepare a brief, outlining how the company could approach BPR, the nature of the changes that would be required and the problems that might be encountered.

2 Consider yourself in the role of a management consultant hired to advise your company on the pros and cons of it pursuing BPR and how it might approach such a task. Present a preliminary report summarising the benefits to the company from pursuing BPR and the key changes from its present state that it would need to make in order to succeed. Is success possible and what are the risks?

REFERENCES

Bambarger, B., 'Osram Sylvania's time-based continuous improvement approach to BPR', *Industrial Engineering*, Vol. 25, No. 12, pp. 14–18, December 1993.

Burnes, B., *A Strategic Approach to Organisational Development and Renewal*, Pitman Publishing, London, 1992.

Carr, D.K. and Johansson, H.J., *Best Practices in Re-engineering: What works and what doesn't in the re-engineering process*, McGraw-Hill, New York, 1995.

COBRA, *Business Restructuring and Teleworking: Issues, considerations and approaches*, A methodology manual for the Commission of the European Communities, provided by Adaptation Ltd, 1994.

Coulson, C.T. (ed.), *Business Process Re-engineering: Myth and reality*, Kogan Page, London, 1994.

Hall, G., Rosenthal, J. and Wade, J., 'How to make re-engineering really work', *Harvard Business Review*, pp. 119–31, Nov/Dec 1993.

Hammer, M., 'Re-engineering work: Don't automate, obliterate', *Harvard Business Review*, pp. 104–12, Jul/Aug 1990.

Hammer, M. and Champy, J., *Re-engineering the Corporation: A manifesto for business revolution*, Nicholas Brealey Publishing, London, 1993.

Hoy, A.H., 'An evaluation of the theory and practice of business process re-engineering', MBA Dissertation, School of Management and Finance, University of Nottingham, Nottingham, 1996.

Lawrence, A., 'BPR – tool of controversy', *Computer Business Review*, pp. 11–14, March 1994.

Manganelli, R.L. and Klein, M.M., *The Re-engineering Handbook: A step-by-step guide to business transformation*, AMACOM: The American Management Association, New York, 1994.

McCloud, J., 'Changing customer demands serve as impetus for BPR at Schlage Lock Co.', *Industrial Engineering*, Vol. 26, No. 6, pp. 30–4, June 1994.

Morris, D.C. and Brandon, J.S., *Re-engineering your Business*, McGraw-Hill, New York, 1994.

Obolensky, N., *Practical Business Re-engineering*, Kogan Page, London, 1994.

Pendlebury, A.J., Johansson, H.J., McHugh, P. and Wheeler, W.A., *Business Process Re-engineering: Breakpoint strategies for market dominance*, John Wiley & Sons, 1993.

Peppard, J. and Rowland, P., *The Essence of Business Process Re-engineering*, Prentice Hall, Hemel Hempstead, 1995.

'Re-engineering slip-ups: Why two out of three efforts to fix corporations fall short', *Information Week*, US, 20 June 1994.

Talwar, R., 'Business re-engineering: a strategy-driven approach', *Long Range Planning*, Vol. 26, No. 6, pp. 22–40, 1993.

Talwar, R., 'Re-engineering: A wonder drug for the '90s?', Chap. 2 in Coulson, C.T. (ed.) *Business Process Re-engineering: Myth and reality*, Kogan Page, London, 1994.

Taylor, S., 'Business process re-engineering: Eastman Chemical strives for better than world class', *Industrial Engineering*, Vol. 25, No. 11, pp. 28–34, November 1993.

Zairi, M. and Sinclair, D., 'Business process re-engineering and process management: A survey of current practice and future trends in integrated management', *Management Decision*, Vol. 33, No. 3, pp. 3–16, 1995.

PART 6
Making it happen

CHAPTER 12

Key management ideas

OBJECTIVES

The objectives of this chapter are to:

- review certain prominent management approaches
- consider the nature and importance of organisation culture
- outline the need for the right type of structure and examine different types of organisation
- explain the purpose and nature of organisation development (OD), its underpinnings and the areas on which it focuses
- consider what stress is, its effects at work and how organisations, managers and workers can deal with the causes of stress and the effects of stress-related problems.

MANAGEMENT ENABLERS

To make changes successfully in today's business climate, it is necessary to focus on particular management enablers in an organisation. They can be classed in three ways:

1 the management approach and culture
2 structure and types of organisation
3 organisation development and stress.

THE MANAGEMENT APPROACH

Attributes of excellence

The approaches and style of management the most senior decision makers in the organisation adopt are crucial to the success of the organisation. Peters and Waterman studied 62 of America's most successful companies and showed that success is achieved by having a culture which fosters more people involvement, better organisation and more emphasis on customer needs. Many organisations would benefit from management adopting their eight attributes of excellence, which are:

1 **A bias for action**: getting things done rather than too much planning.
2 **Close to the customer**: listening to the customer and learning and striving to achieve quality, service and reliability.
3 **Autonomy and entrepreneurship**: pursuing innovation, creativity and risk-taking through the efforts of people with leadership and championing qualities.

4 **Productivity through people**: appreciating the value of workers as a main source of productivity and quality and providing them with training and giving them autonomy to enable them to continue in their productivity.

5 **Hands-on, value-driven**: top management providing a clear understanding of what the business is about and developing an interest in its values throughout the organisation, particularly at shopfloor level.

6 **Stick to the knitting**: carrying on with what is known best in the business and being cautious about acquiring businesses whose core activities are not so well known.

7 **Simple form, lean staff**: keeping structures simple and having a few top-level staff in the pursuit of improved flexibility and communication.

8 **Simultaneous loose-tight properties**: centralising control in terms of the organisation's culture, values and beliefs while decentralising control in terms of encouraging individual innovation, autonomy and entrepreneurship.

Some critics say this approach is flawed (*see* Cummings, 1989), but undoubtedly it laid the foundations for much useful future work. In his book *Liberation Management*, Peters puts much more emphasis on having an appropriate organisation structure and again getting close to the customer through reorganising, networking and paying attention to changes in fashion. Many cases are cited in which the organisations are successful through using the brain rather than the brawn, using the power of their people, being able to customise their products and services, and quickly changing what they do to keep up with the demands of existing and new customers.

Meet both the employees' and customers' needs

In his book *The Frontiers of Excellence*, Robert Waterman explores in depth why a handful of widely-admired American firms do well. From the viewpoints of the middle managers and frontline people in the firms, he learnt that these firms are successful because they manage the intricate interplay between people, strategy, organisational arrangement and customer. According to Waterman, what makes these top-performing companies different is:

- *They are better organised to meet the needs of their* people, *so that they attract better people than their competitors do and their people are more greatly motivated to do a superior job, whatever it is they do.*

- *They are better organised to meet the needs of the* customers *so that they are more innovative in anticipating customer needs, more reliable in meeting customer expectations, better able to deliver their products or services more cheaply, or some combination of the above.*

The ways companies best organise themselves to meet the needs of their people and their customers are shown in Fig 12.1 and are discussed below.

Organising to meet the needs of people

Waterman* considers that too few managers learn that they need to ask, 'What motivates people?' From talking with managers, top executives, psychologists and career

* Text adapted from *Frontiers of Excellence: Learning from companies that put people first* by Robert Waterman; 1994; published by Nicholas Brealey Publishing, 36 John Street, London, WC1N 2AT @ £9.99.

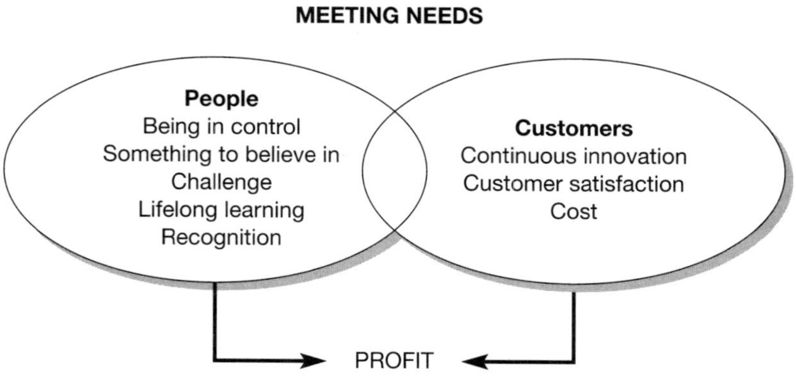

MEETING NEEDS

Fig 12.1 Organising to meet the needs of both people and customers

counsellors he found that motivation was dependent on the following needs – needs which top-performing companies honour:

- **Being in control.** People are happier, healthier and more effective if they find they are in control. Therefore, today's managers should understand that they need to relinquish control to get results. Accordingly, Waterman cites Procter & Gamble as obtaining an estimated 30 per cent gain in productivity through plant workers who are essentially self-directed.
- **Something to believe in.** Although the financial people talk about profit margins or return on investment, many people in the organisation, particularly those in operations, relate more to the everyday tasks that they do. They take a pride in doing their job well. For example, Levi Strauss says that understanding its people's need to believe in what the company stands for and the value of what they do has reaped benefits in productivity.
- **Challenge.** People enjoy solving problems and meeting a challenge. One has only to witness people's absorbtion in sporting activities and hobbies to realise this. When workers have been asked to use their minds and be innovative in order to solve problems and meet challenges, this has proved worthwhile.
- **Lifelong learning.** People also like to learn and keep doing so throughout their careers. Companies have benefited from the payback from their employees when they have provided them with training, development programmes and general opportunities to learn and develop.
- **Recognition.** Although money is a good form of recognition, people also want to stand out in some way as individuals. Many companies have benefited from the power of simple, none-cash recognition systems. Everyone is different, and over time people's interests change; therefore companies need programmes to help them understand their employees' interests and match them with jobs that they can truly enjoy.

Organising to meet the needs of customers

With regard to firms being better organised to meet the needs of customers, Waterman discovered that every successful company sustained its success on the basis of one, or some combination, of four fundamentals: continuous innovation, customer satisfaction, cost and profits.

- **Continuous innovation.** Through continuous innovation many companies stay ahead strategically because they have the ability to out-innovate the competition. These companies are good at innovating, i.e. they are creative at providing new things that customers want. They worry more about the customers than the competition and they are better at innovating because they are better organised to innovate.

- **Customer satisfaction.** The successful companies have embarked upon programmes such as Total Quality or Total Service or cutting the time it takes to respond to the market. They have made these issues strategic by tightly coupling the programmes to the needs of customers. They have achieved this through building relationships with the customers, which are very difficult for the competitors to match. Having determined their customers' requirements, the companies are organised to push control as far down the line as possible, via educational programmes and empowering people.

- **Cost.** Prices can only be kept competitive if costs are kept down. In the companies that Waterman studied, cost competitiveness was found to be a natural outgrowth of unusually productive organisational arrangements. At a minimum, this would be achieved through attention to systems and processes, the shared values in the culture, the way leadership shows what it deems important by what it chooses to pay attention to, the various sets of skills and the people employed, and the structure. Other companies have obtained cost advantages through the enormous productivity gains of self-directed work teams and doing things right first time.

- **What about profits?** Profits should not be put first. Shareholders will benefit if the firm also clearly understands that its people and its customers are just as important. Kotter and Heskett's study of big established companies that adopted this philosophy showed that they did four times better in revenue growth, eight times better in job creation, twelve times better on stock prices and an astounding 756 times better in net income growth.

World-class organisations need to excel in the areas of quality and learning

According to Hodgetts *et al.* world-class organisations are not merely leaders in their field, they are recognised as the best – and they strive to sustain this status. A world-class organisation can be described as being the best in its class or better than its competitors around the world, at least in several strategically-important areas. Thus, any organisation, regardless of size or type, can be world class. Many organisations are exceptional in one or more areas of performance. In recent years, considerable press has been given to organisations with world-class manufacturing, world-class quality management, world-class information systems or world-class purchasing systems. However, few of these are world class as whole organisations.

Hodgetts *et al.* state that world-class organisations include the total quality and learning organisational characteristics and more. To become world class, an organisation must excel in most of the dimensions that are important in both total quality and learning organisations. But in a synergistic and additive sense, there are other dimensions as well. Although it is difficult to delineate all the common characteristics, the authors summarise the major pillars that seem necessary to support world-class stature as:

- customer-based focus
- continuous improvement
- fluid, flexible organisations
- creative human resources management (HRM)
- egalitarian climate
- technological support.

Kanter's strategies for change

Companies need to be aware of their surroundings so that they can stay ahead of their competitors. The three main strategies Kanter proposes, presented in Fig 12.2, suggest how the organisation of the future should operate to cope with changing requirements:

1 **Restructuring to find synergies**: This involves the removal of non-value-adding parts of the business; in practice selling off a company's non-core activities. The remaining parts of the business must be lean and efficient. Kanter notes an important point at this stage, that the essential tasks which were previously carried out prior to restructuring are still undertaken. This can be achieved using computers for monitoring and information gathering, devolving greater responsibility and power down to individual teams, and contracting out services and tasks previously carried out in-house. The purpose of these changes is to create:

> *flatter, more responsive and less complex organisations which have a greater degree of focus than in the past.* (DTI, 1994)

Kanter argues that such changes need to be well planned and executed carefully so that they are successful and that employees are not demotivated.

2 **Opening boundaries to form strategic alliances**: As organisations are slimmed down and some tasks are contracted out, companies need to form alliances with other firms to share ideas, information and resources. Kanter suggests three forms of alliances: service, opportunistic and stakeholder alliances. A *service alliance* is where an organisation joins forces with another to undertake a special project which it would not be able to pursue by itself. An example of this is the alliance between Ford and General Motors in researching the development of new materials for making cars.

An *opportunistic alliance* aims to benefit from a particular advantage which has arisen which will benefit both parties. An example of this is the link between Rover

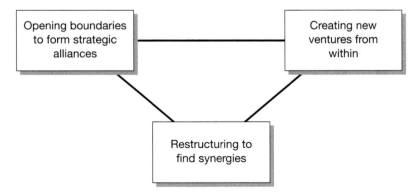

Fig 12.2 Kanter's three strategies for change

375

and Honda, where Rover gains from Japanese know-how and Honda gains greater access to the European market.

A *stakeholder alliance* is more of a partnership than the other two and can be internal, among employees, trade unions and management, or it can be external, between suppliers and customers. Many firms have strong alliances with suppliers and customers so as to build up a flow of information between them and be aware of their present and future needs and concerns. An example of this is in the car industry where manufacturers are involving suppliers in the design and development of new models. This idea from Kanter is reinforced in the DTI report* which concludes that:

> to support their operations and to maximise the exploitation of scarce resources, winning companies are entering into strategic alliances, especially when looking to break into new markets.

3 **Creating new ventures from within – encouraging innovation and entrepreneurship**: Kanter argues that there is a feeling in many traditional organisations that they are missing opportunities due to their inability to give staff the flexibility to pursue new ideas and develop new products. Product development should move away from being the output of strategic planners and R&D departments to being the product of new independent units which are formed to be innovative and to act like entrepreneurs. To achieve this, management must break down old barriers and restrictions so that:

> the innovative potential of employees can be tapped, and a proliferation of new ideas, products and ways of working can emerge.

The need for this innovation among employees at all levels in a company is a strong theme in the DTI report, which says:

> Winning companies constantly introduce new and differentiated products and services.

The report argues that:

> competition forces innovation. Innovation is driven by the goal of being and staying Number One.

This means that managers must have a good knowledge of their company's competitors and communicate the meaning of this competition to workers. Innovation is seen as being the key business aspect to be used to stay ahead of the competition:

> New product development is like getting up in the morning – if you don't develop new products, you don't get very far.

Companies must be able to take advantage of innovation. As the report says:

> The winning companies are focused on all aspects of the business that will enable them to exploit new ideas successfully, whether in the production process through simultaneous engineering and time compression techniques, or in after-sales service.

The production process is seen as being very important in helping to deliver continuously improving products.

---

* *Competitiveness: How the best companies are winning.* Crown copyright. Reproduced with the permission of the Controller of Her Majesty's Stationery Office.

Kanter has described possible strategies to be followed by managers in organisations, which are highly applicable to manufacturing organisations. In his book, Handy also argues that profound changes are taking place in organisational life:

The world of work is changing because the organisations of work are changing their ways. At the same time, however, the organisations are having to adapt to a changing world of work. It's a chicken and egg situation. One thing, at least, is clear: organisations in both private and public sectors face a tougher world – one in which they are judged more harshly than ever before on their effectiveness and in which there are fewer protective hedges behind which to shelter.

CULTURE

To implement these strategies organisations need to have, or acquire, supporting cultures. According to McLean and Marshal, culture is:

the collection of traditions, values, policies, beliefs, and attitudes that constitute a pervasive context for everything we do and think in our organisation.

Handy argues that if the organisation's structure and culture do not match then conflict will arise. Successful change occurs when the culture encourages flexibility, autonomy and group working. Successful firms have cultures which foster learning and continuous improvement. Their aim is to encourage employees to take more interest in their work and continually to examine what they do in order to learn by their mistakes and improve. It is also important to develop an atmosphere of understanding in which the existence and nature of people's fears are recognised and appropriate action taken. The culture should also try to reinforce desired behaviour by pay, recognition, and praise being given to those who achieve the desired goals. If a company does not have a culture which matches how it wishes to operate in the future, it must create one.

According to Hunt, culture evolves from individuals searching for ways to cope with common problems and finding ways of exploiting what is happening. These values and beliefs are then passed down the generations of employees working in the organisation.

Influences on organisational culture

There are a number of factors that influence the development of organisational culture (*see* Mullins, 1994). These include:

1 **History.** The reason the organisation was formed and the way it was formed underpin the organisation's culture, along with how old the organisation is and the philosophy and values of the first senior managers.
2 **Primary function and technology.** The range and quality of products will affect the nature of processes and methods used, which will, in turn, affect the culture of the organisation.
3 **Goals and objectives.** The objectives and strategies followed by the organisation will affect culture. Objectives and goals may also be affected by culture changes.
4 **Size.** The larger the organisation, the more likely it is to be made up of separate departments or split-site operations, which will need to be carefully co-ordinated to avoid communication problems and interdepartmental rivalries. Expansions or reductions in size will also influence culture, as the size of the workforce will change.
5 **Location.** The location and physical characteristics of an organisation often greatly influence its culture.

6 **Management and staffing.** Senior executives can have major influences over culture, but all staff members play a part in shaping this culture. *Culture is also determined by the nature of staff employed and the extent to which they accept management philosophy and policies* (Mullins, 1994). The match between corporate culture and employees' perceptions of the psychological contract is another important influence.

7 **The environment.** Culture must take account of the environment in which the organisation operates.

Analysing organisational culture

Armstrong lists 16 questions, given in Exhibit 12.1, which need to be addressed when analysing organisational culture.

Exhibit 12.1

Analysing organisational culture

1 Do people feel they are given enough responsibility?

2 Do people know what is expected of them in the shape of objectives and standards of performance?

3 Is there adequate feedback to people on their performance, whether it is good, bad or indifferent?

4 Is there sufficient challenge in the jobs given to people and sufficient emphasis on doing a good job?

5 Are people given enough support by their managers or supervisors in the shape of guidance or help?

6 Is the emphasis in the organisation on hard, dedicated work, or is it fairly relaxed?

7 Do people feel fairly rewarded for the work they do?

8 Do people feel promotion policies are fair?

9 Is there an emphasis on positive rewards rather than punishments?

10 Is there a lot of bureaucracy and red tape around the organisation or is the approach to work reasonably flexible and informal?

11 Is there an emphasis on taking calculated risks in the organisation, or is playing it safe the general rule?

12 Is management open about what the company is doing?

13 Is there a general feeling of warmth and good fellowship in the atmosphere?

14 Do managers and other employees want to hear different opinions?

15 Is the emphasis on getting problems out in the open rather than smoothing them over or ignoring them?

16 Do people feel that they belong to a worthwhile company and are valuable members of working teams?

Source: Armstrong, M., *How to be an Even Better Manager*.

Management style and values

Armstrong also believes that the management style and values should be analysed to obtain a clearer picture of how a company's culture is linked to an individual's behaviour and motivation. For example, with respect to *style*, does the organisation tend to be autocratic, i.e. using authority to compel people to do what they are told; or is it democratic, i.e. encouraging people to participate and involve themselves in decision making? Does it tend to be task-centred or people-centred? Do managers tend to be distant and cold or approachable and friendly? Do managers tend to be hard or soft on people? With respect to *values* it needs to be known if the employees are proud of the company and its products or services. Does the company truly believe in producing high-quality products and providing a good service to its customers? Are managers and employees really interested in increasing productivity? Do managers truly believe in the importance of the people who work there? Are they committed to improving the quality of working life, providing better opportunities for growth and development, giving individual attention to the needs of employees? If so, this would involve keeping them informed on matters that affect them and involved in decision making, and maintaining a fair pay system which rewards staff according to their responsibilities and contribution.

Effect of culture on employees

What effect does culture have on employees? Different cultures will require different psychological contracts, reflecting the values and beliefs found within these cultures:

> *Certain types of people will be happy and successful in one culture, not in another.* (Handy, 1986)

If the culture of the organisation matches the psychological contract of the individual, the individual should be satisfied in his/her position (*see* Handy, 1986). Differences in beliefs and values will lead to either a dissatisfied or demotivated employee, or industrial relations conflicts.

Matching values and belief with culture

It can be seen that all organisations hold some form of organisational culture which evolves from those factors mentioned. For employees to be satisfied within an organisation, the culture of the organisation must match the values and beliefs of the individual. It is therefore important that individuals' personalities, beliefs and values are taken into account when recruiting, in order to find someone who will be happy working within the organisation's culture.

STRUCTURE OF ORGANISATION

Organisations of the future

Handy, like Peters, is convinced of the need to acquire the right type of structure for individuals and organisations to operate. He notes the changes that are occurring in British industry as it moves away from being inhabited by labour-intensive organisations, and argues that:

> *fewer, better-motivated people, helped by clever machines, can create much more added value than large groups of unthinking, demotivated ones ever could.* (Handy, 1989)

Again, he believes that emerging firms in the future will be:

> *smaller, more flexible and less hierarchical.*

TYPES OF ORGANISATION

Handy recognises that the changes facing organisations are not identical and has identified three generic types of organisation which would cope with future changes. These are shown in Fig 12.3.

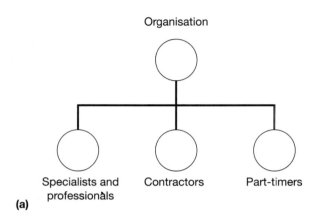

(a)

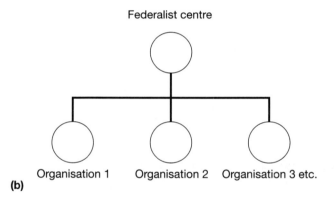

(b)

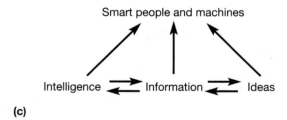

(c)

Fig 12.3 Types of organisation to cope with change
(a) The Shamrock organisation
(b) The Federal organisation
(c) The Triple I organisation

The Shamrock organisation

The Shamrock organisation is named after the plant because it is composed of three distinct groups of workers. The first is the small group of core workers who are a group of specialist, professional workers who form the central part of the organisation and who are seen to be essential to the success of it. They run the organisation and control the 'smart' machines and computers that have replaced, to a large extent, much of the workforce. These workers are summed up as being:

> *half the people, paid twice as much, working three times as effectively.* (Handy, 1989)

This group of workers operates as colleagues and partners in the business as opposed to superiors and subordinates.

The second group of workers is *'the contractual fringe'*. They use machines to replace people and contract out services and tasks to other organisations, and so the size of this group is small in relation to its production capacity. This contractual fringe may or may not work exclusively for the company in question and are paid a fee based on results rather than a wage for time taken. The advantages of having this arrangement are that it is cheaper because companies only pay for what they get; it reduces the size of the workforce, making human management easier; and during times of low demand it is the contractor who bears the impact of the reduced workload.

The third leaf of the Shamrock is made up of a pool of part-time workers with the relevant skills to carry out the necessary tasks. This group mainly comprises women who work and look after a family, and people who prefer to change from job to job rather than follow a single career.

These characteristics allow the Shamrock organisation to be:

> *lean with few hierarchical layers and even less bureaucracy.* (Handy, 1989)

Other advantages of the Shamrock organisation are that it requires less office and factory space, and it becomes very flexible but still operates with highly-skilled staff.

The Federal organisation

Handy defines a Federal type of organisation as:

> *a variety of individual groups of organisations allied together under a common flag with some shaped identity.* (Handy, 1989)

The reasons he gives for its formation are that as firms grow too big, the Shamrock set-up cannot cope with the volume of information available, and that in the ever-changing competitive environment organisations need to be flexible but still call on the resources available to large organisations. This set-up operates with three groups, as in the Shamrock organisation, but they are separated, relating to one another under the control of the Federalist centre. This Federalist centre collates the ideas from the different groups and then sets strategic objectives, with the aim of keeping the business ahead of its rivals. Handy explains how this type of organisation seeks to maximise the innovative and creative potential of workers using the 'inverted doughnut' principle:

> *The doughnut is an American doughnut. It is round with a hole in the middle rather than the jam in its British equivalent...This, however, is an inverted do'nut, in that it has the hole in the middle filled in and the space on the outside...The point of the analogy begins*

> *to emerge if you think of your job, or any job. There will be a part of the job which will be clearly defined, and which, if you do'nut do, you will be seen to have failed. That is the...centre of the do'nut...[but]...In any job of any significance the person holding the job is expected not only to do all that is required but in some way to improve on that...to move into the empty space of the do'nut and begin to fill it up.*

The aim of this is to encourage experimentation and enquiry that leads to higher standards, which will make the organisation more flexible and more capable of competing in a changing environment.

Handy, in *The Empty Raincoat,* uses the term 'doughnut' to describe the way in which organisations as well as individuals have an essential core: a core of necessary jobs and necessary people; a core which is surrounded by an open, flexible space which they fill with flexible workers and flexible supply contracts. The problem of change here is achieving a balanced doughnut – which activities and which people to put in which space. In today's competitive world, organisations are becoming smaller, with a small core of key people surrounded by their necessary partners; such partners being part-timers, consultants and associated businesses and suppliers. Definitely the vertically-integrated organisation – one which wants to own and run the whole of its doughnut – is a thing of the past. Some companies, such as Eastman Kodak, contract out crucial service functions. Obviously, each organisation has to assess its own pros and cons to establish an appropriate balance.

Mills and Friesen, in a similar way, talk about the evolving structure of a learning organisation. They cite The British Petroleum Company evolving a 'cluster' organisation designed for close interchange with customers and for intimate communication internally. Clusters are mission-centred and employees take greater responsibility for work and its quality: they are not 'controlled', 'supervised' or 'managed' in the traditional sense. The middle managers do not supervise: they find the right person to fit the culture and task and then step back (*see* Altany, 1988). Whether we are talking about doughnuts or cluster-type organisations, what needs to be sorted out is the dilemma between necessary control and freedom, of being planned yet flexible, of being more autonomous and yet more of a team, and of being centralised for some things yet decentralised for others.

The Triple I organisation

The Triple I is the last type of organisation outlined by Handy. It is based on *Intelligence, Information* and *Ideas* and will use both smart people and smart machines. The implications of this approach for managers are that they will have to ensure the machines they use are 'smart' enough for the company to remain competitive, and that staff have the skills necessary to control these machines. For such an organisation to be successful it needs constantly to update the skills, knowledge and abilities of its staff. This may include meetings with external professionals, study tours and meetings with fellow workers within the organisation. Information will have to flow freely around the organisation and be available to everyone. Managers and other core workers will be:

> *expected to have not only the expertise appropriate to his or her particular role, but will also be required to know and understand business, to have the technical skills of analysis and the human skills and the conceptual skills, and to keep them up to date.*

Organisations cannot suddenly decide to operate on a Triple I set-up; they have to develop into one.

INFRASTRUCTURE

Project and improvement teams

In organising a company to fulfil best the type of changes that should be made, it also needs an appropriate infrastructure. Infrastructures which include project or improvement teams should be created with an appropriate reporting relationship with senior management. This should not preclude the use of outside consultants. The teams' job is to develop action plans which clearly link the operational requirements to the organisation's plans and strategies. The direction the teams should take should be made clear, and senior management should actively support such teams. This support should take the form of clarifying objectives and providing the necessary resources, support systems, encouragement and advice.

Implementing change is, or should be, the least time-consuming part of the change process. It is the planning and organising of change that takes, or should take, the most time. Burnes and Weekes argued that the companies which achieved successful change tended to spend some 90 per cent of their time in planning and organising change and only about 10 per cent of their time implementing it. Therefore, an infrastructure is needed which best facilitates planning and organising for change.

Communication

One way of combating the uncertainty that changes promote is to establish a regular and effective communications process. Such a process should make people aware of the pressures for change and what the plans for the future are, if the organisation is to survive and prosper. The performance of the different areas within the company should be assessed, and successful performance should be publicised and rewarded. Recommendations to senior managers should be made which clearly define any problems or opportunities and suggest the type of changes and the timescale in which they should be made.

Structure and culture

At present, many companies are finding that it is becoming increasingly difficult to be efficient and effective when they are faced with increased uncertainty, and changes in technology and working practices. As a result, organisations are adopting more flexible structures and jobs. However, as argued by Burnes, the result of these changes can be that in some organisations the existing culture is in conflict with the organisation's competitive needs, and its structure and culture no longer equip it for the environment and market in which it operates. In such cases the relationship between structure and culture needs to be restored to a mutually supportive one if the organisation is to operate efficiently and effectively.

ORGANISATION DEVELOPMENT

Change, whether it be about design, process, technology or systems, involves people and requires people to make it happen. Any influence, external or internal to an organisation, will affect the people within it. In this sense, then, the people side of change cannot be ignored and organisations must carefully consider the human element when they introduce change.

McCalman and Paton put forward the following definition of organisation development:

> *Organisation development is an ongoing process of change aimed at resolving issues within an organisation through the effective diagnosis and management of the organisation's culture. This development process uses behavioural and social science techniques and methodologies through a consultant facilitator and employs action-research as one of the main mechanisms for instigating change in organisational groups.*

Organisation development recognises that for successful management of change considering people is important. Therefore, it shifts the emphasis from the technical aspects of managing change to deal with human resources in the organisation and the ability of social science to assist in the management of change.

Many organisations, even in the '90s, have not taken this on board – perhaps because they are still fighting through the effects of the recession and consider people issues secondary to survival. However, survival long term means considering people, and to do so organisations require a change of emphasis in management thought. They need to recognise that change implementation involves people and that gaining the involvement and active participation of the individual within the organisation will assist the likelihood of success. This can be achieved through the use of organisation development (OD), which has developed since the 1960s and uses techniques from the behavioural and social sciences.

What follows is a summary of the underpinnings of organisation development, an outline of its current areas of focus, together with a process for OD which companies could usefully adopt to manage their organisation development change process.

McGregor and the human side of enterprise

Douglas McGregor worked on changing organisation structures to enhance teamwork and increase decision making at the shopfloor level. This work was termed organisation development. The publication of his work, *The Human Side of Enterprise,* made clear the role of management and created the concept of Theory X and Theory Y. McGregor classified managers' attitudes and perceptions about the worker and the design of organisations as falling into two categories:

- **Theory X assumptions**. The average human being has an inherent dislike of work and will avoid it if he can.
- **Theory Y assumptions**. The expenditure of physical and mental effort in work is as natural as play or rest.

The Tavistock Institute and socio-technical systems

At the time McGregor and others were undertaking research in large American organisations, the researchers Eric Trist, Ken Bamforth and A.K. Rice at the Tavistock Institute of Human Relations in London were developing the model of socio-technical systems design (*see* Buchanan, 1979). The proposition underpinning this influential body of research work was that any organisation exists as both a social and a technical subsystem and that both these subsystems need to be taken into consideration when organisations contemplate change. The Tavistock model is outlined in Fig 12.4.

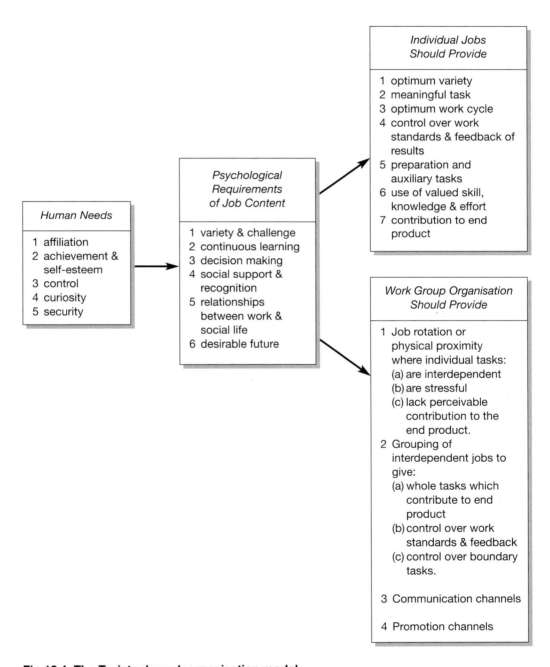

Fig 12.4 The Tavistock work organisation model
Source: Buchanan D.A., *The Development of Job Design Theories.*

In respect of organisation development the significant points of the Tavistock studies are as follows:

1 It is managers who make decisions about work organisation, job allocations, the formation of groups, and the amount of discretion allowed to workers.
2 Mass-production techniques can be replaced by alternatives which maintain or even enhance performance while offering a better quality of working life.
3 Working in groups is the best form of work organisation to meet both technical and social needs within the workplace.

We can learn from the studies, with respect to change management, that there are choices of different work designs that can be made, some of which will be more effective. One contentious example of this is the undertaking of the duties of managers and supervisors by self-managing groups. In certain situations this has proved to be more effective but it does challenge the status and responsibilities of such managers.

In many ways, the above sums up what the organisation development model is about. It is about management choice, the choice an organisation can make to manage change for the better.

Areas of focus of OD

The various areas of OD on which practitioners have focused are shown in Fig 12.5.

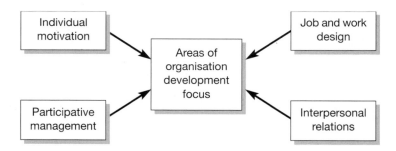

Fig 12.5 Areas of organisation development focus

Individual motivation

The work of writers such as Vroom and Lawler is concerned with what motivates individuals to perform within their organisation. Naturally the understanding of this type of human behaviour in organisations is one of the key areas of organisation development.

Job and work design

Research work in this area, especially that of Hackman and Oldham, looks at how work design leads to greater worker satisfaction. The variables associated with greater worker satisfaction are:

- meaningfulness of the work
- responsibility for the work and its outcomes
- performance feedback.

Hackman and Oldham depict the causal links between job-implementing concepts, such as forming natural work units and opening feedback channels; core job dimensions, such as task identity and autonomy; psychological states, such as responsibility for the outcome of the work and knowledge of the results; and personal and work outcomes such as high internal work motivation and high-quality work performance.

Interpersonal relations

The emphasis placed on developing the individual within the organisation is important in OD. Argyris's work is concerned with individual development towards maturity at work and interpersonal relations within the group at work. According to Argyris, maturity in individuals in the workplace is prevented by the approach of management and the lack of interpersonal competence.

Participative management

With any change process it is important that the organisation design is the best possible to meet the objectives sought. In considering the appropriate approach to adopt when managing people in a particular situation, we can make use of Likert's four models of organisation design. As mentioned in Chapter 7, his studies show that managers adopt systems of management which range from being *exploitative authoritative*, where managers use the techniques of fear and threat to control members of the organisation, through to *benevolent authoritative* and *consultative*; to *participative*, where management uses the technique of group rewards to attain participation and involvement of the workforce.

The organisation development process

Organisation development is concerned with the process of attaining change, and through it change is progressed on a broad front in the firm over the longer period. Important in this is training people in organisation development techniques to provide expertise and skilled resources to help manage the changes which take place.

The attributes of organisation development

Thirteen characteristics common to organisation development, identified by Margulies and Raia, are presented in Exhibit 12.2.

Developing an organisation development strategy

Developing an appropriate organisation development strategy is crucial to achieving effective change.

Exhibit 12.2

Attributes of organisation development

- It is a total organisational system approach.
- It adopts a systems approach to the organisation.
- It is positively supported by top management.
- It uses third-party change agents to develop the change process.
- It involves a planned change effort.
- It uses behavioural science knowledge to instigate change.
- It sets out to increase organisational competence.
- It is a long-term change process.
- It is an ongoing process.
- It relies on experiential learning techniques.
- It uses action-research as an intervention model.
- It emphasises goal setting and action planning.
- It focuses on changing attitudes, behaviours and performance of groups or teams in the organisation rather than individuals.

Source: Margulies, N. and Raia, A., *Conceptual Foundations of Organizational Development*, McGraw-Hill 1978. Reprinted by kind permission of the McGraw-Hill Companies.

Pugh's organisation development matrix

The organisation development matrix developed by Pugh, shown in Fig 12.6, provides examples of the most common strategies used in organisation development. The strategies shown apply to the four levels within the organisation at which change is contemplated: the individual, intergroup, group and organisational levels. Such strategies concern the extent of the change which has to take place, depending on the behaviour, structure and context of the particular situation. Since the matrix shows the most common strategies used in organisation development, it provides an excellent framework for diagnosing and initiating change.

Hopefully, the above provides a clear indication of how to manage change, by developing the organisation and harnessing the most complex, yet potent, asset the organisation has – its people.

Phases of organisation development

Figure 12.7 depicts the seven phases which Warner Burke (summarised in McCalman and Paton*) identifies an organisation experiences during a typical organisation development change process.

Phase 1: Entry

At this point an initial contact is made between the organisation and the consultant to begin the entry phase.

From the organisation's perspective it has to be sure that it has the right person for the job and that the consultant will be able to work with the organisation. The consultant

*Adapted and reprinted with permission from McCalman, J. and Paton, R. A. *Change Management: An effective guide to implementation*, 1992, Copyright © 1992 Paul Chapman Publishing Ltd, London.

Diagnosis and methods of initiation of change

	Behaviour (What is happening now?)	Structure (What is the required system?)	Context (What is the setting?)
Organisational level	General climate of poor morale, pressure, anxiety, suspicion, lack of awareness of, or response to, environmental changes. *survey feedback, organisational mirroring*	Systems goals – poorly defined or inappropriate, strategy inappropriate and misunderstood, organisation structure inappropriate, centralisation, divisionalisation, standardisation: inadequacy of environmental monitoring mechanisms. *change the structure*	Geographical setting, market pressures, labour market, physical conditions, basic technology. *change strategy, location, physical set-up; culture (by saturation OD)*
Intergroup level	Lack of effective co-operation between subunits, conflict, excessive competition, limited war, failure to confront differences in priorities, unresolved feelings. *intergroup confrontation (with third party as consultant), role negotiation*	Lack of integrated task perspective; subunit optimisation, required interaction difficult to achieve. *redefine responsibilities, change reporting relationships, improve co-ordination and liaison mechanisms*	Different subunit values, lifestyle, physical distance. *reduce psychological and physical distance; exchange roles, attachments, cross-functional social overlay*
Group level	Inappropriate working relationships, atmosphere, participation, poor understanding and acceptance of goals, avoidance, inappropriate leadership style, leader not trusted, respected; leader in conflict with peers and superiors. *process consultation, teambuilding*	Task requirements poorly defined; role relationships unclear or inappropriate: leader's role overloaded, inappropriate reporting procedures. *redesign work relationships (socio-technical systems), autonomous working groups*	Insufficient resources, poor group composition for cohesion, inadequate physical set-up, personality clashes *change technology, layout, group composition*
Individual level	Failure to fulfil individual's needs; frustration responses; unwillingness to consider change, little chance for learning and development. *counselling, role analysis, career planning*	Poor job definition, task too easy or too difficult. *job restructuring/modification, redesign, enrichment, MBO*	Poor match of individual with job, poor selection or promotion, inadequate preparation and training, recognition and remuneration at variance with objectives. *personnel changes, improved selection and promotion procedures, improved training and education, bring recognition and remuneration in line with objectives.*

There are two dimensions to the matrix which represent the two main factors that have to be identified during the diagnosis stage of the OD process: level of analytical focus and degree of required intervention.

Fig 12.6 The organisation development matrix
Source: Pugh, D. S., *Planning and Managing Change; Block 4: Organizational Development*, Open University Business School, Milton Keynes, 1986.

also has a number of criteria that have to be satisfied. These relate to factors such as whether he/she can work with the organisation, whether or not there is a readiness for change, the motivation and values of the individual(s) within the organisation calling on the consultant, their position within the organisation as a leverage point for instigating change, and the amount of resources at hand for change (*see* Burke, 1987).

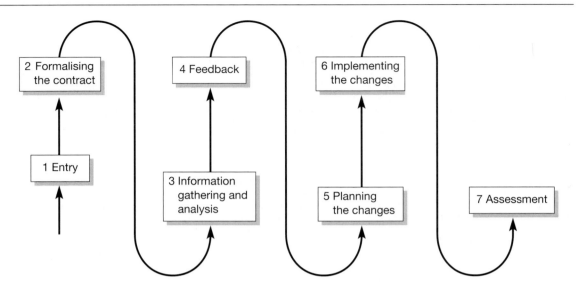

Fig 12.7 Phases of organisation development
Source: Burke, W. *Organisation Development: A normative view*, Addison-Wesley, 1987.

Phase 2: Formalising the contact

The second phase is the drafting of a contract which explains and clarifies what will be done. This is a two-way process in which the consultant lays out his/her intentions but also explains what the organisation is contracting to do. The client organisation will internally discuss the consultant's proposal with its key people and may propose amendments before agreeing to the terms.

Phase 3: Information gathering and analysis

Having successfully negotiated a contract, it is then up to the consultant in conjunction with the client organisation to begin the diagnosis phase. There are two important elements here: getting the information required and making sense of it. Formal information gathering is therefore necessary, and this usually comes in the form of records, interviews and staff surveys. Input from the people likely to be affected by the organisation development change programme will be especially important.

Phase 4: Feedback

Having gathered the data, it is then up to the consultant to analyse and summarise the information, and organise it into a format that can be readily understood by the organisation's members to enable action to take place based on that information. McCalman and Paton recommend that a report of the work carried out, the consultant's conclusions, issues for the future, and proposals for change be distributed to all who took part in the data-gathering stage. This would act as a further source of information or feedback. Also, to facilitate discussion of the data being considered, a presentation should be made to the management body who initiated the organisation development change programme.

Phase 5: Planning the change process

This phase is the action phase of the organisation development intervention – to improve the organisation's processes from their current to their future position. There are two possibilities here. First, the planning for change stage may take place towards the end of the feedback session, as the consultant and organisation get a clearer picture of the steps that are likely to be needed. However, for more complex, larger organisation development issues, the planning process may be lengthened in time and include those likely to be involved in the process itself. The whole point of the planning for change phase is to look at the alternative actions open to the organisation in terms of response to the feedback given by the consultant, and to consider the best way forward or plan of action to take.

Phase 6: Implementing the changes

Once the organisation has decided what action it will take in terms of organisation development intervention, the implementing of changes can take place. The consultant may or may not be involved at this stage, depending on the actions to be taken. (Examples of organisation development strategies were given in Fig 12.6.)

Phase 7: Assessment

The final phase is to evaluate the results of the process. Assessment is useful in that it looks at what has gone before, what the current state of play is, and what action steps need to be taken to move the organisation forward.

STRESS

The nature of stress

Stress is mainly a physical condition resulting from the way our body responds to the demands placed on it by our lifestyle. We continually react to stresses, and often this can bring out the best in us; in fact in an emergency our reactions can save our lives. However, everyone has a different tolerance level to stress and people can become ill or even die as a result of being stressed. It is, however, possible to manage your reactions to stress effectively by first becoming aware of your stress tolerance level.

Stress at work

The sources of stress at work can be physical, such as irregular or long hours; boring, repetitive work; work overload; loud noises; lack of a social centre; and sick offices which typically are hot, unventilated and crowded. The psychological sources of stress may be the setting of unrealistic objectives, lack of autonomy, responsibility without authority and a lack of support.

Constructive and destructive stress

Constructive stress

Stress is not always a negative influence on our lives, and constructive stress can act in a positive way that can increase our efforts, our creativeness and diligence etc. It can help us win races and pass exams. In fact, our stress response enables us to mobilise all our resources to face the many challenges put upon us. Undoubtedly, many people are only happy when they feel they are reacting successfully to challenges.

Destructive stress

Managers should attempt to create conditions that stimulate people and achieve the improved effectiveness created by constructive stress. They should also be concerned that destructive stress can adversely affect people's performance. Destructive stress can manifest itself in the following ways: bad health, aches and pains, upset stomach, tiredness, dizziness, ulcers, skin diseases, heart and circulatory problems, low performance and energy, inability to concentrate, restlessness, poor judgement, unsuitable behaviour, irritability, depression, sleeplessness, short temper, too much smoking and drinking, making frequent mistakes.

The effects of negative stress, if not released from the body after one situation, will remain to influence behaviour in the next. Stress now accounts for about 14 per cent of occupational diseases. Unfortunately, stress needs to be managed properly or it can influence the health and wellbeing of everyone. On straightforward humanitarian grounds, managers should be concerned about the effects of stress on health, and also the effects that stress can have on people's productivity and creativity. This will eventually affect an organisation's return on the investment in the people it employs.

Exhibit 12.3 illustrates how problems at work can tip people into depression and provides advice on health management.

Looking for signs of stress

One way of checking the stress systems of people at work is to look for changes in the following types of behaviour:

From quality work, punctuality, positive approach, good nature and humour, good decisions, accepts change, diligent attitude
To mistakes and errors, lateness, negative approach, poor nature and humour, errors in judgement, rejects change, careless attitude.

Research shows that there are type A personalities who are more prone to stress-related illnesses than type B personalities (*see* Bishop, 1988). They create self-induced stress as a result of constant striving for achievement. In a sentence, '*One person's stress is another person's energiser.*'

A common source of psychological stress at work is role ambiguity or role conflict.

Exhibit 12.3

Managing well includes managing your own health

In 1990, clinical depression resulted in 213 million lost working days, largely among employees aged 30 to 44, according to a study by the Massachusetts Institute of Technology and the Analysis Group, a Cambridge, Mass., consulting company. The researchers put the annual cost of absenteeism and diminished productivity resulting from depression at $23.8 billion.

Problems at work can tip vulnerable employees into depression. Ambiguous roles, an absence of intrinsic job rewards, a lack of organisational commitment, negative work events, and downsizing, among other things, can be significantly related to episodes of depression.

For a business owner or manager, identity is often closely tied to the company's performance. If the company fails to meet financial goals, or a difficult decision has to be made – such as closing a plant and laying off employees – a business owner may be thrown into crisis.

Depression is usually treatable, through therapy, medication or a combination of both, but workplace attitudes and norms can prevent an owner or employee from seeking treatment.

Many people still view depression as a personal weakness rather than an illness that can be treated. The typical workplace environment encourages employees to plough through obstacles and exalt strength at all costs. Depressed employees are often stigmatised.

Business owners and managers should try to promote a work environment where an employee can feel comfortable coming forward and admitting that he or she needs help. A depression-awareness training programme for supervisors and human-resources personnel can enable them to recognise possible signs of depression. Likewise, regular performance reviews can be used to clarify ambiguous roles and responsibilities.

Source: Katz, N. and Marks, I., 'To your health', *Nation's Business*.

Role conflict

At work the organisational norms we experience are often expressed through the behaviour of our superiors, peers and subordinates. They place expectations on the individual. This is called role demand. Often the individual does not perceive or accept this role in the same way. This is called role desire. It may also be that the individual is not interested or motivated by the role, or simply that they do not possess adequate capabilities for the role. If an individual is unsuited to or incompatible with the demands of the role, they are likely to become frustrated, demotivated and as a result suffer from stress. The actual behaviour or role performance is the outcome of these different factors and influences. This process is depicted in Fig 12.8.

The particular types of role conflict which can contribute to such stress are:

- **Role overload**. In this situation the individual, even when performing flat out, cannot meet all the role demands. Some people can overcome this and grow to fulfil the demands of the job. Others follow the Peter Principle when they rise to their level of incompetence.

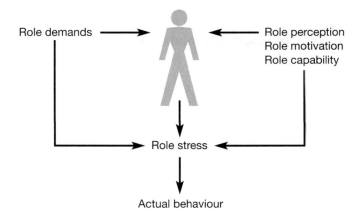

Fig 12.8 Role conflict and stress

- **Role ambiguity**. Here, the individual is placed under simultaneously conflicting demands from particular individuals, groups and other roles. Such conflict of expectations and diversity, and burden of work and tasks can create many problems for the individual. To overcome this problem the necessary requirements and standards to be achieved need to be clarified.
- **Role underload**. Here, the demands of the job are small compared to the individual's talents and capacity for work. The job will be unchallenging and result in low morale and frustration. The person may feel their abilities are being underutilised.
- **Role misalignment**. When an individual is assigned with a role outside their capacity, their performance in that area could be poor and their interest, ownership and enjoyment could be lacking.

Responding to role stress

When faced with any of the above role conflicts, an individual may respond by accepting the situation or endeavouring to overcome it by working harder to meet the expectations. Some people have the drive and energy to do this, but many in trying can ruin their physical and mental health. According to Webber, people respond to stress in the following ways:

- meet all demands
- reject or resign
- modify demands
- change desires
- selective withdrawal
- respond to power or authority
- compartmentalise demands.

Exhibit 12.4 shows how university psychologists help employers tackle problems of work-related stress.

Exhibit 12.4

Psychologists help employers tackle problems of work-related stress

The Centre for Organisational Health and Development at the University of Nottingham is looking at methods of assessing and managing stress in the workforce to create a healthier and more effective workplace. Interest in stress escalated two years ago after a landmark legal victory when a member of staff successfully sued Northumberland County Council for giving him a health-endangering workload.

Dr Amanda Griffiths, Deputy Director of the Centre, says, 'Evidence suggests that a great deal of stress is caused by the way jobs are designed and people are managed – for example, the amount of control people have over what they do in their job is very important. If control is taken away people experience stress. Managers are obligated by European and UK health and safety legislation to assess the risks to health of their employees – risks do not mean just physical or chemical hazards, they can be psycho-social too.

'People can become seriously unwell and ineffective, both physically and psychologically, if their work is not properly managed or designed. Stress can contribute to musculo-skeletal disorders and can be associated with arthritis and coronary heart disease.

'The solutions to stress-related problems can often prove relatively easy to implement – through policy formation, systems development, job redesign, work reorganisation or communication and staff education.'

Source: The NewsLetter, No.134, The University of Nottingham.

Reward systems and worker lifestyle

Reward systems

Kanter, in discussing her post-entrepreneurial model in her book *When Giants Learn to Dance* reveals two areas which could contribute to stress. The first refers to systems which reward or pay bonuses to entrepreneurial, inventive high performers. Unfortunately, not everyone has such talent or opportunity to earn bonuses. Also, if a reward system which is based on seniority and loyalty etc. is scrapped, many older, more experienced and dedicated steady employees will lose out. In outcome, the reward system could become divisive, create conflict and demotivate many people. This will inevitably result in stress and an ultimate reduction in effectiveness of many employees – the exact opposite of what the reward system set out to achieve.

Worker lifestyle

In the second area of stress, worker lifestyle, Kanter considers those high flyers who work long hours and whose social life centres around their work. She comments:

> the fact that one's work lifestyle or goals don't sit well (integrate) with one's personal life could create severe stress. This could manifest itself as physical or mental deterioration and breakup of personal and family relationships.

As illustrated in Exhibit 12.5, the situation is going to get worse for many managers whose interpersonal skills, networks of contacts and trust demanded by their jobs are not easily transferable.

Exhibit 12.5

Whatever happened to leisure?

Technology was going to shorten working hours and leave more time for leisure and a satisfying lifestyle. Where did it all go wrong? British managers now work the longest hours in Europe (though not, it should be said, as long as their US counterparts, or, looking to the East, the Japanese and Koreans). According to a survey in *Personnel Today*, one in eight UK managers currently clocks up over 60 hours a week, while 40 per cent work over 50 hours. The Institute of Personnel Development, meanwhile, reports that one in five middle managers takes work home three or more times a week, with one third of junior managers regularly taking it home at weekends.

'For many, the assumption these days is that they are always on call; this was not always the case,' says Courtaulds chief executive, Sipko Huismans. According to Carole Pemberton, a research consultant at Sundridge Park Management Centre, 'The hard truth is that in the '60s people worked hard to get on, now they have to work hard just to stay in. So where do we stand 30 years on?' According to Geoff Mulgan and Helen Wilkinson, writing in *Time Squeeze* (the October 1995 quarterly from the Demos think-tank), 'The "elite" are working even harder and longer, since the interpersonal skills, networks of contacts and trust demanded by their jobs are not easily transferable. With their types of work, three workers working 50 hours each week are much more efficient than 5 workers working 30 hours a week. At the bottom end, so-called flexibility is also more often imposed than sought, with the important difference that rewards are declining rather than rising. At the middle levels, even though there is little evidence of either long hours or shorter tenure, people are feeling harried.'

What is to be done? 'Down shifting' – changing down a gear of two in terms of career and income aspirations in pursuit of a better quality of life – has become a vulgar concept in the US, but it remains to be seen whether it will be translated into action, in that country or this. Meanwhile, employees could take a more modest step towards a balanced existence by obeying the call of the Long Hours Campaign (launched by the Parents At Work group last September) to 'Go home on time!' on 21 June, the longest day of the year. Get a life!

Source: Van de Vliet, A., 'Whatever happened to leisure?', *Management Today*, Haymarket Publications.

Stress effects on the individual and the organisation

Through stress the individual may suffer physiological effects such as burnout or boredom. The reaction to stress may be alcohol or drug abuse, smoking or overeating. The organisation may then suffer through experiencing accidents, low productivity, impaired decision making, absenteeism, and excessive labour turnover.

Dealing with stress

Prevention of stress is preferable to allowing stress levels to become excessive in the first place. Individuals can attempt to cope with stress in many ways: exercise, healthier eating, time management, career planning, change of job, relaxation, meditation, counselling and prayer. It is helpful to us if we can develop a stress management programme to cope with the constant barrage of stress that we all face in our lives. Listed below are alternative strategies for maximising the benefits of stress and minimising its destructive effects.

- Be realistic about your limits.
- Maintain control over situations to a level that is satisfactory to you.
- Take action to have better control over your life.
- Know when to back off in situations or when to do nothing.
- Pace yourself.
- Be more open to others.
- Take regular exercise.
- Have a healthy diet.
- Do something for others.
- Balance your work with recreation and home life.
- Learn relaxation techniques.

Organisations can play a huge part in dealing with stress-related problems by providing counselling, recreation, training, career and personal development facilities, improved job design and matching the person to the job. Certainly managers need to be constantly aware that work-role ambiguities, job constraints and demands can cause excessive stress. A management by objectives (MBO) programme can help here by bringing managers and workers together to clarify roles and difficulties while attempting to spot and take action to reduce potential stress situations.

SUMMARY

- The building blocks that are fundamental to the effective management of operations and change are referred to as 'management enablers'. They are:

  1 the management approach and culture
  2 structure and types of organisation
  3 organisation development and stress.

- Prominent research and studies show that organisations become the best in their field by adopting management approaches which:

  - have a culture which fosters more people involvement, better organisation and emphasis on customer needs (Peters and Waterman's eight attributes of excellence)

  - are better organised to meet both the employees' and customers' needs (Robert Waterman)

  - restructure to find synergies; open boundaries to form strategic alliances, and create new ventures from within, encouraging innovation and entrepreneurship (Rosabeth Moss Kanter).

● The level of performance in the way an organisation manages its operations and change depends on its culture. The organisation's structure and culture need to match. Cultures are needed which match individual beliefs and values and which foster learning, continuous improvement, understanding, and reinforce desired behaviour.

● Management experts are convinced of the need to acquire the right type of structure for individuals and organisations to operate. Handy identified three generic types of organisation which would cope with future changes: the Shamrock organisation, the Federal organisation and the Triple I organisation. A company also needs an appropriate infrastructure which includes project or improvement teams and a regular and effective communications process.

● Organisation development (OD) shifts the emphasis from the technical aspects of managing change to deal with human resources in the organisation and the ability of the behavioural and social sciences to assist in the management of operations and change. The underpinnings of OD stem from the work of Douglas McGregor on the concept of Theory X and Theory Y and socio-technical systems design conducted at the Tavistock Institute of Human Relations in London. Various practitioners of OD have focused on the areas of individual motivation, job and work design, interpersonal relations and participative management. Developing an appropriate organisation development strategy is considered to be crucial to achieving effective change.

● Stress is mainly a physical condition resulting from the way our body responds to the demands placed upon it by our lifestyle. We continually react to stresses placed upon us and stress at work and often this can bring out the best in us, in fact, in an emergency our reactions can save our lives. However, everyone has a different tolerance level to stress and people can become ill or even die as a result of being stressed. It is, however, possible to effectively manage your reactions to stress by first of all becoming aware of your stress tolerance level. A common source of physiological stress at work is role ambiguity or role conflict. Organisations can play a huge part in dealing with stress-related problems by providing counselling, recreation, training, career and personal development facilities, improved job design and matching the person to the job.

REVIEW AND DISCUSSION QUESTIONS

1 What is an organisation's culture and what issues influence organisational culture?

2 If you were aiming to redesign the organisational structure of your company in order to cope with future changes, what issues would you consider and what types of structure would you propose?

3 Outline the conceptual underpinnings or thrust of organisation development (OD) and describe the ways in which OD can assist in the management of operations and change.

4 Discuss the sources of stress at work and how stress can be effectively managed by both the individual and the organisation.

ASSIGNMENTS

1 Your chief executive has asked you to develop a series of seminars to ensure that the senior managers in the company are fully aware of the latest management thinking and approaches aimed at managing operations and change. Outline the content of your seminars and the ways in which the wisdom contained within them could be used to the company's benefit.

2 As a prerequisite to a new change initiative, your managing director considers that an assessment of the organisation's culture is necessary. Your advice has been sought regarding the validity of this reasoning and the factors you would consider when analysing organisational culture.

REFERENCES

Altany, D.R., 'Decision-making trickles down to the troops', *Industry Week*, p. 34, 18 April 1988.

Argyris, C., *Intervention Theory and Method*, Addison-Wesley, Reading, Mass., 1970.

Armstrong, M., *How to be an Even Better Manager*, 3rd edn, Kogan Page, London, 1990.

Bishop, J.E., 'Prognosis for the "Type A" personality improves in a new heart disease study', *Wall Street Journal*, p. 29, 14 January 1988.

Buchanan, D.A., *The Development of Job Design Theories*, Saxon House, Aldershot, 1979.

Burke, W., *Organisation Development: A normative view*, Addison-Wesley, Reading, Mass., 1987.

Burnes, B., *Managing Change*, Pitman Publishing, London, 1992.

Burnes, B. and Weekes, B., *AMT: A Strategy for Success?*, NEDO, London, 1989.

Cummings, T.G. and Huse, E.F., *Organisation Development and Change*, West, St. Paul, Minn., 1989.

Department of Trade and Industry, *Competitiveness: How the best companies are winning*, report published jointly by the DTI and the CBI, designed and produced by CGI London Limited, 1994.

Hackman, J.R. and Oldham, G.R., 'Development of the job diagnostic survey', *Journal of Applied Psychology*, Vol. 60, pp. 159–70, 1975.

Handy, C., *The Age of Unreason*, Arrow, London, 1989.

Handy, C., *The Empty Raincoat*, Hutchinson, London, 1994.

Handy, C., *Understanding Organisations*, Penguin, Harmondsworth, 1986.

Hodgetts, R., Luthans, F. and Lee, S., 'New paradigm organizations: from total quality to learning to world class', *Organizational Dynamics*, Vol. 22, No. 3, pp. 5–19, 1994.

Hunt, J.W., *Managing People at Work*, 2nd edn, IPM, London, 1986.

Kanter, R.M., *When Giants Learn to Dance: Mastering the challenges of strategy, management, and careers in the 1990s*, Unwin, London, 1989.

Katz, N. and Marks, J., 'To your health', *Nation's Business*, p. 75, June 1994.

Kotter, J.P. and Heskett, J.L., *Corporate Culture and Performance*, Free Press, New York, 1992.

Lawler, E.E., 'Job design and employee motivation', *Personal Psychology*, Vol. 22, pp. 426–35, 1969.

Likert, R., *The Human Organisation: Its management and value*, McGraw-Hill, New York, 1967.

Margulies, N. and Raia, A., *Conceptual Foundations of Organizational Development*, McGraw-Hill, New York, 1978.

McCalman, J. and Paton, R.A., *Change Management: A guide to effective implementation*, Paul Chapman Publishing, London, 1992.

McGregor, D., *The Human Side of Enterprise*, McGraw-Hill, New York, 1960.

McLean, A. and Marshal, J. 'Intervening in cultures', Working Paper, University of Bath, 1993.

Mills, D. Q. and Friesen, B., 'The learning organization', *European Management Journal*, Vol. 10, No. 2, pp. 146–56, June 1992.

Mullins, L.J., *Management and Organisational Behaviour*, 3rd edn, Pitman Publishing, London, 1994.

The NewsLetter, No. 134, The University of Nottingham, 12 April 1996.

Peter, L.J. and Hull, R., *The Peter Principle*, Morrow, New York, 1969.

Peters, T.J., *Liberation Management*, Macmillan, London, 1992.

Peters, T.J. and Waterman, R.H., *In Search of Excellence*, Harper & Row, New York, 1982.

Pugh, D.S., *Planning and Managing Change; Block 4: Organisational Development*, Open University Business School, Milton Keynes, 1986.

Van de Vliet, A., 'Whatever happened to leisure?', *Management Today*, pp. 46–50, May 1996.

Vroom, V.H., 'Industrial social psychology', in Lindsey, G.and Aronson, E., (eds), *The Handbook of Social Psychology*, Addison-Wesley, Reading, Mass., 1969.

Waterman, R.H., *The Frontiers of Excellence*, Nicholas Brearley Publishing, London, 1994.

Webber, R.A., *Management: Basic elements of managing organisations*, pp. 573–7, Richard D. Irwin Inc., London, 1979.

CHAPTER 13

Personal and management development

OBJECTIVES

The objectives of this chapter are to:

- **address issues of people's lifestyle at work and how it relates to job enjoyment, job satisfaction, career development and giving the best to the organisation**
- **develop an understanding and appreciation of the nature and importance of management skills**
- **show how individuals can assess and develop themselves as managers**
- **examine the quality of management education, training and development in Britain in comparison with other developed economies**
- **examine managerial career progress, career development patterns, career development programmes and the management development function**
- **consider the importance, benefits and process of acquiring and using a mentor**
- **investigate more progressive approaches to assessment used by successful organisations, such as 'Upward Feedback/Appraisal' and '360° Feedback'.**

THE IMPORTANCE OF THE RIGHT WORK LIFESTYLE

The lifestyle people experience at work can affect their wellbeing, personal and career development and the contribution they make to the company. Therefore, some important questions need to be asked regarding one's work lifestyle. For example, are you in the right job and does your job suit you? Some people are good at their job and enjoy doing it because they like the element of power that it brings and they are good at company politics. Others may like the enjoyment and pride of practising a particular hard-won skill, even though the pay may not be that good. Some people may put up with doing work they don't particularly like so long as the pay is good. Other people, sadly, are square pegs in round holes. They hate what they do and feel trapped in an occupation to which they are not suited.

Making changes for the better

Obviously, everyone's situation is different, but what is certain is that you can change situations and you can strive to get more of what you really want and like – be it more money, better conditions, the opportunity to do what you are good at or what you like doing. The more positive you are about these aspects, the better chance you have of succeeding. It is important that these issues are addressed now if in the future you wish to progress in your career by making the best use of your talents. Furthermore, since the organisation is paying you, is it really getting the best from you? Perhaps you would get paid more if you were playing to your strengths and doing the things you were best at.

Finding out which aspects of a job best suit you, and looking to see which of these aspects are not present in your current job can provide you with information on the type of job you should be seeking, either in your current company or elsewhere.

Assessing work lifestyle

To start with, you need to assess your current work lifestyle and consider which aspects of it you are happy and content with, which work lifestyle aspects you dislike, and which you would like to have.

Figure 13.1 illustrates the factors that should be borne in mind by an individual when assessing how they feel about their current job, how other jobs in the organisation rate, and what they would prefer to do or be best doing. These factors are:

- **Use and expression of talents and abilities**. What skills (e.g. interpersonal, communication, analytical) are required? To what extent does the job require inventiveness and creativity and does this allow the opportunity to use initiative? Is there the opportunity for personal development and learning?

- **Rewards, recognition and status**. The level of remuneration is important as well as other benefits, job perks and rewards. So too may be the position of authority, the power and status offered, the promotion opportunities and the level of recognition and respect.

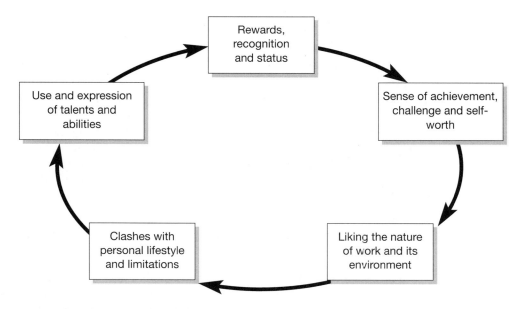

Fig 13.1 Assessing work lifestyle

- **Sense of achievement, challenge and self-worth**. What may be sought is a job that is pioneering, say developing a new drug, which poses a challenge and brings a sense of achievement. What may be sought is a feeling of self-worth and a sense of fulfilment, which may, for example, be achieved through coaching and advising others.

- **Liking the nature of the work and its environment**. People's tastes vary. Some prefer a work environment that is structured, steady, established, prescribed and procedural. The job may be liked because the environment is one where people get on well with their peers and those senior or subordinate to them. Others may prefer a more pressured, ever-changing, organic, more political and chaotic situation. Good working conditions and surroundings are considered paramount by many. However, work, in whatever form, may be sought simply because it has variety, is interesting, enjoyable and appears to offer more job satisfaction. Other reasons may be linked to how supportive the organisation and its managers are as well as the apparent degree of job security. It may be that a job is desirable because it offers the opportunity to work with other people or belong to a team. Alternatively what may be sought is the chance to work alone.

- **Clashes with personal lifestyle and limitations**. Last but not least it is important for the individual to consider how important the characteristics of their jobs are to them in terms of their personal make up and needs; that is how does their present lifestyle match up with their preferred lifestyle? They should also consider their constraints and limitations. For example, they should ignore those factors which it is impractical to pursue in the intermediate future, e.g. perhaps they would like to practise a particular skill that they don't currently possess or they would like to be in the most senior position but are currently in one of the most junior positions. In other words, people need to be realistic so that they can determine which job might best suit them and get them where they want to be.

The benefits of being a properly-positioned employee

Being in the right job is important to individuals because it fulfils their needs both now and possibly in the future. It is important to the company because a properly-positioned employee brings their natural capabilities to the job. Using and developing such capabilities should be to the advantage of that person and hence of the organisation, since it should have a more content, productive and effective employee.

SELF-ASSESSMENT AND DEVELOPMENT

What is involved?

Managers and students of management need to appreciate the nature of personal traits and understand how they should behave in relation to them. They should also consider the important management skills they need and explore these skills in the context of what is perceived as being important in the organisation they work for, and how they match up to these expectations. In particular, they need to consider their particular weaknesses as managers with respect to these management skills. They can then consider the different methods available for personal development in the context of developing their management expertise and career progression. To provide relevant independent feedback, managers and students are encouraged to make use of a mentor who can advise and guide their career development. They should also explore the ways an organisation can be and should be of assistance in terms of career progression and developing them as managers.

Skills required by managers

There are many classifications of the skills which are required by different types of managers. Thamhain identifies three main skill groups required by production, and by implication, operations managers:

- leadership and people skills, e.g. assertiveness, self-confidence, determination
- administrative skills, e.g. delegation, decision making, time management
- technical skills, e.g. manufacturing/operations systems knowledge.

Megginson, Mosley and Pietri use a different categorisation and add an extra set of skills, split off from the administration group of traits:

- administrative skills, e.g. planning, time management
- conceptual skills, e.g. decision making
- human relation skills, e.g. leadership abilities, honesty, fairness
- technical skills.

Work done by Megginson *et al.* shows that the relative importance attributed to these various skills by managers depends upon their managerial level.

Another way of classifying such skills, which encompasses the above categories, is presented in Fig 13.2. The categories of skills are:

- personal traits, e.g. assertiveness, decisiveness, self-confidence
- general management skills, e.g. delegation, decision making, planning
- functional management skills, eg. marketing, finance, personnel
- technical and expert skills, e.g. knowledge techniques and tools in a specific field.

This book is concerned with a combination of the above skills, requiring knowledge and expertise across the board.

Fig 13.2 Skills required by managers

PERSONAL TRAITS

There has always been great debate over whether managers are 'born' or 'made'. It is a highly controversial topic. For example, managers are not born with technical skills; these are taught through certain educational methods. Thamhain carried out a survey examining where managers developed skills, and discovered that, in quantitative terms, the portion of skills the manager 'must be born with' averages five per cent and varies with the particular category. For example, Thamhain considers that conflict resolution skills seem to be more difficult to learn than administrative skills. What has been decided is that managers are made, not born, and success depends upon attitude, experience, and training. However, many think this is not the case for personal traits, since they are often subject to a manager's personality and disposition; examples given being intelligence and leadership. On the other hand, many believe that such traits are developed or can be developed with the correct types of management training.

Many experts have sought to identify the personal traits that make a good manager. Hundreds of trait names are in use and it is not sensible to consider all of them. Exhibit 13.1 lists 20 personal traits most applicable to management success that Brearley and Sewell accord to experienced senior managers.

It is important that individual managers assess their level of ability with respect to particular personal traits. They should be able to understand the nature of personal

Exhibit 13.1

Personal traits applicable to management success

1 **Decisiveness**: I am able to weigh up the factors and readily decide upon a course of action.
2 **Determination**: I show resolution, perseverance and purpose when pursuing objectives.
3 **Diplomacy**: I am subtle and tactful when dealing with others.
4 **Drive**: I am enterprising, with 'get up and go'.
5 **Energy**: I demonstrate vigour, vitality and energy when pursuing objectives.
6 **Enthusiasm**: I am keen and eager about my work.
7 **Fairness**: I possess a sense of balance and fair play.
8 **Flexibility**: I am adaptable, responsive and amenable to change.
9 **Foresight**: I am forward looking and anticipate problems.
10 **Honesty**: I am trustworthy, truthful and ethical.
11 **Intelligence**: I am quick thinking and can readily understand different situations.
12 **Judgement**: I am discerning and make sound decisions.
13 **Leadership**: I enjoy taking responsibility.
14 **Logicality**: I approach things in a rational and analytical fashion.
15 **Loyalty**: I am dependable and maintain allegiance.
16 **Reliability**: I am dependable and stable.
17 **Resilience**: I can cope with difficulties and recover from set-backs.
18 **Self-confidence**: I am assured and do not worry.
19 **Self-control**: I maintain a calm, controlled manner in different situations.
20 **Stability**: I remain calm and steady in different situations.

Source: Brearley, A. and Sewell, D., *The Ernst & Young Management Self-Assessment System.* Crown Copyright. Adapted and reproduced with the permission of the Controller of Her Majesty's Stationery Office.

traits and develop the ability to identify which aspects of different personal traits make a good manager. In this respect, individual managers should consider which of these management traits they think are important and which are perceived as being important in their organisation. Also, they should reflect on which are their strongest and weakest traits to determine the possible need for personal management development and how best they can make use of their abilities.

GENERAL MANAGEMENT SKILLS

A manager in a particular area or function has to learn to use specialist knowledge and technical capabilities in association with his or her general management skills. For example, preparing production schedules requires planning skills as well as effective time management. When dealing with suppliers, materials management and purchasing skills are needed but, just as importantly, so are the skills of communication.

What are general management skills?

General management skills reflect the core functions of a manager, be it an operations manager, a sales manager or any other type of manager. The following are the key areas of management expertise which need to be considered:

- planning
- decision making
- communication
- delegation
- managing time and meetings.

The above skills cannot be isolated from one another. In fact, they are completely interactive with and dependent on one another. For example, decision making may involve deciding which decisions can be delegated and this, in turn, involves strategic planning.

Planning

Planning is the activity of bridging the gap mentally between one's current position and one's desired future position, in terms of accomplishing a task (*see* Adair, 1988). It involves selecting missions and objectives and the actions to achieve them; it requires decision making, i.e. choosing from alternative future courses of action (*see* Torrington and Weightman, 1985). Successful planning is always based on maximising opportunities (*see* Drucker, 1994).

Oldcorn recommends five rules of good planning:

1 Allow plenty of time.
2 Involve all managers.
3 Leave nothing to chance.
4 Quantify (budgets, etc.).
5 Set milestones (intermediate stages when certain things have to be achieved).

Decision making

Decisions are made and actions are taken at every step in the analysis of a business and its economic dimensions (*see* Drucker, 1994). Decision making involves some aspect of problem solving. Oldcorn states that the process of arriving at a decision is usually referred to as 'problem solving' and provides six stages which indicate the underlying elements of problem solving and decision making:

1 Recognise that there is a problem.
2 Diagnose the cause(s).
3 Develop some possible solutions.
4 Evaluate the possibilities.
5 Choose the course of action (i.e. take the decision).
6 Implement the decision.

Communication, delegation, managing meetings, planning and time management all incorporate some degree of effective decision making. For example, Taylor and Watling suggest that whenever and wherever it is possible, delegate decision making within the capabilities of your staff.

Communication

Examine what is being said, not who is speaking.

Arabian proverb

Taylor and Watling define communication simply as being a mutual exchange of thoughts between people, and they identify five fundamental methods: speaking, writing, visual, gestures and listening. Although this is true, the definition does not capture the depth of communication skills.

Oldcorn provides a more thorough explanation:

> *Communication is all about passing on information. Information is required for all aspects of organisational life; to help in planning, for better decision making and problem solving, for creating understanding between people and for effective control.*

Clemmer and McNeil make the point that:

> *Communication is a dynamic and interactive process.*

Managers are likely to spend most of their time engaged in some form of communication process. Even when they are working alone – when studying or preparing reports – they are relying on other people's attempts to communicate with them, or they are preparing to communicate with others (*see* Rees, 1988).

To communicate, individuals must hear and understand what others are trying to convey, not just listen to the particular words or expressions (*see* Clemmer and McNeil, 1990). Other processes work interactively with different types of communication. If the communication process is faulty then everything else can be affected. Accuracy in decision making depends, in particular, on effective communication (*see* Rees, 1988).

407

Stemp proposes four basic ways of improving the fundamentals of communication:

- listen carefully
- write thoughtfully
- read selectively
- present efficiently.

A further development of these skills is suggested by Rees, who provides six methods of improvement:

- coaxing information
- listening effectively
- choice of time and place
- choice of language
- recognising cultural barriers
- interpreting body language.

Communication skills are essential for managers in this electronic age, more so than ever before. As today's market is global, so today's leaders must be able to communicate globally. This does not mean mastering hundreds of languages, but rather mastering the ability to communicate ideas (*see* Clemmer and McNeil, 1990).

Communications in today's flat organisations

An Institute of Management (IM) research report, *Are Managers Getting the Message?* (*see* Aspen Business Communications, 1992), provides a summary on communications in the flat organisation. The key findings are that restructuring continues, and almost two-thirds of managers have been affected by reorganisation in the past two years. Three-quarters of these reported a cut in the number of managers; two-thirds a reduction in the number of management levels. Around six in ten thought that communications had improved in the past two years, yet only four in ten agreed that their internal communications strategy was now clearer.

Personal contact is still important

Personal contact remains the key to good communications. Four in ten managers considered that face-to-face communications (formal and informal meetings, team briefings, etc.) had increased since restructuring. Over two-thirds judged face-to-face communications to be even more effective than communications based on paper or technology. The introduction of technology does not appear to have usurped the role of the memo. Over four in ten managers reported a rise in the number of memos and circulars, and a third reported greater use of paper-based communications in general.

Technology has speeded up communications

Just over half judged paper-based communications to be effective. The use of technology-based communications, i.e. faxes and electronic mail, has increased by a third. Two-thirds of managers said that the introduction of technology has speeded up communications and improved their ability to access information. However, only four in ten believed it made information more relevant to its target audience. Few organisations are reaping the full benefits of information technology (IT). Only 15 per cent of managers thought they fully understood the capabilities of the systems in place; less than a quarter thought that IT was being exploited to its full potential. Restructuring generally has improved the flow of information around organisations, particularly that flowing from the top down. Restructuring generally has had a positive effect on company culture. The majority of managers characterised the flatter organisation as more open, honest, informal, consultative and progressive. There was one exception: organisations were now seen as less caring, and managers lower down the organisation were more likely to think this than senior management.

Restructuring and flatter structures improve communication

The conclusions are that restructuring does speed up communication and improves managers' access to information. Yet much of this communication is poorly targeted. The focus on speeding flow of information appears to have been at the expense of ensuring its relevance.

A flatter structure does appear to lead to a more open management style with more information flowing down the organisation. However, top management was much more likely to have a rosy picture of the effectiveness of communications than managers lower down, who were concerned about a reduction in their ability to take decisions. A number of factors contribute to this upward migration of decision making. In particular, with improved access to information, senior managers may now be in a position to make the decisions previously taken by middle managers.

The information technology potential needs to be realised

The era of information technology appears to have arrived. Yet less than a quarter of respondents felt it was being exploited to its full potential. Is IT being used simply to increase the flow of paper around the organisation?

Appointing an internal communications manager

The recommendations of the report contain a number of practical suggestions for action by managers and their employees, aimed at improving the communication process. These include appointing an internal communications manager. Most organisations in the survey carefully managed their public relations. Fewer nominated someone with clear and unambiguous authority for managing communications with managers and employees. Yet these are likely to be critical to organisational success.

Carrying out a communications audit

Few organisations survey employees to identify the strengths and weaknesses of their internal communications.

Developing a communication strategy

Organisations need an overall strategy to ensure consistency of transmission of messages up, down and across the organisation. Information technology needs to be integrated within the communications process. IT needs to be introduced as an integral part of a communication strategy rather than being added as an optional extra. Its benefits need to be fully exploited through rigorous training.

Delegation

Delegation is a central function of management. It is necessary to allow the range of work for which managers have responsibility to be carried out; to enable managers to concentrate on key aspects of their job; to develop subordinates and widen their experience, and to train successors. Managers who neglect to delegate or 'cannot' delegate are failing to develop the human resources for which they have responsibility (*see* Guirdham, 1990).

Rees defines delegation as a person conferring authority on a subordinate to act on his/her behalf. A less sophisticated definition, yet easier to comprehend, is that given by Stemp, which describes delegation as a key management activity which allows you to achieve through others and free yourself to spend time on priorities.

There are many advantages of delegation. Oates lists as many as fifteen important benefits:

1 leaves delegator free to concentrate on more strategic issues
2 increases job satisfaction for delegator and subordinate
3 helps subordinates to develop new skills
4 helps subordinates to grow in confidence
5 provides an opportunity to assess subordinates' potential
6 fosters teamwork
7 helps create a more motivated workforce
8 enhances morale
9 improves communication through feedback
10 creates fresh insights into work issues
11 helps create a climate for achievement
12 ultimately speeds up results
13 reduces costs (subordinate's time is less expensive than delegator's time)
14 increases chances of promotion for delegator
15 ensures smooth succession when delegator is promoted.

Failure to delegate often results from the manager's fear of losing control (*see* Mullins, 1993).

Managers frequently do not delegate to the extent that is possible. There are a number of barriers to productive delegation. Stewart provides a list of constraints which repeatedly account for the lack of delegation:

- the relative skills of the boss and the subordinate
- task specification
- attitude of boss
- confidentiality
- amount of status differentiation
- origin of subordinate's work
- 'what else can the manager do?'

At the heart of successful delegation lies interaction between the manager and his/her subordinate, during which three tasks must be accomplished: exchange of information, agreement on the scope and nature of the delegation, and establishment of an effective working leadership (*see* Guirdham, 1990).

Time management

Time is a unique resource – you cannot rent, hire, buy or otherwise obtain more time. The supply of time is totally inelastic, time is totally irreplaceable and everything requires time (Drucker, 1994).

Time is the only factor you can do absolutely nothing to increase (Oldcorn, 1988).

General management functions – communication, decision making, delegation, managing meetings and planning – all incorporate the efficient use of time. Much time is wasted completing aspects of these functions.

Managers' attitudes to using and managing time

Research was conducted to assess managers' attitudes to using and managing time in the flatter, leaner organisations of the 1990s (*see* DHL International (UK), 1994).

The key findings can be summarised as follows:

- Individual workloads increased greatly for almost half of the respondents over the previous two years. One in five was working an extra 15 hours per week.
- More managerial time was being spent on new business development, general administration/paperwork and planning/setting objectives than before, indicating a short-term emphasis on the 'harder' skills as the recovery strengthens.
- Online databases, a desk fax and a portable lap-top computer were rated as being very helpful in saving managers' time. Other suggestions included making more use of answering machines, dictaphones, desk-top printers and teleconferencing.

The way forward – practical recommendations for better use of time

There are only 1440 minutes in a day, and on average 480 are taken up by sleep alone, leaving 960 minutes for the completion of all the tasks that have to be performed within a day – tasks including eating, bathing and washing, attending to matters in the home and travelling between places, as well as any duties to be accomplished at work! It would be wonderful if quantities of time could be bought in addition to the daily amount available, but of course this is impossible. The only method of 'creating' time is to eliminate as much wasted time as possible, and thus use time more productively.

Adair proposes a ten-point programme to monitor the wastage of time:

1 Develop a new personal sense of time.
2 Plan ahead.
3 Make the most of your best time.
4 Capitalise on marginal time.
5 Avoid clutter.
6 Do a task **now**.
7 Learn to say no.
8 Use the telephone as a time-saving tool.
9 Delegate as many tasks as possible.
10 Use meetings as a tool of delegation and information dispersion.

Exhibit 13.2 summarises the results of an Institute of Management survey of managers' use of time, showing how to get the most out of the 86 400 seconds in a day.

Managing meetings

Meetings, whether formal or informal, are increasingly an integral part of organisational activity, and it is naïve for people to suggest that meetings are unnecessary.

Exhibit 13.2

Getting the most from your time

The following checklist can help individual managers assess their own time management performance. The manager who uses his/her time to best effect is one who:

- says 'yes' to important, urgent work and 'no' when it has a low priority and could affect progress on high-priority work
- adopts a 'do it now' policy and concentrates first on high-priority work
- sets objectives and plans actions
- schedules resources sensibly and flexibly
- delegates professionally
- holds action-centred meetings, not talking shop
- deals quickly with paper and other routine work
- helps staff and colleagues to manage their time
- reduces their work stress by identifying, confronting and dealing with sources of stress
- looks ahead and develops contingency plans for potentially busy times.

Source: DHL International (UK), *Finding the Time: A survey of managers' attitudes to using and managing time* for the Institute of Management (IM).

Meetings can be part of a constitutional decision-making process, for briefing purposes only, for negotiation, for consultation or for the mutual exchange of views (*see* Rees, 1988).

Properly used, meetings present an excellent opportunity for all people working on a given job, or affected by a specific decision, to get together and share their ideas, viewpoints or problems (*see* Clemmer and McNeil, 1990).

Oldcorn distinguishes between four main types of meetings:

- meetings for the dissemination of information
- problem-solving meetings
- collective-decision meetings
- creative-thinking meetings

Much time can be wasted by the inadequate planning of meetings. Taylor and Watling state several rules necessary for a well-conducted meeting:

1 There must be a clear object.
2 The people who attend must be capable of dealing with the subject.
3 The subject must be within the scope of the meeting's level and ability.
4 The agenda and timing should ensure a quick, successful session.

Although there are countless benefits of meetings, they do have two main disadvantages:

- meetings can lead to unsatisfactory compromise.
- meetings can be indecisive (*see* Oldcorn, 1988).

FUNCTIONAL MANAGEMENT SKILLS

The problem of functionality

An organisation needs communication to occur between its separate functions in order to operate effectively. However, there are often many barriers to effective communication, resulting from each department resenting the others due to a lack of knowledge. Usually each function within a firm perceives itself as the superior and expects the other departments to work around its schedules and specifications. This leads to animosity between functions and, eventually, to a decrease in overall production.

Understanding what other functions do

One method of overcoming such difficulties is to allow members of different departments to acquire skills and knowledge about other sections of the organisation. Workers and managers alike will be able to express their views on matters concerning other departments with much more conviction if they understand what is going on. Also, managers and workers from other departments are more likely to listen to opinions, knowing that those giving them have knowledge of what they are saying.

Experience of other functional areas

Practising managers need to identify the range and depth of functional management skills which they need to acquire over time to become effective. This depends on the situations faced in both their current job and any future jobs. The problem is compounded further in that different companies rely more on certain functions than on others and, even within a function, certain activities will require more focus and expertise than others. Therefore, although the skill requirements are situational and will vary over time, managers would be wise to consider acquiring skills in certain basic disciplines which they can build upon over time, disciplines such as corporate strategic issues, legal issues, organisational issues, finance and accounting, marketing, purchasing, product development and personnel. Depending on the situation, there will be skills which they need to acquire, and those skills which they already have but need to develop further.

TECHNICAL AND EXPERT SKILLS

A technical skill is one which requires the knowledge, tools and techniques of a specific field. Technical skills differ from the other skills groupings in that they are systematically developed through formal and informal methods. These skills can be tested and reviewed by educational and professional bodies. Technical skills are precise and unqueried.

MANAGING OPERATIONS AND CHANGE SKILLS

To focus on managing operations and the associated change problems, it becomes necessary to develop or acquire a wide band of management knowledge and skills, particularly with respect to:

- operations and change strategy development
- planning and controlling the changes
- making use of operations initiatives such as TQM, MRP, JIT and OPT
- managing the people in the change process
- pursuing the initiatives of change, e.g. teams, empowerment, the learning organisation and business process re-engineering
- making things happen by using key management ideas, personal and management development (being discussed in this chapter) and continuous improvement.

Individual managers should consider how good they think their management skills are in each area of management expertise. It should be appreciated that the *emphasis* the top management in the organisation places on each area of management expertise, and how good its management skills are in each one, will determine the 'effectiveness' with which the company pursues 'good practice' in each area.

DEVELOPING YOURSELF AS A MANAGER

Being a successful and effective manager is not an automatic gift, it is something that has to be continually worked on. The following is a structured approach to assessing and developing yourself as a manager:

Clarity of vision

Are you certain about your career aspirations? Think about what you want to achieve and what you want to do. Contrast this with what you can do and what you are willing to strive for. It is important that you build up a picture in your mind of the type of work you wish to do; the management level you would wish to work at; the extent of responsibility you would wish to assume and the salary you would expect. You must ask yourself if your goals are realistic and, if not, what other prospects are realistic?

Management skill gaps

You need to identify your strengths, weaknesses and your main management skill gaps. Your development as a manager will be assisted if you seek to make improvements to your main management skill deficiencies. To do this you will need to consider the three main areas, referred to earlier, of personal traits, general management skills, and functional management skills.

Necessary training and education

Having some knowledge of your management skill gaps, you should consider which types of further training and education you might benefit from. Are you aware of the main types of training and education that may be of help to you? Which programmes can you pursue and what do they entail in terms of content, cost, convenience and overall use to you?

The following is a list of the main types of training and education that may be of help:

- internal courses
- external courses
- coaching
- personal study
- on-the-job learning
- correspondence courses
- management games
- management workshops
- case studies.

Management development and career opportunities

What provision for management development is available and suitable for you within the company? What career opportunities exist in the company for you?

Acquiring and using a mentor

You should find someone in the organisation who is willing to act as a mentor to you. This person should be prepared to listen to you, discuss issues concerning your career problems and offer advice. It should preferably be someone who is a more senior professional manager, who works in a different area to you, who knows about how you work.

Using mentor for advice on skill gaps

With respect to your personal trait skill gaps, show your mentor the list of 20 personal traits presented earlier (Exhibit 13.1) and let him/her know what you consider to be your main strengths and weaknesses and which particular management traits you think are important.

Ask your mentor to consider this information and give their own opinion. If your mentor's views are different from yours then you may wish to reconsider your main strengths and weaknesses. Also, inform your mentor which general management, as well as operations and change management, skills you think you will need to develop and acquire. Discuss the reasons that form your views. Ask if your mentor thinks any key skills listed are missing and where he/she thinks you should develop your skills.

Development of career plan

Having thought about the job that you wish to attain, it is necessary to start working towards that goal. Developing a timescaled career plan will help steer you towards it. In the plan you will need to consider your management skill gaps and the type of further training and education you need. You will need to know what provision for management development within the company is available and suitable for you. In the short and long term, what career opportunities exist in the company for you? If things look bleak, what do you think your next job move should be? Are such jobs available at the moment, and what would be the difficulties associated with moving?

THE MANAGERS IN 2001

The Ashridge Management Research Group, commissioned by the IM to gather views on the skills and competences of the manager in 2001, considers that the important message for individual managers is as follows:

1 To win in a competitive and changing world it will be necessary to have up-to-date knowledge, together with flexible and transferable skills. Managers will need to have a strong sense of the whole organisation to support their interactions. Managers must be strongly tuned into the external environment and see and respond to the constant changes it will throw at them.

2 Effective interpersonal, teamworking, information handling and IT skills will become increasingly important in a knowledge-based economy. These will under-pin a manager's strategic thinking ability, which was identified by the research as the key skill for 2001 and beyond. Task skills (the 'doing' skills) will be highly valued: for example, problem analysis, prioritising and benchmarking.

3 A strongly-focused approach is provided by the management standards, voca-tional qualifications and the national record of achievement. In particular, for individual managers the world of work is changing and the range of options increasing. For employees and potential employees, the changes mean they will have to be prepared to work in different ways and be more flexible about their work arrangements. As the job market becomes even more varied and more volatile, individuals may, in future, be employed on demand for periods of a year or two, followed by periods without work.

4 A clear message from the research was that individuals will take on responsibility for their development. The individual's ability to learn and develop, coupled with the awareness of his or her own strengths and development needs, is important.

Personal development over a lifetime is something which requires a commitment by the individual as well as the employer. Service-sector organisations such as Forte and Marks & Spencer, or high-tech manufacturers such as Ford and Rover, are experi-menting with new forms of commitment involving job security and investment in skills in exchange for greater task flexibility. Recent evidence suggests that genuine progress has occurred. The study indicates that:

- Eight in ten large organisations (501 or more employees) have a formal training pro-gramme for managers.
- One in two organisations have some formal system of management training and development.
- 40 per cent of organisations have a management development and training policy at supervisory level.
- 31 per cent have a formal training policy for senior managers, 35 per cent for junior managers and 35 per cent for middle managers.
- A further one in 20 stated they were planning to introduce a formal training programme.
- Smaller firms (less than ten employees) are half as likely to have any form of management training. This gap is greatest for senior management.

THE TRAINING OF MANAGERS

A summary of a research report on management training in the UK by the Institute of Management (*The Training of Managers*, 1992) showed that training was less frequent among older managers and for those in smaller organisations; 82 per cent of managers undertook some worktime training in 1991, while 49 per cent took part in training in their own time. Overall, 88 per cent had some form of training; 18 per cent of managers had no worktime training in 1991, 51 per cent did not undertake own-time training and 12 per cent had no training of any kind. The average (median) number of days spent training in 1991 was five days for worktime training and eight days for all types of training. Of managers undertaking training in their own time, half paid some or all of the costs.

Attitudes to training

Managers' attitudes to training were generally positive: 89 per cent reported that *the business environment is changing so rapidly that managers need more training than in the past,* and 83 per cent agreed that *organisations should require all of their managers to undertake some training every year;* 81 per cent agreed they *would be a more effective manager if they received more training;* 51 per cent said they had received too little training in 1991; 32 per cent said their organisation does not have a formal management training policy, while only four per cent reported they had received training based on the management charter initiative standard. Around 60 per cent rated their most recent training activity as 'very helpful' or of 'very great help'. Conversely, 40 per cent took a negative view of that training.

Recommendations

The report reinforced the guidelines from the Constable/McCormick and Handy *et al.* reports from 1987. Specifically, Handy *et al.* recommended that leading corporations should be encouraged to set a public standard of five days of off-the-job training each year for managers and that organisations find ways to make individual study, reading and learning more corporately respectable.

The Handy *et al.* report also made new proposals within the framework of the National Training Targets for Lifetime Learning. This is personal development over a lifetime which requires commitment by the individual as well as the employer. Drawing from four existing targets, the Handy *et al.* report calls for discussions between the leading players in the management field to establish clear targets for management training. Each manager should undertake some training each year and for that purpose a target of days per year of manager training should be set. Targets should be attainable and allowances should be made for the difficulties of resourcing management training in smaller companies. Specific targets are required for different types of manager and different types of organisation. Separate training targets should also be established for older managers, since the report shows that companies make least provision for training this group.

Management education, training and development in the USA, West Germany, France, Japan and the UK

According to Handy *et al.*, in their report *The Making of Managers*, there can be little doubt that, by comparison with the other countries in this study, Britain has neglected her managerial stock. With some notable exceptions, companies have asked too little of their would-be managers and given them too little in terms of education, training and development. Quantity does not guarantee quality, but in crude statistical terms it is suggested that we should probably need to be doing nearly ten times as much as we are now, as a nation, if all would-be managers and executives were to be relevantly educated before they start, and each were to spend at least 40 hours a year in off-the-job training, in addition to all the less quantifiable aspects of development. The clear conclusion of this study is that Britain needs to do more to develop her managers and to do it more systematically. The study poses a ten-point agenda, based on the best practice in Britain, the USA, Japan, West Germany and France:

1 Expand educational base by educating people more broadly for more years.
2 Encourage some form of work experience as part of this education.
3 Devise a framework for early business education.
4 Establish a tradition of apprenticeship.
5 Encourage leading corporations to set a public standard of five days of off-the-job training.
6 Encourage further good practice in management by developing and promoting the larger corporations as trendsetters for the rest.
7 Develop mechanisms for the delivery of training.
8 Establish an official statistical and information base, statutorily backed if need be, so that the government and organisations can know what is happening.
9 Find ways to make individual study, reading and learning more corporately respectable.
10 Encourage firms to look for the best in recruiting, to give individuals early responsibility backed by appropriate help and training, and pay them well if they do well.

It would, however, be naïve not to imagine the vast complexities involved and the difficulties many companies would have to face in attempting to fulfil the above ten-point agenda.

CAREER AND MANAGEMENT DEVELOPMENT

A manager's career is divided into various stages: stages through which every manager will pass. During each stage, the goals the manager strives to achieve will change. At some stages, power and autonomy – goals associated with the manager's career – will be of primary importance, whereas at other stages, goals associated with comfort, relationships etc. will be of importance. The goals which appear to be most predominant during these stages, along with the personality of the manager, will affect the way his/her career develops. The more ambitious the manager, the more he/she will seek to achieve his/her work goals.

Changing jobs

The Institute of Management defines a job change as:

> *any move between jobs, or any major alteration to the content of your work duties and activities* (Inkson and Coe, 1992).

Surveys carried out by the IM between 1980 and 1992 found that the frequency with which managers are changing jobs is increasing. Changes in jobs within the same organisation were due to promotion, a change of duties or demotion. Changes in jobs between organisations created no change in status or a change for the better or the worse. The reasons given for changing jobs included:

- to develop one's career
- because of company reorganisation
- because of promotion and reward.

The most common reason for changing job was found to be for career development. More and more people are planning on, and are having careers that involve, working for several organisations during their working life. There are also people who wish to work in multiple occupations. According to Porter *et al.*, studies of graduates indicate that 50 per cent will change organisation within the first five years after graduation. Some of this turnover is unavoidable – it may represent people who take jobs for a short period only. However, Porter *et al.* consider that most of this turnover is controllable, as it stems from people who become dissatisfied with the way their careers are developing. They decide to try a similar job in a different organisation because their current job fails to provide them with the rewards and outcomes they expect. The job in the new organisation is perceived as being more likely to satisfy their needs. This turnover could, of course, be reduced if organisations gave prospective employees a better idea of what the job entailed and provided them with the rewards they wanted.

However, some of the turnover due to dissatisfaction is not controllable. Through their career, people change their goals and their concepts of how well they are capable of functioning in a particular environment (*see* Porter *et al.*, 1975). This causes them to feel that organisations no longer provide them with what they want. Other factors affecting this type of turnover are changes in the skills needed to function effectively in a given occupation: an example of this would be a reduction in a person's ability to perform a particular skill because of the effects of age. There may also be a change in their professional abilities, or a change in perception of the outcomes and rewards available in different organisations and occupations.

Difficulties with career progression

Inkson and Coe report that:

- Managers are changing jobs more often.
- Sideways or downward moves amongst managers are increasing.
- Upward managerial moves are declining.
- Managers are changing jobs for different reasons.
- Managers are increasingly subject to changes imposed by the employer.
- The 1992 recession has had a marked effect on job change.

They conclude that managerial career progress, slow in the 1980s, has slowed even more in the 1990s and, in some cases, even gone into reverse. Managers will need increasingly to take ownership of their own career and, in particular, their own portfolio of skills. They will need, above all, to be prepared for change and to seize it as an opportunity rather than view it as a threat.

The career development pattern

Porter and Lawler believe that people modify their careers as they pass through various periods in their lives. Super suggests there are four stages of development:

1 exploration of career possibilities (age 15–25)
2 establishment in an occupation (age 25–45)
3 holding one's own in the occupation (age 45–65)
4 decline or reduced work involvement (age 65+).

Maslow believes that the levels in his hierarchy of needs will evolve at different points in the life cycle. As the employee advances in his/her career, ego and autonomy needs become the most important. Porter and Lawler presume that as the employee moves towards the middle and end of his/her career, he/she will become more concerned with the need of self-actualisation.

Hunt considers how the priorities for various goals, such as comfort, structure, relationships, recognition, power and autonomy, change for an average manager during his/her career. He considers seven stages a manager is said to move through:*

Stage 1: Career launch (mid-20s to mid-30s). Hunt believes that a person's goal priorities shift very slowly during their twenties, but begin to accelerate once a permanent relationship has been formed. The career profile of the high flyer develops here.

Stage 2: The child-producing years (mid-20s to early 30s). The birth of a couple's child will change the goal priorities of the employee. High achievement goals may become dampened and comfort, physiological change and relationships become much more significant.

Stage 3: Career take off (30–38). Most high achievers will have reached a peak in career motivation by their thirties. More interesting work is found, and the dissatisfaction with work experienced in their twenties begins to disappear. However, in many cases, achievements have not yet been reached, careers are evolving and success is on its way.

Stage 4: Mid career (38–43). Here many people question what they have achieved and what they intend to do for the rest of their lives. These questions arise from both affluence and disillusionment with a career. The majority of employees cope fairly well during this period; however, a third of managers experience a period of intense and sustained depression. This period is most commonly known as a 'mid-career crisis'.

Stage 5: Career peak (mid-40s to mid-50s). For the two-thirds of managers who experience no mid-career problems, the profile of their thirties continues into their forties. However, the circumstances of the employees are now changing: their children have

* This extract is taken from *Managing People at Work* by J. W. Hunt and reproduced with the permission of the publishers, The Institute of Personnel and Development, IPD House, 35 Camp Road, Wimbledon SW19 4UX.

left or are preparing to leave home, careers are reaching their peak, and possessions and other signs of success are now available. It is at this stage that an employee's goals tend to be realigned. They tend to look outside the workplace for motivation through hobbies and other projects. During this period, relationships may be questioned and marriage may be questioned. Managers begin to see that they are no longer the up-and-coming stars of the organisation, and comfort, structure and relationship goals slowly become more important.

Stage 6: Approaching retirement (mid-50s to mid-60s). The goals tend to be ranked equally amongst high achievers in their mid fifties. Employees now believe comfort, structure and relationships justify as much attention as the previous, high-achievement goals of recognition, power, autonomy, creativity and growth. This period appears to be one of contentment – less stress, less aggravation and the approach of retirement.

Stage 7: Decline (mid-60s to mid-70s). Retirement signifies the first time in people's lives when they can do whatever they like when they want to. This period also represents another shift in goals. For the first time there is concern for comfort, structure and certainty, and relationships dominate the high achiever. The average ex-manager is now concerned less with achievement.

Career development programmes

Many organisations have, or are in the process of developing, systems of career planning and development. They believe these programmes are useful, as they allow individuals the opportunity to equip themselves with the skills necessary for their present and future jobs. According to Kakabadse *et al.*, by giving this training to its employees, the organisation is preparing them for promotion to positions of responsibility:

> *It makes sense to identify, prepare and nurture on the job people who will make significant contributions to the development of the organisation.*

Research carried out by Margerison and Kakabadse concluded that the following elements are very important in any career development programme:

1 **Identifying executive potential.** Although successful people place a great deal of importance on achieving results, few organisations test this need. It is believed that actual performance is a good indicator of an individual's drive and thus future performance.

2 **Accountability for profit and loss.** It is essential that employees who are moving towards senior positions are given opportunities to gain any experience necessary at the right time. Many organisations build these opportunities into their manpower planning systems. Positions are designed to give employees challenging jobs and overall accountability for running some part of the organisation. Wherever possible, profit centres are established, enabling young managers to gain experience of leading a team.

3 **Early personal leadership.** For an employee to move into higher positions within the organisation, he/she must learn how to allocate work, resolve differences of opinion, chair meetings, motivate people, resolve conflicts, and many other leadership activities. Organisational structures can be designed to facilitate the creation of leadership positions.

4 **Breadth of business experience.** Leaders need a broad view of the organisation. To learn how an integrated business should be run this view is achieved through experience in two or three functions.

5 **Jobs with challenge and support.** The survey showed that

executives respond to and learn from challenges... The jobs must allow the individual manager sufficient discretion to make decisions and get on with the job in his own way, while having the counsel and support of senior managers.

It is important that jobs be challenging, although not impossible, in order to motivate. Along with this, employees need regular feedback on their performance.

Establishing a management development function

Matheson recommends a central management development service or function that has a responsibility for determining and arriving at the management development policy of the organisation. The policy will impact on several issues, such as:

- performance appraisal
- potential appraisal
- selection
- remuneration
- termination
- training
- organisation review
- placement
- career planning
- communication structure and consultation.

His recommendations are that the management development policy should be arrived at with input from the managing director and board of directors, together with input of needs from line managers. A policy statement should contain certain basic facts about the company and its attitudes, these will include the following:

- What is to be developed and equally who is to be developed?
- Who will be responsible overall for the implementation of the policy?
- How will the implementation be monitored?
- What is the company's likely future growth and profit?
- What manpower will it need over the next five to ten years?
- Are finances and resources available for management development activities?
- Will the organisation look the same in five years' time?
- Are there going to be technological changes?
- Is there a need to rationalise the operational activities?
- What is the current level of management expertise and know-how?

Two examples of company management development statements, cited by Matheson, are shown in Exhibit 13.3.

Exhibit 13.3

Company management development statements

Company A

Management development is regarded as an integral and vital part of every manager's job and the company's policy is based on the following beliefs and assumptions:

- development as a function of line management
- all development is self-development and has to do with improving managerial performance both in the short and long term
- managerial development will require both individual and organisational development. This will involve changing the environment – such as structure, salary scales, job contents – and may require influencing individuals' attitudes or improving individual abilities.

Company B

Management development is regarded as a series of processes, activities and events in the company which are designed to improve the performance now and in the future to provide for future management needs. The main board requirements of a management development programme are:

- a means of defining results expected from managers
- continuous improvement of management performance
- training for tomorrow's job as well as today's at reasonable cost
- a means acceptable to managers themselves of judging their performance
- a flexible succession programme for staffing the business in the future
- motivation of managers and provision of suitable rewards for them
- improvement of communications within the business
- secure and retrain recruits of suitable calibre.

Source: Matheson, C.S., 'Human resource management: Establishing the management development function', *The British Journal of Administrative Management.*

W.H. Smith's approach to developing senior managers

Nixon and Pitts developed a programme for the development of senior managers in W.H. Smith. In their article they describe the objectives of the programme as follows:

1 To identify the key changes occurring in the general business environment and specifically those affecting your situation.
2 To develop a vision of how your part of the business will meet those challenges within the requirements of a large, multinational organisation.
3 To develop practical strategies and plans to realise that vision and the confidence to deal with obstacles and set-backs as they arise.
4 To identify the skills needed to develop the potential of those around you and to create a high-quality relationship at all levels.
5 To develop a support structure to enable you to continue a long-term change and assist others to produce similar quality.
6 To identify and work on your personal development needs as a key issue in the growth of your part of the business and your teams.

The key issues that were agreed by the participants were:

- Examine what is going on in the external business environment.
- Stand back and look at my business.
- Understand how to manage time and increasingly huge pressures.
- Learn how to handle change.
- Develop my ability to get the best out of my team.
- Get feedback from other successful managers.
- Get encouragement to take risks and try new things.
- Learn how to bring more enjoyment into my work and take better care of myself.

The programme was conducted through workshops to provide an empowering structure to help the managers decide which changes they wanted to bring about and to provide support in implementing them. The workshops focused on the issues of:

- their vision for the business
- examining the business environment
- creating strategies to achieve their vision
- identifying and working on key issues
- plans and commitments to action
- recreating the climate
- developing long-term action plans, including support and support groups
- making a personal commitment to learning in a new way.

The initial sessions set out to create a climate in which the managers felt they could trust, open up and talk about what really mattered. This was achieved partly by contracting with them on the desired set-up of the workshop. The sort of things the managers said, and the kind of climate they sought in their organisations, were as follows:

- frankness/honesty – being able to say what I really think
- exciting, fun, humour
- as much giving as receiving
- constructive criticism
- encouraging and challenging
- appreciation
- listened to
- safe – total confidentiality
- respect for differences, tolerance
- time to reflect or to read
- we take a break when we get bogged down
- exercise and time to relax
- balance
- to go at my own pace
- not afraid – not holding back from tackling difficulties or disagreements.

Source: Nixon, B. and Pitts, G., 'W.H. Smith develops a new approach to developing senior managers', *Industrial and Commercial Training*, MCB University Press, Vol. 23, No. 6, pp. 3–10, 1991.

MAKING USE OF A MENTOR

Previously mentioned was the importance of acquiring and using a mentor. However, it is wishful thinking to expect mentoring relationships to develop by themselves. Zey, in studying the mentor situation at AT&T, Johnson & Johnson, Merrill Lynch and Federal Express, found evidence of the need to have implemented policies to develop actively mentor programmes. In his article, Zey states that mentor programmes should be considered from every angle before their implementation, and that the factors that should be considered are:

- who should participate?
- matching the mentor and the protégé
- length of the programme
- mode and frequency of interaction
- mentor responsibilities.

Exhibit 13.4 depicts the stages a typical mentor programme might include.

Management development to the millennium

The Institute of Management considers that the way ahead for management development as we approach the millennium is to appreciate that, in order for the manager to cope with 21st-century work, he/she will need to be adaptable and knowledgeable, rather than mainly task trained. Job functions will be shared and job titles will be blurred. Narrow functionalism is to be avoided and managers will be required to become multi-skilled and develop skills that are of use at certain points in their careers. Valuable transferable skills could include improved computer literacy, proficiency in at least one other language and communication techniques.

The report concludes that individual managers, in particular, will need to anticipate and adapt more than ever before. They will be required and expected to take the initiative for development, which is different from the more paternalistic approach of the 1980s. Work will take on a new perspective in the lives of people, and it will be limiting or dangerous to insist on a single source of full-time employment (*see* Ashridge Management Research Group, 1995).

ASSESSING PEOPLE

Traditional methods of assessment (review, appraisal) to provide people with feedback usually take the form of the manager assessing a subordinate.

More exciting and progressive approaches to assessment are concerned with managers and subordinates assessing themselves, and subordinates assessing their managers. The idea behind these forms of assessment is to compare what managers and those managed think of each other. This should reveal the main problems that each perceives and the common problems that exist.

The types of questions asked of subordinates are, should they:

- be more co-operative?
- work harder?
- take more responsibility?
- be less disruptive?

Exhibit 13.4

Stages in a typical mentor programme

1 Development

The first stage of any form of mentoring programme should be the programme development period in which the goals, criteria of participation, and mechanisms of interaction are specifically spelt out.

2 Notification

The implementing department should issue a memo notifying the target audience of the existence of a formal mentoring programme, the benefits to the company and the length of the programme.

3 Selection

All interested candidates should be interviewed individually, appraised on the specifics of the programme and evaluated according to the set criteria.

4 Orientation

All the senior and junior participants chosen should then attend an orientation meeting to facilitate communication information about the high and low expectations of the programme.

5 Pairing

Some mechanisms for matching the protégé with the right mentor should be established.

6 Implementation of participants' actual mentoring meetings at set times and places

7 Evaluation

The bottom-line concern in evaluating a programme is the extent to which it has met its goals, e.g. management training and development. The better you anticipate potential conflicts and pitfalls, the smoother and more effective your programme will be. Based on the experience of existing programmes, the following seven suggestions are offered:

1 Communicate the programme goals to all participants.
2 Enlist the co-operation of the entire organisation.
3 Make the selection processes as autonomous as possible.
4 Ensure that mentors are committed to the project.
5 Permit withdrawal from the programme.
6 Continually evaluate the programme.
7 Give the programme a long-term test period.

Source: Zey, M.G., 'Mentor programmes: Making the right moves', *Personnel Journal,* February 1985. All rights reserved.

- be more punctual?
- be more reliable?
- be more respectful?
- be more adaptable (flexible)?
- be more loyal?

This should be followed by investigation to ascertain what can be done to assist. For example:

- more understanding given, listen to problems
- more communication
- more training
- better facilities
- improved working conditions
- better working environment
- improved safety
- seek opinion
- better pay
- less hours
- more job variety
- more interesting work
- more holidays
- improved chances of upgrading/promotion.

The types of questions asked of managers are concerned with the following abilities:

- awareness of situations and political awareness
- knowledge of job and competence
- approachability
- willingness to listen, adjust and adapt
- decisiveness, firmness and ability to take action
- communicative, instructive
- considerate, thoughtful, understanding, kind, helpful.

The question that then needs to be asked is what could be done to help the managers and their subordinates?

Upward feedback/appraisal

Upward feedback/appraisal is a form of assessment practised by progressive companies, such as Federal Express, BP, W.H. Smith and Midland Cosmetics in Birmingham, as a means of improving the quality and style of the leadership of their managers. Upward feedback/appraisal is used in addition to downward feedback, which may be considered insufficient. Employees are asked how well management serves them and what they think of their boss. Each person in a team is asked how well their manager performs in areas such as the following:

- behaves in a way that the team respects
- makes well-judged decisions
- helps to reduce uncertainty
- publicly supports and represents the team
- delegates work effectively
- gives both regular and constructive feedback
- provides help, guidance and training
- helps with difficult problems
- is not sarcastic
- is not overpowering
- actively listens

- is open and honest
- is approachable
- has good judgement.

Taking this approach, the feedback report is not made public and the staff are encouraged to sort out problems with their manager. The staff are allowed ownership of the problems and encouraged to develop their creativity and provide ideas. The companies using this approach consider they have developed an environment in which those managers admitting to weakness found in their assessment are seen as being strong and with much potential. Other managers assist in the roles of coach, teacher or mentor.

Federal Express has used and developed this approach over 15 years. The company reinforces the values expressed by the system through extra pay and bonuses based on good feedback. The object is to change the behaviour in a manager by being objective and not making snap judgements with little evidence to support them. The company is careful not to criticise personality. Federal Express's experience with upward feedback shows that:

- it needs commitment from the top
- managers learn about themselves
- benefits arise from coaching by more successful colleagues
- the team benefits as a result
- it provides managers with help and guidance
- teams feel empowered and encouraged to make comments.

W.H. Smith's 360° feedback process

A 360° feedback is a process developed by W.H. Smith as a means of providing an 'all round' view of an individual's performance at work against a set of key factors. It differs from the traditional appraisal or feedback process where the capability of individuals is reviewed based only on judgements from their manager or the person appraising them. The 360° feedback process places importance on understanding how an individual is performing at work by seeking views from all the key groups with which he/she interacts. These groups will probably include the individual's peers, subordinates, internal customers, manager, and, just as importantly, the individual him/herself. Direct and indirect reports may also be used as sources of feedback.

Key factors of the feedback process

To help understand how effective an individual's contribution is, the 360° feedback process provides objective feedback on performance against the following key factors:

- business goals
- professional development objectives
- technical skills and knowledge
- competences.

Achievements required

The achievements required are concerned with specific elements of department or divisional plans and the achievement of agreed objectives, derived from individual key accountabilities of the roles involved and achievement of agreed levels of internal or external customer service. Other achievements concern specific agreed objectives relating to the individual's acquisition and performance of 'sets of key behaviours' of both existing and new technical skills or knowledge needed for a particular role.

Key behaviours

The sets of key behaviours or competences form an important element of the 360° feedback process, and the senior management population uses the same set of 'generic' competences during this process. The key competences are associated with excellent performance within a team. Measurement of key behaviours helps to establish how well individuals are contributing to the effectiveness of their team, department and business. This process is depicted in Table 13.1.

The benefits

The 360° feedback process specifically aims to:

- support and promote the introduction of a new management style
- recognise and reward excellent performance
- increase understanding of how well an individual is performing against a whole range of key factors
- highlight areas where an individual's performance may have improved at the expense of effective performance in another key area
- increase the objectivity of appraisal discussions
- encourage individual ownership of feedback on performance
- highlight specific areas where personal development planning should be focused.

Table 13.1 Questions and requirements for the 360° feedback process

Questions	Requirements
What is the business's purpose?	Business vision
What is my department's purpose?	Department vision
What part does my team play?	Team mission
What part do I play?	Individual key accountabilities
What elements or key factors of my performance will be measured?	Business goals Development objectives Technical skills Competences
How will I know if I'm being effective?	Performance review Coaching

Source: W.H. Smith Group plc.

Maintaining confidentiality

One practical issue that needs to be resolved to enable the system to work effectively is that of maintaining confidentiality, and here a 'third party' independent administrator can be asked to summarise the feedback received from all sources relating to a particular individual.

Integration with other feedback processes

The 360° feedback process is not intended to usurp feedback mechanisms which are currently in place but to supplement or reinforce them.

Selection, development and career planning

Providing feedback on performance of important management competences can be used to underpin selection, development and career planning.

SUMMARY

● Addressing issues of work lifestyle can assist with job enjoyment and satisfaction, career development, making the best use of one's talents and giving the best to the organisation. Work lifestyle can be assessed by examining the following factors: use and expression of talents and abilities; rewards, recognition and status; sense of achievement, challenge and self-worth; liking the nature of the work and its environment; clashes with personal lifestyle and limitations.

● Managers and students of management need to appreciate the nature and importance of management skills, which can be classified as: personal traits; general management skills; functional management skills, and technical and expert skills. The skills and competences predicted for the manager in the year 2001 are: organisational sensitivity; being strongly tuned into the external environment; good task skills; empathy/sensitivity to others; strategic thinking; taking a responsibility for personal development.

● A structured approach which can be used to assess and develop oneself as a manager is to consider: your clarity of vision; your main management skill gaps; necessary training and education; your management development and career opportunities; acquiring and using a mentor; using your mentor for advice on skill gaps and development of your career plan.

● With regard to management education, training and development, Britain, in comparison with the USA, West Germany, France and Japan, has neglected her managerial stock. Britain needs to do more to develop her managers and to do it more systematically.

● Managerial career progress, slow in the 1980s, has slowed dramatically in the 1990s. The career development pattern for the average manager is typically: career launch (mid-20s to mid-30s); the child-producing years (mid-20s to early-30s); career take off (30–38); mid career (38–43); career peak (mid-40s to mid-50s); approaching retirement (mid-50s to mid-60s); decline (mid-60s to mid-70s).

- Career development programmes are valuable to both the individual and the organisation. Research concludes that the following elements are very important in any career development programme: identifying executive potential; accountability for profit and loss; early personal leadership; breadth of business experience; jobs with challenge and support.

- Organisations can benefit from establishing their own management development function.

- The importance, benefits and process of acquiring and using a mentor need to be realised. AT&T, Johnson & Johnson, Merrill Lynch and Federal Express found evidence of the need to have implemented policies to develop actively mentor programmes. Stages in a typical mentor programme are: development, notification, selection, orientation, pairing, implementation of participants' actual mentoring meetings at set times and places, and finally, evaluation.

- Traditional methods of assessment or feedback are where the capability of an individual is reviewed based only on judgements from their manager or the person appraising them. More progressive approaches to assessment are concerned with managers and subordinates assessing themselves, and subordinates assessing their managers. The idea behind these forms of assessment is to compare what managers and those managed think of each other.

- Upward feedback/appraisal is a form of assessment practised by progressive companies as a means of improving the quality and style of the leadership of their managers. Employees are asked how well management serves them and what they think of their boss.

- 360° feedback is a process being developed by W.H. Smith which provides an 'all round' view of an individual's performance at work. The process seeks views from the individual's peers, subordinates, internal customers, manager, and, just as importantly, the individual him/herself.

REVIEW AND DISCUSSION QUESTIONS

1 Discuss the nature and importance of the skills and competences required of today's manager and give your opinion of the requirements that will likely be made of the manager in the future.

2 Outline the important elements in a career development programme and explain how a management development function can assist with its implementation.

3 What benefits can acquiring and using mentors bring to both an organisation and its managers?

4 Explain the rationale and methods behind some of the more progressive approaches to assessment.

ASSIGNMENTS

1 A company has hired you to develop a mentor programme for it. Present an outline of the presentation that the senior executives have asked you to make on the main features of such a programme and how it is to be realised.

2 Consider yourself in the role of a consultant requested to brief the senior management of a company on the rationale and benefits of an upward feedback/appraisal scheme or another progressive scheme of assessment in the company. Outline the important elements of such a scheme.

REFERENCES

Adair, J., *Effective Leadership*, Pan Books Ltd, London, 1988.

Ashridge Management Research Group, *Management Development to the Millennium: The new priorities*, The Institute of Management, Corby, Northants, 1995.

Aspen Business Communications, *Are Managers Getting the Message*? Institute of Management research report, Corby, Northants, 1992. These data were collected through a structured and precoded questionnaire sent to 3000 individual members of the IM in December 1992. The sample was selected to reflect a spread of management levels, types of organisation and geographical location. The response rate was 24 per cent.

Brearley, A. and Sewell, D., *The Ernst & Young Management Self-Assessment System*, The Controller of Her Majesty's Stationery Office, London, 1990.

Clemmer, J and McNeil, A., *Leadership Skills for Every Manager*, Piatkus, London, 1990.

Constable, J. and McCormick, R., *The Making of British Managers*, BIM/CBI, 1987.

DHL International (UK), *Finding the Time: A survey of managers' attitudes to using and managing time*, Institute of Management (IM) research report, Corby, Northants, 1994. The research was conducted in September 1994, and the views of over 1250 managers were obtained from a postal questionnaire sent to a random sample of 4000 individual IM members. This represents a response rate of 32 per cent.

Drucker, P. F., *The Practice of Management*, Butterworth-Heinemann, Oxford, 1994.

Guirdham, N., *Interpersonal Skills at Work*, Prentice-Hall, New York, 1990.

Handy, C., Gowe, I., Gordon, C., Randleson, C. and Moloney, M., *The Making of Managers: A report on management education, training and development in the USA, West Germany, France, Japan and the UK*, prepared for publication by the National Economic Development Office (NEDO) on behalf of the National Economic Development Council (NEDC), the Manpower Services Commission (MSC) and the British Institute of Management (BIM), 1987.

Hunt, J.W., *Managing People at Work*, 2nd edn, IPM, London, 1986.

Inkson, K. and Coe, T., *Are Career Ladders Disappearing*? An Institute of Management report investigating all the job changes experienced over 13 years, from 1980 to 1992, by a sample of more than 800 managers who were members of the Institute of Management.

Kakabadse, A., Ludlow, R. and Vinnicombe, S., *Working in Organisations*, Penguin, London, 1988.

Management Charter Initiative, *Management Development in the UK*, 1992.

Margerison, C. and Kakabadse, A. 'Top executives: Addressing their management development needs', *Leadership & Organisational Development Journal*, Vol. 9, No. 4, pp. 17–21, 1988.

Matheson, C.S., 'Human resource management: Establishing the management development function', *The British Journal of Administrative Management*, April/May 1992.

Megginson, L.C., Mosley, D.C. and Pietri, P.H., *Management: Concepts and Applications*, Harper Collins, New York, 1992.

Mullins, L.J., *Management and Organisational Behaviour*, 3rd edn, Pitman Publishing, London, 1993.

Nixon, B. and Pitts, G., 'W.H. Smith develops a new approach to developing senior managers', *Industrial and Commercial Training*, MCB University Press, Vol. 23, No. 6, pp. 3–10, 1991.

Oates, P., *Leadership: The art of delegation*, Century Business, London, 1993.

Oldcorn, R., *Management: Skills and function*, Pan Books Ltd, London, 1988.

Porter, L., Lawler, E. and Hackman, J., *Behaviour in Organisations*, McGraw-Hill, London, 1975.

Rees, D., *The Skills of Management*, Routledge, London, 1988.

Stemp, P., *Are You Managing?*, Industrial Society, London, 1988.

Stewart, R., *Contrasts in Management*, McGraw-Hill, London, 1976.

Super, D. E., *The Psychology of Careers: An introduction to vocational development*, Harper & Row, New York, 1957.

Taylor, W. J and Watling, T. F, *The Basic Arts of Management*, Business Books, London, 1972.

Thamhain, H.J., 'Developing the skills you need', *Research-Technology Management Journal*, Vol. 35, No. 2, pp. 42–7, 1992.

Torrington, D. and Weightman, J., *The Business of Management*, Prentice Hall, London, 1985.

The Training of Managers: A Summary of the IM Research Report on Management Training in the UK. The full report is based on the responses of 2051 managers to a written questionnaire, which was mailed to 6000 IM members in January 1992.

Zey, M.G., 'Mentor programmes: Making the right moves', *Personnel Journal*, February 1985.

CHAPTER 14

Continuous improvement

OBJECTIVES

The objectives of this chapter are to:

- understand what continuous improvement is together with the activities conducted to achieve it
- understand the management procedure involved in improvement programmes
- appreciate the reasons for, the value of, and the use of, procedures and standards
- understand that everyone's involvement is essential and appreciate the main improvement issues
- be aware of where managers should place their emphasis in order to promote the cycle of continuous improvement
- consider the types of skills required for improvement
- consider the hierarchy of objectives sought in pursuing improvement
- appreciate the effectiveness of continuous improvement groups and suggestion schemes
- appreciate the effectiveness of improvement teams for continuous improvement and the major features of team improvement activities.

WHAT IS CONTINUOUS IMPROVEMENT?

Many companies now employ the latest technology and computerised systems. The managers are well educated and trained, and are able to plan the acquisition of new equipment or get the new design through production to the customer sooner using the latest computer-aided technology, rapid prototyping devices and flexible manufacturing systems (FMS).

In the same companies, management information is not shared and the workforce and union detest and mistrust the management. There is constant 'fire fighting', unused equipment, too many people telling others what to do, too much space, too much inventory and scrap.

What is happening is that the whole organisation has not learned how efficiently to add value to its processes in order to satisfy the customer. The organisations that have learned do so through a process of ongoing improvements which aggregate over a period of time to provide visible proof that things are getting better. This is the process of continuous improvement, which the Japanese call 'kaizen'. It focuses on employee involvement by putting people first.

The practice of continuous improvement aims to improve methods, making them simpler and safer. Mechanisms for continuous improvement include suggestion schemes, continuous improvement teams and individuals who are empowered to suggest and make improvements. The emphasis on where continuous improvement efforts should be directed should reflect the strategic needs of the business. At all levels the business should support continuous improvement. Senior management should emphasise its importance and become involved in promoting it and practising it through communications, training, meetings, open days, displays etc. The intention should be to foster an environment where everyone is encouraged and supported to come up with ideas for improvement which can be assessed with a view to their implementation. Implemented improvements which work should be recorded in terms of their procedures and any new standards they introduce.

A fundamental improvement activity which is effective, but which is often overlooked because it is simple and at the shopfloor level, is that of good housekeeping and workplace organisation.

HOUSEKEEPING AND WORKPLACE ORGANISATION

Improved housekeeping and workplace organisation should be among the first steps that management take in improving factory operations. The management's attention to improving housekeeping reflects its general attitude towards work on the shopfloor. Some of the symptoms of lack of shopfloor management in traditionally-run companies may easily be detected on the shopfloor, for example:

- tools not stored properly
- swarf from machines not cleared
- disorganised work tables
- inspection points not indicated
- machines not cleaned
- personal items not stored away
- rubbish on the floor
- people doing very troublesome and monotonous work
- too much inventory
- parts stored directly on the floor
- dirty toilets and social areas.

A better organised workplace, where people's desire to improve is encouraged, can bring many benefits, e.g. keeping tools closer to the machine and avoiding clutter so that materials can be moved more easily; having clean floors and machines to improve safety and expose problems such as oil leaks; getting rid of redundant or scrap material because it takes up space and causes unnecessary record keeping and carrying costs. Ultimately, these types of improvements all combined have a positive effect on the operator's morale, management labour relations, and assist in getting the product to the customer more quickly, more reliably and at a lower cost to the company.

The main tasks that should be considered in the workplace are:

- how to improve and maintain quality and reduce defects
- how to reduce cost

- how to improve productivity and meet delivery deadlines
- how to increase safety
- how to improve interpersonal relationships
- how to make the job easier.

In approaching these tasks it helps to consider the problems there may be with the following *four M's* of the workplace:

1 **Me:** am I doing things wrong, could what I do be improved?
2 **Machine:** is the capability of the machine adequate, is it maintained properly, is it efficient, does it need replacing?
3 **Material:** is it the right grade, does it arrive on time, have we got too much?
4 **Method:** could the way the job is done be improved?

Many successful improvements are the result of identifying waste and eliminating it.

ELIMINATING WASTE

After years of improvement activities, Toyota identified seven prominent types of waste (discussed in Chapter 6, p. 196):

- waste from overproduction
- waste of waiting time
- transportation waste
- processing waste
- inventory waste
- waste of motion
- waste from product defects.

There are less obvious forms of waste due to being overzealous on tracking orders and costs, as well as unnecessary or too detailed monitoring. Schonberger comments on waste:

> *The worst kind of waste is the waste of not realising what people can offer and not utilising their talent.*

Asking why as many times as it takes

For each factor – poor housekeeping, lack of workplace organisation and waste – you must ask the question 'Why?' and search for the true cause. What you intuitively feel is the cause may not be the whole story; the true cause is usually hidden. You may wish to make use of the cause-and-effect diagram, Fig 14.1, to check back through the different 'generations' of cause until you find the true source of the problem.

MANAGING CONTINUOUS IMPROVEMENT

Discipline and hard work are essential to maintaining continuous improvement. To manage this process company-wide, the following improvement procedure should be adopted.

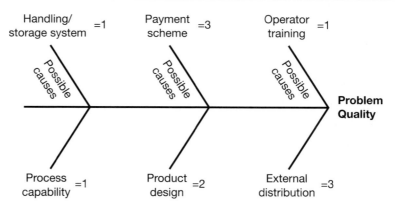

Rank causes and investigate areas to discover what issues and problems need to be faced.

3 = very damaging
2 = damaging
1 = could be improved

Fig 14.1 Cause-and-effect diagram

Identify the problem

The quality of an improvement depends on how deeply you dig to find the root cause. If you immediately jump to a conclusion about the cause, your solutions will most likely produce only temporary relief of the symptoms of the problem. When formulating ideas for making improvements there may be many possible solutions, and the knack is to select the best answer from the different possibilities that are proposed. One way of doing this is to use brainstorming to obtain people's ideas. When you brainstorm, don't put a damper on other people's ideas, but remain open minded. From the range of ideas presented, the feasibility of each one must now be checked by considering factors such as the difficulty of implementation and the cost, time, and labour required. These factors need to be balanced against the benefits of implementation, the adaptability to other situations, and the expected life of the benefits.

If you are relatively new to making continuous improvements, it is wise to start with small improvements. Start by looking for examples of poor housekeeping, lack of workplace organisation and waste that are sure to be around you. The important thing is to identify problems close to you and solve these routine problems one by one.

To assist in understanding the current situation the following tools are available:

- pareto chart – shows the distribution of factors contributing to a problem or situation
- cause-and-effect diagram – provides a systematic and ordered examination of the causes of the problem
- bar graph – makes numbers more meaningful
- checksheet – helps to make a graph based on available data
- scatter diagram – helps to check the correlation among prepared data
- histogram – helps to check the frequency distribution.

Plan

Make it clear what the improvement seeks to achieve. State the objectives that need to be met in the form of a clear statement which, if possible, is quantified and has a time frame; e.g. 'improve the level of downtime in the process area from the current five hours per week to less than one hour per week by next September'. Decide on the means by which the objectives can be achieved.

Consult those who will be involved in the change and develop plans which show what needs to be done, when it needs to be done and with what resources. Communicate this information to those who will be involved.

Implement

Get the approval of the person in charge before implementing the improvement. Encourage people's involvement and get their co-operation to organise the best way to execute the plan. If the improvement is straightforward to implement, get the suggester to implement it.

Follow up

Check the results. It is important to verify if your improvement plan is executed as expected and achieving the desired objectives. Check if the objectives have been achieved as planned, because it is possible for an improvement plan to have detrimental effects.

If the objectives have not been met then analyse why. The plans may need modifying or countermeasures may need to be developed. If improvements have been made, record the procedure and any new standards that may have been established. Unless changes in tasks or improvements in machines and tools are publicised, written in work standard sheets and made familiar to all workers, the improved procedures or equipment can easily be forgotten, neglected, and gradually replaced by the past practices. In other words *make the improvements stick*.

The exact benefits of an improvement are never known until it is implemented. Understandably, more and more companies are using the 'implemented suggestion' system. That is, ideas must be put into effect before credit or a reward is given. If possible, get the employees involved to check the actual results of their suggestions. This way they will learn a lot more about suggesting and making improvements. With the learning that has taken place, is it possible and worthwhile to improve further, or to challenge a new problem, and repeat the improvement procedure again?

Practising the discipline of the improvement procedure means attention and hard work on the part of the management, the team and individuals. If this discipline is not practised, the situation will revert to one of waiting for things to go wrong before changes are made. That is the practice of 'fire fighting' where there is really very little time for proper planning and any progress will be slower and more haphazard. If the improvement procedure can be spread through all areas and established at all levels, the whole organisation will experience a big improvement in its overall performance.

The role of the manager

The role of the manager in work improvement is to:

- show a positive attitude
- give hints to workers
- listen to workers' problems
- make improvement targets clear
- plan competitions and games
- promote involvement
- increase problem-solving capability
- put proposals into practice quickly
- give public recognition.

Exhibit 14.1 provides an example of continuous improvement at Caradon Mira.

Exhibit 14.1

Continuous improvement at Caradon Mira

At Caradon Mira we have a number of old index cam auto bar lathes. Under current legislation they are too noisy and emit oil vapour and fumes. They were run with large component batches.

A cycle of improvements has taken place:

1 Certain machines in the main machine shop were moved into a separate area alongside the machine shop, so that noise and fumes could be isolated.
2 A cell was created using machines and other processes to complete machining of parts.
3 A team of people was appointed to the cell.
4 Cell planning changed from manufacturing orders to JIT schedules, and simplified reporting without paperwork.
5 The batch quantities have been continually reviewed and have been halved on two occasions, and so the batch quantity is a quarter of the initial quantity.

Although improvements have been taking place, a project to replace these with CNC machines has progressed and new machines were delivered between March and May.

The continuous improvement will start again. The cell team is proud of its achievements and will continue to improve the performance of its cell.

Summary

Lead time:	5 weeks to 2 days
Batch quantity:	1 to 1/4
Machine shop scrap:	Down 75 per cent in two years
Delivery performance to schedule:	98 per cent

Source: Adapted from Pummell, D., 'Changing the manufacturing and people culture or can 2 + 2 = 5?', *Control*, August/September, pp. 29–33, 1994, The Institute of Operations Management, Coventry.

PROCEDURES AND STANDARDS

The need for procedures and standards

The reasons for having procedures and standards should be known. They can be a yardstick to measure performance, or for safety or legal reasons. They become the basis for improvement in quality, delivery, flexibility and cost. They also impact on the people who have to work to the standards and procedures in terms of the way they are expected to perform their tasks, the resources they have to work with, the timescales, their safety and morale.

Some of the reasons for setting standards are:

- to establish standards of performance and safety
- as a basis for improvement
- to establish and clarify procedures
- to educate and train
- to act as a performance yardstick
- to facilitate repeatability and consistency.

The value of procedures and standards

The relationship between operating procedures and their effect on methods and people can be used to measure how much value has been added. One way of doing this is to measure the actual performance against the performance standard that has been established. Value has been added if actual performance is greater than planned performance. If the reverse is true then problems exist. Such problems may be:

- excess variability and unpredictability
- lack of awareness of standards or unclear procedures
- scrap or rework
- poor safety
- poor training
- lack of discipline or responsibility
- no fault finding.

By working on these problems, or eliminating them, the workers can continually add value to their own work centres. Striving to meet standards, beating them and then improving the level of standards is a sure way to improve continually the organisation as a whole. To do this requires the capabilities of those involved to be adequate and continually improved. To this end, the procedures and standards can be used to train employees.

A system for managing standards

When changes have been made or new methods or systems have been introduced, they should be recorded in terms of the standards, the aims, and the procedures and checks that need to be maintained. It is important to follow this discipline because these records make clear what the procedures are and provide a baseline from which performance can be measured. This acts as the basis for improvement.

A system needs to be established which manages the establishment of procedures and setting of standards. In the first place, it should be decided in which areas it is important to have procedures and standards. The effort spent on maintaining or creating procedures and standards should be weighed against the reasons they are necessary and the benefits they bring.

It is necessary that people can easily access existing records and that they are made aware of which particular standards refer to them and their environment. The operating procedures should be clearly defined and relate to particular performance objectives such as cost, quality and delivery. Also the procedures should record how they may affect the people who work to them; say in terms of their legal position, safety and morale etc. A standard review procedure is necessary to check the state of standards; i.e. are they applicable and up to date? Do they contain the appropriate level of detail? It may be that the standards have too many parameters with key parameters poorly defined. Are the standards comprehensive enough? The standards may be too general and it may not be clear who does what.

New standards will be continually required and the reason for and place of these standards should be recorded. Thus the priorities for creating the standards will become known and a timescale for their preparation can then be established.

Making use of procedures and standards

There are various approaches to clarifying the content of standards and making sure that they are practised and reviewed. These can range from the use of visual displays and slogans to providing education and training on the setting and use of standards, and establishing improvement groups to improve on them. It is up to the managers and team leaders to provide an atmosphere that fosters such improvement and attempts to involve everybody. Managers will have to adopt a hands-on approach and understand people. They will need to ensure that their workers are provided with adequate resources and tools in order to implement the methods which, if satisfactory, will become the new standards.

The process of using procedures and standards can be summarised as follows:

1 Analyse operations and standardise work procedures.
2 Discover the problems.
3 Develop improved methods.
4 Implement the methods.
5 If satisfactory, establish as standard.

There is no doubt that the ability of a person to practise certain standards and seek further improvements on them reflects the value of that person, and this potential in all the people in the organisation in turn reflects the total potential value of the organisation.

OBTAINING INVOLVEMENT

To maintain and improve implemented suggestions company-wide, everyone's involvement is essential and everyone therefore must know what is to be done and how they can work with others to achieve the targets that have been set.

For example Zytec, a producer of power supplies for computing equipment and a 1991 Baldridge quality prize winner, obtains involvement by getting 20 per cent of its workforce, from all corners of the firm, to share in the development of its five year strategic plan. It even asks a few key suppliers and customers to comment on the plan. Then, every employee and team has a role in translating the plan into action elements with measurable yearly goals (*see* Bemowski, 1991).

If involvement is occurring in a company then the following signs should be evident:

- suggestions being made
- evidence of housekeeping and organisation
- meetings both formal and informal
- management presence and participation in events
- training and education provided
- use made of procedures and standards.

It is of tremendous help if the main improvement issues are kept at the forefront of people's minds through the use of bulletins, newsletters, meetings, performance boards, charts, graphs and pictures. The objectives being sought in each of the areas of quality, cost, delivery, safety, and morale (known as QCDSM measures) should be made clear. For example:

- **Quality:** quality norms, upper quality limits, number of rejects, number of customer complaints, amount of rework and defects
- **Cost:** production, overtime, stock cost, floor space
- **Delivery:** late deliveries, lead time, dependability percentage, volume of production, sales volume
- **Safety:** accident rate, accident types, problem areas
- **Morale:** absenteeism rate, turnover rate, problem priorities.

Table 14.1 shows a performance board which can be used to state the objectives being pursued, how well the area is performing, the main problems and issues, together with the action being taken and associated timescale.

Table 14.1 Peformance board

Objective	Performance	Problem issues	Comments	Action	Timescale (start date)
Safety	Frequency of accidents increasing; limit exceeded	Excessive material traffic flow	Suggestions on space and handling being sought		
Cost	Excessive overtime bookings	Backlogs in particular areas	Possible bottleneck or scheduling problem		

By referring to its respective performance board, each area or team can measure its progress in relation to the objectives set. It can then plan how to take any necessary action.

Whichever mechanism is used to inform people about the objectives and their progress, employee involvement will only be spurred if:

- people have been involved in establishing the objectives
- the objectives are measurable
- the objectives are, in the main, controllable by the group
- the number and difficulty of the objectives match the capabilities of the group
- people are given feedback
- people are recognised for their attempts
- people are given positive criticism with advice when things go wrong.

Establishing, then maintaining and improving standards requires everybody's involvement. To promote the cycle of continuous improvement managers need to work, in particular, on:

- **Creating the right environment for making continuous improvement:** promoting the value of continuous improvement and giving recognition and rewards to those who make improvements.

- **Promoting involvement:** getting people to use their brains and tapping people's creativity, which may require them rethinking and possibly changing their roles and responsibilities. Exhibit 14.2 provides an example of a progressive company that promotes people involvement.

- **Increasing problem-solving capability:** upgrading each individual's problem-solving skill base as they learn to bear more responsibility.

Exhibit 14.2

Self-imposing improvement at Kimberly-Clark Coleshill Mill

Kimberly-Clark Coleshill Mill was voted 1995 Process Industry Highly Commended in the *Management Today* Best Factory Awards. Its business is toilet paper manufacture and its task is to convert waste paper into toilet paper for sale in the highly-competitive market. The company's outstanding features are empowerment and continuous improvement. It is clear that many of Coleshill Mill's employees would be made more than welcome in a lot of other companies. Former electrician Jeff Williamson, operator on one of the state-of-the-art 1.5 million packing lines, is often to be found with a wiring diagram working on another *self-imposing improvement*. Last year, when the unit's electric motors were burning out every couple of months, Williamson traced the cause to oil leaking from gear boxes above the motor. He managed to eliminate the problem by turning them all upside down. Former mechanic and fellow operator Gareth Jones sums up their task: 'We clean the line when it's dirty, fix it when it's broken and feed it when it's hungry.'

Source: Process Industry Best Factory Awards 1995, *Management Today*, Haymarket Publications.

DEVELOPING THE SKILLS

Having to cope with a rapidly-changing business environment is the norm for many companies. Thus an important part of the overall strategy of a progressive company should be the enabling process by which the organisation can respond with more appropriate strategic options for the new environment. One way of achieving this is to raise the overall capability of the organisation through emphasis on three types of skills:

1 **Skills related to maintenance.** These are the skills needed to maintain standards, follow procedures correctly, and complete the job on time without accident or defects.

2 **Skills related to improvement.** These are the skills needed to identify problems and follow through to solve them. With respect to individuals, they relate to the development of analytical and workmanship skills and the move towards self-improvement, even under difficult situations. Where groups are formed, the people in them will need to learn how to utilise their collective wisdom and work together as a team to make improvements. Where management skills are concerned there is a need for managers to look at themselves and address any problems they have with respect to managing themselves. Everyone in the organisation needs to think of ways to simplify and develop processes and systems.

3 **Skills related to innovation.** If the need is for the organisation to be an innovator or a leader then the focus needs to be on the skill level of innovation-related jobs, such as the development of strategies, new products, new manufacturing processes, or developing new skills and upgrading the organisation's capabilities.

Managing skills

An important role of managers is to upgrade people's skills. Unfortunately, however, many managers do not know how to practise this well.

Typical management problems in upgrading people's skills are:

● not realising the importance of upgrading skills

● insecurity about teaching new skills

● assuming that people are not capable of learning

● being selfish and mainly focusing on upgrading their own skills

● not having the skills required to teach or lead people.

We should recognise that money is not the only driver for people to be creative and contribute their ideas. Rather, the environment should be one in which creativity is appreciated and utilised, and through this people realise the benefits in terms of easier, safer, more convenient and more interesting value-adding jobs.

Training and motivating employees to improve key business processes

According to Christopher Jones, the total quality manager at Unisys, in common with other companies such as ICL and the Rover Group, every work group at Unisys is empowered and expected to use its measures of process performance to identify, prioritise and implement 'local' improvements. Proposed process changes should be reviewed by the process owner prior to implementation to determine their contribution to the overall performance of the business process involved. A further review should be undertaken after implementation. If successful, the process owner incorporates the change in the process specification, the revised specification becoming the standard operating procedure (SOP). Jones comments that the planning, measurement and improvement of the key cross-functional business processes is a fundamental element, but only one element in a company-wide improvement strategy. He considers that to fulfil such a strategy it is necessary to have employee training in improvement techniques and employee motivation for improvement.

TYPES OF IMPROVEMENT

To obtain the involvement of people they should know what is required of them and be involved in determining what needs to be done. Schonberger and Knod cite an example of how involvement is achieved at Eicher Tractors Ltd, which operates nine factories in India. Eicher's Faridabad tractor assembly plant intensively trains its workforce and process specification sheets, mostly operator prepared, are posted in each work area. The specification sheets include operating procedures and are an aid to process control, process improvement and cross training. In personal transportation, drivers are assuming ownership of vehicle maintenance and have teamed up on a parking improvement project.

Knowing what needs to be done comes from determining the hierarchy of objectives that need to be pursued. These can be depicted as three types of objectives:

1 Key competitive objectives are the objectives that the manufacturing area of the business needs to pursue to fulfil the strategic aim of the business. Such objectives focus on gaining advantage over the competition by knowing what the customer wants and satisfying the customer in terms of quality, cost, delivery, safety and morale – expressed as QCDSM measures.

Examples of QCDSM Measurement

Q(Quality)   Quality acceptance level improved from 1.0% to 0.1%, number of customer claims reduced by 50%, defects reduced by 60% (0.25% to 0.1%).

C(Cost)   Maintenance cost reduced by 35%, overtime costs down by 20%, energy saved 25%.

D(Delivery)   Lead time cut by 22%, inventory turnover increased by 100% (2 to 4 times/month).

S(Safety)   Number of accidents zero, number of safety related suggestions up by 28%.

M(Morale)   Absentee down by 36%, labour turnover rate down by 15%, number of suggestions increased by 120%.

The following extract from *Management Today* illustrates the importance of safety to a company in terms of saving money and improving productivity.

Frank Davies, Chairman of the Health & Safety Commission comments on accident fatalities that, 'at 1.1 per 100,000 workers, Britain's record is at least twice as good as virtually every other industrialised country . . . Safety is the ordinary man's problem. It is not the boss who usually has the accident. And it is essential for employees to view regulations and safety practices, not as something for the benefit of company management, but for themselves'.

He realises that unfortunately small firms think that safety and health at work are a fine idea but feel that it costs too much in practice. They need to realise that it is the lack of safe and healthy working practices that costs them money. Currently, industrial accident and ill health cost the UK economy a minimum £6bn. Also he points out that Britain in the 1990s is becoming increasingly litigious, American style, and a growing function of trades unions is to pursue claims on behalf of individual workers. He comments, 'It is the TUC's proud boast that its affiliated unions won payments last year of £300 million on behalf of the seven million workers they now represent. He argues that for the small firm an accident can be catastrophe, not just for the individual, but for the very survival of the business. Also he explains that companies do not need to learn the entire rule book but they need to become familiar with the half dozen rules which sensibly apply to their own working practices. Certainly Britain's 1.1 fatalities per 100,000 employees is nothing to be ashamed of, but Frank Davies intends to improve on it by a fair margin yet.

2 Key activity area objectives. These are the objectives that each key activity area in the company needs to pursue to meet the key competitive objectives. Typical key activity areas in many companies are those of product design, process, supply chain, human resources and systems. These key activity areas of business all interlink, as Fig 14.2 shows.

3 Objectives within each activity area and continuous improvement objectives. These are the activities within a particular key activity area that need to be pursued in order to meet the objectives set for that key activity area. Table 14.2 provides a check-list that a company can use to identify elements in each key activity area that could be candidates for continual improvement.

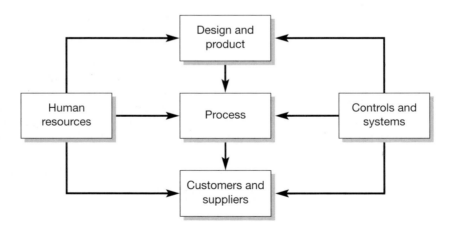

Fig 14.2 Key activity areas of business

Table 14.2 Key activity area improvements

Key activity area	Area of continuous improvement
Design and product	Manufacturability Design features, innovativeness Matching the products and the processes Standard components, modularisation Quality of specification Product cost Product range
Process	Plant type Flexibility Capacity Workplace organisation and layout Process capability and innovation Plant and equipment condition Technology and automation Vertical integration
Controls and systems	Production planning and control, including computer-aided production management Material control Scheduling Maintenance Costing Office technology, computers, networking Supply chain
Customers and suppliers	Information availability and advice Finance options Type and level of service Marketing expertise and effort Up-to-date and accurate supplier information Supplier service, delivery, quality, flexibility, price Sourcing and selecting suppliers Supplier relations and communications
Human resources	Selection, development and training Listening, participative, trusting management style Assessment, incentives, rewards and recognition Involvement and empowerment Experience, qualifications and skills Appropriate culture Motivation and positive attitudes Welfare and safety Knowledge and skills

In practice, the most effective mechanisms for discovering what needs to be done in order to pursue changes for improvement are suggestion schemes and continuous improvement teams.

USE OF SUGGESTION SCHEMES

The value of suggestion schemes is evidenced by the millions of suggestions generated in companies such as Toyota, Matsushita and Toshiba. They often have more than 50 suggestions per employee per year, with a participation rate of more than 90 per cent and an adoption rate of more than 80 per cent. Many of these suggestions have directly saved thousands of pounds and some have made very modest savings. In the latter case, it has been shown that the hidden savings have been invaluable to operators in terms of making their job easier, safer, faster, less tiring, more accurate and more convenient.

Since the number of suggestions represents the total creativity of the organisation, then the top management in your organisation should appreciate that a suggestion programme is important. Managers should become involved to ensure that the programme itself will not fail. Management's attitude should be orientated to be aware of the overall benefits of utilising the brain power that exists at the shopfloor level and show a genuine interest in exploring people's creativity and potential. The emphasis should be on creating an environment where everybody is encouraged and assisted to make continuous improvement and where making suggestions becomes part of the job. Resources should therefore be put into coaching people in data collection and analysis, and problem-solving approaches and presentation techniques. In practice there should be an open style of management where future plans are communicated and ideas are shared.

An approach for making improvements

Outlined below is an approach that managers can use to make improvements to their organisation.

Consider eight improvements that need to be made in the areas that you work in or are responsible for. For each one, describe in Table 14.3 the type of improvement that should be made, giving it a name (in CAPITALS), and the reason why it is considered to be necessary.

Now that you have identified certain improvements that could be made, consider the nature of each together with the reason for the improvement and decide which four are the most important to your work area and should be embarked upon at the earliest opportunity. In Table 14.4 write the name of each improvement and detail the actions to be taken to make the improvement. Carefully consider the type of changes that you are proposing and what actions are required to make the changes and note these in the box. Using this information state in the box what difficulties you anticipate and what obstacles may need to be removed.

Removing the obstacles to continuous improvement

Use the following headings to assist you to write the things you need to do yourself, and what others need to do, in order to remove the obstacles to continuous improvement.

Table 14.3 Making improvements to the work area

Type of improvement and NAME Housekeeping, workplace organisation, waste	Reason Quality, safety, cost, speed, morale
e.g. Type: Improved local lighting Name: IMPROVED LIGHTING	Safety and morale
1	
2	
3	
4	
5	
6	
7	
8	

1 **Information:**
   types of information to create awareness accuracy, speed, content

2 **Capabilities:**
   upgrade of skills, development, new skills

3 **Resources:**
   equipment, machines, funding, time

4 **Infrastructure:**
   systems, empowerment, teams

5 **Culture:**
   attitude, motivation, leadership.

Table 14.4 Identifying obstacles to making improvements

Name of Improvements:
Actions to be taken:
Types of changes:
Difficulties and obstacles:

Virtuous improvement circles

Continued management support and honing of the problem-solvers' skills should result in a further improvement phase where the content of the suggestions improves and many ideas are implemented throughout the company. Once people experience success, just like any winning team, they feel that their perseverance has paid off and they become high spirited. This creates a virtuous improvement circle since people recognise their ability to make improvements and develop a pride in doing so. As these experiences accumulate, they provide added stimulation for solving new problems and moving forward. Success breeds success. The result is a higher morale and more interest in developing problem-solving abilities and making continuous improvements. In many ways people will now perceive that making suggestions is a part of their job. This is echoed by a comment made by a manager about all the company operatives.

Instead of accepting the status quo they go about finding better ways to do the job

An example of a virtuous improvement circle is presented in Exhibit 14.3

Exhibit 14.3

Virtuous improvement circle at Bonas Machine Company

The Bonas Machine Company was voted 1995 Factory of the Year and Electronics Industry Best Factory in the *Management Today* Best Factory Awards. The company produces Jacquard weaving equipment. Its task is to manufacture a complex product to exacting standards of quality, cost and delivery time. Its outstanding feature is a wide range of improvement techniques implemented with unusual thoroughness.

The factory has employed almost every conceivable technique aimed at manufacturing improvement, and done so vigorously and intelligently without simply copying. Supplier rationalisation, Kaizen (continuous improvement activities), routing by walking about – they are all there. Few areas of the factory have been left untouched. Throughout the company people seem to have been galvanised by the new ways of working. Operatives enthuse over slicker set-ups and slashed assembly times; controller boards that used to take 22 hours to complete now take five, and the time needed to put together bus bar assemblies has come down from 17 hours to three.

Some improvements have been felt across the board, cutting set-up and assembly times, and simultaneously reducing material costs. A transformer and power supply redesign, carried out by engineering and manufacturing personnel jointly with suppliers, curbed production time from 24 hours down to four, saving £100 per machine in labour costs and £500 in materials.

What is particularly impressive is the factory's two-day intensive improvement blitzes, carried out by a dedicated, full-time team of engineers. Targeted on productivity, quality and space utilisation, these provide for fundamental analysis and ergonomics investigation of cell layout, parts presentation, motion economy, line balance and any double handling.

Source: Electronics Industry Best Factory Awards 1995, *Management Today,* pp. 98–9, Haymarket Publications.

Improvement programmes can fail

There is a possible down side to suggestion schemes and programmes can fail. In the main this is because management underestimates the potential of people's talent and lacks the willpower to detail the improvements needed in the programme or make them work. For these reasons, if a suggestion programme fails, I would suggest management is 99.9 per cent responsible. Other reasons for failure may be due to too much emphasis being placed on reward – a 'what's in it for me?' attitude. With too long a feedback cycle, people lose interest because others appear uninterested and then everybody starts to forget and the impetus is lost. There may be too great an emphasis on large improvements and the task may seem daunting and never ending. There may be a lack of patience to make suggestions work. There may be a lack of ownership of problems or people may not feel empowered to make improvements; because of this there will always be a reliance on someone else to tackle the problems and implement the improvements.

Developing the appropriate mindset

The reasons why we may not be effective at making improvements are many and varied, but the causes of the above negative situation can be removed if people acquire a different mindset and attitude. Management can assist in this process by using posters, suggestion displays and blocks of time allocated during working hours for people to present the results of their suggestions or present ideas for suggestions. For example, Honda in Japan uses an all-employee event called an 'idea contest', which is held once a year, where refreshments are provided, and all exhibits are displayed in a large field for everybody to look at. Besides stretching the creativity of the minds of the contributors, they have fun and so do the onlookers.

USE OF IMPROVEMENT TEAMS

While suggestion programmes focus on individuals, team-orientated improvement activity is another important way problems can be solved using groups of people. Whether you call them improvement teams, self-managing teams, quality circles, or productivity teams, the emphasis is on a group of people developing their own initiative to address problems and make improvements, usually in their own area. Ultimately, if such teams were suitably empowered they should be able to run as mini companies, while maintaining proper linkages to the total company operation.

Major features of team improvement activities

The emphasis should be on self-managing teams with the team making use of its collective knowledge to decide what needs to be done and by what means it should be achieved. The team may wish to call on outside assistance and expertise. It is important that the team should understand and know how to make use of problem-solving tools that will assist them to manage; for example, time and project management, value engineering, inventory and quality control techniques.

The following checklist can be used to evaluate a team improvement project:

1 **Identify problem.** Has the problem been properly discussed? Does it reflect the real needs of the workplace and the business? Has the team the adequate skills to accomplish the tasks involved?
2 **Describe situation.** Is enough known in terms of the different viewpoints there may be, and are adequate data available?
3 **Set goals.** Are the goals clearly defined? Is there a plan of action?
4 **Analyse root causes.** Is the cause-and-effect relationship clear? Have the people involved contributed their ideas? Has use been made of problem-solving approaches?
5 **Develop options.** Have the views of the parties involved – management, staff, customers, suppliers – been sought? Have the expected benefits of the options been evaluated?
6 **Execute option chosen.** Has people's involvement been sought? Will it be possible to standardise?

7 **Evaluate accomplishments**. Is the monitoring adequate? Have the expected improvements been made?

8 **Standardise.** Have new standards been established? Will they be maintained?

9 **Discuss lessons learned and future plans.** As the programme progresses it becomes necessary to look back and determine if people were adequately trained and resourced. Did the team learn and improve? What lessons have been learned? What are the next steps forward that should be taken to improve this situation and others, and how can the team be better managed?

Small-team activities at Canon

Small-team activity programmes flourish in every Canon factory, and everyone from line workers to plant managers participates in at least one team.

Self-regulated small teams carry out each aspect of their activity independently, from the selection of themes to actual problem solving. Quality, productivity and cost reduction are the most frequently-chosen themes. The teams meet formally for two to four hours a month during regular working hours. The time they spend in meetings after work is also paid for by the company. Typically, a self-regulated small team consists of the workers within a single work centre; some teams, however, are made up of individuals from different work centres or sections who do the same kind of work. These teams have been particularly effective at Canon. Members bring their shared understanding to the problem, and their improvements can be implemented consistently in several work centres at the same time.

Exhibit 14.4 provides an example of small-group achievements at Toshiba Consumer Products UK.

Exhibit 14.4

Small-group achievements at Toshiba Consumer Products UK

Toshiba Consumer Products UK was voted 1995 Engineering Industry Best Factory in the *Management Today* Best Factory Awards. Its activity is to manufacture air-conditioning equipment. Its intention is to achieve Japanese levels of quality and efficiency in a recently-established operation. One of their outstanding features is that of continuous improvement.

According to Neil Lancaster, the manufacturing director, continuous improvement is energetically pursued, with small groups meeting weekly to investigate production problems. One group recently looked at a piece of pipework that was both awkward to braze and a potential source of problems in use. The culprit turned out to be a complicated fitting imported from Japan, but it was found that this could be eliminated altogether using a differently-shaped piece of copper piping. The effect was to cut the number of brazing operations from 17 to 6, giving a 63 per cent reduction in set-up time and a 68 per cent reduction in process time. Best of all, elimination of the imported fitting knocked almost £2 per unit off material costs.

Source: Engineering Industry Best Factory Awards 1995, *Management Today,* Haymarket Publications.

Other examples of successful companies making use of teams in continuous improvement are:

NSK Bearing Europe

NSK Bearing Europe was voted Engineering Industry Highly Commended in the *Management Today* Best Factory Awards 1995. NSK is the second largest manufacturer of ball-bearings. It employs 1700 people and produces over eight million bearings every month. Its task is the low-cost, high-volume and high-quality production for a quality market. Customers include new Japanese arrivals in Europe, such as Toyota, Nissan and Honda, as well as native Europeans such as Rover, Ford, Volkswagen and Bosch. The factory's continuous improvement project focuses sharply on quality and productivity and productivity improvement. Teams compete against one another and members of the winning team spend a week touring Japanese factories.

Merck, Sharp and Dohme

Merck, Sharp and Dohme was voted Household and General Highly Commended in the *Management Today* Best Factory Awards 1995. Its activity is to manufacture prescription drugs in high-volume production to exacting quality standards under tight cost control. Its outstanding features are continuous improvement and people management. Through the use of continuous improvement, teams' clean-down times have been reduced by as many as 300 man hours to 40, achieving substantial savings in energy, fuels and maintenance.

Mutual analysis and counsel method

In addition to small teams at the worker level, Canon also encourages project-centred activities at the foreman level and above. These teams have achieved excellent results that parallel the worker team activities in day-to-day operations. In this type of team, a cross section of the plant's managers and supervisors reviews the problems in a department and investigates opportunities for improvement. On the basis of the advice and counsel received, the managers in that department then carry out the improvements.

Intercompany team programmes

Involving teams in the organisation to pursue continuous improvement could be expanded to include those outside the organisation. It may be that benefit could be derived from including other manufacturers and suppliers, or even companies from unrelated industries, in the process of continuous improvement. For example, in Toyota, study teams are jointly formed with certain suppliers to share the idea of continuous improvement, with an emphasis on those suppliers lowering their production costs through mastering Toyota's production system.

SUMMARY

- The process of ongoing improvements which aggregate over a period of time to provide visible proof that things are getting better is called continuous improvement. The Japanese call this 'kaizen' and it focuses on employee involvement by putting people first.

- A fundamental improvement activity at the shopfloor level is that of improving housekeeping and striving for a better organised workplace.

- Many successful improvements are the result of identifying waste and eliminating it. The main types of waste are: waste from overproduction, waste of waiting time, transportation waste, processing waste, inventory waste, waste of motion, waste from product defects, and, most importantly, the waste of not realising what people can offer and not utilising their talent.

- To manage continuous improvement the following improvement procedure should be adopted: identify the problem, plan, implement and follow up.

- The reasons for and value of having procedures and standards should be known. A system for managing standards should be established. The process of using procedures and standards can be summarised as: analyse operations and standardise work procedures; discover the problems; develop improved methods; implement the methods; if satisfactory, establish as standard.

- To maintain and improve implemented suggestions company-wide, everyone's involvement is essential. Main improvement issues are quality, cost, delivery, safety, and morale. These issues should be made clear through the use of bulletins, newsletters, meetings, performance boards, charts, graphs and pictures.

- To promote the cycle of continuous improvement managers need to: create the right environment (encourage people, attach importance to the quality of the operatives' work life, their safety and the level of their morale), promote involvement, and increase problem-solving capability.

- The overall capability of the organisation to be more responsive to improvement can be raised through emphasis on the following types of skills: skills related to maintenance, skills related to improvement, skills related to innovation and managing skills.

- Involvement is spurred by people knowing what is required of them, and this comes from determining the hierarchy of objectives that need to be pursued; these being: the key competitive objectives, the key activity area objectives, the activities within each area and continuous improvement objectives.

- In practice, the most effective mechanisms for discovering what needs to be done in order to pursue changes for improvement are continuous improvement teams and suggestion schemes.

- Improvement teams are an effective mechanism for continuous improvement. Major features of team improvement activities are: identify problem, describe situation, set goals, analyse root causes, develop options, execute option chosen, evaluate accomplishments, standardise, discuss lessons learned and future plans.

REVIEW AND DISCUSSION QUESTIONS

1 Explain what continuous improvement is and the basic activities that can be done at the shopfloor level to make improvements.

2 What are the reasons for having procedures and standards and in what ways can they be used?

3 What are the main issues involved with gaining everyone's involvement in a continuous improvement programme?

4 In what ways are continuous improvement groups and suggestion schemes effective and how might they fail?

ASSIGNMENTS

1 As the operations director, you have been asked to devise a management programme for initiating continuous improvement in your organisation. Outline the presentation you would make to the potential members of the continuous improvement team that would be involved.

2 As the training manager for your organisation, you have been assigned the task of developing a skills training programme for continuous improvement. Outline the types of skills you would pursue in the programme and explain how you might overcome some of the problems you foresee management may experience with it.

REFERENCES

Bemowski, K., 'Three Electronics Firms win 1991 Baldridge Award', *Quality Progress*, pp. 39–41, November 1991.

Jones, C. R., 'Improving your key business processes', *TQM Magazine*, Vol. 6, No. 2, pp. 25-9, 1994.

Management Today Best Factory Awards 1995, Company reports by New, C. and Wheatley, M., *Management Today*, pp. 106–7, 108, 113, 119, November 1995.

Management Today, 'Striving for a Safer Workforce', Researched and produced by the Aveling Company on behalf of the Health & Safety Executive, pp. 72–3, December 1996.

Pummell, D., 'Changing the manufacturing and people culture or can 2 + 2 = 5?', *Control*, Vol. 20, No. 5, pp. 29–33, Aug/Sept 1996.

Robinson, A., *Continuous Improvement in Operations*, Productivity Press, 1991.

Schonberger, R.J., *Building a Chain of Customers*, Hutchinson Business Books, London, 1990.

Schonberger, R.J. and Knod Jnr. E.M., 'Operations Management', *Continuous Improvement*, 5th edn, p. 12, Richard D. Irwin Inc., Homewood, Ill., 1994.

Suzaki, K., *The New Manufacturing Challenge*, The Free Press, New York, 1987.

Suzaki, K., *The New Shop Floor Management*, The Free Press, New York, 1993.

INDEX